CAMBRIDGE GREEK AND LATIN CLASSICS

SENECA

DE OTIO

DE BREVITATE VITAE

EDITED BY

G. D. WILLIAMS

Associate Professor of Classics,
Columbia University, New York

CAMBRIDGE
UNIVERSITY PRESS

PUBLISHED BY THE PRESS SYNDICATE OF THE UNIVERSITY OF CAMBRIDGE
The Pitt Building, Trumpington Street, Cambridge CB2 1RP, United Kingdom

CAMBRIDGE UNIVERSITY PRESS
The Edinburgh Building, Cambridge, CB2 2RU, UK
40 West 20th Street, New York, NY 10011-4211, USA
477 Williamstown Road, Port Melbourne, VIC 3207, Australia
Ruiz de Alarcón 13, 28014 Madrid, Spain
Dock House, The Waterfront, Cape Town 8001, South Africa

http://www.cambridge.org

First published 2003

Printed in the United Kingdom at the University Press, Cambridge

Typefaces Baskerville 10/12 pt and New Hellenic   *System* LaTeX 2ε   [TB]

A catalogue record for this book is available from the British Library

ISBN 0 521 58223 7 hardback
ISBN 0 521 58806 5 paperback

CONTENTS

PREFACE

It is hoped that this volume can contribute something to the literary study of Senecan philosophy, and make a worthwhile addition to modern scholarship in English on Seneca's *Dialogues* (an area better served in the last century by continental scholarship, especially French and Italian). The completed work has accumulated debts too many to be fully acknowledged here. Professor Therese Fuhrer offered many valuable insights on a draft commentary of *De breuitate uitae*. Professor James E. G. Zetzel commented on several drafts of the whole work with his usual acumen, and gave welcome advice and encouragement at every stage along the way. Professor E. J. Kenney patiently helped the work into its present shape, his experience and learning matched only by his generosity in sharing both. Ms Susan Moore's excellent copy-editing made numerous improvements to the completed MS before Dr Michael Sharp skilfully saw it through the press. Above all, Dr Byron Harries offered inspirational guidance, support and practical help from the work's inception; without his invaluable contribution the present volume would not exist.

CONVENTIONS AND ABBREVIATIONS

1. Unless otherwise specified in the commentary, the text printed is that of L. D. Reynolds (Oxford Classical Text, Oxford 1977). The following editions of (*a*) Seneca's *De otio* and *De breuitate uitae* and (*b*) the *Dialogues* as a whole are cited by editor only:

(*a*) *Ot.*: I. Dionigi, *L. Anneo Seneca: De otio* (*dial. viii*) (Bologna 1983). R. Waltz, *Sénèque: De otio* (Paris 1909).

Breu.: J. D. Duff, *L. Annaei Senecae Dialogorum libri x, xi, xii* (Cambridge 1915).
L. Castiglioni, *L. Annaei Senecae Dialogorum libri ix–x* (Turin 1948).
P. Grimal, *Sénèque: De breuitate uitae* (Paris 1959).
A. Traina, *Seneca: La brevità della vita.* 3rd edn. (Turin 1984).

(*b*) M. C. Gertz, Hauniae 1886.
F. Haase, Leipzig 1852 (Teubner).
E. Hermes, Leipzig 1905 (Teubner).
G. Viansino, Milan 1988–90. 2 vols.

2. In the introduction and commentary the works of Seneca go by abbreviated title as follows.

Ag.	*Agamemnon*
Apoc.	*Apocolocyntosis*
Ben.	*De beneficiis*
Breu.	*De breuitate uitae*
Cl.	*De clementia*
C.S.	*De constantia sapientis*
Ep.	*Epistulae morales*
Helu.	*Consolatio ad Heluiam*
Her. F.	*Hercules Furens*
Her. O.	*Hercules Oetaeus*

Ir.	*De ira*
Marc.	*Consolatio ad Marciam*
Med.	*Medea*
N.Q.	*Naturales quaestiones*
[Sen.] *Oct.*	*Octauia*
Oed.	*Oedipus*
Ot.	*De otio*
Phaed.	*Phaedra*
Phoen.	*Phoenissae*
Pol.	*Consolatio ad Polybium*
Prou.	*De prouidentia*
Thy.	*Thyestes*
Tr.	*De tranquillitate animi*
Tro.	*Troades*
V.B.	*De uita beata*

3. When given in the commentary, textual conjectures are usually assigned to the proposer by name only (e.g. Erasmus).

4. Modern works cited by name and date in the commentary are listed in the bibliography, where abbreviations of periodicals standardly follow *L'Année philologique*. With a few exceptions, standard commentaries are cited by the author's name only (e.g. Courtney on Juv. 2.132, Brink on Hor. *Ars* 152) unless they are abbreviated (so N–H). Abbreviations are as follows:

Arrighetti	G. Arrighetti, ed., *Epicuro: opere.* 2nd edn (Turin 1973).
Basore	J. W. Basore, ed. and trans. *Seneca: moral essays.* 3 vols. Loeb Classical Library (London and Cambridge, Mass. 1928–35).
Berger	A. Berger, *Encyclopedic dictionary of Roman law* (Philadelphia 1953).
Broughton	T. R. S. Broughton, *The magistrates of the Roman Republic.* 3 vols. (vols. i–ii New York 1951–2; vol. iii suppl. Atlanta 1986).

CAH [2]	*The Cambridge ancient history*. 2nd edn (Cambridge 1961–).
CHHP	K. Algra, J. Barnes, J. Mansfeld and M. Schofield, eds., *The Cambridge history of Hellenistic philosophy* (Cambridge 1999).
CIL	*Corpus inscriptionum Latinarum* (Berlin 1863–).
Cooper–Procopé	J. M. Cooper and J. F. Procopé, eds., *Seneca: moral and political essays* (Cambridge 1995).
Diels *Dox. Gr.*	H. Diels, ed., *Doxographi Graeci* (Berlin 1879).
D–K	H. Diels and W. Kranz, eds., *Die Fragmente der Vorsokratiker*. 6th edn (Berlin 1952).
D–S	C. Daremberg and E. Saglio, eds., *Dictionnaire des antiquités grecques et romaines d'après les textes et les monuments*. 5 vols. (Paris 1877–1919).
Dyck	A. R. Dyck, *A commentary on Cicero, De officiis* (Ann Arbor 1996).
E–J	V. Ehrenberg and A. H. M. Jones, eds., *Documents illustrating the reigns of Augustus and Tiberius*. 2nd edn with addenda (Oxford 1976).
E–K	L. Edelstein and I. G. Kidd, eds., *Posidonius, I: the fragments*. 2nd edn. Cambridge Classical Texts and Commentaries 13 (Cambridge 1989).
G–L	B. L. Gildersleeve and G. Lodge, *Latin grammar*. 3rd edn (London 1895).
GLK	H. Keil, ed., *Grammatici Latini*. 8 vols. (Leipzig 1857–70).
Guthrie	W. K. C. Guthrie, *A history of Greek philosophy*. 6 vols. (Cambridge 1962–81).
Hadas	M. Hadas, *The Stoic philosophy of Seneca* (Gloucester, Mass. 1965).
Hofmann	J. B. Hofmann, *Lateinische Umgangssprache*. 3rd edn (Heidelberg 1951).

H–S	J. B. Hofmann and A. Szantyr, *Lateinische Syntax und Stilistik* (Munich 1965).
Kidd	I. G. Kidd, *Posidonius, II: the commentary* (2 vols.); *Posidonius, III: the translation of the fragments*. Cambridge Classical Texts and Commentaries 14A, 14B, 36 (Cambridge 1988–99).
Krebs–Schmalz	J. P. Krebs and J. H. Schmalz, *Antibarbarus der lateinischen Sprache*. 7th edn (Basel 1905–7).
K–R–S	G. S. Kirk, J. E. Raven and M. Schofield, eds., *The Presocratic philosophers*. 2nd edn (Cambridge 1983).
K–S	R. Kühner and C. Stegmann, *Ausführliche Grammatik der lateinischen Sprache: Satzlehre*. 3rd edn, rev. A. Thierfelder. 2 vols. (Leverkusen 1955).
Lausberg	H. Lausberg, *Handbook of literary rhetoric: a foundation for literary study*. Trans. M. T. Bliss *et al.* (Leiden 1998).
Lewis–Short	C. T. Lewis and C. Short, *A Latin dictionary* (Oxford 1879).
Löfstedt	E. Löfstedt, *Syntactica: Studien und Beiträge zur historischen Syntax des Lateins*. 2 vols. (vol. I 2nd edn Lund 1956; vol. II 1933).
L–S	A. A. Long and D. N. Sedley, eds., *The Hellenistic philosophers*. 2 vols. (Cambridge 1987).
LSJ	H. J. Liddell and R. Scott, eds., rev. H. Stuart Jones and R. McKenzie, *A Greek–English lexicon*. 9th edn (Oxford 1968).
Madvig	J. N. Madvig, *Aduersaria critica ad scriptores Graecos et Latinos*. 3 vols. (Copenhagen 1871–84; repr. Hildesheim 1967).

Maltby	R. Maltby, *A lexicon of ancient Latin etymologies* (Leeds 1991).
Mayor	J. E. B. Mayor, ed., *Thirteen Satires of Juvenal.* 4th edn 2 vols. (London 1886–9).
N–H	R. G. M. Nisbet and M. Hubbard, *A commentary on Horace: Odes* I, II (Oxford 1970, 1978).
N–W	F. Neue and C. Wagener, *Formenlehre der lateinischen Sprache.* 3rd edn 4 vols. (Leipzig–Berlin 1892–1905).
*OCD*³	S. Hornblower and A. Spawforth, eds., *The Oxford classical dictionary.* 3rd edn (Oxford 1996).
OLD	P. G. W. Glare, ed., *Oxford Latin dictionary* (Oxford 1968–82).
Otto	A. Otto, *Die Sprichwörter und sprichwörtlichen Redensarten der Römer* (Leipzig 1890; repr. Hildesheim 1962).
*PIR*²	*Prosopographia imperii Romani saec. I, II, III.* 2nd edn (Berlin 1933–).
Pohlenz	M. Pohlenz, *Die Stoa.* 2 vols. 2nd edn (Göttingen 1959).
RAC	T. Klauser, ed., *Reallexikon für Antike und Christentum* (Stuttgart 1950–).
RE	A. F. von Pauly, ed., rev. G. Wissowa *et al.*, *Realencyclopädie der classischen Altertumswissenschaft* (Stuttgart 1893–).
Ribbeck	O. Ribbeck, ed., *Tragicorum Romanorum fragmenta.* 3rd edn (Leipzig 1897).
Rist	J. M. Rist, *Stoic philosophy* (Cambridge 1969).
Shackleton Bailey	D. R. Shackleton Bailey, ed., *Cicero's Letters to Atticus.* 7 vols. Cambridge Classical Texts and Commentaries 3–9 (Cambridge 1965–70).

Summers	W. C. Summers, ed., *Select letters of Seneca* (London 1910).
SVF	J. von Arnim, ed., *Stoicorum ueterum fragmenta* (Leipzig 1903–24).
TLL	*Thesaurus linguae Latinae* (Leipzig 1900–).
Us.	H. Usener, ed., *Epicurea* (Leipzig 1877; repr. Stuttgart 1966).
Vottero	D. Vottero, ed., *L. Anneo Seneca: i frammenti* (Bologna 1998).

INTRODUCTION

1. AUTHOR AND DATE: INITIAL PROBLEMS

Born into a provincial equestrian family of Italian extraction at Corduba (modern Córdoba) in southern Spain, Lucius Annaeus Seneca (c. 1 BC – AD 65) was raised and educated from an early age at Rome. Partly through the influence of his father, whose five surviving books of *Controuersiae* and one of *Suasoriae* (both from his *Oratorum et rhetorum sententiae diuisiones colores*, in at least twelve books) amply reflect his own deep interest in rhetorical theory and practice, the younger S. studied declamatory rhetoric in preparation for a career as an advocate and in politics. But his extensive philosophical education under the Stoic Attalus, Sotion and especially Papirius Fabianus drew him at a young age to the Sextians, so named after Q. Sextius, the sect's founder; heavily influenced by Stoicism and Neopythagoreanism, it was Rome's only native philosophical school.[1] S.'s lifelong attachment to Stoicism was formed in these years, and his early devotion to philosophy may help to explain why he delayed his entry into political life, becoming quaestor when he was past thirty. He won fame as an orator but also the disfavour of one emperor in AD 39, allegedly through Caligula's jealousy of his success; and then of another when, in Claudius' reign, he was accused of adultery with a sister of Caligula and exiled in 41 to Corsica, where he remained until he was recalled in 49 through the intercession of Agrippina, was appointed praetor and became tutor to the young Nero.[2] After Nero's accession in 54 S. was, with the praetorian prefect Sextus Afranius Burrus, one of the two powers behind the throne who oversaw five or so years of good government. But by the time of Burrus' death in 62 S.'s control over the increasingly wayward emperor had declined to the extent that he sought permission in that year to withdraw from public life, only (according to Tacitus) for Nero to refuse both that request and a later one made in 64 (*Ann.* 14.53–6, 15.45.3; cf. Suet. *Nero* 35.5). After 62, however, S. was in effect living in retirement, a phase (62–5) in which he produced or brought to completion the bulk of his extant prose writings: his 124 *Epistulae morales*, the *Naturales quaestiones* and *De beneficiis* (the latter after AD 56 and completed by 64). Charged with complicity in the Pisonian

---

[1] Rawson (1985) 94–5, 318; Sextius in fact wrote in Greek.
[2] For more detail on the first fifty years, Griffin (1976) 29–66.

conspiracy, S. was forced to commit suicide in 65 (Tac. *Ann.* 15.60.2–64.4, Dio 62.25.1–2).

The surviving fragment of *De otio*, in which S. argues that devotion to philosophy from early youth (i.e. total abstention from public service) or upon retirement from a career is fully in accordance with Stoic principles (2.1–2), is conventionally dated to AD 62 or soon afterwards and read as a philosophical justification of S.'s own *de facto* retirement in that year.[3] As for the date of *De breuitate vitae*, most modern scholars have chosen between two main proposals, 49 and 62.[4] Both dates have been manipulated to allow S. to be free of, or at least contemplating withdrawal from, the *negotium* of political life when he urges Pompeius Paulinus, his presumed addressee and the *praefectus annonae* charged with overseeing the Roman grain-supply, to retire to philosophy; for (the standard question goes) how to reconcile the message of *Breu.* with S.'s own life and career if it was written when he himself was actively engaged at court? If written in 49, 'could a prospective praetor . . . have hoped to sound convincing when he insisted that *otium* was preferable to *officium*?'.[5]

But such questions are perhaps too confining, accommodating *Ot.* and *Breu.* to the facts of S.'s life rather than allowing the texts to be evaluated on their own terms, as if the alleged contradictions of both works (how could S. write either if very much *in officio?*) can only be resolved by the convenient dating of *Ot.* and *Breu.* and/or by invoking an 'external', biographical explanation for them. The position taken here, however, is that the philosophical 'message' of *Ot.* and *Breu.* stands regardless of S.'s particular circumstances at the time of writing (whether in office or in retirement or between the two); and that their philosophical importance is too easily compromised or obscured when biographical considerations are allowed to (over-)influence their dating and interpretation. In the case of *Breu.*, S.'s seemingly impractical advice to Paulinus has further encouraged a biographical approach. Unless S. has an ulterior motive for the work, how easy is it to imagine the *praefectus annonae* promptly retiring in the name

[3] For proponents of 62 or thereabouts, Dionigi 48–9 and 49 n. 2; he too holds that *Ot.* was motivated by S.'s withdrawal in 62, suspecting that the work was written before his retirement and not as a *post euentum* justification of it (pp. 52–4).

[4] For proponents of 49, Hambüchen (1966) 28 and n. 2; of 62, 143 and n. 1. See also Hambüchen 23–5 and Griffin (1962) 104 against Justus Lipsius' case for a date in the early 40s on the strength of 18.5 *modo modo intra paucos illos dies quibus C. Caesar perit* . . . (n. *ad loc.*).

[5] Griffin (1962) 111.

of philosophy from his position of vital strategic importance[6] to Rome and the empire?[7] If S.'s message is taken to be more general, how many of his more 'ordinary' Roman readers were in a position to contemplate philosophical retirement without concern for their practical responsibilities in life? So also in *Ot.*, where S.'s argument that abstention from public life is fully compatible with Stoic principles presupposes that the best existence for the *sapiens* is one of self-sufficient isolation from the everyday world – surely no practical possibility for the great majority of S.'s audience. The challenge, taken up below, is how to account for this idealistic dimension to both *Ot.* and *Breu.* without presuming a biographical explanation for either work.

2. THE *DIALOGUES* IN CONTEXT

Ot. and *Breu.* are two of the twelve books, each dealing with an aspect or subject of Stoic ethics (ten treatises in all, as *De ira* occupies books 3–5), preserved under the title *Dialogi* in the *Codex Ambrosianus*, our principal MS. These ten treatises represent only a selection, probably arranged after his death,[8] of S.'s *dialogi*. It is unclear whether he himself used the term *dialogi* of his writings, but late in the first century AD Quintilian refers to S.'s abundant output of *et orationes . . . et poemata et epistolae et dialogi* (*Inst.* 10.1.129). By *dialogi* Quintilian apparently means all of S.'s prose works apart from his speeches and letters; but none of those works is a *dialogus* in the conventional Platonic or Ciceronian sense of a 'real' conversation or debate between named characters in a social setting. How to explain this anomaly? The suggestion that *dialogus* denotes a Greek literary form such as the 'diatribe' has rightly won little favour.[9] A more promising explanation for the title is that it refers to *dialogus* in the technical rhetorical sense of a branch of

---

[6] For which 18.3n. on *orbis . . . rationes*.

[7] Hence Griffin's hypothesis ((1962) 104–7) that *Breu.* was written in 55, when Faenius Rufus was made *praefectus annonae* as part of a politically motivated redistribution of high political offices at Rome; Paulinus, S.'s father-in-law, had to make way for Rufus. *Breu.* is therefore tactical in a face-saving way, supplying the 'official' reason for Paulinus' retirement (he had served his time, was fit for higher things etc.). Highly speculative, but Griffin is careful to stress that this 'secondary purpose' ((1976) 407) accompanies S.'s primary philosophical interest in the competing claims of the contemplative as opposed to the active life.

[8] *Pace* Schmidt (1961), esp. 257–8 (countered by Griffin (1976) 518–19).

[9] Griffin (1976) 413–14, 508–9, and cf. p. 26 below.

the figure prosopopoeia, i.e. words attributed to a definite or indefinite speaker.[10] The more familiar Latin term for this technique is *sermocinatio*; if derived from the Greek term (διάλογος) for this recurrent feature in S.'s writing (e.g. *Ot.* 1.4, 6.1, 6.5, 7.2; *Breu.* 3.5, 7.6, 7.8), the title *Dialogi* may also have helped to assimilate his works to the tradition of the philosophical dialogue extending back to Plato.[11]

While the declamatory fashion of the age is unmistakably reflected in S.'s writing (e.g. in his use of *sermocinatio*), the nature and novelty of his enterprise in *Ot.* and *Breu.* are conditioned by three other basic factors:

(a) The Stoic background [12]

After the foundation of the Stoic school at Athens by Zeno of Citium (335–263 BC), Zeno's teachings in logic, physics and ethics, the three standard parts of Hellenistic philosophy, were refined and systematized by his successors, chief among them Chrysippus of Soli (*c*. 280–207), the third head of the school. Chrysippus' became the standard formulation of Stoicism as a holistic system, complete and self-contained in its different parts, and with a basic emphasis on divine *ratio* (= god, *logos*, mind) as the governing principle of the rational, living and providentially ordained universe. Humans share in the cosmic reason which pervades the universe, so that to live in accordance with our own rational nature is to live in accordance with universal nature. Only the Stoic sage (*sapiens*) who has attained the perfect reason embodied in god (= divine *ratio*) can achieve virtue, the only Stoic good, and live the truly happy life. Not surprisingly, the perfect *sapiens* is hard to visualize in real life and, even if models *do* suggest themselves,[13] he is phoenix-like in his rarity;[14] hence the developments of the so-called Middle Stoa, a stage associated with the innovations of Panaetius of Rhodes (*c*. 185–110 BC), Posidonius of Apamea in Syria (*c*. 135–50 BC) and Hecaton of Rhodes (early first century BC) and leading, in ethics, to a shift away from the remote figure of the *sapiens* to the more

---

[10] Lausberg §§820, 822.9.   [11] Costa (1994) 1 after Griffin (1976) 414–15.

[12] Basic bibliography: *CHHP*, L–S, Pohlenz, Rist (all listed in Conventions and abbreviations pp. x–xii); Arnold (1911), Long (1986), Sandbach (1989), Sharples (1996).

[13] Notably the younger Cato at *C.S.* 2.2–3, 7.1; cf. Lucan 2.284–325, 380–91.

[14] Cf. *Ep.* 42.1, Alex. Aphrod. *Fat.* 199.18 Bruns (= *SVF* III 165.24–5 = L–S I 61 N2); nor did the Stoic masters themselves claim to be *sapientes* (Quint. *Inst.* 12.1.18 = *SVF* I 15.19–24; Plut. *Mor.* 1048e = *SVF* III 166.22–6; further Brunt (1975) 12 n. 17).

ordinary situation of those progressing towards virtue. Panaetius in particular is credited with concentrating more narrowly than his predecessors on
practical ethics, abandoning the *sapiens* as the Stoic behavioural model.[15]
After the rise of Stoic philosophy at Rome in the second and first centuries
BC, with Panaetius and Posidonius important catalysts, this interest in
practical ethics culminates in the marked emphasis on 'philosophy as
a way of life' in Seneca and in the Greek writings of Musonius Rufus
(*c*. AD 30–100), Epictetus (*c*. AD 55–135) and Marcus Aurelius (AD 121–80).

   Panaetius' emphasis not on the perfect *sapiens* but on the philosophical
progress of more ordinary humans extended to political philosophy. The
early Stoics apparently showed little interest in weighing the merits of different regimes and in favouring particular kinds of constitution.[16] Zeno
wrote a *Republic* which differed from Plato's in envisaging a city *only* of the
wise, not one governed by the wise for the common benefit of all. This
'impossibly idealistic society'[17] gave way to the Chrysippean conception of
the world as a universal city; universal not in the sense that it included all
mankind, but in that it united 'gods and sages wherever they may be'.[18]
The relevance of Zeno's *Republic* to contemporary Greek society was of a
negative kind, as the work condemned the world as it is by describing 'not
only the ideal society of the wise, but the wise man's attitude to present society'.[19] For Chrysippus too all regimes in the real world are in error,[20] and
even though the *sapiens* is duty-bound 'to serve the state unless something
prevents him' (*Ot.* 3.2 and n.), the only state or community promoting life
in accordance with cosmic reason and natural law is the universal city. In
later Stoicism, however, the effort to clarify for ordinary people the practical
significance of Stoic ethics led to a shift of emphasis 'from man's first to
his second community',[21] i.e. from the cosmic to the localized city (e.g.
Athens, Carthage etc.); at this point the relative merits of different regimes
were debated. So in a Roman context Panaetius,[22] but Diogenes of Babylon

---

[15] Cf. Cic. *Fin.* 4.79; P. Donini in *CHHP* 727.

[16] Cf. Erskine (1990) 71, suggesting that 'Stoic thought had a democratic bias'
(rebutted by Vander Waerdt (1991) 199–200); Erskine 73 himself rebuts the views
that the early Stoa especially favoured (i) a mixed constitution, or (ii) kingship.

[17] Erskine (1990) 41.   [18] M. Schofield in *CHHP* 768 and (1999) 67–73.

[19] Erskine (1990) 41–2.

[20] Cf. Plut. *Mor.* 1033f, *SVF* III 80.17–19, with further citations in Vander Waerdt
(1991) 202.

[21] Vander Waerdt (1991) 204.

[22] Cf. Brunt (1975) 17 'It was recognized, most emphatically by Panaetius, that
the state answered human material needs and fulfilled men's natural and reasonable

(c. 240 – c. 152 BC), the fifth head of the school, appears to have been 'first responsible for modifying the scope of Stoic political philosophy in such a way as to make it responsive to the needs of practical politics'.[23]

For Stoics in the early Empire, however, 'the claims of citizenship of the universe come to dwarf those of the existing societies in which we find ourselves: the cosmic perspective increasingly overshadows the vantage point of ordinary life'.[24] So S. in *Ot.*, distinguishing the two commonwealths, *maior* and *minor* (4.1), urging that the *sapiens* can best serve the megalopolis in retirement from the distractions of service to its lesser counterpart (cf. 4.2), and arguing that, try as he might, the *sapiens* will never find *any res publica* that will either tolerate him or be tolerated by him (8.1–3). Our task below is to reconcile this detached, cosmic perspective with S.'s (Panaetian) emphasis on practical ethics and philosophy as a way of life in the 'real' world.

(b) The Roman philosophical tradition

For S., as for Quintilian, the outstanding figure in the history of Roman philosophy was M. Tullius Cicero, the great orator and statesman (cf. *Ep.* 100.9, *Inst.* 10.1.123). Roman philosophical prose was not unknown before Cicero,[25] but his prolific writings, many dating from his period of extraordinary productivity in 45–4, set in place a basic Latin philosophical vocabulary and medium independent of the Greek tradition from which they were derived. But if for Cicero philosophy was 'a training for public oratory and a *pis aller* for public life when in retirement',[26] for Seneca the situation was apparently different, philosophy an early priority which delayed his entry into public life. Beyond these personal factors, however, times had changed: even though in the late Republic philosophy was still essentially a Greek subject with many Greek philosophers at Rome, Athens was in decline as the philosophical centre of the Mediterranean world, Alexandria and Rome in the ascendant, fewer young Romans studied in Greece, the

impulse for cooperation.' For Panaetius' alleged advocacy of the Roman Republican system as the best form of government because of its mixture and balance, Brunt (1975) 17–18 with Devine (1970) 331.

[23] Vander Waerdt (1991) 209.

[24] M. Schofield in *CHHP* 770, stressing as 'important for understanding the political thought of the Hellenistic age that this *is* a later development' (his emphasis).

[25] Background: Rawson (1985) 282–97.   [26] Griffin (1988) 140.

Sextians taught a 'Roman' philosophy, and S. himself was raised in a domestic environment which brought him into close contact with committed Roman philosophers such as the Sextian Papirius Fabianus, who worked in Latin; and S. came of age in an era when, for Romans of sufficient wealth and standing, the philosophical life offered a realistic alternative to the more traditional career and *cursus honorum*.[27] In this intellectual climate philosophy was for S. 'not something essentially Greek, for which he might, like Cicero or Lucretius, be a missionary among the Romans. It was not something which *had* to be done in Greek if it were to be done seriously and in one's own voice . . . '[28] He was engaged in 'primary philosophy (rather than exegetical or missionary work) in Latin',[29] thinking and writing creatively in his own language,[30] and so (on the debit side) more elusive than Cicero as a source for Hellenistic ideas; but this independent attitude also reinforces his standing as 'a rare example of first-order Latin philosophy',[31] a fact too often underestimated in modern assessments of his philosophical originality and importance.

(c) From Republic to Empire

In the late Republic and early Empire a favoured thesis in the rhetorical schools was *sitne sapientis ad rem publicam accedere*.[32] In Cicero's day politics was, in general terms, 'the most honourable way of life, and retirement before old age badly in need of defence for a senator'.[33] The same attitude extended down to S.'s time and beyond,[34] but the arrival of the Principate inevitably modified the nature of Roman political involvement. To what extent, then, do *Ot.* and *Breu.* capture the mood of the age by subjecting the traditional Stoic commitment to public life to renewed scrutiny in a time of authoritarian and, especially under Nero, increasingly wayward rule?

Despite Augustus' efforts to present his regime as a restoration of authority to the Senate and people, the realities of his monarchical rule inevitably

---

[27] Inwood (1995) 63–7 for the general picture (an excellent sketch).
[28] Inwood (1995) 67.   [29] Inwood (1995) 68.
[30] Cf. Griffin (1976) 7 'Seneca's choice of Latin as a medium is a sure sign that his interest in writing was at least as great as his interest in philosophy: serious philosophers in his time and immediately after wrote in Greek.'
[31] Inwood (1995) 75.   [32] Cic. *Top.* 82, in Griffin (1976) 315.
[33] Griffin (1976) 344 and n. 2 for references.
[34] Griffin (1976) 344 with Liebeschuetz (1979) 110.

infringed upon the cherished Republican ideal of *libertas*. But after a painful period of transition under Augustus the senate did not decline into insignificance; far from it.[35] What *does* appear to have changed under the Empire, however, is individual motivation for and in public life: because 'senators could no longer feel that they were serving their own state', 'actions are judged less by success or public approval and more by the voice of conscience'.[36] Turning within themselves for guidance, individuals could find assistance in philosophy, which was 'now more than the interesting game it had once been. Ancestral custom and the code of a ruling class no longer provided an adequate guide to living. Philosophy and the philosophical expert had to fill the gaps.'[37] Already in the Republic the expansion and increasing diversity of the empire contributed to the gradual erosion of Roman national identity and, consequently, to the rise of individualism and cosmopolitanism, both of which found a rational basis in Stoicism.[38] Stoicism arguably contributed to 'the growth of a humanitarian spirit at Rome' in the first century AD,[39] while the Stoic emphasis on austere living ran counter to the *paralysis agitans* which Barton[40] associates with the restless appetite in the late Republic and early Empire for the new and the unknown, the exotic and (not least in the gladiatorial arena) the ever more horrific, an appetite resulting from the world being opened up to Rome. And in an age which witnessed a rise in magic, astrology and other forms of superstition offering spiritual comfort in an uncertain world,[41] the Stoic was fortified by his belief in the providence of cosmic reason against the unpredictability of life under the likes of Caligula and Nero; whatever befell him, he was capable of 'the emotional ecstasy of the martyr who feels completely his own man because he delights in going to meet all the trials that can be presented to him'.[42] Astrology also reinforced Stoicism's appeal as a philosophy which correlated human and cosmic reason: granted his dignified place in the universal structure, his future there to be read in the stars, 'this picture of himself gave back to a Roman noble the dignity lost through humiliating submission to an emperor'.[43]

[35] Talbert (1984), esp. 488–91 with Millar (1992) 341.
[36] Liebeschuetz (1979) 109, 112.   [37] Liebeschuetz (1979) 112–13.
[38] Moore (1917) is still rewarding.
[39] Currie (1966) 78; (1973) 21 for Stoicism preaching 'a liberal humanitarianism'.
[40] (1992) 85.
[41] Liebeschuetz (1979) 119–39 with Williams (1978) 171–84.
[42] Williams (1978) 172.   [43] Liebeschuetz (1979) 125.

In the early Empire the Stoic emphasis on virtuous action also served as an antidote to the corruption and hypocrisy of court politics.[44] According to Tacitus, in AD 59 Thrasea Paetus walked out of the senate in protest when thanks were being offered for Nero's safe delivery (by matricide!) from the threat posed by Agrippina (*Ann.* 12.12.1; cf. 16.21.1). There followed a long-running feud with Nero which culminated in Paetus' virtual non-attendance in the senate from 63 onwards (cf. *Ann.* 16.22.1) until 66, when he was forced to commit suicide after his Stoicism was brought as one of the charges against him by Cossutianus Capito, Tigellinus' son-in-law (*Ann.* 16.22). Already by 62 Stoicism was a dangerous allegiance, Rubellius Plautus its first victim when Tigellinus frightened Nero with the insinuation that Plautus 'had the arrogance of the Stoics, who breed sedition and intrigue' (*Ann.* 14.57.3).[45] The punishment of these and other Stoics has given rise to the theory, now generally discredited, that there was an active Stoic opposition under Nero.[46] The Stoics were not against monarchy *per se*;[47] in common with other schools they condemned tyranny, but the fact is that 'there was always a core of senatorial, or better, upper-class resistance to emperors and their power – feelings of friction and resentment that were hardly limited to adherents of Stoicism';[48] Nero victimized non-Stoics as well, as his persecution of the Pisonian conspirators amply attests (nor can it be shown that the conspiracy was Stoic in inspiration). Located in this broader picture of resistance, Paetus' actions are better viewed as those of 'a courageous and upright Roman senator who held Stoic views, not as a Stoic philosopher who happened to be a senator at Rome'.[49]

Despite this qualified view of the Stoic 'opposition' under Nero, S.'s emphasis in *Ot.* on the corrupt condition of the state as a legitimate reason for abstaining from public life (3.3; cf. 8.1–3) has predictably been interpreted as a justification for (his own) retirement under a harsh emperor. But whatever the relevance of *Ot.* to S.'s life, far more important (and interesting) in

[44] A. Wallace Hadrill in *CAH* ² x 305–6.

[45] Cf. Griffin (1989) 20–1 for philosophy brought under suspicion in the late Republic and early Empire because of its potential (i) to divert its followers from participation in public life, (ii) to instil doctrines that were impractical or incompatible with public life, and (iii) to encourage recalcitrance towards authority.

[46] For the theory examined, Griffin (1976) 363–6 and (1984) 171–7.

[47] But for at least the early Stoa cf. n. 16 above.

[48] Shaw (1985) 47, part of a spirited argument (and update of the case) against the notion of a 'Stoic opposition' at Rome.

[49] Wirszubski (1950) 138.

the history of ideas is the cosmic consciousness which he promotes in *Ot.* as an escape from the pressures and involvements of the 'everyday' world. If in the early Empire philosophy was one form of therapy to which people could look for relief and guidance in an age of anxiety, *Ot.* and, in a different way, *Breu.* both contribute significantly to this therapeutic effort.

3. *DE OTIO*

(a) *The view from above*

A precious compensation in exile, S. asserts in the *Consolatio ad Heluiam*, written to ease his mother's sorrow over his banishment to Corsica (AD 41–9), is that wherever we go in the world we are accompanied by universal nature and by our own virtue (8.2). As a citizen of the universe the Stoic can never be exiled (8.5), for 'every place is his country' (*patria*, 9.7): to contemplate the workings (the planetary movements etc.; 8.6) of cosmic reason, of which human *ratio* is a portion, is itself to participate in the universal community, local civic identity being of little consequence by comparison. Hence his repeated emphasis in the *Consolatio* on this 'view from above',[50] that cosmic consciousness which transforms the meaning of exile by changing the compass of our understanding; for 'the view from above . . . leads us to consider the whole of human reality, in all its social, geographical, and emotional aspects, as an anonymous, swarming mass, and it teaches us to relocate human existence within the immeasurable dimensions of the cosmos. Everything that does not depend on us, which the Stoics called indifferent (*indifferentia*) – such as health, fame, wealth, and even death – is reduced to its true dimensions when considered [like S.'s exile in the *Consolatio*] from the point of view of the nature of the all.'[51] From this cosmic perspective S. naturally ends the *Consolatio* on a positive note (20.1–2): released from *occupatio* in the 'everyday' world, the exile is free to rediscover the 'world *qua* world'.[52]

---

[50] As 'a perennial motif in ancient philosophical writing', Rutherford (1989) 155–61.

[51] Hadot (1995) 245; cf. (1998) 173 for his concept of 'the discipline of desire' ('Human affairs, when seen from above, seem very tiny and puny; they are not worthy of being desired . . . ').

[52] Cf. Hadot (1995) 258. For the liberating effects of S.'s exile, also [Sen.] *Oct.* 381–90; but for a grimmer picture, *Pol.* 18.9 – no less strategic (with Ovidian colour; Griffin (1976) 62), albeit in a very different direction, than upbeat *Helu.* 4.1–2 and 20.1–2.

This same contrast between micro- and macrocosmic perceptions of the world is basic to *Ot.*, most obviously in the distinction drawn in 4.1–2 between the localized *res publica* and its universal counterpart. The philosopher who moves from the *minor res publica* to a level of cosmic consciousness in its *maior* counterpart now fully lives *only* through his participation in the megalopolis; the world is his *patria*, his *domus*, his *urbs*, terms whose evocative Roman significance is inevitably lost in their translation to the cosmos.[53] Central to the literary creation of a Roman national consciousness and sense of identity in (and before) the Augustan age is the emotional draw of *patria*, whether in the positive Virgilian representation of Italy as the object of longing and as a near perfect utopia (e.g. *Aen.* 1.380 *Italiam quaero patriam*, 7.122 *hic domus, haec patria est*; cf. the *laudes Italiae* at *G.* 2.136–76), or as the focus of Ovid's exilic nostalgia and lament (e.g. *Tr.* 3.3.53 *cum patriam amisi, tunc me periisse putato*). Through this deeply ingrained sense of attachment to Rome and *patria*, the Augustan writers contributed much to the consolidation of central power and to the intimidating capacity of the institutions which safeguarded *res Italas* (cf. Hor. *Ep.* 2.1.2–3); exiled by Augustus, himself of course *pater patriae* (cf. *Tr.* 2.181, 574, 3.1.49, 4.4.13), Ovid for one paid for his non-conformity at Rome by his exclusion not just from the literal *patria* but from *patria* as the emotional centre of his Roman 'belonging'. S. fully recognizes the force of this draw to one's *patria* (cf. *Ep.* 66.26 *nemo . . . patriam quia magna est amat, sed quia sua,*) even though his own Spanish origins might have predisposed him to think of his *patria* (Spain or Italy?) in a more flexible way. In *Ot.* and *Helu.*, however, his emphasis on Stoic cosmopolitanism liberates the self from this strong sense of local affiliation and allegiance, thus offering scope for individual development and autonomy regardless of any local restrictions.

The cosmopolitan Stoic is also protected against the intimidating sanctions of the state. Living each day as if a complete life (*Breu.* 7.9), superior to fortune (*Breu.* 5.3), complete in his happiness (*V.B.* 4.4) and incapable of losing his inner freedom (*Ep.* 75.18 *absoluta libertas*) whatever his external circumstances, the *sapiens* can no more be affected by exile than by any other state-imposed punishment or threat. In this respect *Ot.* can be read as a politically challenging blueprint for how to survive in the empire by living *extra potentiam principis* with one's self-respect and individual autonomy

---

[53] For cosmic *patria*, *V.B.* 20.5, *Tr.* 4.4, *Ep.* 28.4, 102.21 (Ciceronian: *Rep.* 1.19.5); for *domus* and *urbs*, Cic. *Diu.* 1.131 and *N.D.* 2.154 with Pease.

intact; or as a compromise piece which keeps access to the *minor res publica* open while providing an escape-route to its *maior* counterpart (cf. 4.1 *quidam eodem tempore utrique rei publicae dant operam, maiori minorique*).[54] Whether *Ot.* is dated to the reign of Claudius or Nero, to *c*. 49 or *c*. 62, S. thus promotes a cosmopolitan vision which may also be self-serving, distancing him from (his own involvement in) the ugly political realities of his day. But *Ot.* can simultaneously be read as a more disinterested enquiry into the relationship between different Stoic world-perspectives. S.'s imaginary interlocutor in 1.4, a Stoic committed to *actio* in the *minor res publica*, represents the microcosmic 'view from below' in contrast to the cosmic consciousness and 'view from above' urged by S. through the course of the fragment. The jolting effect of S.'s recommendation to withdraw from public life and from involvement with the 'irrational' majority (1.1–3) is to force a change of perception: 'The utilitarian perception we have of the world, in everyday life, in fact hides us from the world *qua* world. Aesthetic and philosophical perceptions of the world are only possible by means of a complete transformation of our relationship to the world: we have to perceive it *for itself*, and no longer *for ourselves*.'[55] *Ot.*, like *Breu.*, moves and jostles the reader towards 'a complete transformation' of this personal kind, and to a reassessment of how we order our priorities in life. Even if the ideal of retirement in the manner of the *sapiens* in *Ot.* and as urged on Paulinus in *Breu.* remains far beyond us in practical reality, our exposure to the idea may still disconcert us towards a beneficial form of self-examination.

(*b*) *Date, addressee and related problems*

The approach taken thus far is based on no assumptions about the date of the work, its addressee's identity or its possible autobiographical significance. In combination, these three problems have long (over-)influenced the modern interpretation of *Ot.*, but with significant difficulties which are briefly surveyed below. The question of whether or not *Ot.* is complete at its transmitted end also remains to be addressed.

S. may well have identified his addressee in the lost opening sentence of *Ot.* Such is his practice in all of the *Dialogues* but *Tr.*,[56] where Serenus opens

---

[54] Cf. Momigliano (1969) 249 'World-citizenship [sc. 4.1–2] is an alternative solution to the citizenship of the individual State, when the individual State proves to be unsatisfactory.'

[55] Hadot (1995) 254.   [56] Discounting *Pol.*, its opening also lost.

the imaginary debate by addressing S. by name, the latter reciprocating
when he begins his reply in 2.1. In others S. occasionally names his addressee
in the course of the work (Serenus at *C.S.* 5.1, 6.8, *Tr.* 4.1, 17.12; Paulinus
at *Breu.* 18.1), but the loss of the opening section of *Ot.* is compounded
by the absence of any identifying vocative later. Moreover, the name is
effaced in the table of contents in the *Codex Ambrosianus*,[57] its restoration to
Serenus only conjectural; but Annaeus Serenus, prefect of the watch under
Nero (Plin. *N.H.* 22.96), is still commonly accepted as S.'s addressee, not
least because his addressee's 'ardent and stubborn, yet open and honest'[58]
personality as revealed in his imagined words at 1.4 etc. is in keeping with
Serenus' character as represented in *C.S.* and the opening stages of *Tr.*[59] At
Ep. 63.14, written in 63 or 64, S. movingly describes his grief at Serenus'
death, which occurred (according to Plin. *N.H.* 22.96) when the latter was
still prefect. Tigellinus held that office in early 62, subsequently becoming
praetorian prefect after Burrus' death in that year. If Serenus succeeded
Tigellinus as prefect of the watch in early 62, he died in that year or soon
after; but if he preceded Tigellinus as prefect (rather more probable), he
died no later than early in 62.[60]

If, then, *Ot.* is addressed to Serenus (itself far from certain), the work
would seem to have a *post quem non* of 63 at the very latest – a scenario
which allows S. to have composed the work in the general period of his
own withdrawal from court. Three main factors have been cited in support
of this convenient dating of *Ot.* to *c.* 62, but each is open to objection; the
third also usefully leads us to the problem, taken up in (iv) below, of *Ot.*'s
(in)completeness at its end.

(i) Several thematic parallels with the *Epistulae morales* indicate that *Ot.* closely
anticipates that later collection (62–5).[61] But they are insufficient *in themselves*
to prove a close temporal relationship, as S. may well revert in the *Epistulae*
to themes explored considerably earlier;[62] and stylistic analysis of *Ot.* yields
no firm evidence to support the date only suggested by the parallels.

[57] For the table, Reynolds ix.   [58] Griffin (1976) 354 n. 2.
[59] For what little is known of Serenus, Griffin (1976) 77, 89 and n. 8, 253 with
PIR[2] 1 p. 104 no. 618 and *RE* 1 2.2248 *Annaeus* 18.
[60] On the controversy, Griffin (1976) 447–8.
[61] Dionigi 51–2 sets out the parallels.
[62] Cf. Griffin (1962) 113 on the weakness of a parallel argument for *Breu.*'s late
date on the strength of thematic connections between it and the *Epistulae morales*.

(ii) *Ot.* allegedly contains several historical/autobiographical allusions. S.'s second main proposition as set out in 2.2 (*ut possit hoc aliquis emeritis iam stipendiis, profligatae aetatis, iure optimo facere...*) has been interpreted as an allusion to his own proposed retirement at a relatively advanced age after years of service to Nero.[63] But the allusion grows fainter when his emphasis on retirement in old age is seen specifically to answer his interlocutor's commitment in 1.4 to Stoic active service until death. Despite the suggestive coincidence between S.'s emphasis on the active study and teaching of philosophy in retreat (2.2) and his own active retirement (cf. *Ep.* 8.1–2 *in hoc me recondidi et fores clusi, ut prodesse pluribus possem... posterorum negotium ago. illis aliqua quae possint prodesse conscribo*), his theme in 2.2 is woven into a tight sequence of argument that resists simple autobiographical dissection. As for the survey in 3.3 of the various 'official' Stoic grounds for exemption from public service,[64] the first (the state too corrupt to be helped) has invited comparison with Tacitus' indictment of Neronian Rome at e.g. *Ann.* 14.15.3 (AD 59) *inde gliscere flagitia et infamia, nec ulla moribus olim corruptis plus libidinum circumdedit quam illa colluuies*; for the second (the *sapiens* lacks sufficient prestige or power), *Ann.* 14.52.1 (AD 62) *mors Burri infregit Senecae potentiam, quia nec bonis artibus idem uirium erat altero uelut duce amoto, et Nero ad deteriores inclinabat*; for the third (exemption because of illness), *Ann.* 14.56.3 (after S. was refused permission to retire in 62) *rarus per urbem, quasi ualetudine infensa aut sapientiae studiis domi attineretur,*[65] 15.45.3 (after permission was refused in 64) *ficta ualetudine, quasi aeger neruis, cubiculum non egressus*. But despite these suggestive parallels, the grounds for exemption in 3.3 are surely too well attested before S., too conventional rather than personally revealing,[66] to lend unambiguous support to an autobiographical reading.

Further difficulties arise in 8.2–3. True, no exception is apparently made for Rome when (8.3) S. claims that no state is ever to be found which could either tolerate or be tolerated by the *sapiens*.[67] Of his two familiar *exempla*, the hostility of Athens to Socrates and Aristotle (8.2) has been interpreted as a thinly veiled allusion to the persecution of philosophers, especially Stoics, under Nero; and S.'s Carthage, in constant political turmoil and notorious

[63] Dionigi 102–3.   [64] Dionigi 104–6.

[65] Pohlenz II 157 claims that at *Ann.* 14.52–6 Tacitus drew on *Ot.* and *Tr.* as biographical material.

[66] 3.3nn. on *si... possit, si parum... res publica* and *si ualetudo... impediet* with Dionigi 79–86; the point is well made by Ingrosso (1988) 112.

[67] The words *nullam* [sc. *rem publicam*] *inueniam quae...* (8.3) surely undermine Ingrosso's claim ((1988) 112–14) that Rome is in fact distinguished *positively* here from the negative stereotypes of Athens and Carthage.

for its corruption and barbaric cruelty, has predictably drawn comparison with Nero's Rome.[68] But the parallel is fundamentally misguided. Rome is inevitably implicated along with Athens, Carthage and any other *res publica* as an environment unsuitable for the *sapiens*. Whoever the emperor, whether Augustus or Nero, 'good' or 'bad', Rome *must* appear to the remote *sapiens* as a city corrupted by the vices of its population, which (after 1.2–3) inevitably lives in a state remote from the ideal *res publica* envisaged by the *sapiens*. From this detached (cosmic) perspective S.'s attack on Nero's Rome – if *Ot.* is indeed taken to be Neronian – is not so much *ad hominem* as *ad homines*: Rome's corruption is no different from that of any other community. But if S.'s treatment of Athens and Carthage is still pressed into service as an allusion to Nero's Rome, the dating of the treatise to *c*. 62 remains problematic. In observing that when S. refers to Athens and Carthage 'his condemnation inevitably involves Rome', Momigliano for one proposes that 'a date about AD 49 is made probable by the close similarity of thought between the *De otio* and the *De breuitate uitae*'.[69] Claudius' Rome is apparently no less liable than Nero's to Athenian and Carthaginian abuses.

(iii) *Ot.*'s thematic relationship to *Tr.*, which is (also?) addressed to Annaeus Serenus, further complicates the dating of *Ot.* Serenus' change of philosophical position between *C.S.* (itself after 47)[70] and *Tr.* identifies *C.S.* as the earlier work;[71] there an avowed Epicurean (15.4), he follows the Stoics in *Tr.* (1.10); that his Epicurean phase came first may be inferred from *C.S.* 3.2 *si negas accepturum* [sc. *sapientem*] *iniuriam, … omnibus relictis negotiis Stoicus fio* (evidently never yet a Stoic). If, then, Serenus' change of philosophical stance is assumed to have been gradual, *Tr.* would appear to be a relatively late work.[72] At its opening Serenus seeks from S. a remedy for his *displicentia sui* and his 'weakness of good intention' (1.15 *bonae mentis infirmitas*). The prescribed remedy is inner peace (*tranquillitas*); but how to attain it? The best course, claims S. (3.1), is ideally that advocated by the first-century BC Stoic Athenodorus of Tarsus:[73] wholehearted engagement in public life, to the mutual benefit of oneself and others. But because political life is in reality so corrupt, Athenodorus reportedly urged in its place retirement

---

[68] Dionigi 103–4.   [69] (1969) 248.   [70] Griffin (1976) 316.

[71] The conventional view (cf. Griffin (1976) 316) *pace* Grimal (1978) 284–94.

[72] Grimal (1978) 288 assigns *Tr.* to between 51 and 54 (probably 53), but most scholars (e.g. Costa (1994) 4) cautiously opt for an indefinite date after *C.S.* and before Serenus' death.

[73] For whom Griffin (1976) 324 n. 2; the son of Sandon, to be distinguished from the older Athenodorus Cordylion, also of Tarsus.

to the private life (3.2), but not to idle *otium*; through his devoted study and teaching of philosophy the individual can still benefit both himself and mankind in general (3.3–8). In response (4.1–8), S. objects that even if conditions are not conducive to public service, we should withdraw only gradually; but not entirely withdraw, for no state is so corrupt or incapable of improvement that complete retirement is justified. Hence his proposed compromise: *longe ... optimum est miscere otium rebus, quotiens actuosa uita impedimentis fortuitis aut ciuitatis condicione prohibebitur; numquam enim usque eo interclusa sunt omnia ut nulli actioni locus honestae sit* (4.8).

In *Ot.*, by contrast, S. would seem to endorse the Athenodorean position by concluding at 8.3 *incipit omnibus esse otium necessarium, quia quod unum praeferri poterat otio* [sc. the possibility of service in a conducive state] *nusquam est*; and so scholars have found it tempting to identify *Ot.* as the later work, and to detect in S.'s departure there from his position on political participation in *Tr.* a reflection of his changing circumstances under Nero in or around 62.[74] But an immediate objection to this biographical approach is that S.'s shifting positions in *Tr.* and *Ot.* may well be more experimental than a 'sincere' reflection of his own beliefs on either or both occasions. The search for consistency between them as a guide to S.'s changing aspirations under Nero assumes that a biographical pattern can safely be built out of (or imposed on) potentially unrelated texts. Moreover, Griffin for one argues strongly against the conventional view that in *Ot.* S. accepts the Athenodorean position rejected in *Tr.* 4;[75] an argument open to serious objections in point of detail,[76] but which nevertheless draws attention to another major controversy.

(iv) For Griffin *Ot.* is certainly incomplete at its transmitted end.[77] If S. holds that *otium* is 'necessary for all' (8.3) because of the inevitable corruption in all states, and if public service at any age is therefore ruled out, how would it be possible to embark *in the first place* on a career from which eventual retirement is justified?[78] How, in other words, could S. pursue the Athenodorean line in 8.1–3 (retirement necessary in all circumstances) and *still* proceed

[74] The approach is usefully summarized (but not endorsed) by Griffin (1976) 317, 355.

[75] (1976) 332–4.

[76] *Ot.* 8.1 n. on *fastidiose*; nor ridicule of an argument of Chrysippus at 8.4 *si quis ... nauigationem* (8.4 intro. and nn.).

[77] So for most scholars; Dionigi 42 n. 25 for a survey of opinion.

[78] Griffin (1976) 332.

to his second topic as set out in 2.2 (retirement allowable after a career in service)? For Griffin, S. must ultimately have qualified or rejected the Athenodorean view (8.3) before taking a different direction in the hypothetical remainder of *Ot*. Perhaps he argued to the effect 'that, if Chrysippus' law could be interpreted as an injunction to *otium*, then, *a fortiori*, it must be all right for a Stoic to choose *otium* in appropriate circumstances. From there the transition to his second topic [in 2.2] would be easy.'[79]

But the position proposed here is that S. fully answers his second topic (2.2) in the course of the extant fragment; and that his twofold plan of argument as set out in 2.1–2 *primum . . . deinde* is internally complete even if *Ot*. is thought incomplete at its very end (to some, an abrupt and lame finish, but see *Ot*. 8.4 intro.). It is important to stress at the outset that S. can hardly disagree in principle with his interlocutor (1.4) on the Stoic commitment to *actio*. Where they diverge is in the interlocutor's failure to see beyond the narrow confines of the localized *res publica* (4.1) and to appreciate that the detached philosopher who resides intellectually in the *maior res publica* (the cosmic megalopolis) is still fully committed to the goal of *actio* – but not, of course, to *actio* in the conventional sense understood by S.'s interlocutor. In terms of 2.1–2, the Stoic who retires to philosophy after a career in service does not abandon *actio* but rather channels his efforts to that end differently, fulfilling his Stoic duty (1.4 *communi bono operam dare*, 3.5 *hoc nempe ab homine exigitur, ut prosit hominibus . . .*) by teaching (2.2 *hoc . . . ad alios . . . referre*) and by personal example (cf. 3.5 *quisquis bene de se meretur hoc ipso aliis prodest, quod illis profuturum parat*). As for the *sapiens* who abstains *uel a prima aetate* from the *minor res publica*, he belongs to the category of philosopher who makes every effort to seek a tolerant and tolerable state in which to serve (8.1, 3); but from his detached perspective in the *maior res publica*, the pervasiveness of ordinary human corruption in its *minor* counterpart forces his hand (cf. 8.3 *incipit omnibus esse otium necessarium*). But even as he withdraws, the *sapiens* remains committed to *actio* both in the form of 'active' contemplation (for 5.8 *ne contemplatio quidem sine actione est*) and in the form exemplified in *Ot*. by Zeno and Chrysippus. Notorious for advocating public service while never serving in office themselves (1.5n. on *'numquid . . . ibo'*), they nevertheless still served mankind by their philosophical influence and writings (6.4–5). In this way they fully met their Stoic obligation to social *actio* even though they played no active role in the *minor res publica*.

[79] Griffin (1976) 333.

Both parties delineated in 2.1–2, then, – the *sapiens* who withdraws *uel a prima aetate* and the Stoic who withdraws only after a career in service – remain fully committed to *actio* also in retirement. Hence at 7.4 *alii petunt illam* [sc. *contemplationem*], *nobis haec statio, non portus est* S. accounts for both initial topics in 2.1–2 before he concentrates more closely on the first in 8.1–3: for both retired parties in 2.1–2, *actio* will *always* be the ultimate goal (*portus*), *contemplatio* secondary to it as a necessary but temporary 'roadstead' (*statio*) along the way. By thus demonstrating that *actio* remains the priority even *in otio*, S. fulfils the initial task he sets himself in 2.1 *Nunc probabo tibi non desciscere me a praeceptis Stoicorum*. Griffin's objection remains: if service in the *minor res publica* at *any* age is ruled out, S.'s second topic in 2.2 would seem to be redundant because a conventional career will never be an option in the first place. But such a career is ruled out by circumstance rather than by will or intention. If an appropriate state could ever be found, the philosopher would serve for as long as he is practically capable of doing so (hence the emphasis on retirement because of age and infirmity in 2.2 *emeritis iam stipendiis, profligatae aetatis*). In effect, S. necessarily keeps open in 2.2 the possibility of service in a conducive, albeit currently non-existent, *res publica*; for the Stoic commitment to serving the *minor res publica* remains valid in principle even if in grim reality the philosopher is prevented by circumstance from ever meeting that commitment.[80]

4. *DE BREVITATE VITAE*

(a) *Preliminaries*

S.'s argument in *Ot.* is driven by the tension between his persona and his imaginary interlocutor, whose words in 1.4 characterize him as a practical if narrow-minded Stoic more at home in the *minor res publica* than in its

---

[80] From a different perspective, moreover, S.'s two initial propositions can be seen to refer to different parties, in 2.1 the *sapiens*, in 2.2 the more 'ordinary' Stoic who serves the *minor res publica* conventionally enough until (philosophical) retirement. If this difference is conceded, Griffin's words ((1976) 332) warrant qualification: 'If *otium* is *necessary* for a Stoic, how can any kind of public career or *actio*, whenever terminated, be justified?' True only of the *sapiens* (cf. 8.3 *incipit omnibus* [sc. *sapientibus*] *esse otium necessarium*); a public career remains fully justified for the 'ordinary' Stoic who, like S.'s interlocutor, has yet (if ever) to progress to the transforming perspective of the *maior res publica* (cf. 4.1–2). As soon as Griffin's 'a Stoic' is qualified in this way, lifelong abstention (for the *sapiens*) in 2.1 becomes reconcilable with retirement only *after* long service in 2.2.

maior counterpart. This lively approach fully coincides with Nussbaum's characterization of S. and Lucretius as offering 'remarkable models of philosophical-literary investigation, in which literary language and complex dialogical structures engage the interlocutor's (and the reader's) entire soul in a way that an abstract and impersonal prose treatise probably could not'.[81] S.'s idiosyncratic mode of protreptic[82] in *Breu.* is still more engaging in this way, but with a less organized structure than in *Ot.* Grimal for one attempts to offer a detailed plan of the work,[83] but with limited success as S. progresses more by the loose association of ideas than by rigidly following a strict line of argument.[84] Ch. 1: people complain that life is too short. Not so; life is long enough if well managed. After this *exordium* chs. 2–9 survey the countless ways in which life is squandered, time not properly valued. In 10.1, a summary of S.'s theme so far: the preoccupied (*occupati*, a key word in the treatise) inevitably find life too short. In 10.2–17.6, where (*inter alia*) the attractions of true philosophical *otium* are contrasted with the delusions of *otium* as commonly experienced, the different world-perspectives of the *sapiens* and the *occupati* are gradually isolated from each other. The 'view from above' finally prevails in S.'s admonition to Paulinus to retire in 18.1–19.2, where it soars above the lives mired in *occupatio* earlier in the work; the virtual ecstasy of emancipation in chs. 14–15 and 19 is felt in direct proportion to the suffocating effects of preoccupation which are so dramatically pictured in the rest of the treatise. The two 'halves' of the work are coordinated by the transition to positive instruction in 10.1 *tamen ut illis* [sc. *occupatis*] *error exprobretur suus, docendi* [ch. 11 onwards], *non tantum deplorandi* [chs. 2–9] *sunt.* We shall return to this division below.

(b) Date and addressee

Despite continuing controversy, especially about the date,[85] the position taken here is (i) that S.'s addressee is certainly Pompeius Paulinus, a knight of Arelate (modern Arles; cf. Plin. *Nat.* 33.143) and *praefectus annonae* probably from late 48 to 55. On the assumption that he was the father of the Pompeius Paulinus whom Tacitus mentions as a consular legate of Lower Germany in 55–7 (*Ann.* 13.53.2) and as a member in 62 of a commission

---

[81] (1994) 486.
[82] For protreptic as 'the least inept' label for the work, Griffin (1976) 318.
[83] In his edition, 5–13; also (1960).   [84] Traina xv after Albertini (1923) 258.
[85] P. 2 and n. 4.

overseeing the *uectigalia publica* (*Ann.* 15.18.3),[86] our Paulinus was probably born not much after 10 BC at the latest; for the younger Paulinus must have been at least 32 and was probably older when, before AD 55, he held the consulship.[87] The case, now generally accepted, for identifying our Paulinus as S.'s father-in-law rests on Tac. *Ann.* 15.60.4, where Pompeia Paulina is named as S.'s wife (S. refers to her as Paulina at *Ep.* 104.1, 2, 5; cf. Dio 62.25.1).[88] (ii) *Breu.* was written between AD 49 and 55. If born *c*. 10 BC, Paulinus, though apparently still vigorous (cf. 19.2 *nunc, dum calet sanguis, uigentibus ad meliora eundum est*), was clearly of an appropriate age to receive S.'s admonition to retire in *Breu.*[89] The case for dating *Breu.* to before the end of January 50 has been overstated,[90] while Griffin's argument for 55 is intriguing but inconclusive.[91] Hence the case for an open date between 49 and 55, with S. fully engaged in political life even as he urges Paulinus to retire.

(c) Theme and interpretation

Real but not material, time was classified by the Stoics as one of the four incorporeals along with the 'sayable', void and place.[92] Infinite in extension, time is also infinitely divisible on either side, past and future, of the 'limiting' present. For Chrysippus only the present is fully real in the sense that it 'belongs' (ὑπάρχει) to us in a way that the past and the future do not (they ὑφίστανται 'subsist'). But no time is exactly present; as part of a continuum, the present in the strict sense is itself composed of the past and the future, so that when we talk of *now* performing an action we refer to the looser, 'durative' present, which has reality 'only in relation to my consciousness,

---

[86] This against the view (e.g. Herrmann (1937) 110) that S.'s Paulinus was involved in the Neronian commission. For a more detailed account of the father and son distinguished as here, Bérenger (1993) 91–101.

[87] Griffin (1962) 105.

[88] Paulina (*PIR*² VI p. 299 no. 678) is generally assumed to be his second and much younger wife, but for controversy, Griffin (1962) 106 n. 30 and (1976) 57–9.

[89] Cf. Griffin (1962) 113 on Paulinus' age.   [90] 13.8n. on *Auentinum . . . esse*.

[91] Above, n. 7. The case for 62 (above, n. 4) is also unconvincing. True, in addition to 49–55, the list of known *praefecti annonae* can accommodate Paulinus in 62. But in contrast to 49–55 he faces competition for the post in 62 (from Claudius Athenodorus; Griffin (1962) 105); and Paulinus' doubtful identification with his namesake in Tacitus tells further against 62 (above and n. 86; S. does not refer at 18.3 *tu quidem orbis terrarum rationes administras . . .* to Paulinus' involvement in the Neronian commission of 62).

[92] Goldschmidt (1989) 13; L–S I 27D.

thought, initiative, and freedom'.[93] S. exploits the present in the strict sense when it suits his argument (10.6n. on *praesens . . . breuissimum est*), but he, like other later Stoics, moves away from time 'viewed primarily as a problem in physics' to time itself as 'a moral problem'.[94] In *Breu*. time enters the moral sphere because our (Stoic) inner freedom depends on our mastery *over* time; the good and happy life is impossible unless the value of each present moment is understood in relation to 'really' living in accordance with nature.[95]

The Stoics were in agreement with the Epicureans on the importance of seizing the moment (cf. 9.1 *protinus uiue*). But whereas for the Epicurean this liberation from the cares of the past and from anxiety about the future amounts to 'a relaxation, a pure joy of existing', the Stoic insists on 'the effort needed to pay attention to oneself, the joyous acceptance of the present moment imposed on us by fate'.[96] In other words the Epicurean 'enjoys the present moment, whereas the Stoic wills it intensely; for the one, it is a pleasure; for the other, a duty'.[97] By concentrating on the present the Stoic lives in a state of vigilance and presence of mind, a self-consciousness which frees us from the passions and composes life by always acting in accordance with reason. At every moment the Stoic's actions are also harmonized with universal reason so that 'his consciousness expands into the infinity of the cosmos, and the entire universe is present to him'.[98] Because only the present is fully real, the *sapiens* possesses the whole of reality in each instant, his existence always complete (cf. *Ep*. 59.16); his perfect happiness in the moment cannot be increased by longer duration, so that each day is as if a complete life (cf. 7.9 *qui* [sc. *sapiens*] *omnem diem tamquam uitam ordinat*). Because each present moment is lived in this serene way, the *sapiens* is untroubled by regret when he surveys the secure past (cf. 10.3), as if it really is possible for him to envision a fixed 'historical' past as opposed to one always re-created or reinvented in the moment of recollection. By delimiting the present the *sapiens* is also unburdened by the future (cf. 7.9 *nec optat crastinum nec timet*);[99] his mastery over the different parts of time, past, present and future (cf. 15.5), is complete.

[93] Hadot (1998) 136–7; *Breu*. 10.2nn. on *In tria . . . futurum est* and *quod agimus breue est*.
[94] Rist 287, with emphasis on Marcus Aurelius.
[95] For this Senecan emphasis on time mastered, Armisen-Marchetti (1995) and 546 n. 2 for bibliography; Dionigi (1995) 17–22 and Gagliardi (1998), esp. 31–50 on *Breu*.
[96] Hadot (1995) 69.   [97] Hadot (1995) 230.   [98] Hadot (1995) 229.
[99] On this 'appropriation' of the past and future, Armisen-Marchetti (1995) 554–61.

S.'s mode of therapy in *Breu.* thus lays claim to a positive efficiency, with time made a commodity which can be used to better advantage through better management, and clinically divisible (as if like Gaul) into three parts, *quod fuit, quod est, quod futurum est* (10.2), each of them brought under the systematic control of reason. The essential optimism of this approach is well brought out by comparing the Horatian experience of time in e.g. *C.* 2.14 *Eheu fugaces, Postume, Postume,* | *labuntur anni* . . . and gently evoked by the Horatian undertones of *Breu.* 8.5 *nemo restituet annos, nemo iterum te tibi reddet* etc. In Horace the relentless movement of time and life towards old age and death is offset by the compensating pleasures of *carpe diem* (25–8; cf. *C.* 1.11.8), which offer at least a measure of resistance to the universal flow even as the rest of the poem resigns us to it; submission is inevitable, the alleviating effects of *carpe diem* ultimately of little or no consequence.[100] But for S. the Horatian sentiments of 8.5 are there to be confounded by a different understanding of time. *Protinus uiue,* he urges in 9.1, not in the compensating spirit of Horace's *carpe diem* but as if it is enough simply to abolish procrastination by imposing a new discipline on life. In *Breu.* more generally, the positive effect of S.'s descriptions of the 'lost' lives of the *occupati* is to provoke the reaction that we *do* have an alternative, that the self *can* be reclaimed from the predatory demands of others (cf. 2.4, 7.7), that there *is* a way of retaking control of our existence. Hence S.'s intolerant sureness of voice, with 'no serious consideration here, as there is elsewhere in Seneca, of the claims of the condemned activities [e.g. pointless learning in 13.1–8], no admission that they can be pursued for different motives and at different moral levels: their practitioners are all condemned as men driven by passion (2.1–3), or self-disgust (2.5), rather than guided by rational decisions (2.2; 3.3)'.[101] S. offers a radical cure, not just partial comfort; his uncompromising manner ('this way or not at all . . .') is a necessary part of the treatment.

The Senecan treatment requires a 'letting go' of the ordinary encumbrances of life, a change of perspective to which *Breu.* guides us in two stages that correspond to the distinction drawn at 10.1 *docendi, non tantum deplorandi sunt* [sc. *occupati*]. In the first (chs. 1–9) S.'s condemnation of the *occupati* is both comforting and cajoling: comforting because it invites Paulinus (and the reader) to side with the enlightened at a reassuring distance from the

[100] On this Horatian tension between resistance and submission to time, Commager (1962) 281–90.

[101] Griffin (1976) 318.

worse kinds of *occupati*; and yet cajoling because the reader's own life is inevitably subjected to scrutiny along the way. So in e.g. S.'s audit at 3.2–3 of time wasted in a long life, his direct address to his imaginary interlocutor (e.g. 3.3 *repete memoria tecum quando certus consilii fueris . . .*) also speaks directly to the reader, effectively submitting his life to the same audit – a relatively straightforward example of how S. actively involves his reader in the therapeutic work of the text. In the second stage (10.2–17.6) S. only partially modifies his treatment of the *occupati* despite his declared transition in 10.1 to a more constructive approach (*docere*). The same condemnatory tone persists in e.g. his surveys of *otium* squandered on trivial pursuits in chs. 12–13; but these biting descriptions also prepare the way for his change of direction in 14.1 *Soli omnium otiosi sunt qui sapientiae uacant, soli uiuunt*, where he embarks on a strategy which finds important illumination in the *Epistulae morales*.

In *Ep.* 44[102] S. distinguishes two different kinds of *nobilitas*. At this stage in the therapeutic process that the *Epistulae morales* cumulatively represent, Lucilius is pictured at a low point, apparently complaining to S. in (we are to imagine) a recent letter that for reasons of birth and fortune he has failed to rise *ad felicitatem hominum maximam*, i.e. to the highest political and social standing. In response, S. maintains that Lucilius *does* have access to the greatest *felicitas* if he thinks of such happiness from a different, philosophical perspective. To that end S. sets up a countersociety of philosophers, among them Socrates, Cleanthes and Plato (44.3), all of them *nobiles* not because of their rank and station in life (cf. 3 *patricius Socrates non fuit*) but because philosophy made them so; the freedman (*libertinus*) holds his particular place in society, but only the philosopher is truly free (44.6 *liber*). The lesson for Lucilius is that 'giving up Roman values and Roman class- and status-consciousness is a necessary prerequisite for achieving the worth that is most important'.[103] S. delivers a very similar lesson in *Breu.*, where another countersociety is set up in the contrast drawn between different kinds of *clientela* in chs. 14 and 15. While the ordinary Roman client rushes from one humiliation to the next, striving to gain access to his elusive *patroni* (14.3–4; cf. 2.5), the *sapiens always* has open access to all of *his* patrons, whether Socrates or Carneades, Epicurus or Zeno (14.2, 5). In contrast to its real-life alternative, this philosophical *clientela* is (paradoxically) liberating, freeing the *sapiens* to be his own self-sufficient master who 'fully' lives because he alone controls the whole of his time (cf. 15.5). After this releasing vision, S.'s

[102] Analysed by Nussbaum (1994) 354–7.   [103] Nussbaum (1994) 356.

renewed portrayal of the anxieties and delusions of the *occupati* in chs. 16–17 is all the more oppressive, sinking their lives in misery (17.4 *miserrimam . . . , non tantum breuissimam, uitam . . .*) before he finally appeals to Paulinus to retire (18.1 *Excerpe itaque te uulgo . . .*).

The distinction drawn between different kinds of *clientela* in chs. 14 and 15 offers a model of how to 'let go', or how to see the habitual impositions on life from a transforming external viewpoint. So in ch. 18 S. surveys Paulinus' role and responsibilities as *praefectus annonae* from a position of disarming detachment: Paulinus has served for long enough (18.1), greater intellectual stimulation awaits him in retirement (18.2); while important in one way, the task of managing the Roman corn-supply is beneath a man of such wide education and abilities (18.4); lesser men can do the job; so much for the highness of Paulinus' position. S. varies the technique in 19.1–2: from the perspective of the 'view from above', here (as at *Ot.* 4.2, 5.5–6) represented by a sequence of cosmic questions (*quae materia sit dei, quae uoluntas* etc.), Paulinus' official duties as described in 19.1 appear positively mundane in comparison with the 'higher' business of philosophy (*haec sacra et sublimia*);[104] so much for the petty preoccupations of the world when viewed from the cosmic perspective.

And yet all speculation as to whether such procedures actually led Paulinus to retire is surely beside the point.[105] The greater interest of the work lies in the change of attitude that it promotes, as S. creates an inner world of the personal, a self-regard which has its own stimuli and evaluative structure independent of one's public persona and the performance of one's public duties. S.'s advice to Paulinus to retire from his important position is provocative in the extreme, and doubtless an impractical option for most of his 'ordinary' readers. But his exhortation still hits home if it causes them (*us*) to step back from life, to question from a radical, alternative perspective the ordering of our priorities in life, and to conclude that we can be *occupati* in one area of existence (in the workplace, the senate-house, the imperial palace etc.) while still retaining our freedom of conscience and our capacity for self-development in another (spiritual) area – certainly a

[104] For the hint of condescension in S.'s tone cf. Momigliano (1969) 246 'Up to a point his contempt for a great Roman institution like the *annona* is little more than the consequence of his rooted conviction that the human body is something inferior and contemptible . . . '

[105] E.g. Duff xi 'it is possible . . . that Seneca did not in the least expect that his advice would be taken'.

'modern' message given the late twentieth-century interest in alternative living and in psychotherapeutic, chemical and spiritual forms of escape from the depersonalizing pressures of everyday life. If composed when S. himself was *in officio*, *Breu.* is not so much the work of a hypocrite as an embodiment of its message: in urging the taking back of life and our detachment from its pettier preoccupations (pettier at least in the cosmic scheme of things), *Breu.* exercises the very self-consciousness that it promotes.

5. STYLE AND LANGUAGE[106]

(a) *Senecan style: context and general tendency*

A measure of S.'s ancient popularity as a 'modern' stylist is the harshness of Quintilian's criticism of his *corruptum et omnibus uitiis fractum dicendi genus* (*Inst.* 10.1.125), a verdict prompted by S.'s apparently dangerous influence on so many young admirers (125 *tum ... solus hic fere in manibus adulescentium fuit*). While Quintilian commends him for his forceful denunciations of vice and concedes that his writing is not wholly without merit (129), S.'s epigrammatic brevity and apparently faulty expression (129–30) mark the corruption of all that Cicero represents as *Latinae eloquentiae princeps* (6.3.1).[107] But Quintilian's reverence for Cicero was backward-looking in an age when oratory was no longer the living force in Roman political life which it had been in the Republic, and when declamation had become an increasingly elaborate form of exhibitionism in itself rather than a preparation for 'real' public speaking.[108] S. thus reflects the more general tendencies of the so-called Silver period in his striving for immediate impact through bold and arresting forms of expression, point and epigram (*sententia*), dazzling word-play and word-formation – a style much admired and imitated in other

[106] In general: Summers xv–xcv, Bourgery (1922), Leeman (1963) i 264–83, Currie (1966), Coleman (1974), Wright (1974), Setaioli (1980) and (1981 a), and Traina (1987).
[107] See Leeman (1963) i 278–82, 293–6, with mitigating emphasis on the fact that in e.g. *Ep.* 100 and 114 S. himself criticizes the more excessive features of the declamatory style. For both sides of S.'s ancient reputation, Gell. *N.A.* 12.2.1 (with Gellius' own barbs at 12.2.8, 11, 14); Fronto is harsher (p. 153.11–154.13 van den Hout²).
[108] Bonner (1949) 71–83 with Currie (1966) 77 and Wright (1974) 42–3; this is not to deny that 'oratorical skill remained an avenue to wealth, influence and prestige' (Mayer (2001) 15).

literatures through the ages,[109] but also much censured.[110] For Caligula his
style was like 'sand without lime' (Suet. *Cal.* 53.2 *harenam . . . sine calce*), the
charge apparently that S.'s prose lacks cohesion because his excessive cultivation of instant point and effect results in illogicalities, his sequence of
argument broken by repetition, distraction and self-indulgent display. His
casual approach to the rhetorical divisions which conventionally separated
a discourse into its parts contributes to this impression of informality.[111]
But this looseness of form is also characteristic of the mode of popular
philosophical essay often termed 'diatribe' in modern scholarship, as if a
clearly defined genre of lively and combative sermon, full of e.g. rhetorical
exclamations and questions, imaginary interlocutors, colourful everyday
imagery and language etc., was recognized in antiquity. But there is no
compelling evidence that this was so. Many of S.'s rhetorical techniques
doubtless existed in the Hellenistic popular philosophical tradition, but
they were not exclusive to that tradition and so defy simple characterization as constituents of a separate genre of 'diatribe'; the often used term
'Cynic-Stoic diatribe' may especially mislead in this respect.[112]

But while his style reflects (and shapes) the fashion of the age, S. is no
slave to fashion. Far from addressing his audience in the austere language
of technical philosophy, he relies for the therapeutic effect of his writing
on directly engaging each reader in the 'highly personal, vivid, and concrete way' emphasized by Nussbaum;[113] in this respect he hardly lives up to
the Stoics' ancient reputation for subtle and efficient but dry argumenta-
tion with little regard for eloquent style and presentation.[114] Three general

---

[109] Summers xcvi–cxiv offers a brief but convenient survey.

[110] E.g. Macaulay (in T. Pinney, ed., *The letters of Thomas Babington Macaulay* III
(Cambridge 1976) 178 (to Thomas Flower Ellis, 30 May 1836)) 'There is hardly a
sentence which might not be quoted. But to read him straight forward is like dining
on nothing but anchovy sauce. I dislike the man as well as the style.' According to
John Aubrey in his *Brief lives*, the seventeenth-century Oxford scholar Ralph Kittel
'was wont to say that Seneca writes as a Boare does pisse, *scilicet* by jirkes' (ed.
O. Lawson Dick (Ann Arbor 1957) 186).

[111] Wright (1974) 41–2, more measured than Currie (1966) 80.

[112] For 'diatribic' elements in S., Weber (1895) and esp. Oltramare (1926). For the
cautious approach taken here to the diatribe as a genre, Powell (1988) 12–14 with
Griffin (1976) 508–9; in the commentary the term is used with these reservations in
mind.

[113] (1994) 339.

[114] Cf. Cic. *Parad. praef.* 2, *Fin.* 4.7, 78–9 (Panaetius more lucid than earlier Stoics),
De orat. 2.159, 3.66, *Brut.* 114 *exile* [sc. *orationis genus*] *nec satis populari assensioni accom-
modatum*, 118, Quint. *Inst.* 10.1.84 with Currie (1966) 82–3.

characteristics warrant emphasis before his lexical style and technique are
sampled in greater detail.

(i) However 'ramshackle'[115] in general structure, S.'s writing (especially in
Breu.) is ordered by design, albeit loosely, his constant shifts in direction and
angle of approach from chapter to chapter always re-engaging the reader
through a new injection of stimulus. In this respect he follows 'essentially a
literary structure, not a logical one', his technique 'not that of the philosopher, developing a systematic argument with a logical beginning, middle,
and end, but of the preacher'.[116]

(ii) The intrusiveness of second person address: S.'s imaginary interlocutor
in *Ot.* serves as a textual surrogate not just for his addressee (Serenus?) but
also for the reader, who thus 'participates' in the dialogue and becomes
involved at e.g. 2.1 *Nunc probabo tibi*..., 6.1 *aduersus hoc tibi respondeo* etc. as
the direct object of S.'s persuasion. So also in *Breu.* S.'s ambiguous use of
the second person singular at e.g. 7.7 *dispunge, inquam, et recense uitae tuae
dies*...allows him to conflate Paulinus and his reader as his 'primary' addressee even as he may simply be using the indefinite 'you'.[117] S. also uses
changes of addressee from e.g. 'you, the centenarian' in the imaginary audit
in 3.2–3 of a life largely wasted, to 'all of you who live as if you're going
to live for ever' in 3.4 *tamquam semper uicturi uiuitis*, to the second person
singular (possibly indefinite, possibly addressing Paulinus / the reader) in
3.5 *audies plerosque dicentes*..., and then to a different person when S. rounds
on his imaginary interlocutor later in 3.5 (*et quem tandem longioris uitae praedem accipis?*). This free-ranging technique allows him to engage his wider
readership (e.g. 6.4 *Vestra mehercules uita...in artissimum contrahetur*..., 7.7 *uos*
etc.) while still directly addressing Paulinus as well as the individual reader
with e.g. 2.4 *pererra*..., 7.2 *aspice*..., 9.1 *protinus uiue* etc. He thus extends
the 'personal' relevance of *Breu.* to a universal as well as a more private
audience, while the intrusive persistence of his second person imperatives
in particular guides each reader towards self-scrutiny.

(iii) Beyond the engaging lexical and stylistic effects of his writing, S. uses
more general strategies to assist his reader's therapeutic progress through
the text. In *Ot.* his method is shaped by what he portrays as his interlocutor's

---

[115] Cf. Currie (1966) 80.   [116] Coleman (1974) 285–6.
[117] No ambiguity only when S. finally appeals directly to Paulinus (18.1 *Excerpe
itaque te uulgo, Pauline carissime*...).

narrowness of philosophical vision. Very much a citizen of the localized *minor res publica* as opposed to its universal counterpart in 4.1–2, the interlocutor is characterized by his imagined words in 1.4 as a rigid Stoic whose text-book commitment to *actio* to the exclusion of *contemplatio* is matched by his narrow-minded hostility to Epicureanism. In response, S.'s technique is to work within and then gently stretch his interlocutor's narrow horizons in a more enlightened, cosmic direction; his method works in progressive cycles through the fragment.[118] In *Breu.*, on the other hand, S. relies more on techniques of emphasis in order to impress each new point on his audience. His staple method is to introduce an abstract or general idea which is then embedded more deeply in the reader through S.'s concrete re-expression, variation or elaboration of it.[119] One of many typical cases is 9.1, where he embarks on a new theme, taking to task those who boast of their foresight for failing to live in the moment. His remonstrances culminate in the sharp injunction *protinus uiue*, only for the point to be recast through his quotation (9.2) of Virg. *G.* 3.66–7 *optima quaeque dies miseris mortalibus aeui | prima fugit.* S.'s subsequent elucidation of Virgil's meaning (9.2 '*quid cunctaris?*' *inquit* '*quid cessas?* . . . ') remakes the point by spelling out its concrete message; and the consolation process is still unfinished (cf. 9.3 *de die tecum loquitur et de hoc ipso fugiente*). This 'embedding' technique contributes much to the sermon-like atmosphere of *Breu.* Its many variations through the work range from S.'s use of concrete analogy (e.g. 1.4 *sicut amplae . . . opes . . . , si bono custode traditae sunt, usu crescunt, ita aetas nostra bene disponenti multum patet*, 7.10, 10.5) to his adducing of ever further evidence to support a general point (e.g. the ever more extreme cases of *otium occupatum* in 12.2–6 or of *otium* wasted on trivial literary learning in 13.1–8). But perhaps most notable of all is his use of historical *exempla* to illustrate an abstract idea, often allowing S. to construct within the *exemplum* a mini-drama which is especially engaging because it captures and draws the reader's imagination in unusually powerful ways.[120] The 'tragic' potential of the cases of Augustus, Cicero and Livius Drusus at *Breu.* 4.2–6.2, of Xerxes at 17.2 and of Scipio in 17.6 is particularly suggestive in this respect.

[118] See 3 intro. and esp. 4.1–2, 5.1–6, 7.1–3.

[119] Cf. Nussbaum (1994) 338 on 'the focus on the concrete and the use of examples . . . Seneca's practice . . . is to move from concrete context to general reflection, and back again, allowing them to illuminate one another.'

[120] Nussbaum (1994) 339 with Mayer (1991) 165–8 (S.'s use of *exempla* as 'companions of our self-examination'); for their directness, *Ep.* 6.5 *longum iter est per praecepta, breue et efficax per exempla.*

(b) Senecan mannerism, vocabulary, wordplay

S.'s style in *Ot.* is generally less exuberant than in *Breu.*, where his brisker pace and racier tone are more conducive to stylistic display. Even so, in constantly striving to (re-)engage the reader S. uses different registers of narrative mood and tone in both works, from close analytical argument at e.g. *Ot.* 3.2–5 and 7.1–4 to the freer movement of e.g. his portrayal of nature seducing man into contemplation of the universe at *Ot.* 5.2–6;[121] from his melodramatic descriptions, partly satirical in colour, of the *occupati* under stress at e.g. *Breu.* 2.4–5, 7.6–8 and 17.4–5 to the quasi-tragic dramas of e.g. Augustus, Cicero and Livius Drusus at 4.2–6.2; from his brisk, intolerant surveys of *otium* wasted in chs. 12–13 to the calmer flow of e.g. his 'poetic' (Horatian) reflections on time at 8.5 and on literary/philosophical immortality at 15.4. Through *sermocinatio* (e.g. *Ot.* 1.4, 6.1, 7.2, *Breu.* 3.2–3, 3.5, 7.8 etc.), personification (*Ot.* 5.6) and philosophical or poetic quotation (*Ot.* 1.4, 3.2, *Breu.* 2.2, 9.2) different narrative voices speak directly to the reader (or hearer)[122] with multiple variations in pitch, tone and viewpoint. In passages of extended narrative description such as *Breu.* 5.1 (on Cicero) and 6.1 (Livius Drusus) or 18.5 (the food-crisis precipitated by Caligula) complex sentences are sometimes constructed in a 'classical' manner, with elaborate subordination and ornate systems of balance (cf. *Breu.* 5.1 intro.). So also on occasion in *Ot.* (nn. on e.g. 5.7 *cui . . . concutiat*, 6.2 *quomodo . . . sic . . . ostendens*), but more typical of S. generally is his use either of brief sentences with little subordination for added point, or of longer structures whose subordinate clauses follow a straightforward internal design, often with anaphoric repetition for shape (e.g. *Breu.* 3.2 *duc quantum . . . quantum . . .* , 3.3 *repete . . . quando . . . quotus . . . quando* etc.);[123] but he will also use a plain connective between clauses (e.g. *Ot.* 1.2 *aliud ex alio placet uexatque nos hoc quoque . . .*), or no connection (asyndeton) for economy, as at e.g. *Ot.* 1.2 *petita relinquimus, relicta repetimus, alternae inter cupiditatem nostram et paenitentiam uices sunt.*

    In the latter instance the asyndeton makes starker the impact of his antimetabole (n. on *petita . . . repetimus*) and hyperbaton (n. on *alternae . . . uices*; *Ot.* 5.4n. on *labentia*); but however penetrating in the moment, both conceits illustrate a form of narrative stimulus which is spread throughout the

---

[121] On the latter, Hijmans (1966) 243, 247–8 (part of a broader survey of drama and spectacle in Senecan prose).

[122] An important emphasis; Hijmans (1991) 16–19.

[123] For the anaphora, Traina (1987) 31–3, 99–101 (featuring *Breu.* 2.5, 3.2–3, 7.2).

Dialogues, as much to test his readers as to impress them. If his brand of Sto-icism promotes above all a form of self-conscious vigilance in life, his style itself requires a constant alertness to verbal possibility, pattern and fine dis-tinction, so that the audience is actively challenged by his word-craft as well as by his philosophical 'message'. The permutations of his wordplay are far too numerous to be adequately catalogued here,[124] but favoured techniques include (i) polyptoton at e.g. *Ot.* 6.4 *apud omnes omnium gentium homines*, *Breu.* 1.1 *uitae... uita*, 17.5 *spes spem... ambitionem ambitio*; (ii) punning at e.g. *Breu.* 6.4 *uita... uitia*, 11.1 *exeant... extrahantur*, 20.1 *uideris... inuideris*; (iii) pari-syllabic pairings (often punning) at e.g. *Breu.* 7.3 *percepisse... praecipere*, 9.1 *pendet... perdit*; (iv) related words used in combination at e.g. *Ot.* 5.3 *specta-tores... spectaculis*, 6.3 *si non actor deest sed agenda desunt*; (v) different parts of the same word in combination at e.g. *Breu.* 3.4 *uicturi uiuitis*, 6.1 *dicitur dixisse*, 17.4 *bona... bene... optimae*; (vi) word-contrast at e.g. *Ot.* 2.2 *cum didicerunt docent*, 5.7 *immortalium... mortalis* (cf. *Breu.* 15.4), *Breu.* 20.1 *dignitatis... indignitates*; (vii) notable homoeoteleuton at e.g. *Breu.* 15.3 *nobilissimorum ingeniorum*, 19.1 *tranquilliora tutiora maiora*; and (viii) chiasmus (with homoeoteleuton) at e.g. *Ot.* 5.5 *grauia descenderint, euolauerint leuia*, *Breu.* 15.4 *extendendae mortalitatis... in immortalitatem uertendae*. Wordplay naturally figures prominently in his mem-orable 'points' of thought (*sententiae*) as illustrated by e.g. *Breu.* 12.9 *ille otiosus est cui otii sui et sensus est*, 17.6 *otium numquam agetur, semper optabitur*; the com-bination of anaphora, contrast and clausal symmetry makes *Breu.* 3.4 *omnia tamquam mortales timetis, omnia tamquam immortales concupiscitis* an especially impressive case.

At the lexical level his use of colloquial language makes direct contact with everyday life,[125] e.g. in his words to his interlocutor at *Breu.* 3.2 (nn. on *agedum, computationem, rex* and *lis*; cf. e.g. 7.7 *reiculos*, 8.5 *uelis nolis*, 16.3 *con-stitutum, Ot.* 1.4 *bene gnauiter*, 5.1 *quid porro?* etc.). Hyperbole is frequent (e.g. *Breu.* 12.1 *elidi, illidant*, 12.9 *mortuus*, 14.4 *miliens* etc.), especially in the form of bold and often apparently unprecedented metaphor or image (e.g. *Ot.* 1.1 *scindimus, Breu.* 2.4 *offocantur*, 4.5 *exprimerent*, 7.8 *diripitur*, 15.2 *clientelam* etc.). Technical philosophical language is generally avoided and under-stated when it does occur (nn. on e.g. *Ot.* 1.1 *nemo... detorqueat*, 3.5 *prosit*, 6.3 *profectus, Breu.* 1.1 *affectus*); hence the striking effect of his semi-technical language (e.g. *indiuidua* for 'atoms') when it is used much more overtly in

---

[124] See Summers lxx–xcv and Traina (1987), the latter with a useful index (allit-terazione, anafora, antitesi, arcaismo etc.).

[125] Summers xlii–l; rich but more diffuse are Setaioli (1980) and (1981 a).

his purple passages of 'liberated' cosmic enquiry at *Ot.* 5.5–6 and *Breu.* 19.1. His use of archaism (e.g. *Breu.* 10.3 *quoi*) or poeticism as at e.g. *Ot.* 5.4 *labentia, flexili, Breu.* 8.5 *ibit . . . aetas, tacita labetur, curret,* 10.6 *fluit, irrequieta,* 17.2 *lacrimas profudit* etc. occasionally brings notable tonal variation; there are also echoes of poetic rhythm (e.g. *Breu.* 9.3 *ipso fugiente*), but they are rare and faint in comparison with S.'s heavy use of alliteration, assonance and homoeoteleuton (nn. on e.g. *Ot.* 8.4 *in quo . . . rapiant, Breu.* 7.10 *saeua . . . egit?,* 12.4 *componendis . . . canticis* etc.). A favourite technique is to heighten the sound and accelerate the dramatic pace of a passage through 'outraged' rhetorical questions and exclamations, often in bursts of short sentences or clauses coordinated by anaphoric repetition (e.g. *Breu.* 7.7 *quot . . . quot . . . quot* etc., 8.3 *quomodo . . . quomodo,* 14.4 *quam multi . . . quam multi* etc.). For conciseness the future participle is worked particularly hard,[126] replacing a more elaborate subordinate construction at e.g. *Ot.* 3.3, 5.3, 5.4, *Breu.* 3.4, 19.1 etc. Ellipsis is common (e.g. nn. on *Breu.* 1.3 *quam . . . sentimus,* 4.4 *non poterat,* 15.3 *maiora . . . quo . . . diuiseris*), as is adversative asyndeton (nn. on *Breu.* 1.2 *homini,* 3.1 *discurrunt: in uitam,* 7.3 *uiuere . . . discendum est*) and also *correctio* for sharp contrast (*non* x *sed* y; e.g. *Ot.* 4.1, 8.1, *Breu.* 1.3, 7.10, 16.4 etc.). Two further devices, rarer and more striking, which S. uses for strong contrasting emphasis are juxtaposition (nn. on *Breu.* 4.2 *Diuus Augustus,* 9.4 *inciderunt, accedere*) and paradox (12.2 *otium occupatum* and *desidiosa occupatio,* 12.4 *iners negotium,* 16.1 n. on *nihil agunt, occupatos,* 16.2n. on *mortem . . . timent*).

Emphasis is placed in the commentary on aspects of S.'s language and syntax in *Ot.* and *Breu.* which reflect his markedly post-Augustan/Silver usage.[127] A brief list of more significant entries is given here for convenience: nn. on *Ot.* 1.1 *singuli,* 3.5 *hoc . . . exigitur, ut . . . ,* 5.6 *contenta* (+ inf.), 6.5 *discursus; Breu.* 1.1 *gignimur,* 1.2 *exigentis,* 2.2 *plerosque,* 2.5 *dignatus es* and *imputes,* 3.1 *in . . . consentiant,* 3.3 *certus consilii,* 3.4 *in causa,* 7.7 *dispunge,* 7.9 *crastinum* and *de cetero,* 8.2 *annua,* 11.1 *blandiuntur,* 12.5 *exeat* and *enormia,* 12.6 *gestationum,* 13.4 *remittamus,* 13.9 *praestationem,* 14.3 *discursant,* 14.4 *transcurrant* and *uitabunt,* 15.1 *obseruatio,* 18.5 *modo modo,* 19.1 *plena,* 20.3 *plangi,* 20.5 *ambitiosas.* Finally, prose rhythm:[128] *Ot.* and *Breu.* fairly reflect the range and proportion of S.'s favoured clausulae in his prose works generally,[129] with the combinations of cretic + spondee and double cretic most frequent; nn. on *Ot.* 1.4

---

[126] Well analysed by Westman (1961).   [127] Summers li–lxx.

[128] Bornecque (1907) 86 with Bourgery (1910) and (1922) 145–8.

[129] Bourgery (1910) 167–8 tabulates the different combinations according to their frequency.

senili manu, 6.5 *egere*, *Breu.* 2.2 *deprendunt*, 2.3 *est*, 4.5 *quantum ... exprimerent*, *quantum ... tegerent*, 4.6 *residebant*, 9.3 *ipso fugiente*, 10.6 *praecipitatur*, 19.1 *ingentibus ... miraculis*, 19.2 *alta rerum quies*.

6. THE TRANSMISSION OF THE TEXT[130]

The oldest and most important MS of the *Dialogues* is the *Codex Ambrosianus* (known as A), copied in the Benedictine monastery at Montecassino late in the eleventh century. Nothing is known about the text's transmission between the sixth and eleventh centuries, but A probably descends from an ancient book which survived down to late antiquity in southern Italy. The Montecassino Chronicle gives a long list of texts copied at the instigation of the celebrated abbot, Desiderius (1058–87). The list includes an unspecified work by S., but circumstantial evidence strongly indicates that the *Dialogues* are meant; they thus belong to a small group of classical texts (among them Tacitus' *Histories* and *Annals* 11–16 as well as Apuleius' *Golden Ass*) whose modern survival is due entirely to the monks at Montecassino.[131] In the thirteenth century the *Dialogues* grew in circulation in Italy and France and began to reach northern Europe, becoming relatively common in the next two centuries. By 1583 the *Ambrosianus* was in private ownership; later acquired by Cardinal Federigo Borromeo (1564–1631), in 1603 it entered the Ambrosian Library in Milan, founded by Borromeo, where it remains today.

The orginal scribe of A made numerous errors which were corrected by later hands, three of them twelfth-century. The three were able to fill gaps in A by reference to another MS, which indicates that Montecassino housed either the archetype of A or at least one other copy of it apart from A. As for the later MSS, more than a hundred in number and mostly dating from the fourteenth century or later, Reynolds separates them into two groups, β and γ. The former, the bulk of the *recentiores*, derive from the *Ambrosianus* and are therefore of value only when A is lacunose or illegible. The latter are more interesting. Heavily corrected and interpolated, they contain a number of corruptions in common with A as well as readings (more than twenty in the case of *Ot.*) superior to those in A. Shrewd scribal correction may account for many of these better readings, but some appear too impressive to be

---

[130] The following account owes much to Reynolds (1968) and (1983) 366–9 as well as to the *praefatio* (pp. v–xix) of his OCT (1977).

[131] See Reynolds–Wilson (1974) 90, 96–7.

corrections or conjectures. Hence the hypothesis 'that the γ manuscripts go back to a parent which was close to A, and probably inferior to it, but which descended independently from the archetype'.[132] Moreover, γ as well as β can be shown to have originated from Montecassino;[133] but despite the suggestive fact (noted above) that the later hands of A presuppose another copy at Montecassino, the exact relationship there between A and the ancestor of γ remains unclear.

Particular textual problems are discussed in the commentary. This edition follows L. D. Reynolds' Oxford Classical Text with the following modifications: (i) capitalization is standard only at the start of chapters; (ii) orthography is regularized to follow the spelling of lemmata in the *OLD*, so that prefixes are assimilated (e.g. *imb-* for *inb-*) and *-es* replaces *-is* in the third declension acc. plur.; (iii) the present text departs from Reynolds's in the following places:

Reynolds	Williams
Ot. 1.1 <*nisi*>	*nisi*
Ot. 2.2 *emeritis stipendiis*	*emeritis iam stipendiis*
Ot. 2.2 †*ad alios actus animos*†	*ad alios acutissimo animo*
Ot. 3.1 *quoniam*	*quam*
Ot. 3.3 *quam* <*ut*> *adiuuari*	*quam adiuuari*
Ot. 3.5 *prodest quod*	*prodest, quod*
Ot. 5.6 *sint,* [*an*] *in*	*sint, in*
Ot. 5.7 *Qui*	*cui*
Ot. 6.5 <*Non*>	*non*
Ot. 8.1 *Adice nunc* [*huc*]	*Adice nunc huc*
Ot. 8.2 *damnetur*	*damnaretur*
Breu. 2.1 <*At*>	*at*
Breu. 3.5 *perduxerunt!*	*perduxerunt?*
Breu. 4.3 *moratur* [*ut*] *adhuc*	*moratur adhuc*
Breu. 6.2 <*tam*> *praecoquem*	*praecoquem*
Breu. 7.6 [*hinc*] *illos* <*non*>	*illos non*
Breu. 7.9 *tamquam ultimum*	*tamquam uitam*
Breu. 7.9 [*foro*] *fortuna*	*fortuna*
Breu. 7.9 *nec desiderat* <*et*> *capit*	*nec desiderat et capit*

---

[132] Reynolds (1968) 367.   [133] Reynolds (1968) 368–9.

Breu. 8.2 [*aegros*] *uidebis*	*uidebis*
Breu. 9.1 †*sensus hominum eorum dico*†	*esse leuius hominum eorum iudicio*
Breu. 10.1 [*non probat cauillationes*] <*uitia*>	*non probat cauillationes; uitia*
Breu 11.2 *delibatur*	*delegatur*
Breu. 12.4 <*qui*> *in*	*qui*
Breu. 12.4 *ineptissimae*	*inertissimae*
Breu. 12.6 [*et*] *usque*	*usque*
Breu. 13.6 *Depugnant? . . . exterantur*	'*depugnant? . . . exterantur.*'
Breu. 13.8 *auspicante*	*auspicanti*
Breu. 13.8 *falsa sunt aut mendaciis similia*	*farta sunt mendaciis aut similia*
Breu. 14.5 *puta* [*licet dicamus*] *qui*	*putamus? immo id facere illos potius licet dicamus qui*
Breu. 15.5 *transît*	*transit*
Breu. 17.5 *detinetur*	*distinetur*
Breu. 20.2 *natu* <*perorantem*> *et*	*natu et*
Breu. 20.3 *Sex. Turannius*	*C. Turannius*

L. ANNAEI SENECAE
DE OTIO
DE BREVITATE VITAE

DE OTIO

*** nobis magno consensu uitia commendant. licet nihil aliud quod **1**
sit salutare temptemus, proderit tamen per se ipsum secedere: meliores erimus singuli. quid quod secedere ad optimos uiros et aliquod
exemplum eligere ad quod uitam derigamus licet? quod nisi in otio
non fit: tunc potest obtineri quod semel placuit, ubi nemo interuenit
qui iudicium adhuc imbecillum populo adiutore detorqueat; tunc
potest uita aequali et uno tenore procedere, quam propositis diuer-
sissimis scindimus. nam inter cetera mala illud pessimum est, quod **2**
uitia ipsa mutamus. sic ne hoc quidem nobis contingit, permanere
in malo iam familiari. aliud ex alio placet uexatque nos hoc quoque,
quod iudicia nostra non tantum praua sed etiam leuia sunt: fluc-
tuamur aliudque ex alio comprendimus, petita relinquimus, relicta
repetimus, alternae inter cupiditatem nostram et paenitentiam uices
sunt. pendemus enim toti ex alienis iudiciis et id optimum nobis **3**
uidetur quod petitores laudatoresque multos habet, non id quod
laudandum petendumque est, nec uiam bonam ac malam per se
aestimamus sed turba uestigiorum, in quibus nulla sunt redeuntium.

Dices mihi: 'quid ais, Seneca? deseris partes? certe Stoici uestri **4**
dicunt: "usque ad ultimum uitae finem in actu erimus, non desinemus communi bono operam dare, adiuuare singulos, opem ferre
etiam inimicis senili manu. nos sumus qui nullis annis uacationem
damus et, quod ait ille uir disertissimus,

> canitiem galea premimus;

nos sumus apud quos usque eo nihil ante mortem otiosum est ut, si
res patitur, non sit ipsa mors otiosa." quid nobis Epicuri praecepta
in ipsis Zenonis principiis loqueris? quin tu bene gnauiter, si par-
tium piget, transfugis potius quam prodis?' hoc tibi in praesentia **5**
respondebo: 'numquid uis amplius quam ut me similem ducibus
meis praestem? quid ergo est? non quo miserint me illi, sed quo
duxerint ibo.'

2   Nunc probabo tibi non desciscere me a praeceptis Stoicorum; nam ne ipsi quidem a suis desciuerunt, et tamen excusatissimus essem, etiam si non praecepta illorum sequerer sed exempla. hoc quod dico in duas diuidam partes: primum, ut possit aliquis uel a prima aetate contemplationi ueritatis totum se tradere, rationem uiuendi quaerere atque exercere secreto; deinde, ut possit hoc aliquis emeritis iam stipendiis, profligatae aetatis, iure optimo facere et ad alios acutissimo animo referre, uirginum Vestalium more, quae annis inter officia diuisis discunt facere sacra et cum didicerunt docent.

3   Hoc Stoicis quoque placere ostendam, non quia mihi legem dixerim nihil contra dictum Zenonis Chrysippiue committere, sed quia res ipsa patitur me ire in illorum sententiam, quam si quis semper unius sequitur, non in curia sed in factione est. utinam quidem iam tenerentur omnia et in aperto et confesso ueritas esset nihilque ex decretis mutaremus! nunc ueritatem cum eis ipsis qui docent quaerimus.

2   Duae maxime et in hac re dissident sectae, Epicureorum et Stoicorum, sed utraque ad otium diuersa uia mittit. Epicurus ait: 'non accedet ad rem publicam sapiens, nisi si quid interuenerit'; **3** Zenon ait: 'accedet ad rem publicam, nisi si quid impedierit.' alter otium ex proposito petit, alter ex causa; causa autem illa late patet. si res publica corruptior est quam adiuuari possit, si occupata est malis, non nitetur sapiens in superuacuum nec se nihil profuturus impendet; si parum habebit auctoritatis aut uirium nec illum erit admissura res publica, si ualetudo illum impediet, quomodo nauem quassam non deduceret in mare, quomodo nomen in militiam non **4** daret debilis, sic ad iter quod inhabile sciet non accedet. potest ergo et ille cui omnia adhuc in integro sunt, antequam ullas experiatur tempestates, in tuto subsistere et protinus commendare se bonis artibus et illibatum otium exigere, uirtutium cultor, quae exerceri **5** etiam quietissimis possunt. hoc nempe ab homine exigitur, ut prosit hominibus, si fieri potest, multis, si minus, paucis, si minus, proximis, si minus, sibi. nam cum se utilem ceteris efficit, commune agit negotium. quomodo qui se deteriorem facit non sibi tantummodo nocet sed etiam omnibus eis quibus melior factus prodesse potuisset, sic quisquis bene de se meretur hoc ipso aliis prodest, quod illis profuturum parat.

Duas res publicas animo complectamur, alteram magnam et uere **4** publicam qua di atque homines continentur, in qua non ad hunc angulum respicimus aut ad illum sed terminos ciuitatis nostrae cum sole metimur, alteram cui nos ascripsit condicio nascendi; haec aut Atheniensium erit aut Carthaginiensium aut alterius alicuius urbis quae non ad omnes pertineat homines sed ad certos. quidam eodem tempore utrique rei publicae dant operam, maiori minorique, quidam tantum minori, quidam tantum maiori. huic maiori rei **2** publicae et in otio deseruire possumus, immo uero nescio an in otio melius, ut quaeramus quid sit uirtus, una pluresne sint, natura an ars bonos uiros faciat; unum sit hoc quod maria terrasque et mari ac terris inserta complectitur, an multa eiusmodi corpora deus sparserit, continua sit omnis et plena materia ex qua cuncta gignuntur, an diducta et solidis inane permixtum; quae sit dei sedes, opus suum spectet an tractet, utrumne extrinsecus illi circumfusus sit an toti inditus; immortalis sit mundus an inter caduca et ad tempus nata numerandus. haec qui contemplatur, quid deo praestat? ne tanta eius opera sine teste sint.

Solemus dicere summum bonum esse secundum naturam **5** uiuere: natura nos ad utrumque genuit, et contemplationi rerum et actioni. nunc id probemus quod prius diximus. quid porro? hoc non erit probatum, si se unusquisque consuluerit quantam cupidinem habeat ignota noscendi, quam ad omnes fabulas excitetur? nauigant **2** quidam et labores peregrinationis longissimae una mercede perpetiuntur cognoscendi aliquid abditum remotumque. haec res ad spectacula populos contrahit, haec cogit praeclusa rimari, secretiora exquirere, antiquitates euoluere, mores barbararum audire gentium. curiosum nobis natura ingenium dedit et artis sibi ac **3** pulchritudinis suae conscia spectatores nos tantis rerum spectaculis genuit, perditura fructum sui, si tam magna, tam clara, tam subtiliter

ducta, tam nitida et non uno genere formosa solitudini ostenderet.
4 ut scias illam spectari uoluisse, non tantum aspici, uide quem nobis
locum dederit: in media nos sui parte constituit et circumspectum omnium nobis dedit; nec erexit tantummodo hominem, sed
etiam habilem contemplationi factura, ut ab ortu sidera in occasum labentia prosequi posset et uultum suum circumferre cum
toto, sublime fecit illi caput et collo flexili imposuit; deinde sena
per diem, sena per noctem signa producens nullam non partem sui
explicuit, ut per haec quae obtulerat oculis eius cupiditatem fac-
5 eret etiam ceterorum. nec enim omnia nec tanta uisimus quanta
sunt, sed acies nostra aperit sibi inuestigandi uiam et fundamenta
uero iacit, ut inquisitio transeat ex apertis in obscura et aliquid
ipso mundo inueniat antiquius: unde ista sidera exierint; quis fuerit
uniuersi status, antequam singula in partes discederent; quae ratio mersa et confusa diduxerit; quis loca rebus assignauerit, suapte
natura grauia descenderint, euolauerint leuia, an praeter nisum
pondusque corporum altior aliqua uis legem singulis dixerit; an
illud uerum sit quo maxime probatur homines diuini esse spiritus, partem ac ueluti scintillas quasdam astrorum in terram de-
6 siluisse atque alieno loco haesisse. cogitatio nostra caeli munimenta
perrumpit nec contenta est id quod ostenditur scire: 'illud' inquit 'scrutor quod ultra mundum iacet, utrumne profunda uasti-
tas sit an et hoc ipsum terminis suis cludatur; qualis sit habitus
exclusis, informia et confusa sint, in omnem partem tantundem
loci obtinentia, an et illa in aliquem cultum discripta sint; huic
cohaereant mundo, an longe ab hoc secesserint et hic in uacuo
uolutetur; indiuidua sint per quae struitur omne quod natum futu-
rumque est, an continua eorum materia sit et per totum mutabilis;
utrum contraria inter se elementa sint, an non pugnent sed per di-
7 uersa conspirent.' ad haec quaerenda natus, aestima quam non
multum acceperit temporis, etiam si illud totum sibi uindicat.
cui licet nihil facilitate eripi, nihil neglegentia patiatur excidere,
licet horas suas auarissime seruet et usque in ultimum aetatis humanae terminum procedat nec quicquam illi ex eo quod natura

constituit fortuna concutiat, tamen homo ad immortalium cognitionem nimis mortalis est. ergo secundum naturam uiuo si to- 8
tum me illi dedi, si illius admirator cultorque sum. natura autem
utrumque facere me uoluit, et agere et contemplationi uacare:
utrumque facio, quoniam ne contemplatio quidem sine actione
est.

'Sed refert' inquis 'an ad illam uoluptatis causa accesseris, nihil **6**
aliud ex illa petens quam assiduam contemplationem sine exitu; est
enim dulcis et habet illecebras suas.' adversus hoc tibi respondeo:
aeque refert quo animo ciuilem agas uitam, an semper inquietus sis
nec tibi umquam sumas ullum tempus quo ab humanis ad diuina
respicias. quomodo res appetere sine ullo uirtutum amore et sine 2
cultu ingeni ac nudas edere operas minime probabile est (misceri
enim ista inter se et conseri debent), sic imperfectum ac languidum
bonum est in otium sine actu proiecta uirtus, numquam id quod
didicit ostendens. quis negat illam debere profectus suos in opere 3
temptare, nec tantum quid faciendum sit cogitare sed etiam aliquando manum exercere et ea quae meditata est ad uerum perducere? quodsi per ipsum sapientem non est mora, si non actor deest
sed agenda desunt, ecquid illi secum esse permittes? quo animo 4
ad otium sapiens secedit? ut sciat se tum quoque ea acturum
per quae posteris prosit. nos certe sumus qui dicimus et Zenonem
et Chrysippum maiora egisse quam si duxissent exercitus, gessis-
sent honores, leges tulissent; quas non uni ciuitati, sed toti humano
generi tulerunt. quid est ergo quare tale otium non conueniat uiro
bono, per quod futura saecula ordinet nec apud paucos contionetur sed apud omnes omnium gentium homines, quique sunt quique
erunt? ad summam, quaero an ex praeceptis suis uixerint Cleanthes 5
et Chrysippus et Zenon. non dubie respondebis sic illos uixisse
quemadmodum dixerant esse uiuendum: atqui nemo illorum rem
publicam administrauit. 'non fuit' inquis 'illis aut ea fortuna aut
ea dignitas quae admitti ad publicarum rerum tractationem solet.'
sed idem nihilominus non segnem egere uitam: inuenerunt quemadmodum plus quies ipsorum hominibus prodesset quam aliorum

discursus et sudor. ergo nihilominus hi multum egisse uisi sunt, quamuis nihil publice agerent.

7   Praeterea tria genera sunt uitae, inter quae quod sit optimum
quaeri solet: unum uoluptati uacat, alterum contemplationi, tertium
actioni. primum deposita contentione depositoque odio quod implacabile diuersa sequentibus indiximus, uideamus ut haec omnia
ad idem sub alio atque alio titulo perueniant: nec ille qui uoluptatem
probat sine contemplatione est, nec ille qui contemplationi inseruit
sine uoluptate est, nec ille cuius uita actionibus destinata est sine
2 contemplatione est. 'plurimum' inquis 'discriminis est utrum aliqua
res propositum sit an propositi alterius accessio.' sit sane grande discrimen, tamen alterum sine altero non est: nec ille sine actione contemplatur, nec hic sine contemplatione agit, nec ille tertius, de quo
male existimare consensimus, uoluptatem inertem probat sed eam
quam ratione efficit firmam sibi; ita et haec ipsa uoluptaria secta
3 in actu est. quidni in actu sit, cum ipse dicat Epicurus aliquando se
recessurum a uoluptate, dolorem etiam appetiturum, si aut uoluptati imminebit paenitentia aut dolor minor pro grauiore sumetur?
4 quo pertinet haec dicere? ut appareat contemplationem placere
omnibus; alii petunt illam, nobis haec statio, non portus est.

8   Adice nunc huc quod e lege Chrysippi uiuere otioso licet: non
dico ut otium patiatur, sed ut eligat. negant nostri sapientem ad
quamlibet rem publicam accessurum; quid autem interest quomodo sapiens ad otium ueniat, utrum quia res publica illi deest
an quia ipse rei publicae, si omnibus defutura res publica est? sem-
2 per autem deerit fastidiose quaerentibus. interrogo ad quam rem
publicam sapiens sit accessurus. ad Atheniensium, in qua Socrates
damnatur, Aristoteles ne damnaretur fugit? in qua opprimit inuidia
uirtutes? negabis mihi accessurum ad hanc rem publicam sapientem. ad Carthaginiensium ergo rem publicam sapiens accedet, in
qua assidua seditio et optimo cuique infesta libertas est, summa
aequi ac boni uilitas, aduersus hostes inhumana crudelitas, etiam
3 aduersus suos hostilis? et hanc fugiet. si percensere singulas uoluero,
nullam inueniam quae sapientem aut quam sapiens pati possit.
quodsi non inuenitur illa res publica quam nobis fingimus, incipit

omnibus esse otium necessarium, quia quod unum praeferri poterat otio nusquam est. si quis dicit optimum esse nauigare, deinde 4 negat nauigandum in eo mari in quo naufragia fieri soleant et frequenter subitae tempestates sint quae rectorem in contrarium rapiant, puto hic me uetat nauem soluere, quamquam laudet nauigationem.

L. ANNAEI SENECAE

DE BREVITATE VITAE

1 Maior pars mortalium, Pauline, de naturae malignitate conqueritur, quod in exiguum aeui gignimur, quod haec tam uelociter, tam rapide dati nobis temporis spatia decurrunt, adeo ut exceptis admodum paucis ceteros in ipso uitae apparatu uita destituat. nec huic publico, ut opinantur, malo turba tantum et imprudens uulgus ingemuit: clarorum quoque uirorum hic affectus querellas euocauit. inde illa maximi medicorum exclamatio est, 'uitam breuem esse,

2 longam artem'; inde Aristotelis cum rerum natura exigentis minime conueniens sapienti uiro lis est: 'aetatis illam animalibus tantum indulsisse ut quina aut dena saecula educerent, homini in tam multa

3 ac magna genito tanto citeriorem terminum stare.' non exiguum temporis habemus, sed multum perdimus. satis longa uita et in maximarum rerum consummationem large data est, si tota bene collocaretur; sed ubi per luxum ac neglegentiam diffluit, ubi nulli bonae rei impenditur, ultima demum necessitate cogente quam ire

4 non intelleximus transisse sentimus. ita est: non accipimus breuem uitam sed facimus nec inopes eius sed prodigi sumus. sicut amplae et regiae opes, ubi ad malum dominum peruenerunt, momento dissipantur, at quamuis modicae, si bono custodi traditae sunt, usu crescunt, ita aetas nostra bene disponenti multum patet.

2   Quid de rerum natura querimur? illa se benigne gessit: uita, si uti scias, longa est. at alium insatiabilis tenet auaritia, alium in superuacuis laboribus operosa sedulitas; alius uino madet, alius inertia torpet; alium defetigat ex alienis iudiciis suspensa semper ambitio, alium mercandi praeceps cupiditas circa omnes terras, omnia maria spe lucri ducit; quosdam torquet cupido militiae, numquam non aut alienis periculis intentos aut suis anxios; sunt quos ingra-

2 tus superiorum cultus uoluntaria seruitute consumat; multos aut affectatio alienae fortunae aut suae querella detinuit; plerosque nihil certum sequentes uaga et inconstans et sibi displicens leuitas per

noua consilia iactauit; quibusdam nihil quo cursum derigant placet,
sed marcentes oscitantesque fata deprendunt, adeo ut quod apud
maximum poetarum more oraculi dictum est uerum esse non du-
bitem: 'exigua pars est uitae qua uiuimus.' ceterum quidem omne
spatium non uita sed tempus est. urgent et circumstant uitia undique 3
nec resurgere aut in dispectum ueri attollere oculos sinunt, sed mersos et in cupiditatem infixos premunt. numquam illis recurrere ad
se licet; si quando aliqua fortuito quies contigit, uelut profundum
mare, in quo post uentum quoque uolutatio est, fluctuantur, nec
umquam illis a cupiditatibus suis otium est. de istis me putas dicere 4
quorum in confesso mala sunt? aspice illos ad quorum felicitatem
concurritur: bonis suis offocantur. quam multis diuitiae graues sunt!
quam multorum eloquentia et cotidiana ostentandi ingenii occupatio sanguinem educit! quam multi continuis uoluptatibus pallent!
quam multis nihil liberi relinquit circumfusus clientium populus!
omnes denique istos ab infimis usque ad summos pererra: hic aduocat, hic adest, ille periclitatur, ille defendit, ille iudicat, nemo se sibi
uindicat, alius in alium consumitur. interroga de istis quorum nomina ediscuntur, his illos dinosci uidebis notis: ille illius cultor est, hic
illius; suus nemo est. deinde dementissima quorundam indignatio 5
est: queruntur de superiorum fastidio, quod ipsis adire uolentibus
non uacauerint! audet quisquam de alterius superbia queri qui sibi
ipse numquam uacat? ille tamen te, quisquis es, insolenti quidem
uultu sed aliquando respexit, ille aures suas ad tua uerba demisit,
ille te ad latus suum recepit: tu non inspicere te umquam, non audire dignatus es. non est itaque quod ista officia cuiquam imputes,
quoniam quidem, cum illa faceres, non esse cum alio uolebas sed
tecum esse non poteras.

Omnia licet quae umquam ingenia fulserunt in hoc unum con- **3**
sentiant, numquam satis hanc humanarum mentium caliginem
mirabuntur. praedia sua occupari a nullo patiuntur et, si exigua
contentio est de modo finium, ad lapides et arma discurrunt: in
uitam suam incedere alios sinunt, immo uero ipsi etiam posses-
sores eius futuros inducunt. nemo inuenitur qui pecuniam suam
diuidere uelit: uitam unusquisque quam multis distribuit! astricti

sunt in continendo patrimonio, simul ad iacturam temporis uen-
2 tum est, profusissimi in eo cuius unius honesta auaritia est. libet
itaque ex seniorum turba comprendere aliquem: 'peruenisse te ad
ultimum aetatis humanae uidemus, centesimus tibi uel supra premitur annus: agedum ad computationem aetatem tuam reuoca. duc
quantum ex isto tempore creditor, quantum amica, quantum rex,
quantum cliens abstulerit, quantum lis uxoria, quantum seruorum
coercitio, quantum officiosa per urbem discursatio; adice morbos
quos manu fecimus, adice et quod sine usu iacuit: uidebis te pau-
3 ciores annos habere quam numeras. repete memoria tecum quando
certus consilii fueris, quotus quisque dies ut destinaueras cesserit,
quando tibi usus tui fuerit, quando in statu suo uultus, quando animus intrepidus, quid tibi in tam longo aeuo facti operis sit, quam
multi uitam tuam diripuerint te non sentiente quid perderes, quantum uanus dolor, stulta laetitia, auida cupiditas, blanda conuersatio
abstulerit, quam exiguum tibi de tuo relictum sit: intelleges te im-
4 maturum mori.' quid ergo est in causa? tamquam semper uicturi
uiuitis, numquam uobis fragilitas uestra succurrit, non obseruatis
quantum iam temporis transierit; uelut ex pleno et abundanti perditis, cum interim fortasse ille ipse qui alicui uel homini uel rei donatur
dies ultimus sit. omnia tamquam mortales timetis, omnia tamquam
5 immortales concupiscitis. audies plerosque dicentes: 'a quinquagesimo anno in otium secedam, sexagesimus me annus ab officiis
dimittet.' et quem tandem longioris uitae praedem accipis? quis ista
sicut disponis ire patietur? non pudet te reliquias uitae tibi reseru-
are et id solum tempus bonae menti destinare quod in nullam rem
conferri possit? quam serum est tunc uiuere incipere cum desinendum est! quae tam stulta mortalitatis obliuio in quinquagesimum
et sexagesimum annum differre sana consilia et inde uelle uitam
inchoare quo pauci perduxerunt?

4   Potentissimis et in altum sublatis hominibus excidere uoces uidebis quibus otium optent laudent, omnibus bonis suis praeferant. cupiunt interim ex illo fastigio suo, si tuto liceat, descendere; nam ut
nihil extra lacessat aut quatiat, in se ipsa fortuna ruit.

2   Diuus Augustus, cui di plura quam ulli praestiterunt, non desît
quietem sibi precari et uacationem a re publica petere; omnis eius

sermo ad hoc semper reuolutus est, ut speraret otium; hoc labores suos, etiam si falso, dulci tamen oblectabat solacio, aliquando se uicturum sibi. in quadam ad senatum missa epistula, cum requiem 3 suam non uacuam fore dignitatis nec a priore gloria discrepantem pollicitus esset, haec uerba inueni: 'sed ista fieri speciosius quam promitti possunt. me tamen cupido temporis optatissimi mihi prouexit ut, quoniam rerum laetitia moratur adhuc, praeciperem aliquid uoluptatis ex uerborum dulcedine.' tanta uisa est res otium 4 ut illam, quia usu non poterat, cogitatione praesumeret. qui omnia uidebat ex se uno pendentia, qui hominibus gentibusque fortunam dabat, illum diem laetissimus cogitabat quo magnitudinem suam exueret. expertus erat quantum illa bona per omnes terras 5 fulgentia sudoris exprimerent, quantum occultarum sollicitudinum tegerent: cum ciuibus primum, deinde cum collegis, nouissime cum affinibus coactus armis decernere, mari terraque sanguinem fudit. per Macedoniam Siciliam Aegyptum Syriam Asiamque et omnes prope oras bello circumactus Romana caede lassos exercitus ad externa bella conuertit. dum Alpes pacat immixtosque mediae paci et imperio hostes perdomat, dum ultra Rhenum et Euphraten et Danuuium terminos mouet, in ipsa urbe Murenae, Caepionis, Lepidi, Egnati, aliorum in eum mucrones acuebantur. nondum horum effugerat insidias: filia et tot nobiles iuuenes adul- 6 terio uelut sacramento adacti iam infractam aetatem territabant Iullusque et iterum timenda cum Antonio mulier. haec ulcera cum ipsis membris absciderat: alia subnascebantur; uelut graue multo sanguine corpus parte semper aliqua rumpebatur. itaque otium optabat, in huius spe et cogitatione labores eius residebant, hoc uotum erat eius qui uoti compotes facere poterat.

M. Cicero inter Catilinas Clodios iactatus Pompeiosque et 5 Crassos, partim manifestos inimicos, partim dubios amicos, dum fluctuatur cum re publica et illam pessum euntem tenet, nouissime abductus, nec secundis rebus quietus nec aduersarum patiens, quotiens illum ipsum consulatum suum non sine causa sed sine fine laudatum detestatur! quam flebiles uoces exprimit in quadam 2 ad Atticum epistula iam uicto patre Pompeio, adhuc filio in Hispania fracta arma refouente! 'quid agam' inquit 'hic quaeris?

moror in Tusculano meo semiliber.' alia deinceps adicit quibus et priorem aetatem complorat et de praesenti queritur et de futura
3 desperat. semiliberum se dixit Cicero: at mehercules numquam sapiens in tam humile nomen procedet, numquam semiliber erit, integrae semper libertatis et solidae, solutus et sui iuris et altior ceteris. quid enim supra eum potest esse qui supra fortunam est?

6 Liuius Drusus, uir acer et uehemens, cum leges nouas et mala Gracchana mouisset stipatus ingenti totius Italiae coetu, exitum rerum non peruidens quas nec agere licebat nec iam liberum erat semel inchoatas relinquere, execratus inquietam a primordiis uitam dicitur dixisse uni sibi ne puero quidem umquam ferias contigisse. ausus est enim et pupillus adhuc et praetextatus iudicibus reos commendare et gratiam suam foro interponere, tam efficaciter quidem
2 ut quaedam iudicia constet ab illo rapta. quo non erumperet tam immatura ambitio? scires in malum ingens et priuatum et publicum euasuram praecoquem audaciam. sero itaque querebatur nullas sibi ferias contigisse, a puero seditiosus et foro grauis. disputatur an ipse sibi manus attulerit; subito enim uulnere per inguen accepto collapsus est, aliquo dubitante an mors eius uoluntaria esset, nullo
3 an tempestiua. superuacuum est commemorare plures qui, cum aliis felicissimi uiderentur, ipsi in se uerum testimonium dixerunt perosi omnem actum annorum suorum; sed his querellis nec alios mutauerunt nec se ipsos; nam cum uerba eruperunt, affectus ad consuetudinem relabuntur.

4 Vestra mehercules uita, licet supra mille annos exeat, in artissimum contrahetur: ista uitia nullum non saeculum deuorabunt. hoc uero spatium quod, quamuis natura currit, ratio dilatat, cito uos effugiat necesse est; non enim apprenditis nec retinetis nec uelocissimae omnium rei moram facitis, sed abire ut rem superuacuam ac reparabilem sinitis.

7 In primis autem et illos numero qui nulli rei nisi uino ac libidini uacant; nulli enim turpius occupati sunt. ceteri etiam si uana gloriae imagine teneantur, speciose tamen errant; licet auaros mihi, licet iracundos enumeres uel odia exercentes iniusta uel bella, omnes isti uirilius peccant: in uentrem ac libidinem proiectorum inhonesta labes est. omnia istorum tempora excute, aspice quam diu com- 2 putent, quam diu insidientur, quam diu timeant, quam diu colant, quam diu colantur, quantum uadimonia sua atque aliena occupent, quantum conuiuia, quae iam ipsa officia sunt: uidebis quemadmodum illos respirare non sinant uel mala sua uel bona.

Denique inter omnes conuenit nullam rem bene exerceri posse 3 ab homine occupato, non eloquentiam, non liberales disciplinas, quando districtus animus nihil altius recipit sed omnia uelut inculcata respuit. nihil minus est hominis occupati quam uiuere: nullius rei difficilior scientia est. professores aliarum artium uulgo multique sunt, quasdam uero ex his pueri admodum ita percepisse uisi sunt ut etiam praecipere possent: uiuere tota uita discendum est et, quod magis fortasse miraberis, tota uita discendum est mori. tot maximi uiri relictis omnibus impedimentis, cum diuitiis officiis 4 uoluptatibus renuntiassent, hoc unum in extremam usque aetatem egerunt, ut uiuere scirent; plures tamen ex his nondum se scire confessi uita abierunt, nedum ut isti sciant. magni, mihi crede, et supra 5 humanos errores eminentis uiri est/nihil ex suo tempore delibari sinere, et ideo eius uita longissima est quia, quantumcumque patuit, totum ipsi uacauit. nihil inde incultum otiosumque iacuit, nihil sub alio fuit, neque enim quicquam repperit dignum quod cum tempore suo permutaret, custos eius parcissimus. itaque satis illi fuit: iis uero necesse est defuisse ex quorum uita multum populus tulit. nec est quod putes illos non aliquando intellegere damnum 6 suum: plerosque certe audies ex iis quos magna felicitas grauat inter clientium greges aut causarum actiones aut ceteras honestas miserias exclamare interdum 'uiuere mihi non licet.' quidni non 7 liceat? omnes illi qui te sibi aduocant tibi abducunt. ille reus quot dies abstulit? quot ille candidatus? quot illa anus efferendis heredibus lassa? quot ille ad irritandam auaritiam captantium simulatus aeger? quot ille potentior amicus, qui uos non in amicitiam sed in apparatum habet? dispunge, inquam, et recense uitae tuae dies: uidebis paucos admodum et reiculos apud te resedisse. assecutus 8 ille quos optauerat fasces cupit ponere et subinde dicit 'quando hic annus praeteribit?' facit ille ludos, quorum sortem sibi obtingere magno aestimauit: 'quando' inquit 'istos effugiam?' diripitur ille toto foro patronus et magno concursu omnia ultra quam audiri potest complet: 'quando' inquit 'res proferentur?' praecipitat quisque uitam suam et futuri desiderio laborat, praesentium taedio.

9 at ille qui nullum non tempus in usus suos confert, qui omnem diem tamquam uitam ordinat, nec optat crastinum nec timet. quid enim est quod iam ulla hora nouae uoluptatis possit afferre? omnia nota, omnia ad satietatem percepta sunt. de cetero fortuna ut uolet ordinet: uita iam in tuto est. huic adici potest, detrahi nihil, et adici sic quemadmodum saturo iam ac pleno aliquid cibi quod nec desiderat

10 et capit. non est itaque quod quemquam propter canos aut rugas putes diu uixisse: non ille diu uixit sed diu fuit. quid enim si illum multum putes nauigasse quem saeua tempestas a portu exceptum huc et illuc tulit ac uicibus uentorum ex diuerso furentium per eadem spatia in orbem egit? non ille multum nauigauit sed multum iactatus est.

8   Mirari soleo, cum uideo aliquos tempus petentes et eos qui rogantur facillimos; illud uterque spectat propter quod tempus petitum est, ipsum quidem neuter: quasi nihil petitur, quasi nihil datur. re omnium pretiosissima luditur; fallit autem illos quia res incorporalis est, quia sub oculos non uenit, ideoque uilissime

2 aestimatur, immo paene nullum eius pretium est. annua, congiaria homines carissime accipiunt et illis aut laborem aut operam aut diligentiam suam locant: nemo aestimat tempus; utuntur illo laxius quasi gratuito. at eosdem uidebis, si mortis periculum propius admotum est, medicorum genua tangentes, si metuunt capitale supplicium, omnia sua ut uiuant paratos impendere: tanta in illis

3 discordia affectuum est. quodsi posset quemadmodum praeteritorum annorum cuiusque numerus proponi, sic futurorum, quomodo illi qui paucos uiderent superesse trepidarent, quomodo illis parcerent! atqui facile est quamuis exiguum dispensare quod certum est; id debet seruari diligentius quod nescias quando deficiat.

4 nec est tamen quod putes illos ignorare quam cara res sit: dicere solent eis quos ualdissime diligunt paratos se partem annorum

suorum dare. dant nec intellegunt; dant autem ita ut sine illorum incremento sibi detrahant. sed hoc ipsum, an detrahant, nesciunt; ideo tolerabilis est illis iactura detrimenti latentis. nemo restituet 5 annos, nemo iterum te tibi reddet. ibit qua coepit aetas nec cursum suum aut reuocabit aut supprimet; nihil tumultuabitur, nihil admonebit uelocitatis suae: tacita labetur. non illa se regis imperio, non fauore populi longius proferet: sicut missa est a primo die curret, nusquam deuertetur, nusquam remorabitur. quid fiet? tu occupatus es, uita festinat: mors interim aderit, cui uelis nolis uacandum est.

Potestne quicquam esse leuius hominum eorum iudicio qui pru- **9** dentiam iactant? operosius occupati sunt ut melius possint uiuere, impendio uitae uitam instruunt. cogitationes suas in longum ordinant; maxima porro uitae iactura dilatio est: illa primum quemque extrahit diem, illa eripit praesentia dum ulteriora promittit. maximum uiuendi impedimentum est expectatio, quae pendet ex crastino, perdit hodiernum. quod in manu fortunae positum est disponis, quod in tua dimittis. quo spectas? quo te extendis? omnia quae uentura sunt in incerto iacent: protinus uiue. clamat ecce maximus 2 uates et uelut diuino ore instinctus salutare carmen canit:

> optima quaeque dies miseris mortalibus aeui
> prima fugit.

'quid cunctaris?' inquit 'quid cessas? nisi occupas, fugit.' et cum occupaueris, tamen fugiet; itaque cum celeritate temporis utendi uelocitate certandum est et uelut ex torrenti rapido nec semper ituro cito hauriendum. hoc quoque pulcherrime ad exprobrandam 3 infinitam cunctationem, quod non optimam quamque 'aetatem' sed 'diem' dicit. quid securus et in tanta temporum fuga lentus menses tibi et annos in longam seriem, utcumque auiditati tuae uisum est, exporrigis? de die tecum loquitur et de hoc ipso fugiente. num dubium est ergo quin optima quaeque prima dies fugiat mor- 4 talibus miseris, id est occupatis? quorum pueriles adhuc animos senectus opprimit, ad quam imparati inermesque perueniunt. nihil enim prouisum est: subito in illam necopinantes inciderunt,

5   accedere eam cotidie non sentiebant. quemadmodum aut sermo aut
lectio aut aliqua intentior cogitatio iter facientes decipit et peruenisse ante sciunt quam appropinquare, sic hoc iter uitae assiduum et
citatissimum, quod uigilantes dormientesque eodem gradu facimus,
occupatis non apparet nisi in fine.

10   Quod proposui si in partes uelim et argumenta diducere, multa
mihi occurrent per quae probem breuissimam esse occupatorum
uitam. solebat dicere Fabianus, non ex his cathedrariis philosophis
sed ex ueris et antiquis, contra affectus impetu, non subtilitate pugnandum, nec minutis uulneribus sed incursu auertendam aciem;
non probat cauillationes; uitia enim contundi debere, non uellicari.
tamen ut illis error exprobretur suus, docendi, non tantum deplorandi sunt.

2   In tria tempora uita diuiditur: quod fuit, quod est, quod futurum
est. ex iis quod agimus breue est, quod acturi sumus dubium, quod
egimus certum; hoc est enim in quod fortuna ius perdidit, quod in
nullius arbitrium reduci potest. hoc amittunt occupati; nec enim illis uacat praeterita respicere, et si uacet, iniucunda est paenitendae

3   rei recordatio. inuiti itaque ad tempora male exacta animum reuocant nec audent ea retemptare quorum uitia, etiam quae aliquo
praesentis uoluptatis lenocinio surrepebant, retractando patescunt.
nemo nisi quoi omnia acta sunt sub censura sua, quae numquam

4   fallitur, libenter se in praeteritum retorquet; ille qui multa ambitiose
concupiit, superbe contempsit, impotenter uicit, insidiose decepit,
auare rapuit, prodige effudit, necesse est memoriam suam timeat.
atqui haec est pars temporis nostri sacra ac dedicata, omnes humanos casus supergressa, extra regnum fortunae subducta, quam
non inopia, non metus, non morborum incursus exagitet; haec nec
turbari nec eripi potest: perpetua eius et intrepida possessio est.
singuli tantum dies, et hi per momenta, praesentes sunt; at praeteriti temporis omnes, cum iusseris, aderunt, ad arbitrium tuum
inspici se ac detineri patientur, quod facere occupatis non uacat.

5   securae et quietae mentis est in omnes uitae suae partes discurrere:
occupatorum animi, uelut sub iugo sint, flectere se ac respicere non
possunt. abit igitur uita eorum in profundum et ut nihil prodest, licet
quantumlibet ingeras, si non subest quod excipiat ac seruet, sic, nihil

refert quantum temporis detur, si non est ubi subsidat, per quassos foratosque animos transmittitur. praesens tempus breuissimum est, 6 adeo quidem ut quibusdam nullum uideatur; in cursu enim semper est, fluit et praecipitatur; ante desinit esse quam uenit, nec magis moram patitur quam mundus aut sidera, quorum irrequieta semper agitatio numquam in eodem uestigio manet. solum igitur ad occupatos praesens pertinet tempus, quod tam breue est ut arripi non possit, et id ipsum illis districtis in multa subducitur.

Denique uis scire quam non diu uiuant? uide quam cupiant **11** diu uiuere. decrepiti senes paucorum annorum accessionem uotis mendicant; minores natu se ipsos esse fingunt; mendacio sibi blandiuntur et tam libenter se fallunt quam si una fata decipiant. iam uero cum illos aliqua imbecillitas mortalitatis admonuit, quemadmodum pauentes moriuntur, non tamquam exeant de uita sed tamquam extrahantur! stultos se fuisse qui non uixerint clamitant et, si modo euaserint ex illa ualetudine, in otio uicturos; tunc quam frustra parauerint quibus non fruerentur, quam in cassum omnis ceciderit labor cogitant. at quibus uita procul ab omni negotio 2 agitur, quidni spatiosa sit? nihil ex illa delegatur, nihil alio atque alio spargitur, nihil inde fortunae traditur, nihil neglegentia interit, nihil largitione detrahitur, nihil superuacuum est: tota, ut ita dicam, in reditu est. quantulacumque itaque abunde sufficit, et ideo, quandoque ultimus dies uenerit, non cunctabitur sapiens ire ad mortem certo gradu.

Quaeris fortasse quos occupatos uocem? non est quod me solos **12** putes dicere quos a basilica immissi demum canes eiciunt, quos aut in sua uides turba speciosius elidi aut in aliena contemptius, quos officia domibus suis euocant ut alienis foribus illidant, quos hasta praetoris infami lucro et quandoque suppuraturo exercet. quorun- 2 dam otium occupatum est: in uilla aut in lecto suo, in media solitudine, quamuis ab omnibus recesserint, sibi ipsi molesti sunt; quorum non otiosa uita dicenda est, sed desidiosa occupatio. illum tu otiosum uocas qui Corinthia, paucorum furore pretiosa, anxia subtilitate concinnat et maiorem dierum partem in aeruginosis lamellis consumit? qui in ceromate (nam, pro facinus! ne Romanis quidem uitiis laboramus) sector puerorum rixantium sedet? qui unctorum

suorum greges in aetatium et colorum paria diducit? qui ath-
3 letas nouissimos pascit? quid? illos otiosos uocas quibus apud
tonsorem multae horae transmittuntur, dum decerpitur si quid
proxima nocte succreuit, dum de singulis capillis in consilium itur,
dum aut disiecta coma restituitur aut deficiens hinc atque illinc in
frontem compellitur? quomodo irascuntur, si tonsor paulo negle-
gentior fuit, tamquam uirum tonderet! quomodo excandescunt, si
quid ex iuba sua decisum est, si quid extra ordinem iacuit, nisi
omnia in anulos suos recciderunt! quis est istorum qui non malit
rem publicam suam turbari quam comam? qui non sollicitior sit
de capitis sui decore quam de salute? qui non comptior esse malit
quam honestior? hos tu otiosos uocas, inter pectinem speculumque
4 occupatos? quid illi qui componendis audiendis discendis canticis operati sunt, dum uocem, cuius rectum cursum natura et optimum et simplicissimum fecit, in flexus modulationis inertissimae
torquent, quorum digiti aliquod intra se carmen metientes semper
sonant, quorum, cum ad res serias, etiam saepe tristes adhibiti sunt,
exauditur tacita modulatio? non habent isti otium sed iners ne-
5 gotium. conuiuia mehercules horum non posuerim inter uacantia
tempora, cum uideam quam solliciti argentum ordinent, quam diligenter exoletorum suorum tunicas succingant, quam suspensi sint
quomodo aper a coco exeat, qua celeritate signo dato glabri ad
ministeria discurrant, quanta arte scindantur aues in frusta non
enormia, quam curiose infelices pueruli ebriorum sputa detergeant.
ex his elegantiae lautitiaeque fama captatur, et usque eo in omnes
uitae secessus mala sua illos sequuntur ut nec bibant sine ambitione
6 nec edant. ne illos quidem inter otiosos numerauerim qui sella se et
lectica huc et illuc ferunt et ad gestationum suarum, quasi deserere
illas non liceat, horas occurrunt, quos quando lauari debeant,
quando natare, quando cenare, alius admonet; usque eo nimio delicati animi languore soluuntur ut per se scire non possint an esuriant.
7 audio quendam ex delicatis – si modo deliciae uocandae sunt uitam
et consuetudinem humanam dediscere – cum ex balneo inter manus
elatus et in sella positus esset, dixisse interrogando 'iam sedeo?'
hunc tu, ignorantem an sedeat, putas scire an uiuat, an uideat, an

otiosus sit? non facile dixerim utrum magis miserear si hoc ignorauit, an si ignorare se finxit. multarum quidem rerum obliuionem 8
sentiunt, sed multarum et imitantur. quaedam uitia illos quasi felicitatis argumenta delectant: nimis humilis et contempti hominis
uidetur scire quid facias. i nunc et mimos multa mentiri ad exprobrandam luxuriam puta! plura mehercules praetereunt quam fingunt et tanta incredibilium uitiorum copia ingenioso in hoc unum
saeculo processit ut iam mimorum arguere possimus neglegentiam.
esse aliquem qui usque eo deliciis interierit ut an sedeat alteri credat!
non est ergo hic otiosus, aliud illi nomen imponas: aeger est, immo 9
mortuus est; ille otiosus est cui otii sui et sensus est. hic uero semiuiuus, cui ad intellegendos corporis sui habitus indice opus est,
quomodo potest hic ullius temporis dominus esse?

 Persequi singulos longum est quorum aut latrunculi aut pila **13**
aut excoquendi in sole corporis cura consumpsere uitam. non
sunt otiosi quorum uoluptates multum negotii habent. nam de illis
nemo dubitabit quin operose nihil agant qui litterarum inutilium
studiis detinentur, quae iam apud Romanos quoque magna manus
est. Graecorum iste morbus fuit quaerere quem numerum Ulixes 2
remigum habuisset, prior scripta esset Ilias an Odyssia, praeterea
an eiusdem esset auctoris, alia deinceps huius notae, quae siue contineas, nihil tacitam conscientiam iuuant, siue proferas, non doctior
uidearis sed molestior. ecce Romanos quoque inuasit inane studium 3
superuacua discendi. his diebus audiui quendam referentem quae
primus quisque ex Romanis ducibus fecisset: primus nauali proelio Duilius uicit, primus Curius Dentatus in triumpho duxit elephantos. etiamnunc ista, etsi ad ueram gloriam non tendunt, circa
ciuilium tamen operum exempla uersantur; non est profutura talis
scientia, est tamen quae nos speciosa rerum uanitate detineat. hoc 4
quoque quaerentibus remittamus, quis Romanis primus persuaserit
nauem conscendere (Claudius is fuit, Caudex ob hoc ipsum appellatus quia plurium tabularum contextus caudex apud antiquos uoca-
batur, unde publicae tabulae codices dicuntur et naues nunc quoque
ex antiqua consuetudine, quae commeatus per Tiberim subuehunt,
codicariae uocantur); sane et hoc ad rem pertineat, quod Valerius 5

Coruinus primus Messanam uicit et primus ex familia Valeriorum
urbis captae in se translato nomine Messana appellatus est pau-
6 latimque uulgo permutante litteras Messalla dictus: num et hoc
cuiquam curare permittes, quod primus L. Sulla in circo leones
solutos dedit, cum alioquin alligati darentur, ad conficiendos eos
missis a rege Boccho iaculatoribus? et hoc sane remittatur: num
et Pompeium primum in circo elephantorum duodeuiginti pug-
nam edidisse, commissis more proeli innoxiis hominibus, ad ullam
rem bonam pertinet? princeps ciuitatis et inter antiquos principes,
ut fama tradidit, bonitatis eximiae memorabile putauit spectaculi
genus nouo more perdere homines. 'depugnant? parum est. lanci-
7 nantur? parum est: ingenti mole animalium exterantur.' satius erat
ista in obliuionem ire, ne quis postea potens disceret inuideretque
rei minime humanae. o quantum caliginis mentibus nostris obicit
magna felicitas! ille se supra rerum naturam esse tunc credidit,
cum tot miserorum hominum cateruas sub alio caelo natis beluis
obiceret, cum bellum inter tam disparia animalia committeret, cum
in conspectu populi Romani multum sanguinis funderet, mox plus
ipsum fundere coacturus. at idem postea Alexandrina perfidia de-
ceptus ultimo mancipio transfodiendum se praebuit, tum demum
intellecta inani iactatione cognominis sui.
8 Sed ut illo reuertar unde decessi et in eadem materia ostendam
superuacuam quorundam diligentiam, idem narrabat Metellum
uictis in Sicilia Poenis triumphantem unum omnium Romanorum
ante currum centum et uiginti captiuos elephantos duxisse; Sullam ultimum Romanorum protulisse pomerium, quod numquam
prouinciali sed Italico agro acquisito proferre moris apud antiquos
fuit. hoc scire magis prodest quam Auentinum montem extra
pomerium esse, ut ille affirmabat, propter alteram ex duabus causis, aut quod plebs eo secessisset, aut quod Remo auspicanti illo
loco aues non addixissent, alia deinceps innumerabilia quae aut
9 farta sunt mendaciis aut similia? nam ut concedas omnia eos fide
bona dicere, ut ad praestationem scribant, tamen cuius ista errores
minuent? cuius cupiditates prement? quem fortiorem, quem iustiorem, quem liberaliorem facient? dubitare se interim Fabianus noster
aiebat an satius esset nullis studiis admoueri quam his implicari.

Soli omnium otiosi sunt qui sapientiae uacant, soli uiuunt; **14**
nec enim suam tantum aetatem bene tuentur: omne aeuum suo
adiciunt; quicquid annorum ante illos actum est, illis acquisitum
est. nisi ingratissimi sumus, illi clarissimi sacrarum opinionum conditores nobis nati sunt, nobis uitam praeparauerunt. ad res pulcher-
rimas ex tenebris ad lucem erutas alieno labore deducimur; nullo
nobis saeculo interdictum est, in omnia admittimur, et si magnitudine animi egredi humanae imbecillitatis angustias libet, multum
per quod spatiemur temporis est. disputare cum Socrate licet, du- 2
bitare cum Carneade, cum Epicuro quiescere, hominis naturam
cum Stoicis uincere, cum Cynicis excedere. cum rerum natura in
consortium omnis aeui patiatur incedere, quidni ab hoc exiguo et
caduco temporis transitu in illa toto nos demus animo quae immensa, quae aeterna sunt, quae cum melioribus communia? isti 3
qui per officia discursant, qui se aliosque inquietant, cum bene insanierint, cum omnium limina cotidie perambulauerint nec ullas
apertas fores praeterierint, cum per diuersissimas domos meritoriam salutationem circumtulerint, quotum quemque ex tam immensa et uariis cupiditatibus districta urbe poterunt uidere? quam 4
multi erunt quorum illos aut somnus aut luxuria aut inhumanitas
summoueat! quam multi qui illos, cum diu torserint, simulata festinatione transcurrant! quam multi per refertum clientibus atrium
prodire uitabunt et per obscuros aedium aditus profugient, quasi
non inhumanius sit decipere quam excludere! quam multi, hesterna crapula semisomnes et graues, illis miseris suum somnum
rumpentibus ut alienum expectent uix alleuatis labris insusurra-
tum miliens nomen oscitatione superbissima reddent! hos in ueris 5
officiis morari putamus? immo id facere illos potius licet dicamus
qui Zenonem, qui Pythagoran cotidie et Democritum ceterosque
antistites bonarum artium, qui Aristotelen et Theophrastum uolent habere quam familiarissimos. nemo horum non uacabit, nemo
non uenientem ad se beatiorem, amantiorem sui dimittet, nemo
quemquam uacuis a se manibus abire patietur; nocte conueniri,
interdiu ab omnibus mortalibus possunt.

Horum te mori nemo coget, omnes docebunt; horum nemo **15**
annos tuos conteret, suos tibi contribuet; nullius ex his sermo

periculosus erit, nullius amicitia capitalis, nullius sumptuosa obseruatio. feres ex illis quicquid uoles; per illos non stabit quominus
2 quantum plurimum ceperis haurias. quae illum felicitas, quam pul-
chra senectus manet, qui se in horum clientelam contulit! habebit
cum quibus de minimis maximisque rebus deliberet, quos de se cotidie consulat, a quibus audiat uerum sine contumelia, laudetur sine
3 adulatione, ad quorum se similitudinem effingat. solemus dicere
non fuisse in nostra potestate quos sortiremur parentes, forte nobis
datos: nobis uero ad nostrum arbitrium nasci licet. nobilissimorum
ingeniorum familiae sunt: elige in quam ascisci uelis; non in nomen
tantum adoptaberis, sed in ipsa bona, quae non erunt sordide nec
4 maligne custodienda: maiora fient quo illa pluribus diuiseris. hi tibi
dabunt ad aeternitatem iter et te in illum locum ex quo nemo deicitur subleuabunt. haec una ratio est extendendae mortalitatis, immo
in immortalitatem uertendae. honores, monumenta, quicquid aut
decretis ambitio iussit aut operibus extruxit, cito subruitur, nihil non
longa demolitur uetustas et mouet; at iis quae consecrauit sapientia
nocere non potest; nulla abolebit aetas, nulla deminuet; sequens ac
deinde semper ulterior aliquid ad uenerationem conferet, quoniam
quidem in uicino uersatur inuidia, simplicius longe posita miramur.
5 sapientis ergo multum patet uita, non idem illum qui ceteros terminus cludit: solus generis humani legibus soluitur, omnia illi saecula
ut deo seruiunt. transit tempus aliquod, hoc recordatione comprendit; instat, hoc utitur; uenturum est, hoc praecipit. longam illi uitam
facit omnium temporum in unum collatio.

16 Illorum breuissima ac sollicitissima aetas est qui praeteritorum
obliuiscuntur, praesentia neglegunt, de futuro timent: cum ad
extrema uenerunt, sero intellegunt miseri tam diu se, dum nihil
2 agunt, occupatos fuisse. nec est quod hoc argumento probari putes
longam illos agere uitam, quia interdum mortem inuocant: uexat
illos imprudentia incertis affectibus et incurrentibus in ipsa quae
3 metuunt; mortem saepe ideo optant quia timent. illud quoque
argumentum non est quod putes diu uiuentium, quod saepe
illis longus uidetur dies, quod, dum ueniat condictum tempus
cenae, tarde ire horas queruntur; nam si quando illos deseruerunt

occupationes, in otio relicti aestuant, nec quomodo id disponant aut extrahant sciunt. itaque ad occupationem aliquam tendunt et quod interiacet omne tempus graue est, tam mehercules quam cum dies muneris gladiatorii edictus est, aut cum alicuius alterius uel spectaculi uel uoluptatis expectatur constitutum, transilire medios dies uolunt. omnis illis speratae rei longa dilatio est. at illud tempus 4 quod amant breue est et praeceps breuiusque multo suo uitio; aliunde enim alio transfugiunt et consistere in una cupiditate non possunt. non sunt illis longi dies sed inuisi; at contra quam exiguae noctes uidentur quas in complexu scortorum aut uino exigunt! inde etiam poetarum furor fabulis humanos errores alentium, 5 quibus uisus est Iuppiter uoluptate concubitus delenitus duplicasse noctem: quid aliud est uitia nostra incendere quam auctores illis inscribere deos et dare morbo exemplo diuinitatis excusatam licentiam? possunt istis non breuissimae uideri noctes quas tam care mercantur? diem noctis expectatione perdunt, noctem lucis metu.

Ipsae uoluptates eorum trepidae et uariis terroribus inquietae **17** sunt subitque cum maxime exultantes sollicita cogitatio: 'haec quam diu?' ab hoc affectu reges suam fleuere potentiam, nec illos magnitudo fortunae suae delectauit sed uenturus aliquando finis exterruit. cum per magna camporum spatia porrigeret exercitum nec nu- 2 merum eius sed mensuram comprenderet Persarum rex insolentissimus, lacrimas profudit quod intra centum annos nemo ex tanta iuuentute superfuturus esset. at illis admoturus erat fatum ipse qui flebat perditurusque alios in mari, alios in terra, alios proelio, alios fuga, et intra exiguum tempus consumpturus illos quibus centesimum annum timebat. quid quod gaudia quoque eorum trepida 3 sunt? non enim solidis causis innituntur, sed eadem qua oriuntur uanitate turbantur. qualia autem putas esse tempora etiam ipsorum confessione misera, cum haec quoque quibus se attollunt et super hominem efferunt parum sincera sint? maxima quaeque bona sol- 4 licita sunt nec ulli fortunae minus bene quam optimae creditur: alia felicitate ad tuendam felicitatem opus est et pro ipsis quae successere uotis uota facienda sunt. omne enim quod fortuito obuenit instabile est, et quo altius surrexerit opportunius est in occasum; neminem

porro casura delectant; miserrimam ergo necesse est, non tantum
breuissimam, uitam esse eorum qui magno parant labore quod
5 maiore possideant. operose assequuntur quae uolunt, anxii tenent
quae assecuti sunt; nulla interim numquam amplius redituri temporis ratio est: nouae occupationes ueteribus substituuntur, spes spem
excitat, ambitionem ambitio. miseriarum non finis quaeritur sed
materia mutatur. nostri nos honores torserunt, plus temporis alieni
auferunt; candidati laborare desîmus, suffragatores incipimus; accusandi deposuimus molestiam, iudicandi nanciscimur; iudex desît
esse, quaesitor est; alienorum bonorum mercennaria procuratione
6 consenuit, suis opibus distinetur. Marium caliga dimisit, consulatus
exercet. Quintius dictaturam properat peruadere, ab aratro reuocabitur. ibit in Poenos nondum tantae maturus rei Scipio; uictor
Hannibalis, uictor Antiochi, sui consulatus decus, fraterni sponsor,
ni per ipsum mora sit, cum Ioue reponetur: ciuiles seruatorem ag-
itabunt seditiones et post fastiditos a iuuene dis aequos honores
iam senem contumacis exili delectabit ambitio. numquam deerunt
uel felices uel miserae sollicitudinis causae; per occupationes uita
trudetur; otium numquam agetur, semper optabitur.

18   Excerpe itaque te uulgo, Pauline carissime, et in tranquilliorem
portum non pro aetatis spatio iactatus tandem recede. cogita
quot fluctus subieris, quot tempestates partim priuatas sustinueris,
partim publicas in te conuerteris; satis iam per laboriosa et inquieta
documenta exhibita uirtus est: experire quid in otio faciat. maior
pars aetatis, certe melior, rei publicae data est: aliquid temporis
2 tui sume etiam tibi. nec te ad segnem aut inertem quietem
uoco, non ut somno et caris turbae uoluptatibus quicquid est
in te indolis uiuidae mergas: non est istud acquiescere; inuenies
maiora omnibus adhuc strenue tractatis operibus quae repositus et
3 securus agites. tu quidem orbis terrarum rationes administras tam
abstinenter quam alienas, tam diligenter quam tuas, tam religiose
quam publicas; in officio amorem consequeris in quo odium uitare
difficile est: sed tamen, mihi crede, satius est uitae suae rationem
4 quam frumenti publici nosse. istum animi uigorem rerum maximarum capacissimum a ministerio honorifico quidem sed parum
ad beatam uitam apto reuoca et cogita non id egisse te ab aetate

prima omni cultu studiorum liberalium ut tibi multa milia frumenti bene committerentur: maius quiddam et altius de te promiseras. non deerunt et frugalitatis exactae homines et laboriosae operae: tanto aptiora portandis oneribus tarda iumenta sunt quam nobiles equi, quorum generosam pernicitatem quis umquam graui sarcina pressit? cogita praeterea quantum sollicitudinis sit ad tantam 5 te molem obicere: cum uentre tibi humano negotium est; nec rationem patitur nec aequitate mitigatur nec ulla prece flectitur populus esuriens. modo modo intra paucos illos dies quibus C. Caesar perît – si quis inferis sensus est, hoc grauissime ferens, quod uidebat populo Romano superstite septem aut octo certe dierum cibaria superesse – dum ille pontes nauibus iungit et uiribus imperi ludit, aderat ultimum malorum obsessis quoque, alimentorum egestas; exitio paene ac fame constitit et, quae famem sequitur, rerum omnium ruina furiosi et externi et infeliciter superbi regis imitatio. quem tunc animum habuerunt illi quibus erat mandata 6 frumenti publici cura, saxa ferrum ignes Gaium excepturi? summa dissimulatione tantum inter uiscera latentis mali tegebant, cum ratione scilicet; quaedam enim ignorantibus aegris curanda sunt: causa multis moriendi fuit morbum suum nosse.

Recipe te ad haec tranquilliora tutiora maiora. simile tu putas **19** esse utrum cures ut incorruptum et a fraude aduehentium et a ne- glegentia frumentum transfundatur in horrea, ne concepto umore uitietur et concalescat, ut ad mensuram pondusque respondeat, an ad haec sacra et sublimia accedas, sciturus quae materia sit dei, quae uoluntas, quae condicio, quae forma; quis animum tuum casus expectet; ubi nos a corporibus dimissos natura componat; quid sit quod huius mundi grauissima quaeque in medio sustineat, supra leuia suspendat, in summum ignem ferat, sidera uicibus suis excitet, cetera deinceps ingentibus plena miraculis? uis tu relicto 2 solo mente ad ista respicere? nunc, dum calet sanguis, uigentibus ad meliora eundum est. expectat te in hoc genere uitae multum bonarum artium, amor uirtutium atque usus, cupiditatium obliuio, uiuendi ac moriendi scientia, alta rerum quies.

Omnium quidem occupatorum condicio misera est, eorum 3 tamen miserrima qui ne suis quidem laborant occupationibus, ad

alienum dormiunt somnum, ad alienum ambulant gradum, amare
et odisse, res omnium liberrimas, iubentur. hi si uolent scire quam
20 breuis ipsorum uita sit, cogitent ex quota parte sua sit. cum uideris
itaque praetextam saepe iam sumptam, cum celebre in foro nomen,
ne inuideris: ista uitae damno parantur. ut unus ab illis numeretur
annus, omnes annos suos conterent. quosdam, antequam in summum ambitionis eniterentur, inter prima luctantes aetas reliquit;
quosdam, cum in consummationem dignitatis per mille indignitates erepsissent, misera subît cogitatio laborasse ipsos in titulum sepulcri; quorundam ultima senectus, dum in nouas spes ut
iuuenta disponitur, inter conatus magnos et improbos inualida
2 defecit. foedus ille quem in iudicio pro ignotissimis litigatoribus
grandem natu et imperitae coronae assensiones captantem spiritus liquit; turpis ille qui uiuendo lassus citius quam laborando
inter ipsa officia collapsus est; turpis quem accipiendis immorien-
3 tem rationibus diu tractus risit heres. praeterire quod mihi occurrit
exemplum non possum: C. Turannius fuit exactae diligentiae senex,
qui post annum nonagesimum, cum uacationem procurationis
ab C. Caesare ultro accepisset, componi se in lecto et uelut exanimem a circumstante familia plangi iussit. lugebat domus otium
domini senis nec finiuit ante tristitiam quam labor illi suus restitu-
4 tus est. adeone iuuat occupatum mori? idem plerisque animus est:
diutius cupiditas illis laboris quam facultas est; cum imbecillitate
corporis pugnant, senectutem ipsam nullo alio nomine grauem iu-
dicant quam quod illos seponit. lex a quinquagesimo anno militem
non legit, a sexagesimo senatorem non citat: difficilius homines a
5 se otium impetrant quam a lege. interim dum rapiuntur et rapiunt,
dum alter alterius quietem rumpit, dum mutuo miseri sunt, uita
est sine fructu, sine uoluptate, sine ullo profectu animi: nemo in
conspicuo mortem habet, nemo non procul spes intendit, quidam
uero disponunt etiam illa quae ultra uitam sunt, magnas moles
sepulcrorum et operum publicorum dedicationes et ad rogum
munera et ambitiosas exequias. at mehercules istorum funera,
tamquam minimum uixerint, ad faces et cereos ducenda sunt.

COMMENTARY

De otio

1 Seneca's call to withdraw, and the 'official' Stoic response

1.1–3 Withdrawal into self-sufficiency (1.1 *singuli*) under philosophical role-models (1.1 *optimos uiros*) forces 'a radical rupture with regard to the state of unconsciousness in which man normally lives' in collective association (Hadot (1995) 254) and opens the way to 'impartiality, objectivity, and critical judgment' (247; 1.1 *tunc potest ... detorqueat* etc.). Whether or not already present in the lost introduction, this 'view from above' takes programmatic shape in 1.1 before the focus changes in 1.2–3 to a familiar Senecan assault on the blind conformity and lack of principle engendered in ordinary social intercourse. The difference between the perspectives from above and below is brought out in language of political colour (well analysed by Ingrosso (1988)), which sets rational action (1.3n. on *laudandum petendumque*) against herd-like obedience to electoral and other forms of social persuasion (1.3n. on *petitores laudatoresque*).

1.1 ***nobis: in the MSS *Ot.* is joined to *V.B.* without a break. Marc Antoine de Muret, Montaigne's tutor (1526–85; hereafter Muretus), first proposed that what follows *V.B.* 28 *allisos* belongs to a different essay which is known from its title in the contents-list of the *Codex Ambrosianus* (a title otherwise missing from this and other MSS); Justus Lipsius separated the two in his edition of 1605. *nobis* is preceded in the *Ambrosianus* by a single syllable, *ci.*, from which Reynolds (1974) 274 infers *cir* as the transmitted reading (corrected to *cur* and *circi* later in the tradition), against *cit* read by e.g. Gertz and Hermes. But *cir*, no ending for a Latin word, can belong to *Ot.* only if a lacuna is posited both before and after the isolated syllable – a remote possiblility (Reynolds *ibid.*); hence Reynolds *ibid.* locates *cir...* at the end of the incomplete *V. B.* (cf. his OCT 197 in app.). As to the extent of the lacuna before the transmitted beginning of *Ot.*, S.'s initial manoeuvres together strongly suggest that the surviving text begins soon after its opening: (i) the brief case for withdrawal (1.1) and repudiation of *leuitas* (1.2–3; cf. *Breu.* 2.2) in a possible *exordium*; (ii) confrontation with basic Stoic doctrine defined and defended (1.4–5), followed by a *propositio* (2.1 *Nunc ... Stoicorum*, itself announcing his move to *probatio*); (iii) two lines of argument distinguished in a formal *diuisio* (2.1–2; further on these divisions,

Dionigi 40, 58–9). Very possibly, given S.'s endorsement of withdrawal in
1.1, he opened characteristically with the dangers of associating with crowds
(so e.g. *V.B.* 1.4–5, *Ep.* 7.2, 32.2, 103.1–2, 123.6); the collective citizen-body
may therefore be inferred as the possible subject of *commendant*, as freedom
from *uitia* is achieved more by self-sufficient detachment (see below) than
by keeping better company.   **consensu:** of (misguided) popular opinion also at *Helu.* 5.6, discussed with *Ot.* 1.1 *et al.* by Pittet (1955) 38–9; the
first in a series of terms (e.g. *commendant*, 1.3 *petitores laudatoresque*, 1.4 *partes*)
which describe an ethical/philosophical disposition in electoral/political
language (Ingrosso (1988) 106–11).   **commendant** 'make attractive'
(Summers 157 on *Ep.* 7.2); for the political undertone, Ingrosso (1988)
106 together with *OLD* 4a.   **licet . . . singuli:** *secessus* offers relief
as if from illness (cf. *Ben.* 4.12.3 *salubritatis causa et aestiui secessus*). For *salutare*
('curative') in this medical sense, *OLD* 2a, and for *tempto* of 'trying out'
a cure, e.g. *Cl.* 1.9.6, *Ep.* 2.3 *medicamenta temptantur*, Cels. 1 *praef.* 37; for
prosum of helpful relief, *OLD* 3, and for *melior* of the improving patient,
OLD 12a.   **sit:** potential subjunctive.   **ipsum:** nom. with subj. inf.
('the very act of withdrawal will in itself . . . '); rare, but cf. *Oed.* 992 *ipsum
metuisse nocet* and a few examples in Cicero (*Brut.* 140, *Part.* 139, *Att.* 13.28.2),
who uses word-position to avoid the ambiguity S. has here (so *De orat.*
2.24 *me . . . hoc ipsum nihil agere et plane cessare delectat*). Elsewhere S. en-
sures clarity by mixing cases (e.g. *Cl.* 1.4.1, *Ben.* 5.3.1 *nec per se ipse exitus*,
20.6).   **secedere:** of withdrawal from public life (*Breu.* 3.5 *in otium secedam*), first in V. Max. (*OLD* 3b) and then frequent in S. with philosophical
emphasis (e.g. *Ep.* 8.1–2, 19.11, 68.6, 73.4, 82.4) as equivalent to ἀναχωρεῖν
(Rutherford (1989) 29–30).   **meliores:** i.e. morally (*OLD* 2a) because
closer to attaining self-sufficiency (αὐτάρκεια).   **singuli** 'detached from
others', a rare nuance first in S. (*OLD* 3b, also with *N.Q.* 4A *praef.* 2 *quod est mis-
errimum, numquam sumus singuli*).   **quid quod** 'and further', developing
the point (*OLD quis*[1] 13c); this 'old rhetorical transition-formula' (Tarrant
(1976) 221 on *Ag.* 265) also at e.g. *Breu.* 17.3, *Helu.* 1.3, *Ep.* 78.14, 86.13, *Ben.*
3.9.1.   **optimos uiros:** i.e. the transmitted texts of philosophers and
ethical role-models (cf. *Breu.* 14.2 intro., 14.5, 15.1–3), here in contrast to
populo below; not merely the language of socio-political division (Ingrosso
(1988) 107) but extending *meliores*.   **aliquod . . . eligere:** a rational
choice, distinguished from the mass herd-instinct to follow the convention
(*Ep.* 123.6 *consuetudo*) of the majority. What *ratio* and not *consuetudo* introduces
us to is the ideal *exemplum* reinforcing moral *praecepta* with model behaviour,

where personal witness is preferable *quia longum iter est per praecepta, breue et efficax per exempla. Zenonem Cleanthes non expressisset* ('modelled himself on'), *si tantummodo audisset: uitae eius interfuit, secreta perspexit, obseruauit illum, an ex formula sua uiueret* (*Ep.* 6.5–6). Epicurean *contubernium* obviously facilitated this ethical role-imitation (*Ep.* 6.6, 11.8–10), which can otherwise be enacted through selective directed reading (*Tr.* 1.11–12, with the cautionary note from *Ep.* 6.5). For appropriate Greek and Roman models which meet the requirements, esp. the younger Cato, see *Ep.* 11.10, 104.27–34 with Ingrosso (1988) 106 n. 16.   **ad quod . . . derigamus:** final relative clause (G–L §630). *de-* (cf. *Breu.* 2.2) is preferable to *di-* (Dionigi with the MSS), apparently the later form without reliable epigraphical witness before the fourth century A. D. For the regular construction with *ad*, *OLD ad* 35a with Cic. *Mur.* 3.   **quod:** i.e. *aliquod . . . derigamus* (*secedere* already presupposes retreat *in otium*).   **nisi:** suppl. Gronovius.   **tunc . . . tunc:** anaphoric emphasis, the first correlative with *ubi* (*OLD ubi* 9b); while earlier (e.g. Prop. 2.9.17–18) replacing *tum . . . tum* often before vowels, *tunc*, the growing imperial preference, is already asserting itself in S. (H–S 519– 20 for comparative statistics).   **obtineri** (Madvig II 395) 'be kept up', 'maintained' (of aims, attitudes etc., *OLD* 2), even 'achieved' (*Ep.* 76.22 *nulla* [sc. *uirtus*] *. . . obtineri poterit*); *obtinere* MSS, but intrans. *obtineo* (*TLL* IX 2.289.16–27) is not used with a subj. like *decretum* (Madvig II 395), and impersonal *potest* is rare (*OLD* 6b; Löfstedt (1911) 44–5).   **semel:** i.e. 'once and for all' (*OLD* 3).   **nemo . . . detorqueat:** S. draws on the early Stoic doctrine of διαστροφή [cf. *detorqueat*] τοῦ λόγου ('perversion of reason'), acc. to which man is intrinsically good but corrupted by the specious attractiveness of e.g. riches or by the influence of company (*SVF* III 53.8–10, 55.1–4, *Ep.* 94.13, 52–4 with Bellincioni (1979) 145 and 194); but S. perhaps models his expression on Cic. *Leg.* 1.29 *si opinionum uanitas non imbecillitatem animorum torqueret et flecteret . . .*   **qui:** relative clause of tendency (G–L §631.2).   **imbecillum:** i.e. *tener animus et parum tenax recti* (*Ep.* 7.6), with a medical nuance brought out in *Tr.* 17.3 *multum et in se recedendum est; conuersatio enim dissimilium* ('people of a different nature') *. . . quicquid imbecillum in animo . . . est exulcerat*; a favourite adj. with S. in both declensions (cf. *Ir.* 3.28.3 for *imbecille*, which Dionigi 167–8 finds here in a single late MS).   **populo adiutore:** in contrast to *optimos uiros* above, a source of bad *exempla* (*Ep.* 7.6, 123.6).   **detorqueat:** contrast *derigamus* above.   **uita:** nom.   **aequali . . . tenore** 'even and uninterrupted course' (cf. *Tr.* 2.4, *Ep.* 31.8 *aequalitas ac tenor uitae per omnia consonans sibi*,

59.14), which parallels the course of the celestial bodies (*N.Q.* 7.25.6) and combines the 'smooth current of life' (εὔροια βίου) with 'balanced consistency of character' (εὐτονία ψυχῆς) required by the early Stoics for perfect happiness (*SVF* I 46.15–19, 126.20–7, III 4.4–7, 6.10–11, 18.14–16, 66.23).   **uno tenore:** *OLD tenor* 1b.   **propositis** 'aims'; the first plur. in the whole sentence introduces the suggestion of obstructive duplication.   **scindimus:** the more striking because a rare fig. usage before S. (*OLD* 6).

1.2 uitia ipsa mutamus: inconsistency in vices is itself a vice; an ironic variant on the Stoic fault of *inaequalitas*, which usually emphasizes inconsistency itself without reference to the moral status of the alternatives: Cic. *Tusc.* 4.29 *uitiositas . . . est habitus aut affectio in tota uita inconstans et a se ipsa dissentiens.* The prominence of the theme in Horace (e.g. *S.* 1.1.1–19, 3.1–19, *Ep.* 1.1.94–105) reflects its prevalence in diatribe-satire (cf. Dionigi (1980) 38–42), and it is a commonplace in S., e.g. *Ep.* 20.3–5, 34.4, 35.4. At *S.* 2.7.6–20 Horace adds the nuance of fluctuation between vice and virtue: Priscus is *inaequalis* because he belongs to the *pars hominum . . . | . . . modo recta capessens, | interdum prauis obnoxia* (6–8), while Volanerius at least sticks with the same vice of gambling even when physically incapable of taking part without help (15–20). S. also spotlights this *fluctuatio et inter simulationem uirtutum amoremque uitiorum assidua iactatio* (*Ep.* 120.20). Here, however, he descends to the lowest level of *inconstantia,* that between vices themselves, which consequently *non tantum praua sed etiam leuia sunt.*   **contingit:** stressing the absence of self-direction; with inf., poetic and post-Augustan in prose unless *contigit* is read at Cic. *Arch.* 4 (K–S II 240).   **aliud . . . placet:** with the suggestion of μεμψιμοιρία (*Breu.* 2.2n. on *plerosque . . . deprendunt*). **placet uexatque:** *Breu.* 16.2n. on *uexat*; the juxtaposition itself generates unease.   **praua** 'perverse' because of διαστροφή (1.1 *qui iudicium . . . detorqueat*).   **leuia:** *Breu.* 2.2n. on *uaga . . . leuitas*; contrast the *sapiens,* guided by reason (*Ep.* 66.32 *sola ratio immutabilis et iudicii tenax est*) and so *certus iudicii* (*Ep.* 45.9).   **fluctuamur** Gertz, *fluctuamus* MSS. For the intrans. active, *N.Q.* 3.14.1, 4A.2.5 *fluctuat* [sc. *Nilus*], 6.7.6, *Her. F.* 699, but *fluctuor* is far more usual (*Breu.* 2.3, 5.1).   **comprendimus:** as if desperate (cf. *Ep.* 119.4, in hunger).   **petita . . . repetimus:** antimetabole (the antithetical repetition in the second clause of the words used in the first; *Rhet. Her.* 4.39), an obvious structure for a *sententia*; so e.g. *Ep.* 3.6 *quiescenti agendum et agenti quiescendum est,* 29.10, 63.7, 72.3, 94.7 (further examples in Summers xc) with Traina (1987) 31 and Lausberg §§800–3. For the reprocessing of earlier likes and dislikes, *Tr.* 2.6 *hi . . . quibus semper magis placet quod reliquerunt,* Hor. *Ep.* 1.1.97–8 *quid? mea cum pugnat senten-tia secum,* | *quod petiit spernit, repetit quod nuper omisit* (possibly echoed here; Dionigi (1980) 45).   **alternae . . . uices:** far apart around *cupiditatem* and *paenitentiam,* with *nostram* poised at the centre, to illustrate the full ex-tent of our pendulum-like oscillations (cf. 1.3 *pendemus*) between the two. **cupiditatem:** *Breu.* 2.1 n.   **paenitentiam:** contrast *V.B.* 7.4 *summum bonum immortale est . . . nec satietatem habet nec paenitentiam; numquam enim recta mens uertitur nec sibi odio est . . .*

   1.3 pendemus . . . iudiciis: for Stoics a complete (*OLD totus* 4a) sur-render of self-sufficiency as we lay aside even our own *iudicia praua . . .* [*et*] *leuia* (1.2); as a vice, *Tr.* 15.6 *penitus hoc se malum fixit, ex aliena opinione pen-dere,* *Breu.* 2.1 n. on *ambitio.* For *pendeo* of external reliance, *OLD* 13b, adding *Breu.* 9.1, *Ep.* 15.9 *ex fortuna pendere,* Ben. 3.29.1.   **id . . . habet:** a stan-dard point illustrated by different images and analogies at *V.B.* 1.3–5, 2.2, *Ep.* 8.3 *uitate quaecumque uulgo placent,* 29.10–12, 99.17.   **petitores laudatoresque:** electoral jargon (Ingrosso (1988) 106). In strict usage the *laudatores* testify to the good character of candidates for office (*OLD petitor* 3a; cf. Plin. *Ep.* 3.20.5), but the mildly disdainful combination here may suggest more than the standard topos of *mobilis fauor* (*V.B.* 1.5; cf. *Ben.* 4.21.5). There is considerable evidence to suggest that increasingly during the first century emperors who were promoting their own favourites discouraged active can-vassing and even multiple candidature for the higher magistracies (Talbert (1984) 54–5, 341–5 with Griffin (1976) 116). It is, to say the least, coinciden-tal that S.'s disparaging tone here distances him and his addressee from an activity which regularly provoked imperial intervention.   **laudandum petendumque:** *inseparabile* (*Ep.* 66.10). In a technical sense *petenda* are the 'desirable goals' of Stoic ethics (*Ep.* 48.5, 66.6 = αἱρετά *SVF* III 63.26; L–S I 357–9).   **nec uiam . . . uestigiorum:** the unself-critical mass instinct is to follow *antecedentium gregem, pergentes non quo eundum est sed quo itur* (*V.B.* 1.3). The conventional imagery hardly prepares us for the unexpect-edly sinister twist in the following clause.   **ac:** equivalent to *aut*; K–S II 103.   **turba:** abl.   **in . . . redeuntium:** a grim conclusion, allud-ing to Aesop's fable of the lion and the fox (147 Hausrath–Hunger, Babr. 103): the 'sick' lion attracts sympathetic visitors to his care, but the wily fox observes the one-way direction of all the prints. So, for S., gregarious individuals are inevitably swallowed up in social involvement (e.g. *V.B.* 1.3–5, *Ep.* 7.1–7, 94.68–71, 103.1–2). S. knew the story from Horace

(*Ep.* 1.1.70–6; cf. Lucil. 980–9 Marx), and the not dissimilar contexts suggest a shared debt to the function of fable in moral diatribe (Oltramare (1926) 17, 92, 146; Dionigi 174 and esp. (1980) 44–9).

1.4 Dramatic tension is introduced with the reply of an addressee/ interlocutor which identifies him as an orthodox Stoic of relatively narrow horizons, at least in terms of the distinction drawn between the two *res publicae* in 4.1–2. His incredulous response (*quid ais, Seneca? deseris partes?*) confirms his allegiance even before he delivers (*"usque ad ultimum . . . otiosa"*) the Stoic line: an uncompromising *"non desinemus . . . "* introduces an impressive tricolon (*communi . . . manu*) followed by the invoking of Virgil to add prestige. The military and party-political language (nn. on *deseris partes?*, *uacationem, principiis, si . . . prodis?*) fits a man committed to conventional action and reflects the partisanship of a Stoic in permanent rivalry with the Epicurean camp.   **Dices mihi:** *sermocinatio*, or imaginary dialogue inserted into a speech (*Rhet. Her.* 4.65, Quint. *Inst.* 9.2.29–31; Lausberg §§820–5), is characteristic of diatribe (Oltramare (1926) 11). The interlocutor's objections set the stage for S.'s 'forced' response (1.5) and plan of counter-argument (2.1); similar provocation at e.g. *Ep.* 5.7, 8.1, 16.4, 68.10, *N.Q.* 1.1.4.   **quid ais . . . ?:** indicating surprise which carries over into a follow-up question (*TLL* 1 1455.14–55); from regular use in comedy (e.g. Ter. *Ad.* 556) it passes into Cic. and S. (*Ep.* 90.8; Hofmann 43–4). The scribal 'correction' *agis* brings the phrase into line with a more common use in S. (Reynolds 198 in app.), but when as here introducing an interlocutor it often means no more than 'How are you?' (*TLL* 1 1380.21–36).   **deseris partes?:** the political/military terminology (Ingrosso (1988) 107–8; *OLD pars* 16a, b) brings out the character of S.'s interlocutor, whose aggressive tone (cf. *Ep.* 8.1) already hints at 'betrayal' to the Epicureans (cf. *Ep.* 68.10). **partes:** plur. for sing. (Krebs–Schmalz II 244–5); *Prou.* 2.9, *Ben.* 5.10.3. **uestri:** polemical (Griffin (1976) 317 n. 1), pointedly emphasizing S.'s well-known affiliation (cf. *Ep.* 8.1 *praecepta uestra*), and so hardly clear evidence that S.'s interlocutor is not a Stoic (entertained by Pichon (1912) 216).   **usque . . . erimus:** cf. *Ep.* 8.1 *in actu mori*; Sharples (1996) 124 for Roman Stoicism 'contrasted with Epicureanism, as a philosophy of practical involvement'.   **ultimum . . . finem:** not a tautology, as *finis* [sc. *uitae*] in S. can mean 'old age' (*N.Q.* 3 *praef.* 2; cf. Catul. 64.217 *in extrema . . . fine senectae*); for the combination, *OLD finis* 10a.   **in actu:** virtually a Senecan coinage in this general sense (*TLL* 1 451.21–33), circumventing the pejorative overtones of *occupati*. The quasi-adj. construction

with *esse* is Greek (K–S 1 561).   **non desinemus . . . dare:** the early
Stoic (Chrysippean?) theory of οἰκείωσις/*conciliatio* centred on 'appropriation', or 'the process whereby one recognizes something as belonging to
oneself' (Dyck 83), as the basic impulse of all new-born creatures which,
in humans, progresses by stages ('appropriation' to family, to community
etc.) into an ethical concern not just for oneself but also for other people
(more fully Dyck 83–4 with Sandbach (1989) 32–4). The theory appears
to have been developed by Panaetius in the middle Stoa into 'a drive for
the well-being of humanity at large' as a function of Stoic justice (Rist 193);
see esp. Cic. *Off.* 1.11–12, *Fin.* 3.62–3 with Pembroke (1971) 121–32 and
Inwood (1985) 184–94 for complications in the concept and its development from primary impulse to social orientation. The theory underlies S.'s
portrayal of us as social animals born to promote the *commune/publicum bonum*
(e.g. *Cl.* 1.3.2, 2.5.3, 6.3, *Ir.* 1.5.3, *V.B.* 20.3).   **singulos:** contradicting
S.'s *meliores erimus singuli* (1.1) with an appeal to the Stoics' fundamental basis
for society: *fac nos singulos, quid sumus? praeda animalium et uictimae ac bellis-
simus et facillimus sanguis . . . hominem . . . nudum et infirmum societas munit* (*Ben.*
4.18.2).   **etiam inimicis:** i.e. personal enemies, not enemies of the
state (cf. *Ep.* 95.63). Individual attitudinizing must never displace the *mutuus
amor* which binds all human beings in *foedus auxiliumque commune* (*Ir.* 1.5.3,
Ep. 95.52) and renders superficial even distinctions between free and slave
(*Ep.* 47) and all personal enmities (so *V.B.* 20.5 *ero amicis iucundus, inimicis
mitis et facilis, Ep.* 120.10). Pohlenz 1 315–16 locates this broadening of the
scope of Stoic *humanitas* in the early Imperial period, but the influence of
the middle Stoa, not least Panaetius' pupil Hecaton of Rhodes (*Ben.* 3.18.1,
Ep. 6.7, 9.6), may be significant.   **senili manu** provides an important
fulcrum, balancing *usque ad ultimum uitae finem* above with *canitiem* below. S.
favours both the resulting clausula (double cretic) and the adj. (*Ep.* 30.2,
14, *Oed.* 657), which is Haase's widely accepted conjecture for *eniti* of the
MSS. As Alexander (1945) 67–8 argues, *senili* is palaeographically plausible,
and after three inf. phrases (a favoured tricolon) with *communi bono, singulos*
and *inimicis* as (in)direct objs., *eniti* is too imprecise, unqualified *manu*
otiose.   **nos sumus qui:** heavy emphasis on 'we [Stoics]', varied
below; cf. 6.4.   **annis:** possible metonymy (*OLD* 6e).   **uacationem**
'exemption from (military) service' (*Ir.* 3.16.4), anticipating the metaphor
which dominates the interlocutor's thought below; elsewhere of political
service (*Breu.* 4.2n., 20.3).   **quod . . . premimus:** in common with the
earlier Stoics, esp. Chrysippus, S. frequently uses poetic quotation to express

or illustrate a given precept (so *Breu.* 2.2, 9.2; in general, Mazzoli (1970) 103–8). For the clarifying effect of delivering a point of doctrine in verse, *Ep.* 33.6 *facilius . . . singula* [sc. *praecepta*] *insidunt circumscripta* ('marked off') *et carminis modo inclusa*, 108.9–10; general intro. p. 29.   **disertissimus:** of Virgil cf. *Ep.* 59.3, and of other writers, *Ir.* 1.20.6 (Livy), *Ep.* 92.35 (Maecenas), 107.10, 118.1 (Cicero). Virgil, acclaimed by S. as the greatest of Roman poets (*Breu.* 9.2) as Homer is *poetarum Graecorum maximus* (*Ep.* 63.2; *Breu.* 2.2n. on *maximum poetarum*), is cited some 119 times in Senecan prose; on Virgilian citation in S., Setaioli (1965) and Mazzoli (1970) 215–32 (with further bibliography at 215 n. 1).   **canitiem . . . premimus:** *Aen.* 9.612. The context is significant: 610–11 *nec tarda senectus* | *debilitat uires animi mutatque uigorem*; S.'s interlocutor claims for Stoics a share in the pride Numanus Remulus has in the Italian fighting spirit lasting into old age. Such wider relevance is unusual in S.'s quotations of Virgil (Dionigi 180–1; *Breu.* 9.2n. on *'quid . . . fugit'*).   **premimus:** '"confine", with a suggestion of "suppress", "conceal"' (Hardie (1994) 193).   **usque:** pressing *eo . . . ut* to the limit (*OLD usque* 8); *Breu.* 12.5, 6, 8.   **otiosum:** here contemptuous, dismissive in tone (cf. *Ep.* 100.11, *N.Q.* 2.32.7).   **res** 'circumstance'; cf. 3.1, *Ben.* 2.10.4 (Ciceronian; *TLL* x 1.720.63–6).   **otiosa:** extending *otiosum*; the intended ambiguity (after 'idle' above) is neatly brought out by Apul. *Met.* 8.7.4 *illam* [sc. *uiam mortis*] *lenem otiosamque* ('peaceful') *nec telis ullis indigentem sed placidae quieti consimilem*. If the interlocutor alludes also to Stoic suicide (Marastoni (1979) 382 n. 5), its justification as carried out for the sake of one's friends or country (*SVF* iii 187.34 = L–S i 66h with Griffin (1976) 378–9) fits the theme of service to the *commune bonum*. For a different example of 'active' death set by the Stoic Julius Canus (condemned by Caligula), *Tr.* 14.8–10.   **praecepta** 'instructive sayings', often quoted by S. (cf. *Ep.* 8.7–8); continuing the military analogy (n. on *uacationem* above), a possible play on 'military orders' (e.g. Caes. *Gal.* 5.35.1, Liv. 9.31.9, Tac. *Ag.* 37.2).   **principiis** 'military headquarters' of the Stoic camp (*OLD* 10a), but the interlocutor also has in mind the 'basic principles' of Stoicism (8a) which he contrasts with the 'mere sayings' of Epicurus (cf. the distinction between *praecepta* and *decreta* debated in *Ep.* 94 and 95 and defined at e.g. 95.12).   **bene gnauiter** 'completely', 'outright'; colloquial in tone (N–W ii 731–2) after Sisenna *Mil.* 4 *quid tergiuersaris nec bene* [*g*]*nauiter is?*. Since forms in *gn-* appear to have been superseded by *n-* in the first century AD and the more 'stylish' *bene ac/et nauiter* occurs in Cicero and Livy (*OLD nauiter* 2), the phrase contributes to a picture of the interlocutor as harsh and hostile to innovation.   **si ... prodis?:** the alliterative emphasis and constant recourse to military metaphor here betray the inflexible mind-set under pressure; contrast S. himself at *Ep*. 2.5 *soleo ... et in aliena castra transire, non tamquam transfuga, sed tamquam explorator.*

1.5 S.'s initial response gently teases with its own military allusion.   **in praesentia:** i.e. until 2.1 *nunc*; neut. plur. (*OLD praesens* 16b; K–S 1 358 assume abl. sing.), favoured by S. (*Prou.* 1.2, *Ep.* 13.5, 52.15, 72.1, 110.1).   **'numquid ... ibo':** S. wittily exploits a notorious Stoic 'inconsistency' (for which Griffin (1976) 340–1). Zeno and Chrysippus preached public service but never actually performed it (*Tr*. 1.10, *Ep*. 68.1, Plut. *Mor*. 1033b–c = *SVF* 1 11.5–15, D. Chr. *Or*. 47.2 = *SVF* 1 11.20–6); and so 'I shall go not where they send me [i.e. public life] but where they lead by their own example [i.e. the private life]'. S. returns to this 'paradox' at 6.4–5.   **numquid** 'surely you don't ... ?' Implying incredulity as often, favoured by S. (e.g. *Ep*. 9.11, 19.2, 21.4, 22.5); with *amplius*, e.g. Pl. *Merc*. 282.   **ducibus:** philosophical 'generals'; so e.g. Cic. *Tusc.* 3.37 (Epicurus), Lucr. *D.R.N.* 1.638 (Heraclitus), Hor. *Ep.* 1.1.13, Quint. *Inst.* 5.13.59.   **quid ergo est?** 'In that case, what's to be done?'; colloquial (Summers l, Hofmann 67; *TLL* v 2.765.37–55) and frequent in S. before affirmative statement (e.g. *Breu.* 3.4, *C.S.* 10.4, *V.B.* 13.2, 25.1, 2, 3, *Tr.* 16.2; Brink on Hor. *Ars* 353).   **miserint ... duxerint:** fut. perf.; iso-colic *correctio* (*non quo ... sed quo*) with homoeoteleuton. For the point, *Tr.* 1.10 *sequor Zenona, Cleanthen, Chrysippum, quorum tamen nemo ad rem publicam accessit, et nemo non misit.*

2 The plan of argument

The more formal response setting out two *probationes* (Lausberg §349): the first advocates life-long withdrawal, the second keeps the option open into advanced age, exploring the kind of public service (*actio*) contributed in retirement. The requirements of his argument in answer to his interlocutor leave little scope for allusion to S.'s own (plans for) retirement in *c*. 62, but cf. 2.2 intro. below.

2.1 Nunc probabo: the formal *propositio*, whose purpose is to *proponere ... quae sis probaturus* (Quint. *Inst.* 3.9.2; cf. Lausberg §§348–9). **desciscere** 'revolt (from)', 'desert'; more political/military terminology (Ingrosso (1988) 108; *OLD* 1), but elsewhere of philosophical adherence (*OLD* 2).   **praeceptis:** here 'teachings' (cf. *Ep.* 68.1), but the military allusion continues from 1.4 *praecepta*.   **ipsi … desciuerunt** 'were inconsistent' (cf. Cic. *Att.* 2.4.2), esp. if we read – as we naturally do – *a suis* [*praeceptis*]; but *a suis desciscere* is also used absolutely for 'desert one's own (military) side' (*B. Alex.* 7.2, Liv. 6.36.8).   **excusatissimus:** a striking and unprecedented form; the adj. (rare) has strong legal associations (*TLL* v 2.1307.58–77), but for the nuance here cf. *Ir.* 2.32.1 *excusatius peccat*.   **etiam si … exempla:** i.e. by not participating in public life.   **hoc … partes:** rhetorical *diuisio* (Lausberg §393; cf. *Breu.* 10.1 *Quod … diducere*), introducing the two propositions. The first develops along lines which in effect preclude the need to argue the second at any length, a conclusion which may or may not have been drawn explicitly in a missing final section (general intro. pp. 16–18).   **ut … ut:** epexegetic after *hoc* (G–L §557).   **a prima aetate:** not, of course, children, who lack reason (*Ep.* 121.14) and 'the good' (*Ep.* 124.10; Inwood (1985) 72–4), but *facillime … tenera conciliantur ingenia ad honesti rectique amorem, et adhuc docilibus leuiterque corruptis inicit manum ueritas* (*Ep.* 108.12; cf. 26–7, *Helu.* 18.8, *N.Q.* 1.17.4). All schools stress the irrelevance of age to embarking on philosophy, but for the idea possibly in Stoic protreptic, La Penna (1956) 194–5.   **contemplationi ueritatis:** a prelude to the active life, and the first part of Posidonius' definition of the 'end' (τέλος) of life, 'to live contemplating (θεωροῦντα) the truth (ἀλήθειαν) and order (τάξιν) of all things together and [on the active side] helping in promoting it as far as possible, in no way being led by the irrational part of the soul' (Kidd III 248, rendering fr. 186.13–15 = L–S I 63J2). Posidonius' θεωρία is 'something new in Stoic versions of τέλος' (Kidd II 672), and 'it is only after Posidonius that we find echoes of [the relation of θεωρία to action]' (673). Virtue is therefore based on the prior possession of 'the truth' as 'a systematic body of moral knowledge' (Sharples (1996) 105); *beatus enim dici nemo potest extra ueritatem proiectus* (*V.B.* 5.2; cf. *Ep.* 92.3, 95.57).   **rationem:** not just 'a plan' or 'pattern' here (*OLD* 13c), but 'a coherent intellectual basis'; *Breu.* 18.3n. on *uitae suae rationem*.   **secreto:** here 'by' or 'for oneself', 'individually' (*Ep.* 10.1, V. Max. 3.1 *ext.* 1), not in collective social action (for the dangerous influences of which cf. *Ep.* 94.68–71, 123.8–12), and placed to qualify all three infs.; elsewhere 'secretly' (opp. *palam* at *Cl.* 1.13.5).

2.2 For many interpreters the second proposition has autobiographical relevance, anticipating by some years, or even closely coinciding with, S.'s request to Nero in early 62 for permission to retire (Tac. *Ann.* 14.53–6 with Griffin (1976) 93–4, (1984) 81–2 and Dionigi 52–4, 102–3); but general

intro. p. 14.   **hoc:** i.e. the pursuit and practice of *rationem uiuendi*.
emeritis...stipendiis: properly of military service (*OLD stipendium*
2c; *Breu.* 20.4 for retirement at fifty), but often more widely used (*TLL*
v 2.470.35–42).   **profligatae** 'far advanced' (*OLD* 2a), with the hint
of exhaustion (1c); gen. of quality (G–L §365).   **iure optimo** 'with
perfect right'; Ciceronian after Plautus (*TLL* vii 2.699.30–40).   **ad
alios . . . referre:** the subsequent social dimension, when the enlightened
senex can report on his research and training (the obj. of *referre*, as of *facere*,
is *hoc*), as the Vestal parallel confirms.   **acutissimo animo:** because
now fully enlightened; for *acutus* of the mind, *TLL* i 465.15–22 (with *Ep.*
90.13), and esp. of philosophers, 464.72–6; for the superlative phrase,
Vitr. 6.1.10. The MSS have *actus animos*, which arose (i) because any case
of *animus* before *referre* was likely to be assimilated to the acc., though
the common *animos/-um referre* is unparalleled in S. (Dionigi 190); and (ii)
because *hoc* was not understood as obj. of both *facere* and *referre*, one had
to be created for *referre* – most recently Dionigi's *actus animi* 'le attività
dello spirito' (141). But this phrase is too vague for what the enlightened
senex actually achieves, and none of Dionigi's parallels (e.g. *Tr.* 2.9, *Ep.*
113.25, 114.23) is sufficiently similar to support his required sense for the
phrase in an isolated context like this. For other suggestions, Reynolds
199 (OCT) in app.   **uirginum...docent:** the parallel further
distances the philosopher, himself an observer of *sacra* (cf. *Breu.* 14.1 n. on
sacrarum...conditores, 19.1 n. on *sacra et sublimia*), and confers added kudos on
his instruction.   **annis...diuisis:** to sharpen the contrast between
didicerunt and *docent*, S. concentrates on only two of the three stages (*officia*)
in the Vestals' thirty-year career, which are usually distinguished as 'first
for learning, then for performing the traditional rites, and thirdly and lastly
for teaching them' (Plut. *Mor.* 795d, trans. H. N. Fowler), a decade being
apportioned (*OLD diuido* 6a) to each stage (D.H. 2.67.2, Plut. *Num.* 10.1).
didicerunt docent: S. favours the neat juxtaposition (*Marc.* 18.7, *Ep.*
6.4, 94.54), as does Quintilian (*Inst.* 7.10.10, 12.8.4).

3 *Exemption from public service*

S.'s more open-minded approach (a familiar leitmotiv; 3.1 n. on
ire . . . sententiam) first out-manoeuvres strict dogmatic orthodoxy and allows
him to identify common ground between the rival Epicurean and Stoic
schools (3.2), before contracting to a narrower compass of Stoic (notably

Panaetian) argument (3.3). When he resumes expanding his interlocutor's horizons (3.4), S. adds to the latter's emphasis (1.4) on the *commune bonum* a broader vision of public service extending beyond the local community.

3.1 Hoc: resuming the obj. of *facere* and *referre* from 2.2.   **quoque:** i.e. in common with S.   **placere** 'find acceptance with', Ciceronian (*OLD* 3). **mihi . . . dixerim** 'I have made it my rule', a rare idiom (*Ben.* 2.18.4) first found in Livy after Cicero's *legem statuere* (*TLL* VII 2.1246.53–6); a regular subjunctive after *non quia* introducing a rejected reason (e.g. *Ir.* 1.6.4, *Ep.* 122.14) in preference to Classical *non quod* (G–L §541 n. 2, K–S II 385–6). **nihil . . . committere** 'commit no offence (against)', Ciceronian (*TLL* III 1911.6–11).   **dictum** 'any precept' (*OLD* I b).   **res ipsa** 'the simple fact of the matter'.   **ire . . . sententiam** 'to support their opinion'. The technical political phrase (*pedibus*) *in sententiam ire* (Ingrosso (1988) 108–9) denotes either the action of moving closer to a speaker in the Senate to show support for his opinion (*Apoc.* 11.6 with Eden (1984) 127) or, more properly, the act of *discessio* (Plin. *Ep.* 8.14.19, Gell. *N.A.* 3.18.2) by which members voted *after sententiae* had been heard (Ogilvie on Liv. 1.32.12 with Talbert (1984) 279–85 for general procedure). S. favours the analogy (also in Gell. *N.A.* 7.13.9), with opting for a philosophical 'side' on an issue-by-issue basis (*V.B.* 2.1, *Ep.* 66.41) a way of asserting his freedom from partisanship (cf. *V.B.* 3.2 and esp. *Ep.* 21.9). His personal experience as a senator since Gaius' reign and as suffect consul in 56 (Griffin (1976) 44, 73–4) is deployed to advantage, adding weight to what might otherwise appear weak isolation.   **quam:** sc. *sententiam*, but not *illorum* as *unius* ('the same one', *OLD* 5a) at once confirms. S. often uses this licence in referring to an antecedent, and rather more audaciously at *Marc.* 1.1 *. . . dolori tuo, cui* [sc. *dolori*, but not *tuo*] *uiri . . . haerent* (cf. *Helu.* 2.1), but it is also found in prose and verse elsewhere (examples in Dionigi 193). Emendation has substituted a conjunction (*quoniam* Reynolds after Gertz (1874) 133; *nam* Madvig II 395), requiring an awkward zeugma which S. could easily have avoided with *unam*.   **unius:** for the hint of a possible slight against Epicureanism here, *Ep.* 33.4 *non sumus* [sc. *Stoici*] *sub rege: sibi quisque se uindicat. apud istos* [sc. *Epicureos*] *quicquid Hermarchus dixit, quicquid Metrodorus, ad unum refertur; omnia quae quisquam in illo contubernio locutus est unius ductu et auspiciis dicta sunt.*   **sequitur:** of supporting a proposal (*sententiam*) in the Senate etc., *OLD* 13.   **in curia . . . est:** a rhetorical antithesis; there were of course supporters' groups in the Senate with members shifting from issue to issue (Talbert (1984) 276–7), as S. well knew (cf. *Apoc.* 9.6, where Hercules tries to put one together: '*noli mihi inuidere, mea res agitur; deinde tu si quid uolueris, in uicem faciam: manus manum lauat*'), but there were not established parties (*OLD factio* 4a). Madvig's conjecture (II 395) as retained here neatly simplifies Lipsius' more ingenious solution (*non id curiae sed iam factionis est*) to the nonsense in the MSS, though *in factione esse* seems to be unparalleled. For the continuing political terminology, Ingrosso (1988) 109.   **utinam quidem:** a favoured combination (*Cl.* 1.19.4, *Helu.* 17.4, *Ben.* 3.15.1, *Ep.* 19.5, 68.12, 89.1, 104.17), classified by Solodow (1978) 72–3 with other examples of contrasting *quidem* (= μέν) without a following adversative (in *nunc . . . quaerimus* below).   **tenerentur** 'were understood' (*OLD* 23a).   **in aperto et confesso** 'obvious and generally accepted'; together only here, but each is paralleled separately with this sense (*in aperto: Ben.* 4.32.1, *TLL* II 224.9–13; *in confesso: Breu.* 2.4, *Ben.* 3.11.2, *TLL* IV 232.81–233.8), making Reynolds' adaptation of *inoperta confessa(que)* in the MSS and of previous conjectures very persuasive.   **decretis:** philosophical, *quae Graeci uocant dogmata* (*Ep.* 95.10; cf. 94.2 *ipsa decreta philosophiae*, 4, 13, 31–2).   **eis:** sc. *Stoicis proceribus* at *V.B.* 3.2, where S.'s active participation is fully documented: *aliquem sequar, aliquem iubebo sententiam diuidere, fortasse . . . nihil improbabo ex iis quae priores decreuerint . . .*

3.2 maxime: with *dissident*.   **et in hac re . . . sed** 'also on this question [sc. involvement v. *otium*], while in fact' (*sed* with limiting force; *OLD* 7a).   **dissident sectae:** Ciceronian vocabulary; for the philosophical 'school', *OLD secta*¹ 2a, adding e.g. *Ep.* 83.9, 85.3, 92.5, 97.14 (further examples in Dionigi 197); for *dissidere* with doctrinal reference, *TLL* V 1.1467.47–1468.4 and esp. *C.S.* 16.3.   **mittit** 'directs' (*Ep.* 68.2); distinguished at *TLL* VIII 1172.6–10 as a rare post-Classical nuance. **Epicurus . . . impedierit:** closely parallel constructions highlight the trivial differences which can underlie such apparently irreconcilable positions.   **Epicurus ait . . . Zenon ait:** not direct quotations but summative antitheses contrived by S.   **non . . . interuenerit:** fr. 8 Us. (= L–S I 22Q5) 'the wise man . . . will not engage in politics', *S.V.* 58 (= L–S I 22DI) 'we must liberate ourselves from the prison of routine business and politics' with Arrighetti 566; but for the crucial exception (*nisi . . . interuenerit*), *Ep.* 22.5 *rogat* [sc. *Idomeneum Epicurus*] *ut quantum potest fugiat et properet, antequam aliqua uis maior interueniat et auferat libertatem recedendi*, Cic. *Rep.* 1.10.1. A striking number of Epicureans in fact engaged voluntarily in politics in the first century BC; Griffin (1989) 13 with Sharples (1996) 7.   **accedet ad** 'take part in'. So 8.1, *Tr.* 1.10 (Ciceronian; *TLL* I 260.37–46); opp. *secedere* (1.1).   **nisi si quid interuenerit** 'unless in exceptional circumstances'. *nisi si* (*OLD nisi* 7a, K–S II 417) is rare in S. but as here at *Tr.* 13.2 (cf. also *Ben.* 2.15.1, 4.35.1, *Ep.* 74.34).   **accedet . . . impedierit:** D.L. 7.121 (= *SVF* III 175.3–4) 'the Stoics say that the wise man will participate in politics if nothing prevents it', attributed to Chrysippus; not an innocent misattribution on S.'s part (esp. given 8.1 *e lege Chrysippi*) but Epicurus as founder of one school must face his Stoic counterpart (Dionigi 59 n. 6 and 200).   **nisi . . . impedierit:** Stoic 'reservation' (*exceptio*, ὑπεξαίρεσις), important for the constancy of the *sapiens* because his 'firm decision and intention always remain integral, even if an obstacle should arise which prevents their realization' (Hadot (1998) 194); cf. *Ben.* 4.34.4–5 with Cooper–Procopé 303 n. 75, *Tr.* 13.2–3, *SVF* III 149.29.

3.3 ex proposito 'as a necessary consequence (*OLD ex* 18a) of his thesis' = κατὰ πρόθεσιν, προηγουμένως.   **ex causa** 'only for good reason' (*OLD causa* 6a), here as equivalent to κατὰ περίστασιν (lit. 'depending on circumstances') in the standard Stoic antithesis (*SVF* III 101.24, Epict. *Diss.* 3.14.7).   **causa . . . patet** 'but these grounds are wide-ranging' (*OLD pateo* 7d), illustrated by three traditional cases (cf. *Ep.* 68.2): (i) the state is hopelessly corrupt (*si res publica . . . impendet*; cf. 8.1); (ii) exclusion by the state itself (*si parum . . . res publica*; cf. *Ep.* 14.14); (iii) ill health (*si ualetudo . . . impediet*).   **si . . . possit:** so at *Tr.* 3.2 the first-century BC Stoic Athenodorus of Tarsus (for whom Griffin (1976) 324 n. 2) urges withdrawal *quia in hac . . . tam insana hominum ambitione tot calumniatoribus in deterius recta torquentibus parum tuta simplicitas est . . .* Depending partly on the dating, there are possible autobiographical undertones given S.'s efforts to withdraw from Nero's court in AD 62 and 64 (Dionigi 104–5). But Griffin (1976) 355–7 is rightly sceptical, and the topos of the 'corrupt state' with its recurrent features deriving from Pl. *Rep.* 496c-e (Dionigi 83–6) supplies an adequate point of reference; cf. esp. Sall. *Cat.* 3.3–4.2, *Jug.* 3.1, Cic. *Rep.* 1.9.1–2, *Off.* 1.69 (general intro. p. 14).   **corruptior** 'too diseased'; of the state, Sall. *Cat.* 14.1 and esp. Tac. *Ann.* 3.27.3 where, as here, it 'initiates a complex series of illness metaphors' (Woodman–Martin (1996) 255).   **quam:** *quam <ut>* Reynolds, but Erasmus' addition is superfluous; for the usage, Goodyear (1972) 158 n. 1 with examples in K–S II 300–1.   **si . . . malis:** extending the medical analogy to explain *corruptior* (*OLD occupo*[1] 4a, *malum*[1] 7b). Less probably, *malis* is dat. of agent (Dionigi 203), i.e. the malefactors by whom the state is 'taken over' (cf. Sall. *Jug.* 31.12 *at qui sunt ii, qui rem publicam occupauere? homines sceleratissumi*); such ambiguity is rare in S.'s use of the case (e.g. 3.4 *quietissimis*, *Breu.* 10.3 *quoi*).

non . . . impendet: the wasted effort is given central emphasis in the chi-astic arrangement (*nitetur* and *se . . . impendet* around *in superuacuum* and *nihil profuturus*). S. perhaps recalls the semi-autobiographical allusion in Pl. *Rep.* 496d to the philosopher who, powerless to counter popular corruption, 'would be destined, before he could be of any service to his country or his friends, to perish, having done no good to himself or to anyone else' (trans. F. M. Cornford); cf. *SVF* III 173.19–22.   **in superuacuum:** first in S. (*OLD* 2c, adding *Ir.* 2.11.1, *Ep.* 70.18, 106.12); such formations are generally post-Classical, under the influence of Sallust (H–S 276). For bare *superuacuus*, *Breu.* 6.3n.   **se . . . impendet** 'expend himself'; post-Classical, also with dat. in S. (*OLD impendo* 3a, adding *Ep.* 42.7, *N.Q.* 6.3.4).   **profuturus:** i.e. 'given that . . . '; Westman (1961) 116.   **si parum . . . res publica:** the grounds for this disqualification are self-appraisal by the *sapiens* with reference to the third of four distinctive aspects of the human self (*personae*) defined by Panaetius: universal rationality, indi-vidual nature, personal circumstances determined by fortune, self-directed career-choice (further Dyck 269–70 on Cic. *Off.* 1.107–21 with Griffin (1976) 341–2). A full illustration of self-appraisal in relation to the third of these aspects occurs at *Tr.* 6.2–3.   **auctoritatis:** 'power and influence, but not such as derives from the tenure of magistracy or can be defined by legal enactment' (Syme (1958) 413).   **uirium** 'capacity to direct the course of events' (*OLD* 25b).   **nec:** explicative, 'nor, for that reason . . . ' (K–S II 42).   **admissura** 'ready to accept'; Westman (1961) 71.   **si ualetudo . . . impediet:** e.g. arising from work-stress; cf. *Tr.* 6.2 *alius in-firmum corpus laborioso pressit officio.* Exclusion on individual health-grounds, with appeal to the second of Panaetius' *personae* (Cic. *Off.* 1.71 with Dyck 201), is given a malicious twist when Tacitus has S. give ill health as a pretext for political withdrawal in AD 62 after Nero refuses him permission to retire (*Ann.* 14.56.3 *Seneca . . . rarus per urbem, quasi ualetudine infensa aut sapientiae studiis domi attineretur*), and again in 64 (*Ann.* 15.45.3 *ficta ualetudine*).   **quomodo nauem . . . non accedet:** familiar rhetorical clichés (cf. André (1962) 29), perhaps wittily parodied in S.'s words to Nero at Tac. *Ann.* 14.54.2 *quomodo in militia aut uia fessus adminiculum orarem, ita in hoc itinere uitae senex . . . praesidium peto.* There is no reason to infer (with Dionigi 106) autobiographical over-tones here, where the hackneyed similes support S.'s portrayal of the *causae* for exemption as established wisdom transmitted over centuries from the founders of the school. For pursuit of a career as a voyage cf. *Tr.* 5.5 and more generally Galasso (1995) 203–4 on Ov. *Pont.* 2.3.25–9; as military service,

TLL VIII 958.56–63; as a journey, *Cl.* 1.19.5, *Ep.* 101.1 (*cursus*).   **nauem quassam:** cf. Ov. *Tr.* 5.11.13.   **nomen . . . daret:** of military enrol-ment, *OLD nomen* 21 b.   **debilis** [sc. *sapiens*] 'if a cripple' (cf. Summers 230 on *Ep.* 55.1); emphatic by position.   **inhabile** 'awkward', 'difficult to accomplish' (Tac. *Ag.* 36.1), and so in conflict with *Tr.* 6.3 *debet . . . semper plus esse uirium in actore quam in opere.*   **sciet** 'know to be' (*OLD* 2d).

3.4 Taking up the first of S.'s two initial propositions (2.1 *primum . . . secreto*), dedication to the contemplative life from an early age is here jus-tified if the novice meets any of the *causae* for exemption in 3.3.   **et** 'even'.   **cui . . . sunt** 'who has all options still open'; *OLD integer* 2d and Summers 337 on *Ep.* 108.21.   **experiatur:** simply temporal; the po-tential nuance of the subjunctive is often diluted in Livy and has largely disappeared in S. (K–S II 366–7, Summers lxiii).   **tempestates:** *Breu.* 18.1.   **subsistere** 'stop short'; cf. *Ep.* 8.3.   **bonis artibus:** not 'liberal studies' in general (*OLD ars* 6a) here, but rather 'moral education' (cf. *Ep.* 88.28, *Ben.* 3.31.5), as *uirtutium cultor* confirms.   **illibatum** (Madvig II 395) 'pure', *sine ulla . . . deductione* (*Ben.* 2.4.3).   **exigere:** of 'spending' *otium*, post-Augustan and rare (*TLL* V 2.1465.59–62).   **uirtutium:** for the form, *Breu.* 19.2 and 12.2n. on *aetatium*; as with *cupiditatium* (*Breu.* 19.2, *C.S.* 14.1, *Tr.* 12.1, *Ep.* 5.7, 117.25), -*um* is a regular variant in the MSS (e.g. *Prou.* 1.5, *Ir.* 2.13.2, 3.8.2, *Ot.* 6.2; *cupiditatum:* *Ep.* 19.6, 20.1, 55.5, 82.6).   **cultor:** of Stoic virtue(s), *V.B.* 20.6, *Ep.* 71.28 (*honesti, V.B.* 4.2); cf. *V.B.* 9.1, *Ep.* 36.3.   **exerceri:** of strengthening the virtues by practice, *V.B.* 25.8, *Ep.* 94.45 (with Bellincioni (1979) 180, and also 186–7 on 94.47 *exercitatione*), 109.12.   **quietissimis** 'those furthest from public life' (*OLD* 2c); for dat. of agent, rare in Classical Latin (K–S I 325; Skutsch on Enn. *Ann.* 399), 3.3n. on *si . . . malis, Breu.* 3.2, 10.3, 12.3, *C.S.* 15.5, *Ir.* 2.5.2, *V.B.* 20.2. In the contemplative life *uirtus* commands the same respect as in the world of public affairs (cf. Zetzel (1995) 98–9 on Cic. *Rep.* 1.2.1).

3.5 In accordance with οἰκείωσις (1.4n. on *non desinemus . . . dare*), 'the dis-tinction between altruism and egoism collapses into a single beneficial rela-tion of mutual betterment' (L–S I 377 on 60P = *SVF* III 160.20–2; cf. 160.13–15, *Ep.* 81.19). Even without this broader opportunity the *sapiens*, who 'bene-fits himself' by perfecting his own virtue, still has a public role (cf. 2.2): *Tr.* 3.3 (in the voice of Athenodorus) *hominum . . . maximae in seducto actiones sunt. ita tamen delituerit ut, ubicumque otium suum absconderit, prodesse uelit singulis uniuersisque ingenio uoce consilio; . . . qui iuuentutem exhortatur, qui . . . uirtutem instil-lat animis . . . in priuato publicum negotium agit.*   **hoc . . . exigitur, ut:** rare (with antecedent demonstrative not before S.; *Prou.* 6.1, *Ep.* 63.1, 93.7 with *ne*), reinforcing the obligation: *V.B.* 24.3 *hominibus prodesse natura me iubet*; Cic. *Fin.* 3.65 *impellimur . . . natura ut prodesse uelimus quam plurimis . . .*).   **prosit:** Stoic ὠφελήματα have the widest possible terms of reference; common to all as a feature of *omnis homini erga hominem societas coniunctio caritas* (Cic. *Fin.* 3.69).   **si fieri potest . . . sibi:** the tetracolic anaphora narrows the focus towards climactic *sibi* (marking 'il trionfo dell' io interiore', Traina (1987) 19); for *si minus* (colloquial; Hofmann 146) repeated with different rhythmic effect, *Ep.* 85.40.   **proximis:** perhaps incl. his enlightened associates (τινα τῶν πλησίον, *SVF* III 160.14–15).   **cum . . . efficit:** putting into practice Chrysippus' doctrine of the social utility of all good-ness (D.L. 7.98–9 = *SVF* III 22.3–12).   **commune . . . negotium:** i.e. he meets the Stoic duty to public service (1.4), and he receives as well as gives; *Tr.* 3.1 *cum utilem se efficere ciuibus mortalibusque propositum habeat, simul et exercetur et proficit qui in mediis se officiis posuit communia priuataque pro facultate administrans.*   **quomodo . . . parat:** the inevitable social con-sequences of individual choice and action preclude the possibility of to-tal isolation, good and bad effects being equally influential in extent and moral impact. This evenly balanced contrast is emphasized in the overall coordinating structure and the alliteration in *p*- which closes each of the paired clauses.   **non . . . tantummodo . . . sed etiam:** Livian (K–S II 57) and rare in S. (5.4, *Pol.* 15.3), placing *sibi* and *omnibus* as ordered here in inverse relation to the more familiar Socratic/Stoic idea that to harm others is also to harm the self (cf. *SVF* III 71.6–9, 160.21).   **melior factus:** in protasis.   **bene . . . meretur** 'serves himself well' (Cooper–Procopé 175; *OLD mereo* 6a).   **hoc ipso** 'by this very act' (sc. *quod bene de se meretur*).   **quod . . . parat:** causal, neatly drawing attention to the time-lapse between the act and its wider effect.   **profuturum** = *id quod proderit*; cf. Sall. *Jug.* 1.5 *nihil profutura.*

4 *The two commonwealths*

The positive claims for *otium* are now raised to a more ambitious level, as S. unapologetically invokes the old Stoic vision of the two commonwealths. Zeno's 'dream' in his *Republic* of a universal civic awareness, itself influenced by earlier (notably Cynic) ideas (see Sharples (1996) 125), was adapted by Chrysippus to become the 'cosmic city' of later Stoics – a departure from Zeno despite Plut. *Mor.* 329a-b (*SVF* I 60.38–61.7 = L–S I 67A; Schofield

(1999) 104–11 with Sharples (1996) 125). A central idea in this more elaborate framework is that rational beings (gods and men; 4.1n. on *di atque*
homines) are guided 'by prescriptive [i.e. Stoic cosmic] reason instructing
them how to treat each other as social animals' (Schofield (1999) 72) in line
with οἰκείωσις (1.4n. on *non desinemus . . . dare*). For S. and other Stoics of the
early Empire the claim of this universal citizenship overshadows that of
the local, the shift being one of emphasis rather than substance (Schofield
in *CHHP* 770; general intro. pp. 5–6). S. shows little or no interest in using
the 'cosmic city' either as a supportive blueprint for or as an ideal in conflict
with Roman imperial government (see Griffin (1976) 238–9, 249).

4.1 animo complectamur 'try to take in', conative (G–L §227 n. 2).
magnam: the greater is treated more expansively, with double subordination (*qua . . . in qua*).   **publicam** 'common to all'; in this sense (*Breu.* 1.1),
mostly post-Augustan in prose (*OLD* 5a).   **di atque homines:** a
common periphrasis for *omnes* (*TLL* v 1.909.32–8) but here echoing
Chrysippus' 'the world is . . . the structure consisting of gods and men
and of the things made for their sake' (*SVF* II 168.11–14; cf. 169.23–
5 = L–S I 67LI, *Marc.* 18.1–2, *Ep.* 95.52 with Pease on Cic. *N.D.*
2.154).   **angulum:** contemptuous, as often in S., e.g. *Ep.* 28.4 *cum*
hac persuasione uiuendum est: 'non sum uni angulo natus, patria mea totus hic
mundus est', 68.2.   **terminos . . . metimur:** for the hyperbole, *Rhet.*
Her. 4.44 *'imperii magnitudinem solis ortu atque occasu metiemur'*; for the idea,
Ep. 102.21 *nullos sibi poni nisi communes et cum deo terminos patitur* [sc. hu-
manus animus].   **nostrae:** i.e. Stoic; for *ciuitas* of the Stoic *mundus*,
Cic. *Leg.* 1.23, *Fin.* 3.64.   **ascripsit** 'enrolled' as citizens (*OLD* 2b).
condicio nascendi 'accident of birth' (Summers 166 on *Ep.* 11.6).
aut Atheniensium . . . aut Carthaginiensium: not chosen at ran-
dom, as S. already identifies two major centres of political opposition
to free philosophical speculation which return in 8.2. Both also have
turbulent histories (*C.S.* 6.8, *Marc.* 17.4, *Tr.* 5.1–3) with their prime
long past (cf. in general *Ep.* 91.10), but on this point alone Carthage is
more generally linked with Corinth or Numantia (*Pol.* 1.2; *TLL Suppl.* II
215.46–52).   **aut . . . urbis:** contrast *Ep.* 102.21 for the soul not limited to any 'humble birthplace' (*humilem . . . patriam*, Ephesus or Alexandria),
as *patria est illi quodcumque suprema et uniuersa circuitu suo cingit, hoc omne con-*
uexum . . . .   **alterius:** equivalent to the gen. of *alius* (*OLD alius*[1]; so
7.2, *Breu.* 2.5, 16.3); rare in combination with *aliqui* (*Breu.* 16.3), *aliqui(s)*

alius being more usual (K–S I 636, N–W II 474).   **pertineat** 'reaches out to include' (with *ad*, Cic. *Off.* 1.92); subjunctive in relative clause of tendency (G–L §631.2).   **quidam eodem ... tantum maiori:** the triple anaphora (*quidam ... minorique, quidam ... minori, quidam ... maiori*) points to three distinctive groups, doubtless with individuals changing membership from time to time. To *quidam ... minori* belong e.g. Augustus, Cicero and Livius Drusus as portrayed at *Breu.* 4.2–6.2, and also S.'s Paulinus (cf. *Breu.* 18.1 *maior pars aetatis ... rei publicae data est*); to *quidam tantum maiori* belong the philosophical *otiosi* depicted at e.g. *Breu.* 14.1–2. For the combination of the two (*quidam ... minorique*) cf. *Tr.* 4 where, in response to Athenodorus' advocacy (3.2) of complete retirement from public service because of the corruption rampant in politics, S. favours only gradual and partial withdrawal (4.8 *longe ... optimum est miscere otium rebus*, where *otium* embraces philosophical pursuits). This category is also commended elsewhere as preferable by far (e.g. *Ep.* 3.6 *et quiescenti agendum et agenti quiescendum est*), so that the weighting of the arguments in *Ot.* and *Breu.* in favour of withdrawal has been read as a radically new departure by S. with implications for their dating (general intro. pp. 2–3, 12–20). This is unjustified by the evidence of the treatises: the first (as we have it) advocates withdrawal for someone denied by external circumstances the chance to make an effective contribution, the second for someone whose personal circumstances after years of active service justify elevation to better things. Neither denies the wider advantages, or indeed the inevitability, of the 'mixed commitment' for the great majority, nor is it suggested in 4.1 that the three groups (*quidam ... quidam ... quidam*) are roughly equal divisions of humanity. On the contrary, the whole preceding sentence emphasizes that we all belong to both commonwealths; circumstances affect the extent or desirability of our contribution to either without impairing our dual identity. For other arguments against inconsistency and their implications for dating, Griffin (1976) 331–4.

   4.2 et 'even'; the ironic understatement continues with *immo uero ... melius.*   **deseruire** 'serve with devotion'; with *res publica*, Cic. *Ver.* 3.228.   **immo uero** 'or *rather*'; *immo* frequent in S. but rarely with *uero* as its intensifier (*Breu.* 3.1, *Pol.* 15.3, *Ep.* 7.3, 9.12).   **nescio an:** with affirmative emphasis (*OLD nescio* 4a), as also after corrective *immo* at *C.S.* 4.3, *Helu.* 12.1.   **ut:** epexegetic after *huic ... possumus* (*OLD* 39a), setting out the model programme (*Breu.* 18.2n. on *maiora, Ep.* 68.10, 73.4) of the *maior res publica*. Of the three standard divisions of the Stoic curriculum – logic, physics and ethics (*Ep.* 89.9; L–S I 158–62 with Kidd II 350–1) – S. here begins with ethics (*quid... faciat*) and then progresses to physics (*Breu.* 19.1 n. on *quae... miraculis?*), first the nature of the material cosmos (*unum... permixtum*), then its divine governance.   **quid ... sint:** elaborated at *Ep.* 95.55; L–S 1 383–4 for Socratic/Platonic influence on the formulation of these questions.   **quid sit uirtus:** for Stoics, 'rational consistency' (*SVF* 1 50.3 λόγον ... ὁμολογούμενον = L–S 1 61 B8), by which the controlling intelligence harmonizes perfectly all sense-perceptions, thoughts and responses so that every act of the *sapiens* will be morally good (Rist 15); cf. *Ep.* 66.32 *nihil... aliud est uirtus quam recta ratio*, 76.10.   **una pluresne sint:** not the radical division it first seems. For S. the primary Stoic virtues (practical wisdom, justice, moderation and courage, canonical since Plato; *Breu.* 13.9 n. on *cuius... minuent?*, 19.2 n. on *uirtutium*) are distinguished as variously applicable 'aspects' (*species*; *Ep.* 66.7) of *uirtus* itself, implying one another and only conceptually separable (*Ep.* 67.10, 90.3, 113.14; on the ἀντακολουθία τῶν ἀρετῶν, Dyck 338 on Cic. *Off.* 1.152–61). This unitary thesis is traced through the early Stoa (Zeno, Ariston) back to Menedemus but modified by Chrysippus' emphasis on the qualitative differentiation of the virtues (Plut. *Mor.* 440e–441 b = L–S 1 61 B1–7), to which S. draws attention with *pluresne* here.   **-ne:** with second alternative in indirect question (*OLD -ne* 5c, K–S 11 528), rare in S. (*V.B.* 24.3, cited by Bourgery (1922) 336).   **natura ... faciat:** long contested (e.g. Pl. *Meno* 70a), with Sophists in particular having a vested interest in asserting the claim of 'nurture' over 'nature' (Guthrie 111 250–60). S. elsewhere follows the Stoic position (e.g. *SVF* 111 52.17–20) that goodness is not a natural endowment (*Ep.* 90.44 *non... dat natura uirtutem: ars est bonum fieri*, 46; cf. *Ir.* 2.10.6, *Ep.* 49.11, 88.32, 123.16); nature supplies the raw potential (*Ep.* 108.8 *fundamenta... semenque uirtutum*, 120.4; *SVF* 1 129.18 ἀφορμάς, 111 51.23) for the acquisition of virtue by 'analogy', i.e. by inference from observation (Long (1986) 201–3). This is the basis for Quintilian's view *nihil praecepta atque artes ualere nisi adiuuante natura* (*Inst.* 1 *praef.* 26).   **ars:** the usual antithesis to *natura/ingenium* (*TLL* 11 669.49–670.80), embracing *doctrina, exercitatio* (*OLD* 4), *experientia* (*OLD* 3), *ratio, diligentia*.   **bonos:** predicative.   **unum ... sparserit:** for the interminable debate on the uniqueness or endless reduplication of the universe see Pease on Cic. *N.D.* 1.53, incl. Aetius' summary (*Plac.* 2.1.2–3 = Diels *Dox. Gr.* p. 327): one universe features in e.g. Thales, Pythagoras, Plato, Aristotle and Zeno of Citium, multiple universes in e.g. Xenophanes, Democritus and Epicurus *inter alios*.   **unum sit hoc quod ... complectitur:** *N.Q.* 2.3.1 *omnia* *quae in notitiam nostram cadunt aut cadere possunt mundus complectitur*, *V.B.* 8.4, *Ep.* 92.30; n. below on *toti inditus*. The three major divisions within the enclosed Stoic *mundus* are into *caelestia*, *sublimia*, *terrena* (*N.Q.* 2.1.1 with Hine (1981) 124–6 on the Greek background).   **maria terrasque:** i.e. *terrena*; *N.Q.* 2.1.2 *tertia illa pars de aquis terris arbustis satis quaerit et . . . de omnibus quae solo continentur.* The plur. is common (e.g. *Prou.* 1.2 . . . *ut infusa uallibus maria molliant terras*; *TLL* VIII 377.79–82) and with *terra* normal (e.g. *Helu.* 20.2; *OLD* 9a).   **mari ac terris inserta** 'the things connected to earth and water', i.e. *sublimia* in the sublunary region of the four elements: *N.Q.* 2.1.2 *secunda pars tractat inter caelum terrasque uersantia. hic sunt nubila imbres niues . . . quaecumque aër facit patiturue*, *Helu.* 20.2. The looseness of the phrase reflects the variable contents which philosophers assign to this division: S. follows Aristotle in including earthquakes among *sublimia*, but like Aetius places seas and rivers among *terrena* (Hine (1981) 126–7). The precise mention of water and earth here (next n.) rules out the higher celestial phenomena.   **mari:** here 'sea-water' (*OLD* 5), the exhalation (*halitus*) from which *umidus est, in imbres et niues cedit*, while *uapor* from the earth causes *uentos fulmina tonitrua* (*N.Q.* 2.12.4). The theory is Aristotelian (Hine (1981) 238–40). S. may possibly be avoiding the very rare dat. plur. (N–W I 625), but could have more neatly done so with *illis inserta.*   **inserta:** *OLD insero²* 2a; cf. *N.Q.* I *praef.* 14 *terris uicina*, 2.4.2 *aër . . . et caelo et terris cohaeret.* **multa . . . sparserit:** despite the suggestive Lucretian language (*D.R.N.* 6.922–3 *spargi . . . necessest* | *corpora* = atomic particles), no straightforward allusion to atomist theory, acc. to which *deus* of course plays no part in the random formation of innumerable worlds. S. here simply means 'distributed'.   **continua . . . et plena** 'continuous and with no intervals of space' (*continua* not temporal, given the contrast with *diducta*). In defending this proposition himself (*N.Q.* 2.7.2 *nihil ergo opus erit admixto inani*), S.'s obvious target is the atomists' assertion of the necessity of void to explain motion (cf. Lucr. *D.R.N.* 1.329–417). Earlier refutations of void are inevitably most uncompromising among the Eleatics (Guthrie II 33, 104, 139), but probably Plato (*Tim.* 58a), certainly Aristotle (*Phys.* 4.6–9) and Zeno of Citium (*SVF* I 26. 20–2, 27–30) deny any void *within* the universe as opposed to outside it (cf. *SVF* II 170.38, 171.33–6, 172.15–16; 5.6n. on *utrumne . . . cludatur*).   **materia . . . gignuntur:** Stoic matter is the amorphous Aristotelian substrate (*SVF* II 115.23 ἄποιον σῶμα) which god/reason fashions into recognizable sensibles (*SVF* I 110.26–7), as S. explains at *Ep.* 65.2–3.   **diducta . . . permixtum:** so *N.Q.* 2.7.1 *quidam*

[sc. *Epicurei*] *aëra discerpunt et in particulas diducunt, ita ut illi inane permisceant.*
The original argument that void is essential to facilitate motion (Epic. *Ep.*
Her. 39–40 = L–S 1 5A1) is elaborated in Philodemus (cf. Hine (1981) 195)
and Lucr. *D.R.N.* 1.418–550; further Pease on Cic. *N.D.* 2.82.   **quae sit**
dei sedes: moving on to theology, the final stage in physical studies (L–S
1 26c), S. reopens the debate on the location of the divine (*OLD sedes* 5b)
which Lucretius engages with at *D.R.N.* 5.146–55: *illud item non est ut possis*
credere, sedes | esse deum sanctas in mundi partibus ullis (146–7). The Stoic reply is
given by Cato (Luc. 9.578–9) in answer to Labienus' appeal that he consult
the oracle of Ammon: *estque dei sedes nisi terra et pontus et aër | et caelum et uirtus?*.
quae 'what kind of?' (*OLD qui*[1] 2a); the issue is not merely one of location.
Dionigi's preference after Gertz for *qui sit deus* here draws on parallels at
N.Q. 1 *praef.* 3, 13 (cf. also *Breu.* 19.1, Stat. *S.* 5.3.21 *quis deus . . .*), but these
all introduce a much wider range of questions about the divine nature
than the specific issue on which S. concentrates.   **opus . . . inditus:**
elaborating the relation of god(s) to the universe, the issue to which the
divine *sedes* is indissolubly linked.   **spectet** 'looks on in detachment',
as at Lucr. *D.R.N.* 2.2, Luc. 2.289; no need for a qualifier (for *sedes, sedens*
Dionigi with later MSS; *deses* Gertz), here redundant whether 'in his position' or 'inactive'. For the fuller Epicurean picture, *Ben.* 4.4.1 = fr. 364 Us.
deus . . . securus et neglegens nostri, auersus a mundo . . . nihil agit with Pease on Cic.
N.D. 1.51.   **tractet** 'actively controls', as at *N.Q.* 7.30.3; cf. *Prou.* 1.1, 2.9
intentus operi suo deus, *Ep.* 58.28 *cura regentis*, *Breu.* 19.1 n. on *uoluntas*. Cicero
(*N.D.* 2.75) uses *administrare* to convey the Stoic view of divine involvement.
utrumne . . . an: in S. -*ne* is rarely attached to *utrum* introducing a disjunctive indirect question (*OLD utrum* 2b; cf. 5.6, *Pol.* 6.1, 2, 9.9, 11.4, Bourgery
(1922) 336); possibly for emphasis here (cf. K–S II 529), reinforcing the
incompatibility of the positions on this (for Stoics) most solemn of subjects.   **extrinsecus . . . sit** 'he encompasses it [sc. *operi suo*] from without'; approximate examples are supplied by Plato's demiurge in the *Timaeus*
(Guthrie V 259–62) and Aristotle's 'unmoved mover', which activates the
universe but is not inside it (Guthrie VI 246–62). Dionigi 223 rightly stresses
that the Epicurean gods are located in the *intermundia*/μετακόσμια, the
spaces between the Epicurean worlds (Kenney (1971) 77–8 on Lucr. *D.R.N.*
3.18–22), and so do not provide the neat and absolute antithetical case the
alternative question requires.   **toti inditus** 'implanted in the whole'
(τὸ ὅλον), i.e. the finite (Stoic) cosmos (*mundus* below and at 5.5, 6, *Breu.*
19.1) as opposed to 'the all' (τὸ πᾶν), i.e. the cosmos *and* the void beyond it

(*SVF* II 167.4–9, 10–14 = L–S I 44A with Sambursky (1959) 114). For Stoic belief in the pervasive immanence of god (= *ratio*, λόγος) throughout 'the whole', *Ep.* 90.29 *aeternam . . . rationem toti inditam, Ben.* 4.7.1, *N.Q.* 2.45.3 *partibus suis inditus* [sc. *Iuppiter*].   **immortalis . . . numerandus:** the Stoic *mundus* undergoes periodic destruction and recreation (*Marc.* 26.6, *N.Q.* 3.28–30), which S. distinguishes from final mortality: *Ep.* 58.24 *mundus . . . , aeterna res et inuicta, mutatur nec idem manet,* 71.13 *quicquid est non erit, nec peribit sed resoluetur.* This orthodox position on 'everlasting recurrence' (L–S I 308–13) differs from Epicurus' view of an infinite succession of worlds formed by the disintegration and re-formation of atomic structures (*Ep. Her.* 73–4, Lucr. *D.R.N.* 1.215–64, 2.294–307) in the emphasis it gives to the role of divine providence as much as in the physics of its cosmological picture. For, although Epicurean atoms are everlasting (cf. Lucr. *D.R.N.* 1.221 *aeterno . . . semine*), the never-ending interaction of the divine mind with matter (L–S I 44C7, D4) enables S. to present the Stoic *mundus* as never totally annihilated despite its periodic destruction. For Aristotle's imperishable universe, *Cael.* 1.11–12 with Guthrie VI 267–8; for earlier views, Hahm (1977) 185–95.   **inter . . . numerandus:** distinguishing, like Aristot. *Cael.* 279b 12–17, between the atomists' perishable world (*OLD caducus* 8) and the purely temporary (cf. Cic. *Off.* 1.27 *breuis est et ad tempus, Amic.* 53, Liv. 28.42.5) structures of Empedocles and Heraclitus, which alternate in unremitting cycles of formation and dissolution.   **contemplatur:** possibly hinting at the cosmos as a *templum*; Pease on Cic. *N.D.* 2.37, Zetzel (1995) 232 on *Rep.* 6.15.2.   **praestat** 'bring about' (with *ne*, *OLD* 12a).   **ne . . . sint:** inverting the very common idiom in which the *di immortales* are invoked as witnesses of *human* undertakings and achievements. So also Epict. *Diss.* 3.26.28 'Does God so neglect his own . . . witnesses (μαρτύρων), whom alone he uses as examples to the uninstructed, to prove that he both is, and governs the universe (τὰ ὅλα) well, and does not neglect the affairs of men . . . ?' (trans. W. A. Oldfather; cf. 3.24.112–14).

5 Contemplation and action

Itself 'active', *contemplatio* is inseparable from *actio*. Section 4.2 has introduced the multiple disjunctive question as a stylistic device for stimulating *contemplatio*. Now, advancing to his new stage of *probatio* (5.1), S. deploys the device on a much more ambitious scale (5.5–6) to define the scope and

procedures of *cogitatio* ('rational reflection'), and so trains the basic inves-
tigative instinct in the discipline of intellectual analysis.

5.1 Solemus [sc. *Stoici*] **dicere:** introducing common expressions, *Breu.*
15.3, *Ben.* 4.36.1, 5.7.2.   **summum ... uiuere:** Cleanthes' formula
(L–S I 63B3) had from the start been given various interpretations (Cic. *Fin.*
4.14–15 preserves these), but the major difference in emphasis reflected
in S.'s regular use lies between conformity with one's 'particular' nature
(*Ep.* 41.8 *secundum naturam suam uiuere*; *V.B.* 3.3) and with the universal *lex
naturae* of the physical world (*Ep.* 107.8–9, *Ben.* 4.25.1). The serious logical
problems which had arisen from this (Long (1986) 179–84) are minimized
in S. by presenting the *summum bonum* as a harmonizing of the individual *ratio* with the guiding intelligence of the universe through *cogitatio* (*Ep.*
66.12, 39, 76.9–11, 92.27 *ratio ... dis hominibusque communis est: haec in illis
consummata est, in nobis consummabilis*), with *Ot.* 5.4–7 esp. training the rational faculty in the appropriate analytical method.   **natura ... actioni:**
terms which reflect the debt of the old Stoa (*SVF* III 173.5–6) to early
Aristotle: *Protr.* fr. 61 p. 72.17–19 Rose = Düring (1961) 129 C52: 3 = Cic.
Fin. 2.40 ... *hominem ad duas res ... ad intellegendum et <ad> agendum esse natum quasi mortalem deum*; Inwood (1985) 18–21.   **ad utrumque ... et
contemplationi rerum et actioni:** such variety of construction without antithesis is rare in S. (Summers lxxx–lxxxi); *rerum* is not redundant but
weights the balance of the dicolon (*et ... et*) in favour of its first part (Dionigi
227), with *contemplatio* subsequently (*nunc ... diximus*) given priority until *actio*
is reintroduced in 5.8.   **quod prius diximus:** i.e. *natura nos genuit contemplationi rerum.*   **quid porro?** 'what more to say?', implying that the
question following has an obvious (desired) answer; colloquial (Summers l)
and favoured by S. (*Prou.* 5.3, *V.B.* 28.1, *Ep.* 66.9, 77.18, 78.20).   **erit
probatum** emphasizes already completed action; *Ben.* 6.1.1, *Ep.* 95.48,
K–S I 165.   **se ... consuluerit** 'asks himself'. S. likes this rare trans.
use of the reflexive to introduce an indirect (*N.Q.* 4A *praef.* 18, *Ag.* 51) or
even direct (*Ir.* 2.28.8) question.   **unusquisque** 'each individual person', emphatically restrictive (K–S I 648). S. starts the *probatio* from the
narrowest point of introspection, which will then be aligned with the wider
range of human aspirations (5.2 *quidam, populos*, 5.3 *nobis, nos*), so introducing
reader-awareness (5.4 *ut scias ... uide*) to the shared adventure of the intellect (5.4 *nos, nobis*, 5.5 *uisimus, nostra*, 5.6 *nostra*). At the same time the object
of thought will itself be enlarged from individual motivation (5.1 *quantam*

cupidinem habeat) to encompass the principles of natural science (5.5) and exploration beyond the visible cosmos (5.6), as S. re-applies the technique of presentation – the expanding of his interlocutor's narrow horizons – already used in 1.4–4.2 (3 intro.; general intro. pp. 27–8). **cupidinem ... ignota noscendi:** basic inquisitiveness, which responds well to every banal and fantastic report brought back by travellers, adventurers and the like. A natural progression from this to philosophical enquiry and the search for wisdom is already suggested by Cic. *Fin.* 5.49 *omnia quidem scire, cuiuscumque modi sint, cupere curiosorum, duci uero maiorum rerum contemplatione ad cupiditatem scientiae summorum uirorum est putandum.* The protreptic zeal with which S. here sets about transforming mere *curiosi* into *summi uiri* may well be another echo of Aristotle (n. on *natura...actioni* above; Dionigi 88–90) but possibly also of Antiochus of Ascalon, whose 'Old Academic' views are represented in *Fin.* 5 (Dionigi 92–5, with cautionary remarks in Barnes (1989) 65–6). **quam:** adv. of exclamation, here modifying a verb in indirect question (*OLD* 1b). **ad:** lit. 'in response to', effectively causal (*OLD* 33a, K–S 1 522); *Helu.* 10.5, *Ep.* 67.14, 108.7. **fabulas:** Cic. *Fin.* 5.52 *quid cum fictas fabulas, e quibus utilitas nulla elici potest, cum uoluptate legimus?*; often suggestive of mendacity in S. (*Breu.* 16.5, *Ben.* 1.4.5–6, *Ep.* 82.16, 108.6).

5.2 This inquisitive instinct can lead to extraordinary feats of endurance. In fact, almost all ancient (and modern) exploration was undertaken for motives of trade, colonization, plunder and conquest, with literary *curiosi* like Herodotus and the periegetes Pausanias and Polemon generally confining themselves to already explored areas. S.'s *quidam* may enlarge the field of awareness after *unusquisque* (5.1 n.), but in real terms will have included only a handful of brave individuals, possibly like Pytheas of Massalia. The improbable thesis that such motivation was widespread is a convenient one for Greek protreptic, which can exploit the etymological link between θέα (*spectaculum*) and θεωρία (*contemplatio*) as Aristotle apparently did (*Protr.* fr. 58 p. 69.15–21 Rose = Düring (1961) 66–7 B44), and is therefore influential in Cic. *Fin.* 5.48 *ad eas res* [sc. *cognitionem et scientiam*] *hominum natura nullo emolumento inuitata rapiatur* (5.1 n. on *cupidinem ... ignota noscendi*). S. carefully positions the idea in his structured expansion of the reader's horizons. **nauigant ... remotumque:** separation of the verbs with extended polysyllables intervening suggests the arduous length of such voyages, the final positioning of *remotum* their ultimate goal. **una mercede** 'for the sole reward', abl. of price (G–L §404); the usual connotation is financial (*OLD* 1b). **perpetiuntur:** strategically hemmed in on both sides by the single, overriding motive. S. may adapt the idea from Cic. *Fin.* 5.48 *nonne uidemus eos ... omnia ... perpeti ipsa cognitione et scientia captos ... ?*   **abditum remotumque:** emphasis is intensified by juxtaposition (Apul. *Met.* 4.18.1 *monumentum quoddam ... procul a uia remoto et abdito loco positum*; further parallels in *TLL* 1 58.71–4) as well as by position.   **haec ... contrahit:** the protreptic theme of popular entertainments (theatrical, gladiatorial etc.) as a magnet for public curiosity (Aristot. *Protr.* fr. 58 p. 69.15–21 Rose = Düring (1961) 66–7 B44) here overrides S.'s disapproval of them elsewhere (*Ir.* 2.8.1, *Ep.* 76.4, 80.2; *Breu.* 13.6n. on *et Pompeium primum ... edidisse*).   **haec res:** for neut. pronoun, a Senecan mannerism (Bourgery (1922) 210).   **contrahit** 'assembles'; with *ad* ('for') *spectaculum*, Livian (45.33.3).   **praeclusa ... gentium:** the *congeries*, one of the four *genera amplificationis* (Lausberg §406), expands the mind's horizon to encompass remoter areas of time and place.   **praeclusa:** as neut. plur. substantive, apparently only here (*TLL* x 2.494.50–2).   **rimari** 'pry into things' (*OLD* 3a); here with the positive connotation of *N.Q.* 7.29.3 (pejorative at *Ep.* 68.4, 110.9).   **secretiora:** sc. *quam quae praeclusa sunt.*   **exquirere:** in this scientific sense paralleled in S. only at *N.Q.* 4B.5.3.   **antiquitates euoluere** 'to uncover the past' (*OLD euoluo* 4b) by reading through (6a) works on antiquity (*antiquitas* 2b), perhaps esp. Varro's famous *Antiquitates rerum humanarum et diuinarum* (Rawson (1985) 233–49). Contrast *Ep.* 88.39 *annales euoluam omnium gentium ... ?*, in a context where S. rails against 'useless' learning (*Breu.* 13.1 n. on *litterarum inutilium studiis*) like Varro himself at *Men.* 505 Astbury *ruminaris antiquitates.* The different emphasis here is conditioned by protreptic discussion of the intrinsic interest of all historical detail (Cic. *Fin.* 5.51–2, esp. 52 *multa ... minime necessaria*), and by the need to mark a level of reader-response above that of reacting to the stimulus of *fabulae.*   **mores ... gentium:** not the *fabulae* of travellers but serious essays in the ethnographical literature represented for us by Tacitus' *Germania.*   **barbararum:** not Roman or Greek.   **audire:** at a *recitatio*, where audiences confronted with long treatises or poems could be surprisingly docile (*Ep.* 95.2, 122.11).

5.3 S. elevates the subject from awareness of the self (5.1) and of societies in the wider contexts of time and place (5.2) to universal *natura*, who exercises a quasi-divine *mens* in the purposeful ordering of her arrangements for human admiration. The uniquely human 'response' to nature, which is in fact to participate in the invention of an abstraction and its elaboration in personified guise, is presented as uniform across the boundaries of culture, race and nation. So, in conjunction with the universalizing of the object of perception comes the further expansion of the range of perceivers, from the single *unusquisque* (5.1) and collective *quidam/populos* (5.2) to the appropriately all-embracing *nobis/nos*, forging a common human identity out of a common awareness and a value-system accessible to all through the discipline of *cogitatio*.   **curiosum** 'eager for knowledge', here with positive value (*Ep.* 108.39, *N.Q.* 1 *praef.* 12, 7.25.5) but not always so; *OLD* 3b with Pease on Cic. *N.D.* 1.10 (full discussion in Joly (1961)). The negative slant is emphatic in Cic. *Fin.* 5.49 (5.1 n. on *cupidinem . . . ignota noscendi*), which is explained by the demarcation of *curiosi* and *summi uiri* into sharply opposed groups. S., in contrast, invites every reader to follow a rational progression from an initial stimulus via *curiositas* to the summit of the intellectual life.   **et . . . ostenderet:** the familiar teleological view of the purpose of human life for the cosmos and of the cosmos for human life (4.2n. on *ne . . . sint*; Powell (1988) 253 on Cic. *Sen.* 77), with possible traces of protreptic influence in *spectatores nos . . . genuit*; so Iambl. *Protr.* 9 p. 51 Pistelli = Düring (1961) 54–5 B18, 19: Pythagoras 'used to say he was an observer of nature and it was for this he had come into being. Asked why anyone would choose to be born and live, Anaxagoras allegedly answered "To observe the heavens and the stars, moon and the sun in them", everything else being worth nothing.' Even so, S.'s presentational skill imitates something of nature's brilliance, subtlety and variety by conveying the well-known idea through a sequence of images drawn from aesthetics, the theatre, agriculture and intellectual reflection, with a striking paradox at its climax (next nn.).   **artis:** *censet . . .* [sc. *Zeno*] *artis maxume proprium esse creare et gignere, quodque in operibus nostrarum artium manus efficiat id multo artificiosius naturam efficere . . . atque hac quidem ratione omnis natura artificiosa est . . .* (Cic. *N.D.* 2.57 = *SVF* 1 44.3–5, 11–12; also 2.83 *arte naturae*, 142).   **sibi:** with *conscia* (*OLD* 3a).   **pulchritudinis:** Cic. *N.D.* 2.15 with Pease; at 2.58 *eximia pulchritudo* is classed as one of the three principal objectives of the Stoic *mens mundi*, itself related in the same passage to 'designing' nature.   **spectatores . . . spectaculis:** assimilation of viewer to object viewed emulates the ideal relationship of man to nature; for the theatrical metaphor (the original sense; *OLD spectator* 1b), Pease on Cic. *N.D.* 2.140, 155. These cosmic *spectacula* stand in contrast to those at 5.2 *haec . . . contrahit*.   **perditura . . . sui** 'since she would be sure to lose [Westman (1961) 201] all pleasure in herself'; *OLD fructus* 6, but the metaphor of agricultural fertility (*OLD* 3) is esp. marked after *genuit*

(Cic. *N.D.* 2.37 *fructus quos terra gignit,* Plin. *N.H.* 16.95, 117, 17.178) and *perditura* (Cic. *Fam.* 4.6.2 *existimabam . . . omnes me . . . industriae meae fructus . . . perdidisse*).   **tam . . . tam . . . tam . . . tam:** the seamless perfection of nature in her different characteristics (*magna* etc. neut. acc. plurs.).   **subtiliter ducta** 'finely contrived' both in texture (*N.Q.* 1.3.4, *OLD duco* 23a) and intellectual judgement (*OLD subtiliter* 3).   **non uno genere formosa:** *N.Q.* 7.27.5 *non ad unam natura formam opus suum praestat sed ipsa uarietate se iactat;* for the phrase, *Ep.* 36.1.   **solitudini ostenderet:** the striking paradox in fact reflects S.'s realistic assessment elsewhere of the likely level of interest in what he proposes: *Ep.* 80.2 *cogito mecum . . . quantus ad spectaculum non fidele* ('genuine') *et lusorium fiat concursus, quanta sit circa artes bonas solitudo.*

5.4 ut scias: directing reader-awareness, through a proposition then developed or substantiated (*uide . . . dederit*), to a demonstration of *contemplatio* (5.4–6) accessible only to the *summi uiri.* The device is favoured by S. (*Ir.* 1.1.3, 3.2, 2.4.1, *Marc.* 7.3, *Ben.* 4.18.1).   **spectari . . . aspici:** *Thy.* 416 *cum quod datur spectabis, et dantem aspice* where, however, *aspice* urges *careful* scrutiny (Tarrant (1985) 151) and not the mere 'glance' appropriate here.   **in media . . . constituit:** *nos* (suitably placed) rather than *locum,* so confirming the 'central' significance of the human race to nature's whole creative design (*Ben.* 6.23.4–7). The cosmological picture is Stoic and earlier (Cic. *N.D.* 2.98 with Pease on 1.103), but S.'s emphasis is anthropocentric rather then geocentric like theirs (*SVF* II 180.12–13, 28). The first of six perf. main verbs stresses what nature has *already* provided; all we need do is look and understand.   **sui:** so *partem sui* below, *Ben.* 6.23.6; the reflexive, like *sibi* and *sui* in 5.3, is not redundant but stresses nature's total self-sufficiency (*Ben.* 4.9.1).   **circumspectum omnium** 'a commanding view of the universe' (n. on *uultum* below).   **erexit . . . hominem:** *Ep.* 92.30 *corporum nostrorum habitus erigitur et spectat in caelum,* 94.56 with Bellincioni (1979) 202, *N.Q.* 5.15.3; the divine teleological significance of human stature is a familiar idea from Aristotle's biological works (H. Bonitz *Index Aristotelicus* (Graz 1955; 2nd edn) 58a 42–7) which in Cic. *N.D.* 2.140–1 is already fully elaborated to explain the sense-organs and other upper parts in the same terms (later examples of the topos in Pease *ad loc.*).   **habilem** 'adaptable (to)'; with dat. in this sense (*Ep.* 92.10), Livian and then mostly post-Augustan in prose (*OLD* 2).   **factura:** final; Summers lxvii, Westman (1961) 97–8.   **ut . . . posset:** the cosmic panorama liberates the viewer from the ties of domestic trivia and provides *hoc . . . argumentum diuinitatis suae,* *quod illum* [sc. *animum*] *diuina delectant; nec ut alienis sed ut suis interest* (*N.Q.* 1 *praef.* 12).   **sidera** 'constellations'.   **labentia:** poetical of heavenly bodies (*OLD labor*¹ 2); the hyperbaton directs the reader, like the viewer, to take the wider perspective.   **uultum** 'gaze', post-Augustan in prose (*OLD* 3a); *circumspectum omnium* above paralleled in *uultum...circum-...cum toto*.   **toto:** 4.2n. on *toti inditus*.   **sublime:** to view the heavens; Cic. *N.D.* 2.140.   **flexili:** poetical for *flexibilis*; in prose, first here and in Pliny (e.g. *N.H.* 11.177, 216).   **sena...sena...signa producens:** the zo-diac supplies an example of the unending self-display nature has provided for study. All twelve of its constellations cross the sky every twenty-four hours, with six above the horizon at any time but of course invisible by day (*N.Q.* 1.1.11): 'The arc [sc. of the ecliptic] that moves above the earth equals the arc that is sunk beneath the gulf of the ocean, and every night six twelfths of the circle always set and the same number rise' (Arat. *Phaen.* 553–6, trans. D. Kidd). The smooth regularity of this picture is reflected in S.'s use of alliteration, phrase-balance and poetical vocabulary (cf. Cic. *Arat.* 555–6 [336–7], Man. 3.242, *Aetna* 235b; *bis sena* of the zodiac, *Tro.* 386, *Oed.* 251), but is purely theoretical. Two centuries before S. Hipparchus of Rhodes had demonstrated (*Comm. in Arat.* 2.1.7–12 = pp. 126.4–128.11 Manitius) that the required division of the circle into mathematically equal segments conflicted with the widely differing dimensions of the actual con-stellations, so that observation could not be the basis for accurate time-keeping at night.   **signa** = *sidera* above; Var. *L.* 7.14.   **producens** 'causing (a constellation) to rise', *OLD* 3c (only verse, not before Manilius). **nullam non:** strongly affirmative (i.e. not only the zodiacal constella-tions); *Breu.* 6.4, *Ir.* 2.28.7, *Ep.* 45.12, 76.22 (further Traina (1987) 29–30 with *Breu.* 2.1 n. on *numquam non*).   **partem sui:** as defined at *N.Q.* 2.3.1–6.1 (not as 'element' at *N.Q.* 2.2.1, *Ep.* 117.23); Hine (1981) 164–71. **explicuit** 'has revealed to view', a nuance first in the elder Seneca (*TLL* v 2.1727.36–54).   **ut...ceterorum:** this at first appears to be follow-ing Cic. *Tusc.* 5.69 *horum* [the motions of the stars, planets etc.] *nimirum aspectus impulit illos ueteres* [esp. the early Ionian philosophers; cf. 1.45] *et admonuit ut plura quaererent. inde est indagatio nata initiorum*...S., however, in-serts into the natural composition of every individual (*hominem* above) an active orientation which for Cicero is the attribute of the *sapiens* (*Tusc.* 5.68). **cupiditatem** 'keen interest in' = *studium* (*TLL* IV 1416.72–81); Cic. *Tusc.* 1.44 *insatiabilis quaedam cupiditas ueri uidendi*.   **faceret** 'arouse'; *Ep.* 52.14, 100.12 (*OLD* 11 a).   **ceterorum:** introducing the list (5.5–6) of abstruse matters inaccessible to human sight because of remoteness in time or space; *plura* serves the same purpose in Cic. *Tusc.* 5.69 above.

5.5 From our reliance on sight (*uisimus*) we progress through a combination of visual and mental discernment (*acies*, *OLD* 2a, 5) to deduction and discovery possible only through disciplined reflection (*inueniat*, *TLL* VII 2.143.7–28). The change to first pers. plur. marks the inclusion of the universal human being (5.1n. on *unusquisque*) in the collective group now graduating to advanced study. There is also a significant change in the dominant verb-tense in 5.5 and 5.6: nature has completed her masterpiece and need only sustain it, but bringing the human race to perfection is an on-going process actively engaging our present concern.   **tanta ... quanta sunt** 'their real dimensions'; only the foolish think *se ... metiri mundi magnitudinem posse* (Cic. *Off.* 1.154) or are able *solem ... metiri* (*Luc.* 128), though Archimedes famously attempted to do the latter in his *Sand-reckoner*.   **aperit ... uiam:** in prose, Livian and later (*TLL* II 219.12–22).   **fundamenta ... iacit** 'lays a basis for the truth'; Ciceronian (*TLL* VII 1.38.78–39.20) but almost always with the gen. as at *Helu.* 17.4, the dat. apparently only here and at Cic. *Flac.* 4. **inquisitio** 'investigation', 'research'; as such, post-Augustan (*TLL* VII 1.1820.48–64).   **ex apertis in obscura:** carrying forward the sense of *aperit* to present the process as one of continuity and not as the antithetical contrast suggested in Greek scientific and rhetorical parallels quoted by Dionigi 238 and Pease on Cic. *N.D.* 3.38, S.'s possible point of reference here.   **aliquid ... antiquius:** as with the goal of our search, the end of the clause (*antiquius*) grows entirely out of what precedes it (*aliquid ipso mundo inueniat*), again stressing the continuity of the educative process. This ultimate topic is not so much another universe before our own (for which e.g. *Marc.* 26.6) but the primeval state of things which gave rise to present phenomena, or *initia uniuersorum* (*Ep.* 65.19, where a similar set of questions follows).   **unde ... haesisse:** from the ultimate goal (*antiquius*) issues a stream of indirect questions, which separate off from one another and grow in length and complexity like nature's own multiple cosmic creations out of primeval matter (n.b. *exierint, in partes discederent, mersa et confusa diduxerit*).   **unde ... exierint:** i.e. the constellations we have been looking at (5.4 *sidera ... labentia*). Stoics, influenced by Heraclitus (L–S I 277–8), think of 'designing fire' (n. below on *altior aliqua uis*) as actively participating in transforming matter first into air and then water, evaporation subsequently causing the rarefied fire of which the heavenly bodies consist

(L–S 1 46A–D with Long (1986) 154–8).   **quis . . . discederent:** in the period after a universal conflagration and before divine fire has again begun to act in matter (L–S 1 44B–C, 270–1, 278–9).   **status** 'physical condition', a Lucretian nuance (*D.R.N.* 5.829) in post-Augustan prose (*OLD* 5).   **singula . . . discederent** 'the distinct elements began to separate to form its parts'; cf. *N.Q.* 3.30.1. For the subjunctive, 3.4n. on *experiatur.*   **quae . . . diduxerit:** more expansively presented at *Ep.* 65.19 *quis omnia in uno mersa et materia inerti conuoluta discreuerit? . . . quis . . . confusa distinxerit . . . ?* The more usual picture is less turbulent: *materia iacet iners, res ad omnia parata, cessatura si nemo moueat; causa autem, id est ratio, materiam format et quocumque uult uersat, ex illa uaria opera producit* (*Ep.* 65.2 = *SVF* II 111.25–8). Imagined independently from infusion by the fire-principle, matter is not in motion of any sort (*SVF* II 112.40 ἀκίνητος . . . ἐξ αὐτῆς καὶ ἀσχημάτιστος). **mersa et confusa** 'plunged into darkness and obscurity'; this powerful Virgilian sense of *mergo* (*Aen.* 6.267, 429, 11.28) returns in Senecan tragedy as well as in post-Augustan prose (*OLD* 7a). For examples in S. of neut. pples. used (very appropriately here) without defining substantives (already 5.2 *praeclusa*), Summers lxi (c).   **loca . . . assignauerit:** cf. of the constellations Germ. *Arat.* 435–6 *semel assignata tuentur | immoti loca nec longo mutantur in aeuo.*   **suapte . . . leuia** 'by their *own* nature . . .', the balance (cf. *Breu.* 19.1 *grauissima . . . leuia*) reflected in the chiastic arrangement of *grauia . . . leuia*, with homoeoteleuton in both sets of antonyms. S. is chiefly alluding to Epicurean atomic bodies, as *prima mouentur . . . per se primordia rerum* (Lucr. *D.R.N.* 2.133; cf. 84 *grauitate sua*, 218 *ponderibus propriis*), though in fact the picture is not as harmonious as his sentence-structure implies. Since all bodies fall at equal speed through a void whatever their weight (*D.R.N.* 2.235–9), it is the random 'swerve' (*declinatio*, L–S 1 52) which then enables the denser and lighter formations thus compacted to assume their 'natural' positions (cf. 2.240–50). The very spontaneity of these (re-)formations ensures that the process is eternally continuous and not part of some teleological cosmogony.   **suapte natura:** regular abl. phrase in S. (*Marc.* 11.3, *Ben.* 4.17.2, *N.Q.* 3.27.8), with *suapte* disyllabic at *Ag.* 250 (Tarrant (1976) 219). The emphatic suffix is most commonly found in prose of all periods with the abl. sing. of the possessive adj. (N–W II 373–4), occasionally with other cases (374–5) or pronouns (366).   **euolauerint** 'flew up'; Lucr. *D.R.N.* 6.314 *euolat ignis* (*OLD* 2b).   **praeter . . . corporum** 'quite apart from the pressure [pushing them up] and their own weight [pulling them down]'. The Epicurean context strongly suggests such a contrast, as self-driven motion is always downwards (*D.R.N.* 2.190 *pondera, quantum in se est, ... deorsum cuncta ferantur*; 6.335–6); upward motion (flames, spouting water, floating objects etc.) is caused by other atomic bodies pushing from below or behind (2.193, 204 *expressae*).   **altior aliqua uis:** for the Stoics an active principle (= god, *ratio*, λόγος) identified by Zeno with 'designing fire', by Chrysippus with pneuma, and acting on a passive principle, matter (*Breu.* 19.1 n. on *materia ... dei*); but the allusion is general enough to embrace e.g. the Heraclitean fire-principle (L–S 1 277–8), the Platonic demiurge, or the *deus et melior ... natura* of the poetical cosmogonies (Ov. *M.* 1.21 with Bömer for the major parallels). **altior:** of a divine being, usually poetical (*TLL* 1 1777.39–49); of *uirtus*, *V.B.* 7.3.   **legem ... dixerit** 'laid down the law'; 3.1 n. for a different nuance.   **illud ... quo ... probatur** 'that argument which strives especially to prove ... '; G–L §227 n. 2.   **homines ... haesisse:** Stoics believe the rational human soul to be a portion of the universal fiery divine breath, *ex isdem quibus diuina constant seminibus compositum* (*Helu.* 6.8; cf. 6.7, *Ep.* 41.5, 66.12, 120.14 with *Breu.* 19.1 n. on *quis ... componat*). For the specifically astral dimension, Cic. *Rep.* 6.15.3 *iis* [sc. *hominibus*] *... animus datus est ex illis sempiternis ignibus quae sidera et stellas uocatis*; it extends back through Plato (*Tim.* 41 d–42b) to the Presocratics and beyond (Zetzel (1995) 233). Heraclitus is said (D–K 22 A 15 = Macr. *S. Scip.* 1.14.19) to have called the soul *scintillam stellaris essentiae* (K–R–S 205), though S.'s *ueluti ... quasdam* suggests the metaphor in Latin was by no means hackneyed.   **partem ... haesisse** 'namely that some part ... ', explaining *illud* above.   **desiluisse:** with an inanimate subj., first here in prose (*TLL* v 1.722.37–45).   **alieno ... haesisse** 'were held in a place not their own', i.e. bodily confinement; a familiar Platonic image (e.g. *Phd.* 62b, 67c–d) which offers philosophy as the only route to liberation (*Marc.* 23.2, 24.5, *Helu.* 11.7, *Ep.* 65.16, 21, 79.12). Although *OLD haereo* suggests otherwise, *loco* is most likely to be abl. (*Breu.* 13.8 n. on *illo loco*; Cic. *Rep.* 6.18.3).

5.6 In a climax which parallels that of the philosopher's soul achieving liberation (*Ep.* 73.15 *itur ad astra*; 41.5), we leave the ambiguity of *acies* (5.5 intro.) and questions relating to visible cosmic phenomena for the exclusivity of *cogitatio*, whose object lies *ultra mundum*. The collective grouping indicated by *nostra* accordingly embraces here the *summi uiri* for the final stage of the ascent, but these are not advocates of any particular school (as is the interlocutor in 1.4) promoting their own agenda. No effort is made to disguise the sources of the hypotheses, and equally no attempt is made to label them with sectarian affiliations. The sets of disjunctive questions are not a contest between competing schools – answers would in any case be dependent on pre-determined frameworks in physics and ethics – but a model of what engages every (i.e. *nostra*) discriminating mind at its highest operational level, matters of personal indifference reflected upon without reference to partisan loyalty and authority.   **cogitatio … perrumpit:** dynamic thought takes us even beyond the wide confines of *Helu.* 11.7 *cogitatio eius* [sc. *animi*] *circa omne caelum it…*, perhaps after Lucr. *D.R.N.* 1.72–4. The mind's freedom to travel beyond the cosmos was a protreptic common-place (Russell (1964) 166 on [Longin.] *Subl.* 35.2–36), perhaps traceable to Aristotle's *Protrepticus* (Bignone (1973) II 460–1).   **perrumpit:** as if an irrepressible force; *Helu.* 20.2 *peragratis humilioribus ad summa perrumpit* [sc. *animus*] *et pulcherrimo diuinorum spectaculo fruitur.*   **contenta:** with inf., only poetic until post-Classical prose; some twenty occurrences in S. (Bourgery (1922) 358; *TLL* IV 680.15–56, adding e.g. *Ep.* 85.1, 95.10, 119.14). **ostenditur** 'appears to the eye'; middle, as e.g. *Ep.* 79.2 *longius nauigantibus solebat ostendi* [sc. *Aetna*] (*TLL* IX 2.1124.3–9).   **inquit:** prosopopoeia here makes the extreme remoteness of such *cogitatio* seem more accessible, even companionable, as at *Ep.* 95.10 where *philosophia 'totum' inquit 'mundum scrutor nec me intra contubernium mortale contineo'*. But elsewhere the dramatic effect of the device is different: *natura* (*Marc.* 17.6–7) and *fortuna* (*Prou.* 3.3) try to reconcile us to their being no respecters of persons; *iracundia* exposes the cruelty of her malice (*Ir.* 1.18.6), *ratio* steers us towards right action (*Ep.* 84.11). Commonly associated with the diatribe (Weber (1895) 20–2), the device was transmitted through Bion of Borysthenes, who had already given a self-justifying conversational voice to abstractions (Kindstrand (1976) 117 fr. 17.1 πράγματα, 17.5 πενία with 212–13 *ad loc.*).   **mundum:** the visible cosmos (4.2n. on *toti inditus*).   **utrumne … cludatur:** Sorabji (1988) 125–41: 'Is there infinite or extracosmic space?' Lucr. *D.R.N.* 1.954–7 *quod inane* ('void') *repertumst | … peruideamus utrum finitum funditus omne | constet an immensum pateat uasteque profundum* helps to establish S.'s agenda and phrasing. For Epicurus and earlier atomists an infinite number of atoms had presupposed an infinite void (Rist (1972) 43, 56–7), while Stoics held that there had to be extracosmic void into which the cosmos could expand through transformation into fire during conflagration (L–S I 296–7). Since this requires only a limited void, *an et hoc ipsum* [sc. *quod ultra mundum iacet*] *terminis suis cludatur* may allude to Stoic debate on whether the void is infinite or (a view ascribed to Posidonius but with complications; Sandbach (1985) 77 n. 96 with Kidd II 391–4) sufficient only to accommodate the expanded cosmos in conflagration. **utrumne ... an:** 4.2n. **profunda uastitas** 'boundless immensity'. In this sense the adj., favoured by Lucretius (e.g. *D.R.N.* 1.957, 1108, 2.96, 222), is apparently first in prose in S. (*OLD* 4; cf. *profundum* 4), as is *uastitas* (*OLD* 2a, adding *Ep.* 99.10 *temporis profundi uastitatem*). **cludatur:** the spelling of *claudo* (*OLD* 10c) in compounds appears independently in the first century AD (Lindsay (1894) 40). **exclusis:** sc. *his quae extra mundum sunt*, the substantive (5.5n. on *mersa et confusa*) as unprecedented as apparently the possessive dat. with *habitus*. **informia ... discripta sint:** the succession of three neut. plur. pples. and one adj. with no definite point of reference until we meet (the not very helpful) *illa* conveys the undifferentiated and unrecognizable nature of (any) matter beyond the visible cosmos. The imprecision also offers an area of reference wide enough to suggest both Stoic primordial matter at one moment and Epicurean atoms at another. **informia et confusa:** resembling primordial chaos out of which our cosmos was formed *cum in hunc habitum ex informi unitate discederet* [sc. *mundus*] (*N.Q.* 3.30.1); for *confusa*, 5.5n. **in ... obtinentia** 'taking up the same space in all directions', i.e. in the undifferentiated state of primordial matter *antequam singula in partes discederent* (5.5). **et illa** 'they too'. **cultum** = κόσμον (*OLD* 5c), opening the possibility of endless other worlds on the Epicurean model (L–S I 13A, D1) with no teleological dimension. **discripta** 'divided up', 'arranged' (5.5 *diduxerit*). **cohaereant** [sc. *illa*] 'are physically attached to', *Marc.* 17.2, *N.Q.* 6.25.2. *Pace* Viansino II 622 and Dionigi 244–5, not an allusion to Stoic συνέχεια or 'sustaining' action (L–S I 288), which constitutes coherence *within* the cosmos but cannot apply outside it, where there is in any case only void (n. above on *utrumne ... cludatur*). **mundo:** 4.2n. on *toti inditus*. **longe ... secesserint:** given *indiuidua* of atoms immediately below, a likely allusion to atomist/Epicurean cosmogonies, which 'separate off' atoms from the infinite (ἀπὸ τοῦ ἀπείρου) to form each world-system (D.L. 9.30 with Guthrie II 406–7; Epic. *Ep. Hdt.* 73–4 = L–S I 13C). **et ... uolutetur:** a contingent necessity after *longe ... secesserint*; this (*hic*) world would then be unattached to anything (*OLD uacuus* 6a) and appear to rotate at the outer perimeter (Epic. *Ep. Pyth.* 88 = L–S I 13B, Lucr. *D.R.N.* 5.510–33), though *uolutetur* (Waltz for MSS -*entur*) is better taken to suggest the cosmic 'whirl' or δίνη of the early atomists (*OLD* 2; Bailey (1928) 138–48). **indiuidua ... mutabilis:** do atoms form worlds and dissolve them, or is voidless Stoic matter subject to change in phases of the cosmic cycle (n. on *mutabilis*)? The first *per* = 'by means of' (*OLD* 14a) and is not instrumental (15a) as atoms *in themselves* could never cause worlds to form (Lucr. *D.R.N.* 2.216–50 = L–S 1 11H); the second = 'throughout' (*OLD* 4a).   **indiuidua:** of atoms, *OLD* 1 b.   **natum futurumque:** the two tenses convey the sequence of formation, dissolution and reconfiguration, with the certainty of the last confirmed by the peri-phrastic fut. (Westman (1961) 51).   **continua . . . materia:** 4.2nn. on *continua . . . et plena* and *materia . . . gignuntur*.   **eorum:** sc. *per quae struitur omne quod . . .*   **totum:** 4.2n. on *toti inditus*.   **mutabilis:** in Stoic cos-mogony matter is formed by god into the elements, with fire changing into air, water and earth in fixed order, and these changing back into fire in reverse (*N.Q.* 3.10.1–5, L–S 1 47A2–3 and 286–9). Atoms, by contrast, are immutable (ἀμετάβλητα Epic. *Ep. Hdt.* 41).   **contraria . . . pugnent:** Epicurean elements are perpetually hostile to each other (Lucr. *D.R.N.* 5.380–95, with the same metaphors), recalling the imagery already familiar from Anaximander (Guthrie 1 78–81) and restructured in the more complex Love/Strife principles of Empedocles (II 152–9). S.'s phrasing here attracted Tacitus at *Ann.* 13.57.1.   **per . . . conspirent:** Stoic *discordia concors* (Man. 1.142); *N.Q.* 7.27.4. An obvious influence here is Heraclitus' 'harmony of opposites' (Guthrie 1 435–49) mediated through the Aristotelian theory of elements (Long (1986) 156).   **per diuersa** 'in different ways'; *Ir.* 1.16.4, *N.Q.* 5.18.1.

5.7 Against the background of this immense intellectual challenge, the climax surprisingly introduces a tragic paradox: there is infinitely more to be known than the highest level of dedication in the longest life-span can enable anyone to know. As the point of universal relevance, the first pers. plur. forms, which have gradually become more exclusive in 5.5 and 5.6, are now replaced with a return to the third pers. sing. (5.1 n. on *unusquisque*), presently to be identified simply as *homo*.   **haec:** i.e. the whole range of issues in 5.1–6.   **natus:** emphasizing *natura* as the source of our com-mon vocation (5.1 *secundum naturam*, 5.8); the pple agrees with the subj. of *acceperit* rather than *aestima*.   **quam . . . temporis:** not litotes for *quam paulum*, as Cic. *Brut.* 270 shows by making the contrast: . . . *ut intel-legatis primum ex omni numero quam non multi ausi sint dicere, deinde ex eis ipsis quam pauci fuerint laude digni.* S. is careful to begin the conclusion gently, so as to avoid inducing despair by suggesting that the task and available time are hopelessly mismatched. The calculation (*aestima*) that 'we have

no time to waste' fits well with the emphasis in *Breu.* 1.3 against the traditional protreptic theme of the excessive shortness of human life *per se*
(*Breu.* 1.2n. on '*aetatis...stare*'), and is reinforced in *N.Q.* from the perspective of a *senex* (3 *praef.* 1–4) and of our fluctuating *inter studia ac uitia*
(7.25.4).   **sibi uindicat:** *Breu.* 2.4n.; the retained indicative stresses
plain fact ('even if he *does...*').   **cui...concutiat:** structured to represent the minute attention to detail and orderly arrangement which characterize the life of total self-control, before it is ultimately frustrated in the
final paradox. The first of the two concessive constructions balances paired
anaphoric patterns of *nihil*, instrumental abl., inf., with delayed *patiatur*
locking the formation; the second extends to three ever longer units, each
rounded off with a verb of respectively two, three and four syllables.   **cui**
[sc. *tempori*]: dat. of disadvantage with both *eripi* (*Prou.* 3.7, *Ir.* 1.17.7, *Ep.*
77.17) and *excidere* (*Ir.* 3.24.4, *Ep.* 81.23, *N.Q.* 6.29.2; *Breu.* 4.1n. on *excidere*
uoces). Reynolds has *qui*, adducing Abel's parallel with *Ep.* 98.3, but the
lectio difficilior in all MSS is an unlikely corruption of a straightforward
nom. which greatly weakens the ultimate impact of *homo* in the main
clause.   **facilitate...excidere:** 'obligingness' (*OLD facilitas* 6) in the
face of demands on one's time (*Breu.* 7.6–8) has a less reprehensible connotation than *neglegentia* 'carelessness'; they are (*Ep.* 120.8–9) *specie quidem*
uicina, re autem plurimum inter se dissidentia. A similar distinction contrasts
the two infs.: *Ep.* 1.1 *tempus quod adhuc...excidebat* ('was let slip') *collige et*
serua...quaedam tempora eripiuntur nobis...turpissima tamen est iactura quae per
neglegentiam fit.   **auarissime:** not pejorative; scrupulous use of time is
the unique instance of *honesta auaritia* (*Breu.* 3.1).   **seruet:** of time, *Breu.*
8.3, *Ep.* 1.1.   **ultimum** 'the furthest'; not tautological but Livian and
later for *extremum* (Krebs–Schmalz II 689–90).   **aetatis...terminum**
'limit of the [general] human life-span', in contrast with *horas suas; termi-*
nus of life at *Breu.* 1.2, 15.5, *Marc.* 21.5, *Ep.* 101.7.   **nec...concutiat:**
with five letters in common, *natura* and *fortuna* make a familiar contrast
(*TLL* VI 1.1195.41–50, adding e.g. *Ep.* 16.8, 44.1, 98.14) enhanced by
the isosyllabic wordplay (*natura constituit fortuna concutiat*).   **illi:** as *cui*
above.   **tamen...est:** two factors contribute to the tragic force of
the paradox. All human intellectual endeavour is thwarted in attempting to realize the very purpose of its existence (*ad haec quaerenda natus...*),
with the barely adequate span of a well-spent life (*non multum...temporis*)
now inevitably doomed to premature curtailment (*nimis mortalis*). Also,
the protreptic enterprise by which S. has led each individual reader to

share in the collective vision of the *summi uiri* seems to be undermined by
a universal human incapacity (*homo . . . mortalis est*). This darker perspective
is reminiscent of the fatalism of the tragedies (*Her. F.* 448 *mortale caelo non
potest iungi genus*; 5.8 intro.). In Horatian terms, the emphasis here lies more
with *immortalia ne speres* (*C.* 4.7.7) than with *non omnis moriar* (*C.* 3.30.6).
ad 'in relation to' (*OLD* 37).   **immortalium:** here primarily the
celestial phenomena (*TLL* VII 1.493.78–80); for the wordplay, *Breu.* 3.4, 15.4,
Pol. 1.1.

    5.8 Equally, however, the chapter has established its initial assertion that
intellectual activity is an unavoidable component of human life. The conclusion draws on the tradition that *contemplatio* (θεωρία) offers *ad aeternitatem iter
et . . . illum locum ex quo nemo deicitur* (*Breu.* 15.4 and n. on *haec . . . uertendae*), without attempting to resolve the dilemma in which the noblest aspirations are
finally confronted by a fatalistic awareness of our limitations. This dilemma
is central to the tragic experience, and is given dramatic force in e.g. the am-
bivalence of the long denouement of *Her. O.*, where Alcmena's great *planctus*
for the ultimate futility of her son's superhuman striving (1863–1939, esp.
1903–14) is imperfectly answered by Hercules' secure reassurance (1942–3
iam uirtus mihi | in astra et ipsos fecit ad superos iter, 1965–71). So here in *Ot.*,
the confidence of the conclusion (*ergo*) and the totality of self-commitment
(*totum . . . dedi*) are qualified by a realistic awareness that both will be dis-
appointed.   **ergo:** 5.1 *nunc id probemus . . .*   **secundum . . . uiuo:**
5.1 n. on *summum . . . uiuere*, where S. began from a premiss his interlocutor
could share (*Solemus dicere . . .*); here the change to the first pers. sing. shows
the consensus is not assumed to have lasted to the end, and prepares for
the interlocutor's reply in 6.1.   **si totum . . . sum** defines the formula
in terms now familiar from the argument of the chapter: *si . . . dedi* sum-
marizes the two concessive clauses in 5.7; *admirator* and *cultor* distinguish
the two levels of response in 5.3–6, the first primarily cosmological (5.3–4;
admirator only post-Augustan in prose), the second devoted to intellectual abstraction (5.5–6; *TLL* IV 1317.81–1318.25).   **natura . . . facio:** the conclusion is reinforced by three devices: (i) ring-composition (*natura . . . uacare*;
5.1 *natura . . . actioni*) recapitulates the opening premiss with an important
modification in expression. The additional emphasis to emerge from the
argument of the chapter, that *actio* and *contemplatio* cannot be isolated as different life-choices but are fully realized in the same rigorous intellectual activity, is highlighted (ii) by enclosing the pair centrally between the emphatic
repetition of *utrumque facere . . . utrumque facio* and (iii) by using the same verb

to be compatible with *agere* and *contemplationi uacare*.   **quoniam ... est:**
demonstrating the appropriateness of *facio* with a triumphant flourish, as
actione is indeed present in con<u>templatio</u>. S.'s contribution to the old debate on
how to reconcile the two is not merely this final witticism. The whole chapter has deployed ingenuity of expression to stimulate 'active' engagement
with abstruse questions which alter the reader's perspective and sense of
values, and will be the basis of further discussion in 7.1–2. In the *Epistles*
the approach is more defensive (8.6, 68.2 and esp. 95.10–12, recalling the
discursive treatment and rather different emphasis in Cic. *Fin.* 5.48–58),
but for a closer parallel to what S. is asserting here see the attempt by Rorty
(1980) to explain and harmonize the practical and contemplative lives in
Aristotle: 'The objects of contemplation are the best and most perfect substances. By and in contemplation one becomes actively identical with the
formal character of those substances ... Such a contemplator not only lives
his life, he is that life as an eternal and unified self-contained whole. His
contemplation and his living become one, immutable and unchanging, because contemplating is the best human activity and because the mind is
actualized as and in what it thinks' (388, but more generally 378–88).

6 *Active* otium; *the cases of Zeno and Chrysippus*

There is a note of irony in the interlocutor's imagined response to what
precedes. S. has succeeded in making the reflective life appear *so* satisfying
that he may have overlooked the possibility of attracting people to it for
the wrong reason. With this focus on motivation the interlocutor shows
up a weakness in S.'s attempt (3.2–5) to establish that Epicurus and Zeno
say what is in effect the same thing from opposing viewpoints; the pleasure
motive could never be enough to justify Zeno's retirement (3.3) but would of
course attract Epicurus *nisi si quid interuenerit* (3.2). S. now answers with three
points (6.1 *aeque ... respicias*, 2–3 *quomodo ... perducere?*, 3–4 *quodsi ... erunt?*),
which lead into an alternative assessment of Zeno and the early Stoa based
on the conclusions of the preceding chapter.

6.1 illam: sc. *contemplationem*, as *ex illa*.   **uoluptatis causa:** i.e. *only*
for pleasure, since protreptic consistently presented philosophical initiation as attractive *as well as* morally beneficial; *Ep.* 50.9 *philosophia pariter et
salutaris et dulcis est*, Aristot. *Protr.* fr. 52 p. 63.5–6 Rose = Düring (1961)
72–3 B56 μεθ' ἡδονῆς ἡ προσεδρεία γίγνεται ('it is pleasant to sit down

to philosophy'). The interlocutor appeals to Chrysippus' disapproval of self-gratification as the *only* motive (*SVF* III 176.15–21 = L–S I 67x, itself with an obvious allusion to Epicurus) to focus on S.'s attempted reconciliation of Epicurus and Zeno in 3.2–3, in the knowledge that the motive cannot be endorsed by S. (*V.B.* 5.3–15.5, *Ep.* 92.6–10, *Ben.* 4.2.3–4, 7.2.2–4).   **accesseris:** 3.2.   **exitu:** both of result (*OLD* 5a) and time (3a; cf. *assiduam*).   **dulcis ... suas:** *dulcis* is tainted by the disreputable *illecebras* (only here in S.), a combination similarly ambivalent at Virg. *G.* 3.217. For the noun's association with Epicurean *uoluptas*, Cic. *Fin.* 3.1, *Tusc.* 4.6 with Zetzel (1995) 248 on the exceptional *suis te oportet illecebris ipsa uirtus trahat ad uerum decus* at *Rep.* 6.25.2.   **suas** 'special', 'distinctive'.   **aduersus:** prep., not adv.; with *respondere*, Livian (*TLL* I 857.46, 50–1) and frequent later.   **aeque ... respicias:** the first rejoinder exploits the interlocutor's implicit concession that a single motivation (*assiduam ... sine exitu*) is reprehensible by countering with the opposite case of *assidua inquies*. The antitheton (Lausberg §795) prepares for the reassertion of the position that a balanced combination is best.   **animo** 'frame of mind' (*OLD* 10a).   **ciuilem** 'political' (*OLD* 5, adding *Tr.* 2.9, 3.1, 6.2); the example is provocative to a disciple of Zeno (1.4), as the βίος πολιτικός was one of the principal life-choices commended in the early Stoa (*SVF* III 172.14–22 = L–S I 67w1–3; Griffin (1976) 340–6).   **inquietus** 'without (Stoic) peace of mind' (*Ep.* 3.5), here explicitly defined in *nec ... respicias*.   **tibi ... tempus:** *Breu.* 18.1 n. on *aliquid ... tibi*.   **quo ... respicias:** i.e. 'become wise' by acquiring 'scientific knowledge of the divine and the human' (L–S I 26a = *SVF* II 15.4–5; *Ep.* 31.8, 88.33, 89.5 with Dyck 367–8 on Cic. *Off.* 2.5); as an early Stoic definition, esp. relevant to the outlook of the interlocutor.   **quo:** final relative (G–L §630), expressing time within which (§393), as at *Ir.* 3.2.5, *Ep.* 49.5.   **respicias:** *Breu.* 19.2.

    6.2–3 quomodo ... perducere?: the second rejoinder (mis-)represents the interlocutor as taking *contemplatio* to be a kind of solipsistic indolence, and so makes it easy for S. to reply by again invoking the antitheton (*res ... operas*).

    6.2 quomodo ... sic ... ostendens: the antithesis is reinforced by chiasmus (1 *res ... operas*, 2 *minime probabile est*, 2 *imperfectum ... bonum est*, 1 *in otium ... ostendens*), with each of the paired extremes characterized by inner deprivation (*sine ullo ... ingeni / sine actu*) and their ideal combination (*misceri ... debent*) appropriately balancing them in the middle, the suggestive *inter se* at its centre. In addition, the first colon (*quomodo ... probabile est*) has its own triple chiastic structure: 1 *res* 2 *appetere* 3 *sine ullo ... ingeni* 3 *nudas* 2 *edere* 1 *operas*. As the whole sentence is designed to show similarities in antithetical opposites, closer analysis reveals further pairings: the possession of *uirtus* is contrasted with its absence (*sine ... amore*), of ethical wisdom (*id ... didicit*) with a crude indifference to its intellectual distinction (*sine cultu ingeni*; *OLD ingenium* 4a); quiet concealment (*numquam ... ostendens*) is set against an exhibitionism (*OLD edo²* 11) which has nothing to show for itself (*nudas*), eager acquisitiveness (*appetere*) against letting one's assets go to waste (*proiecta*; *OLD proicio* 6d).   **uirtutum amore:** 3.4n. on *virtutium*, *Breu.* 19.2n. on *amor.*   **sine ... ingeni:** [Plut.] *De liberis educandis* 10 (= *Mor.* 8a) 'the practical [life] with no place for philosophy lacks culture (ἄμουσος) and taste (πλημμελής)'.   **ingeni:** rare in S. (*Marc.* 24.2, *Pol.* 2.6, 18.2, *Ep.* 29.4), *-ii* far more frequent (e.g. *Breu.* 2.4, *Ep.* 7.9, 11.1 etc.) in keeping with the tendency for stems in *-io* to form the gen. sing. in *-ii* in the first century AD (G–L §33 R.1; N–W I 134–54).   **nudas:** stressed by position, defining *sine ullo ... ingeni.*   **edere operas:** military idiom ('do service'); *Prou.* 2.10 *ferrum istud ... bonas ... ac nobiles edet operas,* 5.1 *militare* (inf.) *et edere operas.*   **probabile** 'commendable' behaviour, capable of being endorsed by *probabilis ratio* ('a reasonable account', Cic. *Fin.* 3.58; *SVF* III 22.15, 26.18).   **(misceri ... debent):** *Tr.* 4.8 *longe ... optimum est miscere otium rebus, Ep.* 3.6 *inter se ista miscenda sunt: et quiescenti agendum et agenti quiescendum est.* The Stoic emphasis in [Plut.] *De liberis educandis* sees human perfection in those able to combine and mix their capacities for politics and philosophy (10 = *Mor.* 7f τὴν πολιτικὴν δύναμιν μεῖξαι καὶ κεράσαι τῆι φιλοσόφωι [sc. δυνάμει]); the examples (8b Pericles, Epaminondas etc.) support what is in essence a Stoic position (Dionigi 97–8) from which S.'s interlocutor can hardly dissent.   **sic ... ostendens:** already in Cic. (*Off.* 1.153) the solitary contemplative who ignores *societatem humani generis* might as well be dead (*... excedat e uita*); for *cognitio contemplatioque naturae manca quodam modo atque inchoata sit* [cf. S.'s *imperfectum ac languidum*], *si nulla actio rerum consequatur* – the third of three arguments in §153, all in fact with significant weaknesses (Dyck 340–2). For S. virtue is defective if *sine actu* because (i) the practice of virtue consolidates the possession of it (*Ep.* 94.47 with Bellincioni (1979) 186–7); (ii) the *sapiens* guides others by example (*Ep.* 52.8, 120.11); and (iii) virtue manifests itself through its 'active' employment (Cic. *Rep.* 1.2.1 *nec uero habere uirtutem satis est ... nisi utare; ... uirtus in usu sui tota posita est* with Zetzel (1995) 98–9).   **languidum** 'feeble', 'idle'

(*OLD* 4, 5b).   **in ... proiecta** 'given up to' (pejorative), even 'wasted (on)' (Cooper–Procopé 177).   **ostendens:** in order to teach (*TLL* IX 2.1125.37–48); cf. the dynamic example set at *Ep.* 64.4 where, inspired by Q. Sextius' writings, *illius animum induo qui quaerit ... ubi uirtutem suam ostendat.*

6.3 quis negat ... ?: the second point in S.'s reply concludes with a decisive *interrogatio* (*Marc.* 7.1, 17.1, *Ep.* 94.43, 116.3; *quis negat?* alone at *Ep.* 14.15, 73.5, 98.1, *Ben.* 4.34.1), a figure 'intended to humiliate the opposing party' (Lausberg §767).   **profectus** 'stages of advancement'; post-Augustan equivalent of προκοπή 'progress', one of the Stoic προηγ-μένα 'preferred indifferents' (not in themselves good but useful for attaining a desirable goal; *SVF* III 31.2–3, 32.40–2, Cic. *Fin.* 3.51 with Inwood (1985) 197–9). S. has both the noun and *proficere* (= προκόπτειν) in this sense (e.g. *C.S.* 17.3, *Ep.* 5.1, 11.1).   **in opere temptare** 'try out in action' (*Ep.* 75.7).   **quid faciendum sit:** 1.3n. on *laudandum petendumque*; *Ep.* 94.12 *qui habet exactum iudicium de fugiendis petendisque scit quid sibi faciendum sit* (= τὸ ποιητέον, *SVF* III 61.13, 17).   **cogitare** 'deliberate'.   **aliquando** neatly supports the balanced compromise being commended to the interlocutor.   **manum exercere** 'act decisively'; poetic before S. (*Ir.* 3.18.2, *Thy.* 166, *Cl.* 1.7.4, *N.Q.* 7.14.1). In fact the option S. advocates elsewhere: *Ep.* 52.8 *eligamus ... eos qui uita docent, qui cum dixerunt quid faciendum sit probant faciendo*, 94.48.   **ea ... est** = 6.2 *id quod didicit*; the MSS have *sunt*, which Gertz corrected to make *uirtus* subj. here as already of *debere ... exercere.* The pass. past pple occurs in all periods (*OLD meditor* 1–3, 5 with K–S I 111), but very exceptionally in S. (*Prou.* 2.10 *diu meditatum opus*).   **ad uerum perducere** 'bring to the fullness of reality' (opp. *mendacio pasci*, *N.Q.* 1.16.9). After a tentative start (*temptare*) and the occasional gesture (*aliquando ... exercere*), S. ends this point on a climactic note; cf. *Ep.* 98.17 *hoc* [sc. observing how bravely the *homo prudens* confronts terminal illness] *est ... philosophiam in opere discere et ad uerum exerceri.*

6.3–4 quodsi ... erunt?: the third response can now define a secure detachment for the *sapiens*, after the accusation of cosy self-indulgence (6.1) has been refuted. Drawing on grounds for exemption already explored (3.3) and the distinction between the two *res publicae* (4.1–2), S. will show (2.1 *probabo*, 3.1 *ostendam*) how his view of *otium* can be compatible with the teaching, practice and example of the early Stoa. His argument again employs the mind-enlargement technique which extends thought from the particular to the general, the local to the universal, the temporary to the permanent (3 intro.; general intro. pp. 27–8).

6.3 quodsi...desunt: S. draws only on the first of the grounds for withdrawal in 3.3, society's denial to the *sapiens* of any opportunity for intervention. Any allusion to personal doubt or incapacity in the *sapiens* himself would be out of place now that he has been led through the rigorous educative training of *Ot*. 4–5 and is (supposedly) at the height of his powers.   **quodsi:** adversative emphasis.   **per...mora:** *Breu.* 17.6; colloquial (e.g. Ter. *An.* 593; Tarrant (1985) 233 on *Thy.* 1022).   **non...desunt:** strong *correctio* with double wordplay on *desum* (*Helu.* 12.7, *Ep.* 9.4, 70.24) and *agere* with cognates (cf. 6.5 *egisse...agerent*, *Ep.* 3.6, 16.3, 85.38; Summers lxxxv–lxxxvii).   **agenda** = *officia*, 'functions to fulfil' (*TLL* 1 1379.56–61).   **ecquid...?** 'surely...?' = *nonne* (Summers 189 on *Ep.* 21.10); with a hint of impatience (*Prou.* 6.9, *Helu.* 3.2, *Ep.* 89.22; *OLD* 1 b), as the interlocutor in turn is required to make a concession.   **secum esse:** of retreat into the self, *Ep.* 9.16 *in se reconditur, secum est* [sc. *sapiens*], 58.32 with Traina (1987) 60 and, more generally, Powell (1988) 201–2 on Cic. *Sen.* 49; attainable only by the trained philosopher, as mere physical isolation can be an opportunity for vice (*Tr.* 3.6–8, *Ep.* 25.5–7).

6.4 quo animo...secedit?: counterbalancing 6.1...*quo animo ciuilem agas uitam*.   **ad otium...secedit:** 1.1 n. on *secedere*; *ad* indicates purpose and not merely direction like the non-philosophical *in otium secedam* at *Breu.* 3.5.   **ut sciat** 'in the knowledge that'; *ut* in epexegetic relation to *quo animo* above (cf. 4.2).   **acturum:** emphatic.   **posteris:** as an anagram of *se...prosit*, the future shows itself to be formed out of the contribution (*prosit*) of preceding thinkers (*se*). Cicero (*Off.* 1.155–6) had already cited philosophers like Plato whose instruction actively contributed to the politics of their age and whose writings helped to form political awareness in later generations. S.'s vision is more expansive and universal: the early Stoa spoke not to a political class or society, then or later, but *toti humano generi* and *omnes omnium gentium homines*, and this emphatically different perspective enables S. to claim that Zeno and Chrysippus *maiora egisse quam si...leges tulissent* (nn. below). The difference has implications for S.'s view of his own programme: *Ep.* 8.2 *secessi non tantum ab hominibus sed a rebus...: posterorum negotium ago. illis aliqua quae possint prodesse conscribo*.   **nos...dicimus:** an ironic retort to the interlocutor's *nos sumus qui...* in 1.4; on *this* point at any rate he and S. are at one.   **maiora...tulissent:** a bolder claim than Cicero's (*Off.* 1.155), whose examples – Plato's instruction of Dio, Lysis the Pythagorean's of Epaminondas – are essentially of formative and supplementary contributions adding distinction to larger political/military achievements, so that those instructed *meliores ciues utilioresque rebus suis publicis essent*. S.'s larger assertion (*Ep*. 8.6 *mihi crede, qui nihil agere uidentur maiora agunt: humana diuinaque simul tractant*) strengthens the case for the intellectual life *per se*.   **si . . . tulissent:** homoeoteleuton in -*issent* and -*es* with heavy sibilant stress lends appropriate *grauitas* to such feats; but for the notorious fact, Plut. *Mor*. 1033b-c (= *SVF* I 11.8–11) 'and yet [despite their writings] in the career of none of them [sc. Zeno, Cleanthes and Chrysippus] can there be found any military command or legislation or attendance in council or advocacy at the bar or military service in defence of country or diplomatic mission or public benefaction . . . ' (trans. H. Cherniss).   **quas:** here international and not civic laws; for the relative modifying the sense of its antecedent, 3.1 n. on *quam*.   **toti . . . generi:** part of the first of the two *res publicae* distinguished in 4.1; for the idea, *Ep*. 14.14 *ad hos te Stoicos uoco qui a re publica exclusi secesserunt ad colendam uitam* ('improving human existence') *et humano generi iura condenda sine ulla potentioris offensa* ('without offending the local powers that be').   **quid . . . quare** 'So, then, why ever should . . . ?'; a colloquial idiom (1.5 n. on *quid ergo est?*) favoured by S. (*V.B*. 25.1, *Ep*. 17.4, 71.15, 106.1, *Ben*. 6.16.4; Bourgery (1922) 336).   **uiro bono:** here amalgamating the political and civic *uir bonus* (*TLL* II 2082.30–2083.19) with the moral and philosophical one (2084.8–50).   **futura . . . homines:** the two verbs transfer to the *maior ciuitas* the language of government in the *minor*.   **ordinet** 'manage', 'direct' (*OLD* 3b).   **contionetur:** Cicero's contemplative *sapiens* also needs to perfect his rhetorical skill because *cogitatio in se ipsa uertitur, eloquentia complectitur eos quibuscum communitate iuncti sumus* (*Off*. 1.156 with Dyck 347). The rhetorical voice of *contionetur* is expressed in the balanced phrasing (*apud . . . apud*; *quique . . . quique*), contrast (*nec . . . sed* in *correctio, paucos . . . omnes, sunt . . . erunt*) and wordplay (*omnes omnium*).   **omnes omnium:** a consistently recurring example of polyptoton, in early comedy, Classical prose and verse (*TLL* IX 2.620.3–19) and S. (*Marc*. 25.2, *Tr*. 17.2, *Pol*. 11.4, *Ben*. 4.27.3, *N.Q*. 3.10.1, 4); Summers lxxxv–lxxxvi.   **-que . . . -que:** rare in prose; in relative clauses, *OLD* -*que*¹ 3b (incl. *Cl*. 1.16.5), K–S II 35.

     6.5 After these three points in reply, S. challenges his interlocutor's standard Panaetian (6.5 n. on '*non . . . solet*') interpretation of the early Stoics' exclusion from active politics, applying the position he has established by argument: their *activity* is their formative influence on successive generations far beyond their local communities, which a loyal disciple like the interlocutor (1.4) can hardly contest. **ad summam** 'to sum up'. Colloquial (*Ep.* 31.2, 119.9, *Apol.* 11.3, *Ben.* 6.19.1; Weber (1895) 36), as regular Petronian use (*OLD summa* 7c) confirms. **quaero ... sudor:** a sequence of quick exchanges is conclusive: (i) S.'s straight question (*quaero ... Zenon*); (ii) the interlocutor's assumed response, attempting to avoid the trap set for him (*non ... uiuendum*); (iii) S. forces the issue (*atqui ... administrauit*); (iv) fuller defence by interlocutor (*'non ... solet'*); (v) conclusive rebuttal by S. (*sed ... sudor*). **quaero:** technically *quaesitum* (πύσμα) rather than *interrogatio* (ἐρώτημα), as the supplied response shows (Lausberg §770). **ex** 'in accordance with'; *Ep.* 6.6 *obseruauit illum* [sc. *Zenonem Cleanthes*], *an ex formula sua uiueret* (*OLD* 20a). **Cleanthes:** 331–232 BC; Zeno's successor as head of the Stoa, Chrysippus (*c.* 280–207) succeeding him; Zeno (335–263) last here as the founder of the school. **non dubie:** litotes (*C.S.* 10.3, *Ep.* 9.11, 36.4, 51.10). **dixerant:** the retained indicative stresses the plain fact of the matter. **atqui:** introducing a rejoinder to a fictional interlocutor, with a change of speaker implied (*Ep.* 17.5; *OLD* 1 a, b). **nemo ... administrauit:** the point bluntly exploits an evident discomfiture. **'non ... solet':** as resident metics (cf. Plut. *Mor.* 1034a = *SVF* I 11.1–3), Zeno and Cleanthes were never eligible to hold political or legal office in Athens, which Aristotle had defined (*Pol.* 1275a 22–3) as the main distinguishing privilege of citizenship. It is implied by Antipater of Tarsus (*SVF* III 257.23–6) that Chrysippus did become a naturalized Athenian, but this will have conferred full civic privileges only on his children ([Dem.] 59.92; Rhodes (1981) 510–11). All three are therefore 'exempt' from office on grounds coinciding with Panaetius' third *persona* (options limited by circumstances and chance; 3.3n. on *si parum ... res publica*), which explains the change of tense from the historically contextualizing *fuit* to the general principle suggested by *solet*. **fortuna** 'condition of birth'; so e.g. Cic. *Fin.* 5.52, Prop. 3.9.2. **dignitas** 'civic status', ἀξίωμα; *OLD* 3a. **admitti** 'allow admission to' (3.3 *admissura*). **tractationem** 'management' (*OLD* 3; *Tr.* 3.1). **non segnem:** litotes. **egere:** the syncopated form is rare in S. but found occasionally (also *Pol.* 13.4, *N.Q.* 3.26.3) in the penultimate position more widely favoured for the resulting clausula (H–S 720). **quemadmodum ... sudor:** a familiar topos (Cato, *Orig.* 1 fr. 2 p. 4.2–3 Jordan, Sall. *Jug.* 4.4, Cic. *Off.* 1.156; Dionigi 73–5, 259) more sharply pointed by S.'s concrete imagery. **ipsorum** (Gemoll): emphatic, stressing '*their particular* kind of inactivity' as opposed to 'other people's hyperactivity'; not merely a superfluous substitute-reflexive, for which *illorum* (MSS, defended by Dionigi 259–60) might serve as well in any period (K–S I 611 –12).   **discursus** 'bustle', in this sense apparently not before S. (*OLD* 3; *Breu.* 14.3n. on *discursant*); in contrast to *otium*, Plin. *Ep.* 1.9.7 *strepitum istum inanemque discursum . . . relinque teque studiis uel otio trade.*   **egisse . . . agerent:** 6.3n. on *non . . . desunt*; *Ep.* 8.6 *mihi crede, qui nihil agere uidentur maiora agunt.*   **uisi sunt** 'can be seen', 'are deemed' (Cooper–Procopé 178).

7   The three modes of life

After successfully showing how *otium* is compatible with traditional Stoicism, S. can now confidently anticipate the interlocutor's next move: what of the even older tripartite division of life-choices? By enforcing that traditional division the interlocutor may strive still to separate *contemplatio* from *actio*; but taking advantage of what has already been conceded, S. argues in response that exclusivity is here as impossible as it was earlier misleading in the cases of Zeno and Epicurus (3.2).

7.1 Praeterea: introducing a new stage in the argument, here more radically than at *Ep.* 78.22 *Praeterea duo genera sunt uoluptatum . . .*   **tria . . . actioni:** these were already used to construct ethical value-systems in Plato and his predecessors (Joly (1956) 12–104) and formularized in Aristotle (*E.N.* 1095b 17–19), before the Stoics taught the supremacy of the rational life (*Ep.* 76.9–12) as a formative priority for the contemplative and the active (*uoluptas* being discredited by its Epicurean associations; *SVF* III 173.4–5). A tendency to emphasize the 'ladder of ascent' and group-exclusivity, most famously in *E.N.* 1177a 12–1178a 8, thus gives way to shifting balances within a tripartite structure. The three modes listed here, along with the allusion to a graded hierarchy (*quod . . . solet*), strongly suggest the appeal to venerable authority which characterizes the interlocutor's preferred sphere of reference (1.4), and with his Stoic/Epicurean division now convincingly out-manoeuvred, a quick retreat to the older model is obviously anticipated by S.   **quod . . . solet:** even within Aristotle there is no one incontrovertible answer. For recent attempts to reconcile apparently conflicting statements in *E.N.*, see e.g. the essays by T. Nagel, J. L. Ackrill, K. V. Wilkes and A. O. Rorty in Rorty (1980), 7–33, 341–57, 377–94.   **uacat** 'is devoted to'; 5.8, *Breu.* 14.1.   **primum . . . indiximus** [sc. *Stoici*]: this time S. is more forthrightly ironic in neutralizing the interlocutor's aggressive intransigence in advance, his greater confidence expressed in the anaphoric polyptoton *deposita . . . deposito* (strongly emphatic; Lausberg §§638.3a, 643–4 with Summers lxxxv–lxxxvi) and in so readily distancing himself from the formal voice of authority in *indiximus*.   **primum:** with *deposita/-oque*.   **contentione:** among philosophers, *TLL* IV 676.1–35, with the sequence *odio . . . implacabile* placed to show the stages by which the interlocutor's hardened intransigence is quickly reached. For Stoics in conflict with Peripatetics, Cic. *Fin.* 2.68, 3.41; with Epicureans, 1.4, *Ben.* 4.2.1, Cic. *N.D.* 2.3, Quint. *Inst.* 5.7.35.   **implacabile:** postponed position (K–S II 311–12).   **sequentibus:** usual dat. with *indico*; philosophical (*OLD* 12b).   **indiximus:** Senecan extension (*TLL* VII 1.1156.62–5) of the usage with *bellum*.   **uideamus . . . perueniant:** for Griffin (1976) 147 'irritation . . . directed, in typical Roman fashion, to the hair-splitting of Greek philosophers, who concentrate on verbal differences rather than on substantial similarities'. But S.'s tone is triumphant rather than impatient, deploying subtlety rather than aiming to discredit it. His verbal paradigm will cleverly show the same interdependence of *genera* to be a functional necessity for the Aristotelian model as his earlier argument (*Ot.* 3–6) did for the Stoic/Epicurean one.   **ut** 'how', *OLD uideo* 10, K–S II 495 (not equivalent to *quomodo*; Powell (1988) 158 on Cic. *Sen.* 26); rare in S. (*Ir.* 2.21.7, *Ep.* 114.5, *N.Q.* 3.30.2, *Tro.* 945).   **haec:** sc. *genera uitae*.   **sub . . . titulo** 'under this name or that' (*OLD alius* 4b).   **nec ille qui . . . nec ille qui . . . nec ille cuius:** each of the *tria genera* is identified at the centre of a relative clause introduced by *nec ille* in triple anaphora, with the third neatly varied in subject (*uita*), number (*actionibus*) and voice (*destinata est*); each of the outer cola concludes with *sine contemplatione est*, and this time the middle one varies the epiphoric pattern; the overall balance is itself varied by progressive expansion in *probat . . . inseruit . . . destinata est*, and by the different construction each verb requires in its clause. This combination of anaphora with epiphora is rhetorical *complexio* (Lausberg §§633–4), here demonstrating how coherence and consistency are compatible with interdependence, change and shifting internal balances.   **probat** 'commends', 'sanctions'; in philosophical use, Ciceronian (*TLL* X 2.1463.38–55).   **contemplatione:** not of course at the highest level requiring total commitment (5.8, 7.1 *contemplationi*); the broad spectrum covered in *Ot.* 5 began (1–2) at the widest possible point of human access.   **inseruit:** special devotion (V. Max. 1.8 *ext.* 2 *quibus* [sc. *litteris*] *praecipue inseruerat*), underscored by the verb's rarity in S. (only here unless *inseruisse* is retained at *Ep.* 104.29); cf. 4.2 *deseruire.*   **uoluptate:** the *dulcedo* attendant upon the rational life (6.1–2, *V.B.* 11.1, *Ben.* 7.2.3–4) rather than the (Epicurean) 'primary goal' in *unum uoluptati uacat* above. **uita … contemplatione est:** different phrasing shows this is not the case of the 'advanced' philosopher in 5.8 (*ne contemplatio quidem sine actione est*), with *destinata est* in particular stressing the extent of commitment (*Breu.* 3.5, *Ir.* 3.42.4; *OLD* 4a) to a busy life-style.

7.2 'plurimum … accessio': after S.'s *tour de force* in 7.1, the interlocutor's response centres only on how, not whether, the modes interact. Effectively conceding the basic issue, he wants to recast S.'s position in strictly Stoic terms of definition.   **plurimum … discriminis est:** heavily ironic (by S.); in fact the distinction amounts to a notional technicality.   **propositum:** the 'ultimate aim' (τέλος, *SVF* III 3.16–20) of effort and intention, carefully defined by Stoic analogy (τέλος = σκοπός, *SVF* III 3.24) at Cic. *Fin.* 3.22 (the right aim, not the attainment of that aim, is the *summum bonum*).   **alterius:** 4.1n.   **accessio:** the 'accessory'/'by-product' (ἐπιγέννημα, *SVF* III 19.29–30, 43.10–11) of the *propositum*, already regarded with disdain at Cic. *Fin.* 2.42 … *qui ad uirtutem adiungunt … uoluptatem, quam unam uirtus minimi facit …, accessione utuntur non ita probabili.* For the contrast, *V.B.* 9.2 *uoluptas non est merces nec causa uirtutis sed accessio.*   **sit … discrimen:** concessive or jussive in force (K–S I 189–90), S.'s reply is launched with an extravagantly ironical gesture (*OLD sane* 7). *plurimum* above is proportionally matched by *grande*, which is not found with *discrimen* before S. (*Ep.* 82.15, *TLL* VI 2.2184.58–9); *magnum discrimen* is more usual (*Pol.* 17.2, *Ben.* 1.6.2, *N.Q.* 4B.11.5).   **nec ille sine actione … in actu est:** augmentation of the list of *discrimina*, at the same time (*tamen*) confirming their interdependence by ordering them in a different pattern. *nec ille … contemplatur* rounds off the second definition in 7.1, *nec ille tertius … sibi* the first, but *nec hic … agit* merely repeats the third, perhaps partly to distance Stoic *actio* from the disreputable associations of the Epicurean's *uoluptas* (cf. *de quo male existimare consensimus*), but also to re-emphasize the connection between *actio* and *contemplatio* in 5.1, 8.   **tertius:** first to be listed in 7.1, relegated to show his true status (*V.B.* 7.3 *uoluptas humile seruile, imbecillum caducum*, *Ep.* 123.16).   **de quo … consensimus:** calculated to appease the interlocutor before S. asserts (8.1–3) a position seemingly as remote as possible from the interlocutor's narrow Stoic outlook in 1.4. The tense may be significant ('have come to agree') if the addressee is Serenus, whose conversion from Epicureanism (*C.S.* 15.4) to Stoicism is revealed at *Tr.* 1.10 (Griffin (1976) 316–17; general intro. p. 15); but S.'s usage elsewhere (*Ben.* 3.6.2 'we are in agreement') complicates matters. **uoluptatem . . . sibi:** though the context obviously identifies the position as Epicurean, S. is careful to phrase it in a way with which his orthodox Stoic can hardly disagree. The Stoic case for admitting pleasure controlled by reason is fully argued at *Ben.* 7.2.1–4, more loosely in the identification of 'acceptable' *uoluptas* with *gaudium* at *Ep.* 59.1–4 (cf. *Ep.* 4.1 *alia . . . illa uoluptas est quae percipitur ex contemplatione mentis . . .*), but an Epicurean could appeal to the master's own definition: Epic. *Ep. Men.* 131–2 = L–S 1 21B5 '. . . when we say that pleasure is the end, we do not mean the pleasures of the dissipated and those that consist in having a good time [cf. S.'s *uoluptatem inertem*], . . . but freedom from pain in the body and from disturbance in the soul. For what produces the pleasant life is . . . sober reasoning [λογισμός; cf. S.'s *ratione*] which tracks down the causes of every choice and avoid-ance . . .' (cf. *V.B.* 12.4, Cic. *Fin.* 1.37).   **inertem** 'idle' in making no effort to exercise rational control (*Ben.* 4.11.5 *inertissimum uitium, uoluptas*). **probat:** 7.1n.   **ratione:** while the formulation here may not trouble an orthodox Stoic (n. above on *uoluptatem . . . sibi*), the Epicurean makes plea-sure itself the criterion of rational discrimination; *Ep. Men.* 130 = L–S 1 21B3 'we have to make our judgement on all these points [sc. choosing between or avoiding pleasures/pains] by a calculation (συμμετρήσει) and survey of advantages and disadvantages', 131, *Ratae sententiae* 19 = L–S 124CI, Cic. *Fin.* 1.32 with Gosling–Taylor (1982) 397–9 and (for problems with the theory) 407–13.   **efficit:** *actio* emphasized.   **firmam** 'stable', 'sure', corre-sponding in Epicurean terms to 'katastematic' pleasure (not being thirsty) as opposed to 'kinetic' (drinking to relieve thirst); Sharples (1996) 92 with L–S 1 21N (Plut. *Mor.* 1089d = Epic. fr. 68 Us.) 'The comfortable state of the flesh, and the confident expectation of this, contain the highest and most secure [βεβαιοτάτην = S.'s *firmam*] joy for those who are capable of reasoning.' For difficulties in interpreting the *testimonia* in Cic. *Fin.* and Plut., Gosling–Taylor (1982) 382–94.   **ita** 'accordingly'.   **uoluptaria:** with *in actu* to suggest the mixed *genera*, but from a Stoic perspective (*de quo . . . consensimus*) with the pejorative shading already in Cicero (*Tusc.* 2.18, 3.40, *Fin.* 1.37).   **secta:** 3.2n.   **in actu:** like the Stoics (1.4).

7.3 S. further provokes his imaginary interlocutor by again (cf. 3.2) identifying common ground between Epicureans and Stoics, both of them in their different ways committed to *actus* and to reason as the deter-minant of action.   **quidni** 'how could it not be . . . ?', with the usual

potential subjunctive (*Breu.* 7.7, 11.2, 14.2; K–S II 495–6).   **cum** 'since'.
In the present S. uses temporal *cum* with the indicative (e.g. 3.5, *Breu.*
3.5, 8.1; Waldaestel (1888) 6–7); *Ep.* 75.4 *ille promissum suum impleuit qui
et cum uideas illum et cum audias idem est* is exceptional, but S.'s use of the
indefinite second pers. subjunctive explains the anomaly (Summers lxiii).
aliquando ... sumetur?: Epic. fr. 442 Us., paraphrasing the 'computa-
tion' (συμμέτρησις) in *Ep. Men.* 129 = L–S I 21B3 '... we sometimes pass
over many pleasures in cases when their outcome for us is a greater quantity of discomfort; and we regard many pains as better than pleasures in
cases when our endurance of pains is followed by a greater and long-lasting
pleasure'; L–S I 122, Cic. *Tusc.* 5.95, *Fin.* 1.33. The procedure is carefully
measured out in S.'s chiastic antithesis, setting *uoluptate, dolorem* within the
opposing fut. infs., while the two cola of the conditional clause contrast
natural consequence (fut. active) with deliberative action taken (fut. pass.)
to avoid it; Dionigi 269.   **imminebit ... sumetur:** the retained indicative in *oratio obliqua* marks the thought as Epicurus' own (Handford
(1947) 152).   **minor pro grauiore:** Setaioli (1988) 246–7 suggests
that this further nuance derives not from Epicurus directly but from an
intermediary (Cicero? Cf. *Fin.* 1.33 *ut ... perferendis doloribus asperiores repellat*
[sc. *sapiens*]).

   7.4 S.'s conclusion satisfies both his initial propositions in 2.1–2.
quo pertinet ... ? 'What is the point of ... ?'; signalling the conclusion
to an extended argument, cf. *Ir.* 3.5.1, *Ep.* 124.21, *N.Q.* 3.19.4 *quorsus hoc
pertinet? ut appareat ... (OLD pertineo* 3a).   **placere:** 3.1 n.   **omnibus:**
those committed to the three *genera uitae* of 7.1; Epicureans, Stoics and presumably Peripatetics.   **alii:** i.e. for whom *contemplatio* is the final and
highest goal.   **petunt** anticipates the nautical metaphor in *nobis ... est*
below (*Ep.* 71.3 *ignoranti quem portum petat nullus suus uentus est*).   **nobis:**
Stoics; the interlocutor is assumed to assent to the conclusion.   **haec**
[sc. *contemplatio*] **statio, non portus est:** for the contrast, Vell. 2.72.5
cum ... exitialem ... tempestatem fugientibus statio pro portu foret, where 'the former must be temporary, the latter permanent' (Woodman (1983) 175). For
Stoics, committed to public service (1.4) if circumstances allow (3.2–5) and
'active' for the public good even *in otio* (5.1, 8, 6.3–5), *otium/contemplatio*
will always be a *statio* ('roadstead'; *Ep.* 120.18, Virg. *G.* 4.421, *Aen.* 2.23)
and not, as for the Peripatetics, an ultimate destination (*Breu.* 18.1 n. on
in ... portum ... recede). The distinction refers back to both propositions in
2.1–2: in the case either of withdrawal to the contemplative life *a prima*

aetate (2.1) or retirement to it after a career in service (2.2), the Stoic remains committed to action (here equivalent to *portus*) in accordance with
the orthodox view represented in 1.4; for even in retirement his *contemplatio* is
directed towards *actio* for the social good (cf. 3.5 *aliis prodest*), whether in the
form of teaching (2.2 *hoc . . . ad alios . . . referre*) or by his writings and general
public influence (cf. 6.4 for Zeno and Chrysippus; general intro. pp. 17–18).

8 *Necessary abstention*

In addressing the first of his argument's initial objectives (2.1), S. now ex-
tracts from his earlier list of Stoic 'exclusion-clauses' (3.3–5) the life-long
exemption allowable to a philosopher in a radically corrupt society; but
this can be invoked only if we adopt so bleak a view and deeply pessimistic
an outlook on civic society in general as to regard no state as sufficiently
tolerant of or tolerable to the *sapiens*. What gives this argument here a
compelling force it did not have in 3.3–5 is the intervening elaboration of
the highly sophisticated intellectual life identified with *contemplatio* (5.3–8)
and the demonstration that it is not self-serving but of use to the wider
human community (4.2) and to posterity (6.4). Led stage by stage through
this argument, we now acknowledge (with the interlocutor) the difficulty
of integrating such an elevated, idealized icon-figure into the morally ambivalent ethos prevailing in any actual city. Lifelong exemption, then, will
always be an open possibility, indeed a necessity, for those whose universal
contribution can justify their status.

8.1 Adice . . . quod: the transitional formula is colloquial (Summers l),
post-Augustan and frequent in S. (*Prou.* 5.1, *C.S.* 9.3, *Ir.* 3.27.5, *Ep.* 15.2,
33.10; *TLL* I 674.16–17), here leading back to the first stated aim (2.1).
huc: i.e. to the previous point; Sen. *Contr.* 4.5 *adice huc et quod*, Quint.
Decl. 341 = p. 309.5–6 Sh. B.   **e lege** 'in accordance with the prescrip-
tion'; legal phraseology (*TLL* v 2.1108.50–62), and so an ironic comment
on the interlocutor's rigid mindset (1.4).   **Chrysippi:** obviously along
the lines of *'accedet . . . impedierit'*, attributed to Zeno in 3.2. The change is not
a casual slip. S. has consistently paired Zeno and Chrysippus (3.1, 6.4–5) to
counter the interlocutor's strong tendencies to show a partisanship (e.g. 1.4
in ipsis Zenonis principiis) which S. elsewhere deplores (3.1). By referring the
lex, though not the same quote, to *both* (cf. 3.1 *illorum sententiam*), he reaffirms
his freedom of party spirit in the presence of a *homo factiosus.*   **otioso:**

predicative, with indirect obj. of *licet* understood; *Ben.* 2.31.5, 5.1.4 (Bourgery (1922) 353), *TLL* VII 2.1360.63–83.   **non dico ut ... ut** 'I do not mean (to the effect) that ...'; explanatory *ut* (G–L §557).   **patiatur:** because reluctantly excluded from public service on the grounds set out in 3.3. **eligat:** i.e. 2.1 *ut possit aliquis ... contemplationi ueritatis totum se tradere, rationem uiuendi quaerere atque exercere secreto.*   **negant:** emphatic by position (*V.B.* 7.1, *Ep.* 49.5, 71.17, 88.12, 102.3), summarizing the first *causa* for exemption in 3.3.   **quamlibet:** not just *any* state (*OLD quilibet*[1] 1b) regardless of its condition; *Ep.* 68.2 *nec ad omnem* ('any whatever') *rem publicam mittimus.* **quid ... res publica est?:** the first *causa* is interpreted in a way which turns Zeno's simple exemption-clause (3.2 '... *nisi si quid impedierit*') into the basis of a universal, life-long opt-out: as the ethos of any society will be in some way objectionable, the (Stoic) philosopher always has the choice of invoking the exemption-clause in any individual case. The *probatio* of the proposition first stated in 2.1 does not now seem the cynical manoeuvre it might have then, for two reasons: (i) the intervening description of the ambitious intellectual content of *contemplatio* (4–5) and its universal relevance (6.4–5) suggests the most distinguished, elevated (and therefore rare) *sapiens* whom we can easily accept as fitting the picture in 8.1; and (ii) the examples (8.2) will both confirm this exclusive status as a qualifying requirement for the philosopher, and present a much more pessimistic political outlook to make any objection and exemption readily understandable. S. can now discard the second and third *causae* of 3.3; by 8.4 he will have established his case.   **quid ... interest quomodo ..., utrum ... an:** for a variant on this elongated construction, *Ben.* 2.6.1; apparently not before S. (*TLL* VII 1.2286.22–4).   **res publica illi ... ipse rei publicae:** chiasmus and polyptoton help clinch the point.   **si** 'if we can suppose that ...' **omnibus:** sc. *fastidiose quaerentibus* below.   **defutura ... est:** the periphrastic fut. signals pessimistic resignation to an unalterable state of affairs (Westman (1961) 53).   **fastidiose** 'with a hard critical eye' (*TLL* VI 1.313.30–40). Griffin (1976) 332–3 interprets the word pejoratively ('fussily', *OLD* 2), but the *sapiens* who emerges in 4–6 is not arrogantly disdainful of political responsibility in the *minor res publica*, merely without a useful ('relevant') role to play (3.5).   **quaerentibus:** by now firmly established as the proper 'activity' for the *sapiens*; 2.1 *rationem uiuendi quaerere*, 3.1 *ueritatem ... quaerimus*, 4.2 *ut quaeramus ...*, 5.2 *secretiora exquirere*, 5.5 *inquisitio*, 5.7 *ad haec quaerenda natus*, 6.5 *quaero an ...*, 7.1 *quaeri*. The opposite approach surfaces in e.g. 6.2 *res appetere*.

8.2 Earlier examples are now reconsidered. Athens and Carthage were previously (4.1) neutral illustrations of the city-state to which the philosopher, like the rest, is tied by the *condicio nascendi*; the intervening analysis has produced a *sapiens* who is more self-fulfilled, remote and fastidious, and an image of the *res publica* which is as a consequence *per se* more menacing and even repressive. The change enables the opt-out of 2.1 to be invoked, while the examples ensure its relevance to democratic as well as oligarchic states. The rhetorical tone is heavily ironic.   **interrogo ... accessurus:** '*interrogatio* seeks by indirect, ironic means, to prove the [asking] party's superiority in relation to the matter' (Lausberg §766n. = p. 340 n. 1); with 8.3 *si ... possit*, possibly an echo of Pl. *Rep.* 497a–b (Dionigi 85–6): '[Adeimantus] But is there any existing form of society that you would call congenial to philosophy? [Socrates] Not one. That is precisely my complaint: no existing constitution is worthy of the philosophic nature ... ' (trans. F. M. Cornford). Socrates' own fate below will confirm the point. **ad Atheniensium ... fugit?:** Athens tried and executed Socrates (*Tr.* 5.3, *Ep.* 104.28 with Bogun (1968) 152–4); after Alexander's death in 323 anti-Macedonian feeling caused Aristotle to leave, allegedly recalling the Socratic precedent as he went (Ael. *V.H.* 3.36). An Athenian might well respond with a *tu quoque*: a senatorial decree of 161 BC had ordered the praetor to keep philosophers out of Rome (Gell. *N.A.* 15.11.1), and – esp. ironic if *Ot.* is dated to *c.* AD 62 – important Stoics in particular fell victim to Nero (Griffin (1976) 362–6 and (1984) 171–7; general intro. p. 9), while Epictetus would be expelled with others by Domitian (Gell. *N.A.* 15.11.3–5).   **damnaretur:** primary or historic sequence is permissible in clauses dependent on a historic pres. (*fugit*), with historic predominant in Imperial prose (K–S II 176–8); *Apoc.* 7.1, 12.1 (inconsistent) with Eden (1984) 128, 13.1, 14.1 (both primary). Such evidence does not compel acceptance of Reynolds' *damnetur* after Gertz (1874) 134.   **fugit:** intrans., i.e. *in qua ... ne damnaretur* 'to avoid condemnation in which [state]' (contrast *fugiet* below).   **inuidia:** the Platonic Socrates attributes his own condemnation to popular enmity and malice (*Apol.* 28a διαβολή τε καὶ φθόνος), but S. makes the point sufficiently imprecise for it to be almost universally applicable and so ensure a possible opt-out for the discriminating *sapiens*. For *inuidia* as a constant hazard, *Ir.* 3.31.1, *Breu.* 15.4, *Ep.* 74.4 *perniciosum optimis telum.*   **negabis:** in answer to the *interrogatio* (n. on *interrogo ... accessurus* above).   **ad Carthaginiensium ... hostilis?:** for the parallel with Athens, Plut. *Mor.* 799c–d. S.'s Roman stereotype (Bogun

(1968) 245–6) bears little relation to the flourishing cultural and administrative centre of the contemporary province of Africa Proconsularis, which would presently produce Apuleius and Tertullian. The passage has been read as a covert allusion to Nero's Rome (Dionigi 103–4, 275–6), but general intro. pp. 14–15.   **seditio . . . libertas est:** a combination also supporting the parallel with Athens, explicitly criticized at *Ben.* 6.37.1 as *seditiosa ciuitas et intemperanter libera* and more fully characterized as such in *Tr.* 5.1–3.   **assidua seditio:** the stereotype was well grounded; for factional in-fighting among the ruling families and competing power-groups in fourth-century Carthage, Picard (1968) 131–71. Pompeius Trogus had given detailed accounts in his Augustan *Historiae Philippicae*, epitomized by Justin 18–22.   **optimo . . . libertas est:** within the sequence *seditio . . . crudelitas* this must denote the unrestrained 'licence' of populist domination, as when Socrates lives *in libertate bellis ac tyrannis saeuiore* (*Ep.* 104.27). At Carthage royal and aristocratic rulers were esp. vulnerable, with Hanno I the Great, Suniatus (Just. 20.5.12 *potentissimus . . . Poenorum*) and the general Mago all sentenced to death there in the mid-fourth century (Picard (1968) 132–9, 158–60), the royal commander Hamilcar in 313 (dying just before his condemnation, Just. 22.3.2–7) and his nephew King Bomilcar in 308 (Just. 22.7.8–11, esp. 9 *Bomilcar magno animo crudelitatem ciuium tulit adeo ut de summa cruce ueluti de tribunali in Poenorum scelera contionaretur*; Picard (1968) 168–71).   **summa . . . uilitas:** an extreme antitheton encasing a pair of synonyms.   **aequi ac boni:** a standard combination (*TLL* 1 1041.9– 80), = καλοκἀγαθία.   **uilitas** 'contempt for', lit. 'the state of being held in low esteem' (*OLD* 2; in this sense apparently not before S.). For Carthage's legendary deceitfulness, e.g. V. Max. 9.6 *ext.* 1 *ut ipsum fontem perfidiae contemplemur, Carthaginienses . . .* , Hor. *C.* 3.5.33, Polyb. 6.56.1–4.   **aduersus hostes . . . hostilis:** so Plut. *Mor.* 799d has the Carthaginians both 'harsh to their subjects' and 'most savage when angered'. For their proverbial cruelty in Roman eyes, e.g. Cic. *Phil.* 14.9 *crudelitatem Carthaginiensium*, Liv. 21.57.14, Sil. 6.531–2.   **aduersus hostes:** a Roman would think instinctively of the consul M. Atilius Regulus, returning to Carthage to face *quae sibi barbarus | tortor pararet* (Hor. *C.* 3.5.49–50) along with the Roman prisoners there (17–18; cf. Gell. *N.A.* 7.4.3, V. Max. 1.1.14, 9.2 *ext.* 1, Liv. *Per.* 18). The whole story is now considered an apocryphal justification for Roman reprisals (Walbank (1957) 93–4).   **aduersus suos:** even Justin retained details of what was done to Hanno the Great (n. above on *optimo . . . libertas est*): *. . . capitur uirgisque caesus effossis oculis et manibus cruribusque fractis, uelut a*

singulis membris poena exigeretur, in conspectu populi occiditur; corpus uerberibus lacera-
tum in crucem figitur. filii quoque cognatique omnes, etiam innoxii, supplicio traduntur . . .
(21.4.7–8). S. may also be alluding to the regular Carthaginian practice of
sacrificing children to Ba'al Hammon (Porph. *Abst.* 2.56.1, Picard (1968)
46–7), with two hundred being publicly butchered as the invading army
of Agathocles approached the city in 310 (D. S. 20.14.4–7).   **fugiet:** cf.
fugit above.

   8.3 si . . . possit: 8.2n. on *interrogo . . . accessurus.*   **percensere**
'make a complete survey of' (*OLD* 3), so giving effect to 8.1 *fastidiose*
quaerentibus; in combination with *inueniam*, *Helu.* 6.4, *Ben.* 7.3.1. S.'s own
thoroughness may be judged from the fact that both his examples
had for at least two centuries been in a very different condition.
quae . . . quam . . . possit: relative clauses of tendency ('of the kind
which'; G–L §631.2) with double polyptoton, the first clause gen-
eralizing the case of Athens and the second that of Carthage.
quodsi . . . nusquam est: the final *probatio* of the proposition stated
in 2.1 and now demonstrated as applicable to the *sapiens* delineated in
4–6.   **nobis fingimus** 'construct for ourselves with the mind' (*OLD*
fingo 8a = LSJ πλάσσω III); so Cic. *Rep.* 2.3.2, contrasting the extended
intellectual fabrication of the Platonic Republic with the long 'true' story
of Rome's foundation.   **incipit . . . esse** 'turns out to be', as a consequence of the argument; Senecan, *Ir.* 1.10.3, *Ep.* 9.15 (*TLL* VII 1.919.19–25).
necessarium 'the inescapable option' (*OLD* 5a), and therefore rightly
chosen (8.1 *eligat*) *a prima aetate* (2.1) by all those *fastidiose quaerentibus*, enabling them alone *maiori rei publicae et in otio deseruire* (4.2) without infringing
praecepta Stoicorum (2.1, 3.1, 8.1).   **quod . . . otio:** i.e. *actio* in a tolerable
and tolerant state. Chrysippus' law (8.1) remains valid; the *sapiens* chooses
ex causa.   **poterat:** the so-called 'tense of disappointment' (G–L §254
R.2) denotes what might be the case but is not (cf. *Ep.* 98.6 *expectatione uen-*
turi praesentia, quibus frui poterat, amittet).   **nusquam est** 'is non-existent'
(*OLD* 2a).

   8.4 The concluded argument is rounded off with an ironic adaptation
of the recurring maritime analogy (1.2, 3.3–4, 7.4), familiar from its conventional use in political contexts ('sailing the ship of state'; Hor. *C.* 1.14
with N–H 179–81) and moral discourse ('hazards of ambition and foolish
risk-taking', Smith (1913) 246–7 on Tib. 1.3.37–40). Both these aspects are
clearly relevant to an essentially moral argument with an obvious political
dimension. S. often draws on such familiar associations of the analogy to

illustrate inner turbulence and external menace (*Breu.* 7.10, *Ir.* 2.10.8, *Tr.* 5.5, 11.7, *Helu.* 19.5, *Ben.* 1.1.10, 7.15.1, *Ep.* 14.7–8, 74.4, 87.28, *N.Q.* 5.18.8), but what makes it esp. appropriate to emphasize them here is the adventurous use of sea-travel daringly undertaken by the philosophically uninitiated *una mercede . . . cognoscendi aliquid abditum remotumque* (5.2). In contrast, *cogitatio nostra* (5.6) is shown to embark on its intellectual voyage in a securer vessel; so S. adopts an ironic tone when the analogy introduces as incompatible *contraria* two propositions ('best to sail' but 'sail not in troubled waters') which, at the philosophical level, his preceding argument has now successfully reconciled (n. on *nauigationem*).   **dicit . . . deinde negat:** the sharp dichotomy suggests a speaker (*si quis*, i.e. not the interlocutor) unfamiliar with even the preliminary modifications discussed in 3.2–5, who therefore resembles the *rector nauis* (below) in being irresistibly drawn *in contrarium*. S.'s successful reconciling of the contraries enables him to assume an ironic detachment from their crudely conceived reaffirmation here in quasi-poetical style.   **optimum** 'the best course' (*OLD* 10b, adding *Ir.* 1.7.1, 8.1, *Tr.* 4.8, *Ben.* 2.1.3).   **in quo . . . rapiant:** assonance, alliteration and homoeoteleuton intensify the highly poetical impression: *naufragia fieri soleant et frequenter subitae tempestates sint quae rectorem in contrarium rapiant*).   **puto** 'unless I am mistaken'; ironic condescension (*OLD* 8) towards the speaker's failure to present his thoughts clearly (*dicit . . . deinde negat; uetat . . . quamquam laudet*). The parenthetical use is a familiar colloquialism (*Ep.* 22.7, 58.31, 66.1, 24; Hofmann 106–7).   **quamquam** 'however much', more often with the subjunctive in S. (*Ir.* 3.19.1, *V.B.* 26.7, *Ben.* 7.5.3, also restored at *Ep.* 121.24; Bourgery (1922) 345–6).   **nauigationem:** like the interlocutor at the start (1.4), the speaker envisaged in *si quis* stresses inflexible *contraria* now at odds with the resolution of the argument. By rounding off with the maritime analogy in this way, S. suggests that his speaker is too timid to venture upon even the most mundane of risky voyages (5.2 *nauigant quidam . . .*) which can progressively (5.3–6) lead the voyaging mind to the fullest satisfaction of intellectual curiosity. Irony is therefore an appropriate response for the secure, rationally self-justified *sapiens* confronted by the speaker's incoherence and vacillation.

Ot. is not alone in lacking a *subscriptio* in the *Codex Ambrosianus*; *Helu.* is similarly deprived while in other respects fully intact, and only at the end of *V.B.* is a definite loss of text the probable explanation. The later MSS R and V, independently transmitted from the archetype (Reynolds xvii; cf. general intro. pp. 32–3), have no *subscriptiones* to any of the *Dialogues*, but do have an *inscriptio* at the head of each, even of *Tr.* which lacks one in the *Ambrosianus*. The transmission of *Ot.* as an *addendum* to *V.B.* in the MSS may be a relevant factor (speculative theories in Dionigi 43–6), though a copyist confused by this would have been alerted to the discrepancy by the list of contents in the *Ambrosianus* (Reynolds ix).

De breuitate uitae

1 Exordium

In a characteristically brisk opening S. establishes the trajectory of his argument by countering what he portrays as popular but misguided opinion: life is too short. Not so: life is long enough if well managed. Far from coaxing Paulinus (and his general reader) into agreement, S. affects a dogmatic tone which is sustained throughout the treatise. Hippocrates and Aristotle are made to lend support to the case against which S. will argue; he thus ennobles his own status as a corrector of even distinguished opinion, but not without subtly manipulating the Hippocratic and Aristotelian evidence on which he draws (1.1 n. on *'uitam ... artem'*, 1.2 n. on *'aetatis ... stare'*). Echoes of Sallustian moralizing can also be heard (1.1 n. on *conqueritur*).

1.1 malignitate 'meanness', as opposed to the kindly generosity attributed to nature in S.'s riposte (2.1 *illa se benigne gessit*); cf. against parallel charges of meanness *Marc.* 16.1, *Ben.* 7.1.6.   **conqueritur:** S. uses the compound verb sparingly, here to consolidate the massed chorus of complaint as at *Pol.* 2.2 *conqueramur* 'let us lament together', 3.3. But S. also modifies Sallust's use of *queror* at *Jug.* 1.1, a passage conspicuously echoed here: *falso queritur de natura sua genus humanum, quod imbecilla atque aeui breuis forte potius quam uirtute regatur.* Through verbal and thematic reminiscence S. arguably pays homage to Sallust (Traina (1987) 164; modifications in Borgo (1989)); but whereas Sallust begins by summarily dismissing mankind's groundless protestations (*falso queritur ...*), S. delays his rejoinder (1.3 *non exiguum temporis habemus*), first constructing a hierarchy of misguided opinion (*imprudens uulgus / clari uiri /* Hippocrates and Aristotle) before finally supplying his corrective.   **quod ... gignimur, quod ... decurrunt:** *decurrunt* Reynolds after Gertz (1874) 146. Most editors read *decurrant* with the MSS, thereby (over-)straining to distinguish the universal truth of the first *quod* clause from the opinion reported in the second ('Not everybody feels that "life fails us just as we begin to live"', Alexander (1945) 81).   **gignimur:**

with *in* + acc., a post-Augustan variation on *nasci* with the same construction (*TLL* VI 2.1992.29–32; McKeown on Ov. *Am.* 1.9.41–2); favoured
by S., e.g. 1.2, *Ir.* 2.13.1, *Ben.* 4.4.3. For the temporal phrase accompanying the verb, *Ir.* 3.42.2 *tamquam in aeternum genitos.*   **aeui:** perhaps 'le temps du Monde' (Grimal 15) as opposed to 'the mortal span'
(*OLD* 5a), thereby distinguishing the meaning of *in exiguum aeui* and
dati nobis temporis spatia; the twofold complaint (*quod . . . quod*) is then that
(i) in the context of universal time man lives only for a moment (*Ep.*
77.20, 99.10, 31), and (ii) within that moment the time granted to
us passes too quickly. Cf. *Ep.* 74.10 *quicquid nobis dedit* [sc. *prouidentia*]
breue est et exiguum si compares mundi totius aeuo.   **tam . . . rapide:** the
anaphoric arrangement of advs. (used synonymously) redoubles time's
swift progress; *uelociter* rare in S. (*Ep.* 89.2, 110.7, *N.Q.* 1.14.5, 7.5.2), *rapide*
only here, but cf. in combination *Marc.* 16.7 *rapidum ueloxque tempus*, *Ep.*
108.25 *uelocitatem rapidissimae rei*, also of time.   **spatia decurrunt:**
the laps of life 'run their course', so to speak (*OLD decurro* 5c). The verb is
more often used transitively with *spatium* in reference to elapsed time (Pl. *St.*
81 *decurso aetatis spatio*; *OLD decurro* 8b).   **exceptis . . . paucis:** the abl.
abs. neatly isolates the very (*admodum*) few who live long enough to break the
general rule (*ceteros . . . destituat*).   **in ipso . . . apparatu** 'while they are
still only getting ready to live'. Cf. 9.1 for ridicule of those who waste their
lives in always preparing to live better.   **uitae . . . uita:** for the polyptoton to underline a paradox, 9.1 *impendio uitae uitam instruunt*, *Ep.* 22.9, 62.3,
97.14 (cited by Traina (1987) 83).   **destituat** 'leaves in the lurch' (*OLD*
3b).   **publico** 'universal'; *Ot.* 4.1 n.   **ut opinantur** qualifies *malo*; S.
distances himself from the popular view.   **turba . . . et . . . uulgus:** the
contemptuous combination also at Lucr. *D.R.N.* 2.920, Stat. *Theb.* 3.606.
ingemuit: of unreasonable or irrational complaint also at *Ep.* 99.3, 115.16,
120.13.   **quoque** 'even' (*OLD* 4a).   **affectus** 'feeling'. Pejorative,
equivalent to πάθος: the *sapiens* who subordinates the passions to reason is
ἀπαθής and hence immune to disturbance (*Ep.* 85.9 *si ratio proficit, ne incipient
quidem affectus*). For the Stoic ideal, *SVF* III 108.21–109.14 with Rist 25–7 on
ἀπάθεια.   **maximi medicorum:** Hippocrates of Cos, similarly described at *Ep.* 95.20.   **exclamatio** 'dictum', post-Augustan (e.g. Tac.
Dial. 31.6).   **'uitam . . . artem':** a close rendering of the first two cola
of Hippocrates' first aphorism (ὁ βίος βραχύς, ἡ δὲ τέχνη μακρή, IV 458
Littré), but with chiastic rearrangement to emphasize the contrasting adjs.
S. imposes a loaded interpretation on the aphorism; for to assert that life

is short in relation to the vast demands of one's art is not to complain (as S. would have it) that life *itself* is too short. The interpretation was much debated in antiquity, e.g. by Galen (xvii 2.346–56 Kühn), who also reports in *De sectis* (i 82–3 Kühn) that the Methodist school asserted by contrast that life is long, the medical art short if stripped of its many superfluities. This Methodist position is not incompatible with S.'s assertion (1.3) that life is long enough if released from superfluous *occupationes*; but other possible influences on S. have been claimed. The aphorism is much quoted in exhortations to make good use of time, e.g. by Zeno (*SVF* i 70.5–6) and by Philo (*De uita cont.* 16); since in Philo (*De somn.* 1.9–10) the aphorism is followed directly by the kind of lament which S. goes on to attribute to Aristotle (1.2), Baumgarten (1970) 320–3 conjectures that S. (like Philo) followed diatribic precedent in grouping both citations together.

1.2 exigentis 'expostulating with (*cum . . :*)', a rare post-Augustan usage (*Ep.* 27.1 *mecum exigo*, Plin. *Ep.* 6.12.3).   **sapienti uiro:** general ('philosopher') rather than specific ('Stoic *sapiens*') in meaning. **'aetatis . . . stare':** already Cic. *Tusc.* 3.69 *Theophrastus autem moriens accusasse naturam dicitur, quod ceruis et cornicibus uitam diuturnam . . . , hominibus . . . tam exiguam uitam dedisset . . .* Duff 94 among others (e.g. Reynolds in OCT 239) supposes that S. wrongly attributes the saying to Aristotle through a lapse of memory, but Viansino ii 707 better appreciates his tactical acumen: the saying is attributed to Aristotle, not Theophrastus, because S. chooses the weightier candidate to partner Hippocrates, *maximum medicorum*.   **aetatis illam** [sc. *naturam*]: Gertz's restoration ((1874) 147) of the corrupt text; *aetatis* a partitive gen. dependent on *tantum*, the acc. obj. of *indulsisse* ('nature had bestowed so much time on animals that . . . '). **saecula:** human life-spans (Prop. 2.13.46 *Nestoris est uisus post tria saecla cinis*); hence the distributives *quina* and *dena*. The longevity of the crow and the stag was proverbial, the former allegedly living nine times longer than man, the latter four times longer than the crow (Hes. fr. 304.1–2 M–W, Ov. *M.* 7.273–4, *Eleg. Maec.* 115–18, Plin. *N.H.* 7.153); both animals figure in Theophrastus' parallel complaint as reported at Cic. *Tusc.* 3.69 (quoted above), but S. eschews particular examples to emphasize the general difference between animals and man.   **educerent:** imperf. subjunctive even though the verb introducing Aristotle's reported words (*[lis] est*) is in primary sequence; for if a present verb introduces opinions reported from the extant writings of a dead author, dependent clauses within the quotation may take either a present or a past subjunctive (K–S ii 177); so e.g. Cic. *N.D.*

1.40 *idemque* [sc. *Chrysippus*] *disputat aethera esse eum quem homines Iouem appellarent...*, *Off.* 1.87. **homini:** dat. of advantage with *stare* ('a much shorter limit is set for a human being'). Adversative asyndeton (Summers xcii–xciii) points the difference between animals and man. **terminum:** *Ot.* 5.7n.

1.3 non exiguum ... perdimus: strong *correctio* (*non* x *sed* y) in pointed answer to the preceding grievances. **in ... consummationem:** life is long enough 'for the accomplishing of the greatest things'. Striking language describes striking achievement: *consummatio* in this sense (rare; *OLD* 3) is paralleled in S. only at 20.1 (a different nuance at *Helu.* 18.9); it here fulfils the potential of 1.2 *homini...genito*. **collocaretur:** imperf. subjunctive denoting action unfulfilled in present time: 'life has been given to us in generous measure, if the whole of it were [being] well spent; but life is wasted...' Of 'spending' or 'applying' time etc. (Ciceronian), *OLD* 12. **per luxum ... diffluit:** a familiar moralizing point tinged with Sallustian colour (1.1 n. on *conqueritur*). For *diffluo* with *per* + acc., an extremely rare formulation (Traina (1987) 163), *Jug.* 1.4 *ubi per socordiam uires tempus ingenium diffluxere, naturae infirmitas accusatur*; for life wasted *per luxum ac neglegentiam*, *Jug.* 2.4 *per luxum et ignauiam aetatem agunt*. **ultima ... cogente:** death presses; for *necessitas* so used (notably in Tacitus), *OLD* 4b. After *ultima*, *demum* is tautological for emphasis ('the very last...'; cf. *Ep.* 118.16). **quam ... sentimus** '[the life] which we did not realize was passing we perceive to have passed away'. As often, S. omits the antecedent to a relative pronoun; so e.g. *Ir.* 2.22.3 *quae inuiti audimus libenter credimus*, *Helu.* 2.3, *Ep.* 66.17. **ire:** of time/life, a poetic usage introduced into prose by S. (e.g. 8.5, 16.3, *Ep.* 61.1, 108.25; *TLL* v 2.645.16–37).

1.4 ita est 'so it is'; colloquial (Summers l) and often in S. to introduce a summary conclusion or an evident truth (e.g. *Ben.* 2.29.6, *Marc.* 23.5, *Pol.* 1.1, *Ep.* 97.13). **non accipimus ... sumus:** *uariatio* on the point at 1.3 *non exiguum...perdimus*, with *correctio* (*non...sed...nec...sed*) again to sharp antithetical effect. **breuem:** predicative in relation to *facimus* ('we are not given a short life, we make it so'). For the combination of verbs, *Ep.* 44.3 *Platonem non accepit nobilem philosophia sed fecit*. **prodigi:** for the idea, *Tr.* 3.8 *alii parce illo* [sc. *tempore*] *utimur, alii prodige*. **sicut ... patet:** in closing illustration to round off the *exordium*, the first leg of the correlative (*sicut...ita*) construction is elegantly symmetrical: around the pivotal *at*, *amplae...opes* is balanced and contrasted by *quamuis modicae*, *ubi...peruenerunt* by *si...traditae sunt*, *momento dissipantur* by *usu crescunt*. **peruenerunt ... traditae sunt:** the first verb is loaded in meaning;

whereas wealth is entrusted to the responsible guardian, it merely 'passes into the hands' of the irresponsible owner (*dominus*).   **momento** 'in an instant'; Livian and then common in Silver prose (*TLL* VIII 1395.11–31). **dissipantur:** of squandering wealth, Cic. *Flac.* 90, *Phil.* 2.35, Tac. *Ann.* 13.34.1; of time, *Ir.* 3.42.2 *quid iuuat ... breuissimam aetatem dissipare?* **quamuis modicae** 'however modest'.   **usu:** careful deployment as opposed to careless dissipation; cf. *Ep.* 94.72 *laudet paruo diuitem et usu opes metientem.*   **aetas ... patet:** for the person who 'maps out' time well (*OLD dispono* 5b), life 'extends greatly' (i.e. 'gives ample room', Duff 96); 15.5 *sapientis ... multum patet uita.*

2 Human folly

Elaboration of the initial argument: man, not nature, makes life too short. Acclaimed in antiquity for his vigorous denunciations of vice (Quint. *Inst.* 10.1.129 *egregius ... uitiorum insectator,* Lact. *Diu.* 5.9), S. lives up to that reputation in this vibrant description of the myriad ways in which life is squandered. The account is panoramic in scope, surveying the nooks and crannies as well as the thoroughfares of Roman life to show that, wherever one looks, evidence will be found to support the same general picture. By delivering a serious message in satirical vein (σπουδογέλοιον), S. draws in part on the ethos and certain staple features of Roman diatribe-satire, but without reproducing the affected coarseness of satirical diction; significant parallels with that tradition are noted below. The provocative message is unpalatable: the reader is induced to view other people's lives (and, by implication, one's own) from a different, decidedly (self-)critical perspective.

2.1–2 S.'s opening defence of nature against the charge of *malignitas* (1.1) conditions the catalogue of vices which follows. As 'the intelligent director of everything' (Long (1986) 164), Stoic nature is beyond human reproach, life long enough if lived in accordance with the governing *ratio* of nature. But the vices which S. goes on to describe – *auaritia, ambitio, cupiditas* etc. – are corruptions of Stoic reason and therefore unnatural passions (*SVF* III 95.14–15 'passion is an irrational movement of soul and contrary to nature'; 1.1 n. on *affectus*). S.'s list owes much to Stoic tradition; cf. e.g. D.L. 7.111 = *SVF* III 110.38–41, where Diogenes (drawing on Chrysippus' *On the passions*) specifies greed, drunkenness and lack of restraint among the Stoic πάθη. But the Senecan list is also invaded by elements familiar in

literary σχετλιασμοί (rhetorical protests) against e.g. avarice, mercantilism, sea-travel and war (nn. below on *insatiabilis ... auaritia, praeceps cupiditas*
and *quosdam ... militiae*); traces of the σχετλιασμός tradition here appropriately import 'the idea, largely due to the Cynics and Stoics, that the
downfall of man [sc. from the Golden Age] has been accomplished largely
by his own discoveries and inventions' (Smith (1913) 245–6; S. treats the
theme at length in *Ep.* 90). The contemporary aspects of S.'s list, however,
such as his satirical allusion to the *clientela*-system as 'voluntary slavery', pre-
vent the passage from being merely a reproduction of traditional Stoic and
other literary themes; he fashions a critique which is distinctively Imperial
Roman in cultural identity.

    2.1 benigne: in contrast to 1.1 *malignitate*; nature has acted both benev-
olently (*OLD* 1a) and generously (3).   **si uti scias** 'if you know how
to use it'. Not just Paulinus; indefinite second pers. subj. as at e.g. *Ep.*
12.4 *plena* [sc. *senectus*] *est uoluptatis, si illa scias uti* (general intro. p. 27 with
Summers lxiii).   **at:** suppl. Pauly to avoid the very harsh asyndeton in
the MSS.   **alium ... alium:** the first two elements in an anaphoric
sequence varied in case-ending (*alius ... alius ... alium ... alium*) before giving way to different terms (*quosdam, sunt quos, multos, plerosque, quibusdam*); the
device hurries on S.'s busy description of lives overwhelmed by preoccupation.   **insatiabilis ... auaritia:** portrayed elsewhere as a disease
of the soul (*Ep.* 56.10, 75.11, 85.10, 106.6); for φιλαργυρία (= *auaritia*) as a
νόσημα like the other πάθη, e.g. *SVF* III 25.17, 102.37–9 with Rist 26–7.
For such avarice as unnatural, *Ep.* 90.18 (primitive man, living at one with
nature, limited his wants to the extent of his needs; cf. in familiar schetliastic
nostalgia for the Golden Age e.g. *Phaed.* 527–8, [Sen.] *Oct.* 425–6, 433–4).
tenet: of passion holding sway, *C.S.* 14.1 *tanta quosdam dementia tenet*, *Ep.*
50.7, 74.11; *OLD* 10.   **in superuacuis ... sedulitas:** diligence of the
sort expended on trivial literary problems at 13.1–8; cf. *Tr.* 12.1 *ne aut in
superuacuis aut ex superuacuo laboremus*. For *operosa* of painstaking but misguided industry, 9.1, 13.1, 17.5; *operosa sedulitas* perhaps after Hor. *Ep.* 1.7.8
officiosa ... sedulitas (Mayer (1994) 158).   **alius ... madet:** for drunkenness as a vice, 7.1, 16.4, *Ir.* 2.10.7, *Ep.* 83.18; *SVF* III 102.39, 110.40. The
sapiens may occasionally drink to relax the mind, but with the same moderation which controls all his actions (*Tr.* 17.8–9); for drunkenness excites
the passions (*Ep.* 83.19–21) and, if habitual, bestializes the soul (*Ep.* 83.26).
inertia: in contrast to *sedulitas* above; contemptible because (*inter alia*) (i) a
life of contemplation and action is in accordance with nature (*Ot.* 5.1, 8),

(ii) virtue cannot be attained without active effort (*V.B.* 25.5–6), (iii) the *sapiens* is toughened by toilsome experience (*Prou.* 2.6, 5.9, *Ep.* 81.2), (iv) inertia leads to un-Stoic disquiet (*Tr.* 2.6–7). **ambitio:** listed as a vice with avarice, lust etc. at e.g. *Ep.* 47.17, 56.10, 69.4; for such φιλοδοξία as a sickness of soul (ἀρρώστημα), *SVF* III 103.4. Ambition for (political) advancement is thus a πάθος deplored by S. (*Ep.* 51.8); and because such *ambitio* is 'always contingent on others' judgement' (*ex alienis . . . suspensa*), the passionate careerist inevitably lacks Stoic self-sufficiency (*Ot.* 1.3n. on *pendemus . . . iudiciis*). **praeceps cupiditas:** clearly pejorative, as at Cic. *Phil.* 5.50 *cupiditatem dominandi praecipitem et lubricam.* The Stoic view of ἐπιθυμία (= *cupiditas*) as an 'irrational stretching' (*SVF* III 95.20 ἄλογος ὄρεξις, 115.35) coincides with the schetliastic rejection of mercantilism and seafaring in literary depictions of the Golden Age (*Ep.* 90.24, *Med.* 318–28, *Phaed.* 530–1; so already e.g. Tib. 1.3.37–40, 2.3.39, Ov. *Am.* 3.8.43–4, 49–50). **circa . . . maria:** the merchant's travels are as boundless as his (unnatural) desire; *Ep.* 39.5 *necesse est . . . in immensum exeat cupiditas quae naturalem modum transilit.* **quosdam . . . militiae** 'passion for active service torments some men'. The *sapiens* is immune to any such torture (*Ep.* 119.2 *non torqueberis*); *cupido militiae* typifies human degeneration in S. (*Ep.* 95.30–1, *N.Q.* 5.18.5–12) and is regularly set in contrast to the natural peace of the Golden Age (*Phaed.* 533–5, 544–52, [Sen.] *Oct.* 400–2, 418, 425; so already Tib. 1.3.47–8, 1.10.7–10, Ov. *Am.* 3.8.48, *M.* 1.98–100, 142–4). **numquam non:** stronger than *semper*, and sparingly used by S. for special emphasis (*N.Q.* 1.3.11, 1.8.3, *Ep.* 11.4). **alienis periculis:** dat. with *intentos* ('bent upon inflicting dangers on others'). **suis:** abl. with *anxios* ('worried by their own dangers', and so far from Stoic in their nervous excitement). **sunt quos . . . consumat:** relative clause of tendency (G–L §631.2). **ingratus . . . cultus** 'thankless attendance upon the great' (Basore) in performance of the daily *salutatio* etc.; with satirical colour (for the trials and tribulations of the *cliens*, e.g. Juv. 1.95–146, 3.182–9, 5 *passim* etc.). **uoluntaria seruitute:** *Ep.* 47.17 *nulla seruitus turpior est quam uoluntaria*; in Stoic terms, the servile client is no more his own master than the voluntary slave to passion.

2.2 affectatio 'wishing they had other people's luck'; more boldly construed as 'pursuit of others' wealth' (*OLD fortuna* 12), a possible allusion to legacy-hunting, a commonplace in Roman satire (e.g. Hor. *S.* 2.5, Petr. 116.6–9, Juv. 4.18–19, 5.132–45, 12.93–130). Cf. *affecto* applied to the hunt at *C.S.* 9.2 *magno labore affectata hereditas*, Quint. *Decl.* 342

p. 314.14 Sh. B.   **querella:** Madvig's conjecture (II 397), i.e. 'complaining about their luck'; for the obj. gen., *Ben.* 7.29.1 *querella amissi beneficii*. By contrast the *sapiens*, content with his lot (*V.B.* 6.2, *Ep.* 45.9), craves nothing.   **detinuit** 'keeps busy'; gnomic perf., as often in S. (Bourgery (1922) 328–9); here *uariatio* (continued by *iactauit*) after a succession of verbs in the present.   **plerosque . . . deprendunt:** those whose aims in life are constantly shifting are juxtaposed with those who have no clear aims of any sort. Both lack Stoic constancy of purpose; *Ot.* 1.2nn., *Ep.* 3.5, *Tr.* 2.6. The topos of restless boredom/discontent with one's lot in life (μεμψιμοιρία) is a commonplace in ancient moralizing (N–H on Hor. *C.* 1.1.17) and recurrent in Roman diatribe-satire; e.g. Lucr. *D.R.N.* 3.1053–75 with Kenney (1971) 238, Hor. *S.* 1.3.11–17 (quoted by S. at *Ep.* 120.20), Pers. 3.58–62.
plerosque: not 'most people' (the familiar usage in all periods; *OLD* 1–3), but '(very) many' (*OLD* 4) as at 3.5, 7.6, 20.4 and often in Silver Latin.
uaga . . . leuitas: in Stoic terms a vice (*Tr.* 14.1 *leuitas, inimicissimum quieti uitium, Ep.* 13.16).   **per:** causal ('by reason of', *OLD* 13a) or instrumental ('through the agency of', 15a).   **quibusdam nihil . . . placet:** more extreme than (mere) *sibi displicens leuitas*.   **quo . . . derigant** 'to which end they may direct their course' rather than 'by which . . .' (Basore); so too perhaps *Ep.* 71.3 *errant consilia nostra, quia non habent quo derigantur, Ep.* 78.8.   **marcentes oscitantesque:** closely paralleled at *Tr.* 2.6; Lucr. *D.R.N.* 3.1065 *oscitat extemplo, tetigit cum limina uillae* (restless boredom at home), Pers. 3.58–9 *laxum . . . caput . . . | oscitat hesternum* ('yawns off yesterday').   **deprendunt:** death 'takes them by surprise' (*OLD* 5a); *rapiunt* is more usual with *fata* (Liv. 26.29.9, Ov. *Am.* 3.9.35, Luc. 9.825), but rhythm may influence S.'s choice of verb as *deprendunt* yields a favourite clausula (cretic + spondee).   **quod . . . uiuimus:** *Ot.* 1.4n. on *quod . . . premimus.*
maximum poetarum: the identity of the poet is much disputed. S. refers to Virgil as *maximus uates* at 9.2, to Homer as *poetarum Graecorum maximus* at *Ep.* 63.2 (cf. 58.17), but no trace of the dictum '*exigua . . . uiuimus*', which does not scan, is to be found in either. Perhaps S. mistakenly attributes another's saying to one of the two (Reynolds 240); but the saying has also been attributed to Simonides, Euripides, Menander and Ennius (Setaioli (1988) 474–82 for bibliography and a survey of opinion). But whatever S.'s source, his appeal to 'the greatest of poets' is designed to lend special weight to a relatively simple proposition ('much of life is wasted').   **more oraculi:** i.e. as if a divine utterance, in reference to poets already a Lucretian idea (*D.R.N.* 1.731); *Ep.* 108.26 *inhaereat istud animo et tamquam missum oraculo placeat*

(S. goes on to quote Virg. *G.* 3.66–7; at *Breu.* 9.2 Virgil is *uelut diuino ore instinctus*). Claudius is similarly credited with oracular utterance at *Pol.* 14.2; cf. of Cato *Ep.* 94.27, Sen. *Contr.* 1 *praef.* 9, Plin. *N.H.* 7.171. But the words *'exigua . . . uiuimus'* are also oracle-like in their riddling wordplay (next n.). **'exigua . . . uiuimus'** 'scant is the part of life in which we *really* live'; *Ep.* 99.11 *intelleges etiam in longissima uita minimum esse quod uiuitur.*   **quidem:** equivalent to γε (Solodow (1978) 106), here emphasizing *ceterum* (adj.) rather than qualifying the previous sentence (so rightly Duff 98); i.e. 'as for all the rest of existence (*ceterum . . . spatium*), that is not "living" but merely time'.

2.3 S. delves more deeply into the vices underlying his description thus far of squandered lives.   **urgent . . . sinunt:** vice assails mankind in hostile fashion; *OLD urgeo* 5a, *circumsto* 2a. For *resurgo* of rising to fight on, *Ep.* 13.2 (of a wrestler), and (fig.) *Ir.* 1.8.3 *quomodo . . . ratio occupata et oppressa uitiis resurget, quae irae cessit? urgent* and *circumstant* emphatic by early position; wordplay (*urgent . . . nec resurgere . . .*) conveys the relentlessness of attack as *uitia* overwhelm *uitam.*   **dispectum** 'clear discernment', as at *Ir.* 1.1.2 *dispectum aequi uerique*, 2.10.1, *Ep.* 94.36, 109.16; not found before S. and Pliny (*N.H.* 34.7).   **attollere oculos:** often in a context of failure to raise one's eyes in circumstances of surrender, shame, despair *uel sim.*; e.g. *Ben.* 1.3.1, Virg. *Aen.* 4.688, Ov. *M.* 2.448, 6.605–6 (*TLL* II 1149.62–78). **mersos et . . . infixos premunt:** MSS *immersos* and *emersos*, but *mersos* is supported by *C.S.* 8.3 *damna et dolores . . . quae sapientem . . . non mergunt* (cf. *Ep.* 85.12); for the pples. with *oculos*, *OLD mergo* 9, *infigo* 5.   **recurrere ad se** 'to return to their true selves' (Basore), free from all disturbance. A common emphasis in middle and later Stoicism (Grilli (1953) 149–56 with Traina (1987) 19–20); *Tr.* 14.2 *animus ab omnibus externis in se reuocandus est . . .*, *Ep.* 7.8, 9.16, 25.6 (where S. renders a similar Epicurean maxim (= fr. 209 Us.)).   **si . . . contigit:** in contrast to that permanent state of inner repose (*V.B.* 4.5 *quies mentis in tuto collocatae*) which hardly 'befalls' the *sapiens* by chance.   **uelut . . . uolutatio est:** *Tr.* 2.1 *sicut est quidam tremor etiam tranquilli maris, utique cum ex tempestate requieuit* (minor repercussions after grave illness are likened to the ripples of the sea).   **quoque** 'even' (*OLD* 4a), qualifying *post uentum.*   **uolutatio:** of waves at *Prou.* 1.4, but more often in S. of restlessness of mind (e.g. *Tr.* 2.10, *Ep.* 48.8, 71.27, 101.9); given the latter connotation, the word anticipates the explicit metaphor in *fluctuantur* (next n.).   **fluctuantur:** sc. *homines*, but the verb also embraces *profundum mare* (conjectured by Gertz (1874) 148); if *profundo mari* is read with the MSS (surely not abl. as claimed by Traina 5 but dat.

after *contigit*), the elegant fusion of lit. and fig. meanings is lost. For the fig. application of the verb, e.g. 5.1, *Ot.* 1.2n., *Pol.* 9.6, *Ep.* 4.5, 52.1.   **otium:** only here in S. with *a* + abl., denoting 'relaxation from desires'; cf. Hor. *Epod.* 17.24 *nullum a labore me reclinat otium* with Mankin (1995) 279.   **est:** so Reynolds in remedy of the MSS; *stat* Madvig II 397 ('is fixed', 'is calm'; 1.2 *homini . . . terminum stare*, *Ep.* 101.7 *stat . . . terminus nobis*), but the verb is unparalleled with *otium*, *est* more straightforward, a favourite clausula (double cretic) also resulting (for the effects on clausulae of monosyllabic forms of *sum* in terminal position, Bornecque (1907) 226–8).

2.4 S. allows no exceptions to the general rule: the prosperous, like the less fortunate, scarcely live life to the full.   **istis:** a strong demonstrative, here denoting one group as opposed to another (*illos* below; the two pronouns in similar combination at *Ep.* 47.4, 95.36, 119.11); perhaps also dismissive in tone (*OLD* 5b) given what follows (*quorum . . . sunt*).   **in confesso . . . sunt** 'are unquestioned'; *Ot.* 3.1 n.   **aspice:** often used by S. to introduce an idea which is then qualified or developed in a separate construction (*bonis . . . offocantur*); so e.g. *Helu.* 6.7, *Ep.* 51.11, 56.7, 114.26.   **concurritur** 'people flock to . . .'; for the impersonal use, rare in S. but well suited to his economical style, *Ep.* 36.2, 98.9.   **offocantur** 'are choked' by their own blessings, a striking, apparently novel image. The verb is unknown before S., as is *effocantur* (also in the MSS and preferred by some editors); but a tentative argument in favour of *off-* is its greater currency in later Latin.   **quam multis:** the start of an anaphoric sequence of four exclamations which quicken the narrative pace, enlivening S.'s tone with renewed vigour; *quam multis . . . -orum . . . -i . . . -is* because *quot* cannot stand independently as a noun (Krebs–Schmalz II 470).   **graues:** i.e. because of the attention which wealth draws to itself (*Ep.* 119.11 *excaecant populum et in se conuertunt opes*).   **quam multorum . . . educit!:** for the exhausting demands made on the gifted orator's talent and time cf. 7.6, 8 below. **cotidiana . . . occupatio** 'daily preoccupation with' (+ gen., *Ep.* 15.2 *occupatio exercendi lacertos*, which supports Gertz's conjecture of the noun for MSS *spatio*).   **ostentandi:** for the hint of ostentatious self-display, *Prou.* 4.4 *militares uiri gloriantur uulneribus, laeti . . . sanguinem ostentant*, *Helu.* 10.10, *Ep.* 87.41.   **sanguinem educit** 'drains the blood', thereby enfeebling the orator; the image is boldly contrived from *educo* used of 'drawing off' liquids (Vitr. 2.10.2 *sol . . . ex arboribus educit umores*; *OLD* 5a).   **pallent:** for pallor associated with enervating pleasure, *V.B.* 7.3 *uoluptatem . . . pallidam*, *Ben.* 4.13.1.   **nihil liberi** 'no freedom' from besieging clients. For the phrase,

Ep. 36.5; the use of *nihil* with a defining gen. of adj. goes back to comedy (*OLD* 3b).   **circumfusus** 'spread around' (*Ep.* 59.15 *circumfusa clientium turba*), as if like a besieging army (*OLD circumfundo* 6).   **populus** 'multitude' (*OLD* 4a); S. elsewhere prefers the phrase *turba clientium* (*Marc.* 10.1, *Ep.* 59.15, 68.11, 76.12).   **istos:** that cross-section of Roman society to be found in the law-courts.   **pererra** 'survey', a nuance found only here in S.; the rare usage is not found before Virgil (*Aen.* 4.363, 5.441–2, 11.766–7). **hic . . . iudicat:** in legal terminology *aduocat* refers to a given party's summoning of counsel to plead the case in hand (*TLL* I 894.22–34), *adest* to the counsel (*aduocatus*) who answers the call (*TLL* II 923.30–42), *periclitatur* to the defendant standing trial (*OLD* 5a). The phrase *ille defendit* suggests that the advocate just summoned (*hic . . . adest*) acts for the plaintiff before the presiding official (*ille iudicat*). The contrasting enumerators *hic . . . ille* (*OLD hic¹* 7) are a variation on *alius . . . alius* etc. in 2.1.   **nemo . . . uindicat** 'no one asserts his claim to himself' (Basore), a play on the technical meaning of the verb in legal contexts (*OLD* 1a 'to claim as one's own what is in the possession of another'); the opposite of Stoic freedom at *Ep.* 33.4 *non sumus* [sc. *Stoici*] *sub rege: sibi quisque se uindicat* (cf. *Ep.* 1.1, 113.23).   **in alium consumitur** 'is wasted on/for another'; the verb is here fig. (*TLL* IV 608.60–9), lit. (= *perdere, delere*) at e.g. *Ep.* 24.18 *mors nos . . . consumit*; for the force of *in*, *OLD* 10, 11a.   **interroga . . . uidebis:** S. often uses an imperative in place of a conditional protasis with *si* when the notional apodosis takes a fut. verb (cf. n. on *aspice* above); in Latin of all periods (K–S II 165). So e.g. *Ep.* 4.8, 13.17, 15.7; the two clauses are connected at e.g. *Ep.* 13.16 *considera quid uox ista significet . . . et intelleges . . .* , 99.11, 110.3. **istis . . . ediscuntur:** i.e. influential citizens whose names are studiously memorized (for greeting) by their inferiors.   **his . . . dinosci . . . notis** '[to be] known apart by the following marks'; examples of the verb with abl. of means are rare and post-Augustan (*TLL* V 1.1219.50–5).   **illos** refers back to *istis*: the distinctions governing the usage of demonstrative pronouns in Classical Latin are less rigidly enforced in the Silver period (Duff 100 with Bourgery (1922) 380).   **ille . . . illius:** A cultivates B (*illius*), B (*hic*) cultivates C (*illius*).   **suus nemo est:** the idiom extends back to comedy (*OLD suus* 4b); it here suggests the opposite of Stoic self-mastery as portrayed at e.g. *Ep.* 62.1 *ubicumque sum, ibi meus sum*, 75.18 *inaestimabile bonum est suum fieri* (further Traina (1987) 12–13).

2.5 In satirical climax to the chapter, a biting portrayal of a *cliens* whose frustrations command little sympathy.

dementissima ... indignatio est: for the insult of being denied an audience, *C.S.* 10.2 *ille me hodie non admisit, cum alios admitteret* (the reported words of a disgruntled caller). The *sapiens* is immune to this or any other kind of insult (*C.S.* 2.1 *nullam ... sapientem nec iniuriam accipere nec contumeliam posse,* 10.1–3, *Ben.* 2.35.2; *SVF* III 152.28–9).   **fastidio:** haughtiness (*OLD* 4a) mingled with disdain (4b).   **ipsis ... uolentibus:** dat. dependent on *uacauerint* ('they did not have time for ...'). *ipsis,* for *sibi,* circumvents the technical ambiguity of the reflexive; but S. (like earlier writers) occasionally uses *ipse* where the reflexive could have served, esp. in oratio obliqua (e.g. 20.1, *Ep.* 6.3, 21.9, *N.Q.* 4B.7.1; Setaioli (1981a) 25).   **audet ... uacat?:** the rhetorical question indignantly answers the *indignatio* of the disappointed caller.   **alterius:** *Ot.* 4.1n. **sibi ... uacat?:** contrast the (Stoic) time to oneself indulged by S. in exile (*Helu.* 20.1 *animus omnis occupationis expers operibus suis uacat*) and urged at *N.Q.* 3 *praef.* 2 *sibi totus animus uacet*; he lives long who devotes to himself whatever time he has (cf. 7.5).   **ille ... ille ... ille:** for the anaphoric tricolon, sparingly used by S., e.g. *Ep.* 7.11 *satis sunt ... satis est ... satis est,* 94.63, 97.11; the effect here is to set up the emphatic contrast, activated by *tu* below, between the great man's attention to his client and the client's inattention to himself.   **tamen:** despite the rebuff described above, the client is not always so treated.   **quisquis es** 'whoever you are' in terms of lowly obscurity.   **respexit:** for the look of condescension, Juv. 3.184–5 *quid das ...* | *ut te respiciat ... Veiiento ... ?*   **aures ... demisit:** unparalleled in the sense of 'deigned to listen to', the phrase conveys the lit. condescension of the gesture (*OLD demitto* 10c); *demitto aures* usually describes ears made or allowed to sag (Hor. *S.* 1.9.20, *C.* 2.13.34–5, Virg. *G.* 3.500, Stat. *Theb.* 11.745).   **ad latus suum:** the client is accepted as a companion (*OLD latus*² 4a).   **non ... non:** emphatic by position; whereas the great man deigned to look (*respexit*) and to listen (*aures ... demisit*), the client does neither in respect to himself.   **non inspicere te:** contrast the introspection urged at *Tr.* 6.1 *inspicere ... debebimus ... nosmet ipsos,* where S. echoes the middle Stoic doctrine that one's choice of duties should be contingent on appraisal of one's capacities (*Ot.* 3.3n. on *si parum ... res publica*). For variations on *inspicere te* (*se excutere/ scrutari/ obseruare*), *Ben.* 7.28.3, *Ep.* 16.2, 20.3, 65.15, 118.2.   **dignatus es:** *dignor* + inf., post-Augustan in prose, only twice in S. (cf. *Helu.* 10.3).   **non ... quod** 'And so there is no reason to ...' (*quod* lit. = 'in respect of what ...'). *non est quod* + subjunctive, common in

S., is accompanied by *itaque* in third position at e.g. 7.10, *C.S.* 6.2, *Marc.* 21.6, *Ep.* 71.17 (but first position at 7.5, *Pol.* 8.2, *Ep.* 36.2). From Livy onwards *itaque* is regularly placed second or later in its sentence (*OLD*; K–S II 130).   **ista:** here in its traditional sense as demonstrative of the second person ('those services of yours', e.g. the *salutatio*); cf. 2.4n. **imputes:** mostly post-Augustan in the sense of 'claim credit for' (the client expects a return for his services); *Ep.* 79.4 *non est autem quod istam curam imputes mihi* (i.e. 'you've no right to expect me to be grateful for . . .') with Summers 272 and *OLD* 3a, adding e.g. *Tr.* 7.1, *Ep.* 73.2, *Ben.* 3.18.1, 3.31.4. **non . . . poteras:** an elegant construction, with partial chiasmus (*non esse cum alio . . . tecum esse non*) and the balancing of isosyllabic verbs (*uolebas, poteras*), rounds off the period and aptly concludes the chapter; for the crowning insinuation is that the *occupati* busy themselves only to escape themselves (cf. Lucr. *D.R.N.* 3.1068 *hoc se quisque modo fugit* with Kenney (1971) 240–1).   **tecum esse non poteras:** contrast the self-sufficiency of the *sapiens* (*Ep.* 9.16 *in se reconditur, secum est*).

3 *Accounting for time*

Four stages of argument: (i) demonstration by analogy that to waste time is folly: material possessions are jealously guarded, but time, the most precious possession of all, is squandered (3.1); (ii) in an imaginary address to a centenarian (3.2–3), estimation (*computatio*) of how much time has been wasted in a long life: by adopting the tones of 'everyday' speech, with an ordinary cast of characters (money-lender, mistress etc.) and traces of colloquial diction, S. addresses 'the common man' in appropriate style; (iii) taking stock (3.4): too few people are aware of their own mortality and of the preciousness of the time they have; (iv) illustration of the point (3.5): to plan to begin living the contemplative life only in retirement is folly; death is no respecter of advanced planning.

S. appeals above all for self-conscious reflection on the value of time and the way we use it. His approach is brazenly provocative: how many ordinary people, ancient or modern, could realistically hope to be any more free of life's time-consuming distractions than the centenarian addressed in 3.2–3? How many are in a position jealously to guard their own time in the everyday running of busy lives? The analogy drawn between time and material property in (i) also presupposes that time given to, or allowed to be 'invaded' by, others is necessarily squandered (like wasted wealth); but

S. fails to account either for the very real benefits (e.g. personal satisfaction) which may induce a person ostensibly to 'waste' time on others, or for the duties which *force* so many (e.g. devoted parents) to divide their precious time. And in (ii), it is contrary to human experience to suppose that every moment of life can be made to yield a measurable profit like an investment. A wrong turning in life, a fallow period, a bout of listlessness or depression can be seen in the longer perspective to have contributed to the depth and quality of experience; but acc. to the Senecan *computatio* of 'wasted time', the gathering of a variety of experiences – some trivial in themselves – into a rich harvest of mature reflection on life is impossible. But even as S. provokes such objections, each (dubious) argument contributes to an impressive sequence of analogy, illustration and point which challenges the reader to step back from the ordinary involvements of life and to take stock of its general course and priorities in the broader context of one's existence; it is this wider perspective which the old man (3.2–3) and the ambitious planner (3.5) signally lack.

3.1 Omnia . . . mirabuntur: S. addresses the general condition of folly (*caligo*) exemplified in the previous chapter. The sentence is not strictly part of a developing argument, but designed to fortify his already confident position. By appeal to the consensus of all the brilliant intellects who ever lived, he not only exaggerates his own 'enlightened' sense of wonder at such folly; he also defies anyone to fly in the face of such influential opinion. **in . . . consentiant** 'agree upon this one point', i.e. the folly of squandering life; with *in* + acc. (post-Augustan), *Ben.* 4.4.2.   **caliginem:** the darkness of folly, a recurrent metaphor in S. (13.7, *Ir.* 2.10.1, 3.27.2, *Helu.* 12.3) and already in Cicero (*Tusc.* 1.64 *ab animo tamquam ab oculis caliginem dispulit* [sc. *philosophia*]; cf. Lucr. *D.R.N.* 1.146 *terrorem animi tenebrasque*); the enlightened (*fulserunt*) see into the darkness.   **praedia . . . inducunt:** the first of three doubtful analogies (3 intro.) in which S. foreshadows the argument developed at 8.1: since time is incorporeal its true value is unappreciated, unlike that of material objects. Cf. D. Chr. *Or.* 20.4–6: men are pained by loss of money but not of time; they take care to conserve their property but are careless accountants of time.   **a nullo:** in Classical and later Latin the adj. is often used as a noun in place of the gen. and the abl. (sometimes also the dat., rarely the acc.) of *nemo* (*OLD nullus* 2a; Krebs–Schmalz II 140–1 *nemo*); more exceptional is S.'s use of the nom. adj. as a noun (*Pol.* 14.2 with Duff 209, *Ep.* 7.11).   **exigua . . . finium** 'a trivial

dispute about the limit of their lands'.   **ad lapides ... discurrunt:**
for the frenzied rush to arms, *Ir.* 3.2.3 *ad arma protinus ignesque discursum est.*
discurrunt: in uitam: adversative asyndeton strongly opposes the two
halves of the analogy; so in the two following illustrations (*nemo ... distribuit!*;
astricti ... auaritia est).   **incedere** 'trespass upon', forging the analogy between lit. and fig. territories (*praedia* and *uitam*).   **immo uero:** *Ot.* 4.2n.
ipsi ... inducunt: S. extends the metaphor, initiated by *incedere*, of life's
'territory': *possessor* can refer to 'land-holder' (*OLD* 1 a), *induco* to his installa-
tion in ownership or possession (8a).   **nemo ... uelit:** relative clause of
tendency; G–L §631.2.   **quam multis:** 2.4n.   **distribuit:** gnomic
perf. (2.2n. on *detinuit*).   **astricti** 'parsimonious' (*Ep.* 123.13 *uictus*
astrictior), in contrast to *profusissimi* below.   **simul** presupposes 'but'
(asyndeton); sometimes without *atque/ac* in Classical Latin (*OLD* 10, 11),
the conjunction is always unaccompanied in S.   **ad ... uentum est**
'it is a question of ...'; *Ep.* 66.19, 87.5, *N.Q.* 4B.11.5.   **in eo ... est** 'in
the only case in which it is right to be miserly'. For this connotation of *auari-*
tia, *Ir.* 1.21.2, *N.Q.* 1 *praef.* 6 (*Ot.* 5.7n. on *auarissime*); for *auaritia* generally as
a Stoic vice, 2.1n.

3.2 Directly addressing a centenarian, S. conducts an audit of time
wasted over the years; but for radical weaknesses in his strategy, 3 intro.
For his use of *sermocinatio*, *Ot.* 1.4n. on *Dices mihi*; elements of the colloquial
style and tone affected by S. in this 'everyday' address are noted below. La
Penna (1956) 192–5 relates the passage to (*inter alia*) Hor. *Ep.* 1.1.20–6 and
D. Chr. *Or.* 20.4–6 to suggest a shared topos; but S. may also be influenced
by Lucretius' spirited portrayal of Nature haranguing an old man, ailing
but reluctant to die, at *D.R.N.* 3.952–62.   **itaque:** 2.5n on *non ... quod.*
comprendere: aggressive in connotation ('to seize upon'), setting the tone
for the address which follows.   **ad ultimum:** the neut. adj. is already
used as a noun by Livy (e.g. 3.17.7 *ultimum orationis*); cf. 1.1 *in exiguum aeui.*
centesimus ... annus: centenarians were rare in antiquity. Lucian assembles famous examples, Greek and Roman and ranging from the plausible to the fantastic, in his Μακρόβιοι (1 73–81 Macleod); Stoics figure
prominently in his list of enduring philosophers (18–21; Zeno apparently
starved himself to death at 98, Cleanthes at 99).   **tibi ... premitur:**
while old age presses hard on most (*N.Q.* 3 *praef.* 2 *premit a tergo senectus*,
Ep. 108.28), S.'s addressee achieves an ironic reversal by 'pressing hard'
on his hundredth year (and more). For dat. of agent, *Ot.* 3.4n. on *quietis-*
simis.   **agedum:** with an imperative (*reuoca*), colloquial (*OLD ago* 24)

in keeping with the informal tone of S.'s address.   **computationem** 'audit'. First attested in Varro (*L.* 6.63), the word resurfaces only in S. (*Ben.* 4.11.2, 7.10.4, *N.Q.* 4A.2.9) and later prose.   **reuoca:** (i) 'recall your life' (*Helu.* 2.2 *obliterata mala reuocare*), and (ii) 'submit it to an audit' (*OLD* 19a).   **duc ... discursatio:** the anaphoric repetition of *quantum*, used seven times with the governing verb (*abstulerit*) suitably placed in the middle of the sequence, represents the *computatio* in action.   **duc** 'calculate', a technical nuance (*OLD* 29a) to commence the audit.   **isto:** 2.5n.   **rex** 'patron', a colloquial usage beginning in comedy (*OLD* 8); *Ir.* 3.43.1 *quid regi, quid clienti tuo irasceris?*.   **lis uxoria ... discursatio:** after an initial cast of four characters (money-lender, mistress, patron, client), S. varies the sequence with three abstract nouns, the last two of them linked (for ringing effect) by homoeoteleuton (*-tio*).   **lis uxoria** 'arguing with your wife'; a popular dilution, first in comedy, of the legal term (*OLD lis* 2).   **coercitio:** punishment (*OLD* 2), not general repression. **discursatio:** only here in S., unattested before him and rare afterwards; if not a neologism (Bourgery (1922) 257), then perhaps drawn from ordinary usage (Summers xlvi–xlix). Cf. 3.1 *discurrunt*, 12.5, 14.3 *per officia discursant* (where the verb is also unprecedented).   **adice ... adice:** after sevenfold anaphora, a brisk pairing which is both idiomatic ('consider also'; *OLD* 11) and topical ('add to your calculations').   **morbos ... fecimus:** diseases caused 'artificially', i.e. through one's own fault; for *manu* (opp. *natura*), *Ir.* 2.9.3 *pestilentiam manu factam*, *Ep.* 58.32 (of suicide), 115.2 (of hairstyle). For a florid description of illnesses 'unnaturally' induced by high living, *Ep.* 95.14–29.   **adice et ... iacuit** 'add, too, the time which has lain idle'.   **uidebis ... numeras:** the result of the audit, crisply delivered in a paradoxical *sententia*. For the construction (apodosis after the notional protasis supplied by *duc ... adice ... adice*), 2.4n. on *interroga ... uidebis*.

3.3 repete ... intelleges ... mori: structurally similar to the previous period but with a new emphasis: after estimating the amount of time lost or snatched away over the years, S. now invites his addressee to review his (mis-)management of time. The alliterative sequence of indirect questions (*quando ... quotus ... quando* etc.), its intense progress and the profusion of second person pronouns (*tecum ... tibi ... tibi* etc.) make the passage vigorously confrontational in tone; S. *forces* introspection on his addressee.   **quando:** i.e. 'how rarely'.   **certus consilii** 'resolute of purpose'. The construction, first found in Virgil (*Aen.* 4.554 *iam certus eundi*), is post-Augustan in prose (K–S 1 437–8); *Ep.* 45.9 (the Stoic *beatus* is *certus iudicii*).   **quotus ... dies:** lit. 'what fraction of the total is each day that ... ', i.e. 'how few days'.   **cesserit** 'turned out'. The MSS have *recesserit* ('passed away'; *Thy.* 892 *dies recessit*): Castiglioni's conjecture, supported by impressive parallels (*Ir.* 3.6.5 *contra quam proposuerat aliqua cesserunt, V.B.* 25.3 *omnes mihi ex uoto dies cedant*), improves the sense. **usus tui** 'being at your own disposal', with control over your time; unlike the *senex*, the *sapiens* never lacks such control (*Ep.* 73.10 *arbitrium sui temporis*).   **in statu ... intrepidus:** the two clauses complement each other, for the face which 'wears its natural expression' reflects inner calm (*Cl.* 2.5.5 *eandem semper faciem seruabit* [sc. *sapiens*], *placidam, inconcussam*); but the *senex*, so rarely free from anxiety (*intrepidus*), inevitably reveals as much in his countenance (*Ir.* 1.1.7 *neque ... ulla uehementior intrat* [sc. *mentem*] *agitatio quae nihil moueat in uultu*).   **facti operis:** partitive gen. dependent on *quid*.   **diripuerint** 'have plundered', a rare image (*OLD* 4) here for exaggerating effect.   **uanus ... conuersatio:** in Stoic terms, a catalogue of vices. The adjs. are not otiose, since Stoics place both *uoluptas* (cf. *laetitia*) and *dolor* among the indifferents (i.e. intrinsically neither good nor bad; Gell. *N.A.* 12.5.4, 12.5.7 *uoluptas quoque et dolor ... et in mediis relicta et neque in bonis neque in malis iudicata sunt*); the folly (ἀφροσύνη) suggested by the accompanying adjs. is ἐν ταῖς πρώταις [sc. κακίαις] ('in the first rank of vices', *SVF* III 65.18–19). The *sapiens* no more succumbs to grief or desire than to any other πάθος/ *affectus*; he alone knows true and lasting joy (*Ep.* 72.8 *laetitia fruitur maxima, continua, sua*), which is anything but frivolous (*stulta*; *Ep.* 23.4 *uerum gaudium res seuera est*); and his self-sufficiency insulates him from *blanda conuersatio*, i.e. 'keeping company with those you flatter / with those who flatter you' (Duff 103 for the possible ambiguity of *blanda*). **de tuo:** sc. *tempore*, but S. perhaps plays on a financial idiom as part of the audit ('from your own store'; *Ben.* 1.9.1 *quia de tuo non possum, de meo dabo*, 7.4.1, *Ep.* 8.7, 10).   **immaturum** 'before your time'.

3.4 The audit over, S. takes stock.   **quid ... in causa?** 'What, then, is the cause of this [sc. the squandering of life]?'; *Ot.* 1.5n. S. rarely uses post-Augustan *in causa* (*Helu.* 7.8, *Ep.* 56.8, 116.8, *N.Q.* 6.20.1).   **tamquam ... sit:** by shifting to the second person plur. (*uiuitis ... uobis ... uestra* etc.), S. moves from the particular to the general, provocatively challenging his readers with the charge that they too fail to appreciate the value of time.   **uicturi uiuitis:** S. frequently uses the fut. pple in wordplay, e.g. *Ben.* 1.9.2 *eadem facturi odere facientem, Ep.* 7.4, 79.6. The fut. pple often serves, as here, to depict the precariousness of the present (Traina (1987) 28, citing e.g. *Prou.* 5.7 *accipimus peritura perituri, Ep.* 91.12; Westman (1961) 190). **fragilitas:** of human frailty (common; *OLD* 2), e.g. *Ben.* 6.3.2, *Ep.* 15.11, 101.1. **obseruatis** 'keep a careful eye on'. **ex pleno et abundanti:** normally adverbial phrases (*OLD plenus* 5b, *abundans* 3b), but here a noun ('source') must be supplied. **perditis:** sc. *tempus.* **cum interim ... ultimus sit:** the subjunctive is potential ('may be your last'), not dictated by the *cum interim* construction, which takes the indicative (K–S II 341). For S.'s own Stoic recognition that each day may be his last, *Ep.* 12.8, 61.1 *id ago ut mihi instar totius uitae dies sit ...*, 93.6, 101.7; the *sapiens* who lives this *perfectam uitam* is free from anxiety about each tomorrow (cf. 7.9). **donatur** 'is given over to'. **tamquam mortales:** inconsistent with *tamquam semper uicturi* above, but not 'certainly irrelevant' (Duff 104) or designed only to give balanced arrangement to the *sententia*; the inconsistency reproduces the pendulum-like swings in human posturing and self-delusion, the oscillations arising from images of ourselves which are themselves inconsistent. **immortales:** *Ot.* 5.7n. **concupiscitis** stresses ardent desire.

3.5 audies ... dicentes: *Ot.* 1.4n. on *Dices mihi.* **plerosque:** 2.2n. **otium:** not philosophical withdrawal of the sort urged on Paulinus at 18.1–19.2 below, but (pending sixty) only partial retirement from active life, presumably incl. exemption from military service (20.4n. on *lex ... non legit*). **sexagesimus ... dimittet:** the speaker ambitiously plans ahead. For retirement at sixty, Juv. 14.197 with Courtney. S. reports at 20.4 that after sixty attendance at the Senate was not compulsory; the elder Sen. specifies sixty-five (*Contr.* 1.8.4), prompting speculation that Claudius lowered the age (Talbert (1984) 152–3). **officiis** 'official duties' (*OLD* 5b) in professional life, different from the client's *officia* in 2.5. **et:** often used to introduce an indignant question (*OLD* 15a); e.g. *Ep.* 27.8 *et quomodo possum?*, 82.24. **tandem** 'may I ask?', expressing impatience (frequently in questions; *OLD* 1b). **quem ... praedem accipis?** 'what guarantee do you have?' The noun, only here in S., lit. = 'guarantor'; for combination with the verb, Liv. 5.55.3 *praedibus acceptis*, Curt. 5.4.13. **ista** 'your planned course'; 2.5n. **disponis:** cf. 1.4 *bene disponenti.* **reliquias** 'remnants', as at *Ep.* 102.2 *reliquias aetatis infractae.* **bonae menti:** common in S., denoting wisdom acquired through philosophy; e.g. *Ep.* 17.1 *ad bonam mentem ... tende*, 23.1, 27.8, 53.9. **quod ... possit?:** i.e. time which, after retirement, cannot be applied to any business (*rem*). **tunc ... est:** *Ep.* 23.11 *quidam uero tunc*

incipiunt [sc. *uiuere*] *cum desinendum est.*   **uiuere** '*really* to live'; 2.2n. on
'*exigua . . . uiuimus*'.   **quae tam stulta . . . ?:** cf. *Ep.* 82.4 *quae tam emu-
nita . . . uitae quies . . . ?*, *Tro.* 981–2, 1057–8, interrogative in all three cases.
Some editors (e.g. Duff, Reynolds) print the sentence as an exclamation,
but on the punctuation of Luc. 1.8 Housman (1927) vi rules that '*quae tanta
licentia!* is not Latin: the exclamatory *quis* or *qui* cannot consist with *tantus*'
(Housman prints line 8 as a question). If tentatively applied to S.'s use
of *tam* + adj., Housman's ruling supports the interrogative reading here
(there are no compelling parallels in S. or elsewhere to defend the exclamatory reading).   **tam stulta . . . consilia:** awareness of one's mortality
places precious value on the time one has; *Ir.* 3.42.2 (on how anger can be
controlled) *nec ulla res magis proderit quam cogitatio mortalitatis* (life too short to be
wasted on anger).   **inde . . . quo . . . perduxerunt?** 'from that point,
to which few have lived' (lit. 'have protracted life', emphasizing remoteness
of age).

4–6 Three exempla

4.1 Thus far S. has concentrated primarily on 'normal' lives, appealing for
a sense of perspective on time, its value and how it is used in the everyday run of things. He now turns to the lives of the more exalted – men of
high position who, the argument goes, crave relief (*otium*) from the stresses
of their responsibilities. S. draws on familiar moralizing themes to portray the precariousness of high office (nn. on *si tuto liceat* and *in se . . . ruit*).
The passage is gnomic in general appeal, but with a warning of immediate relevance to Paulinus: to remain in office when honourable retirement
is apparently possible (as in Paulinus' case; cf. 18.1–2, 19.1) is perilous;
for experience shows, and the three following *exempla* will illustrate, that
those who cannot lay aside the exceptional burdens which they take upon
themselves risk the catastrophic dissolution of their own fortunes.   **in
altum sublatis** 'highly positioned'; not otiose after *Potentissimis*, for S.
raises the powerful to the heights from which, disenchanted, they subsequently long to descend (*cupiunt . . . descendere* below).   **excidere uoces:**
revealing words are inadvertently 'dropped'. Applied to words 'uttered' or
'let fall', the verb can take a dat. in prose (*hominibus*) as at e.g. Cic. *Phil.* 10.6
uerbum tibi non excidit . . . fortuito, Curt. 4.15.11, Quint. *Inst.* 6.3.23, Plin. *Ep.*
6.20.17.   **uidebis:** incongruous with sound as the obj., but *OLD* 9b.
optent 'pray for', with two further verbs (*laudent, praeferant*) to intensify the

longing; not even those who enjoy immense *felicitas* are free from μεμψιμοιρία (2.2n. on *plerosque ... deprendunt*).   **interim** 'sometimes', mostly
a post-Augustan nuance (13.9, *Ir.* 1.16.3, *Ben.* 1.11.1, *Ep.* 64.6).   **si tuto
liceat:** an illusory prospect given e.g. *Tr.* 10.6 *multi quidem sunt quibus necessario
haerendum sit in fastigio suo, ex quo non possunt nisi cadendo descendere* (on the topos
of the dangers of high position, Tarrant (1976) 182 (a)). For the resultant
anxiety of those *in fastigio, Ep.* 94.73; the powerful thus crave *otium* as here (cf.
Ep. 94.74).   **ut:** concessive.   **lacessat:** milder disturbance than the
turmoil denoted by *quatiat* (Duff 105).   **in se ... ruit:** *ipsa* in contrast
to *extra* ('fortune *under its own weight* crashes down upon itself'); *se* acc. (Hor.
S. 2.7.88 *in quem* [sc. *sapientem*] *manca ruit semper fortuna*; *OLD ruo* 5). For the
idea, 'predominantly Roman' (Tarrant (1976) 182) and variously applied
in late Republican and Imperial literature (e.g. Hor. *Epod.* 16.2 *suis ... ipsa
Roma uiribus ruit*, Liv. 6.19.6, Luc. 1.81), cf. *Prou.* 3.10, *C.S.* 2.2, *Ag.* 87–9. S.
himself lived out the lesson: Plin. *N.H.* 14.51 *... Annaeo Seneca, principe tunc
eruditorum ac potentia, quae postremo nimia ruit super ipsum.*

   4.2 The first *exemplum*: Augustus. S.'s treatment of Augustus is in two
stages: (i) an account of his alleged aspirations to retire (4.2–4), and (ii) a
description of the stresses from which he apparently yearned to escape
(4.5–6). In (ii) the Senecan picture is carefully structured to bear out the
closing *sententia* in 4.1 (*ut nihil extra lacessat aut quatiat, in se ipsa fortuna ruit*):
after describing Augustus' rise to power, S. moves from *externa bella* to Rome
itself and to the various conspiracies hatched against the emperor (4.5 *in
ipsa urbe ... mucrones acuebantur*); then S. enters the imperial house (4.6) to address the domestic scandals which troubled Augustus from 2 BC onwards.
The emphasis on Augustus' consolidation of the near and more distant
empire (4.5 *dum Alpes pacat ... dum ultra Rhenum ... terminos mouet*) is important; for even though on these external fronts Augustus' rule was allegedly
untroubled (4.1 *ut nihil extra lacessat aut quatiat*), the contrasting emphasis on
troubles ever closer to home (conspiracies *in urbe*, scandal *in domo*) offers its
own illustration of fortunes collapsing upon themselves (4.1 *in se ipsa fortuna ruit*). This artful structuring of events cautions against taking S.'s claims
in (i) entirely at face value. Whatever the true extent of Augustus' aspirations to retire (4.2n. on *non desît ... uicturum sibi*), his example here does
not only offer a model illustration of the frustrated desire to descend from
a high but dangerous position (4.1 *cupiunt ... descendere*). Augustus' escapist
longing for *otium* and his reliance on the mere 'sweetness of words' (4.3 *uerborum dulcedine*) – the illusory prospect of retirement – to sustain him as he

stoically shoulders the burdens of office also suggest a profound imbalance in life from which Paulinus might learn – even though the burdens of the *princeps* were obviously in so many ways unique.   **Diuus Augustus:** juxtaposition with *in se ipsa fortuna ruit* (4.1) creates an ominous effect, as even those acclaimed as gods are subject to the batterings of *fortuna*. That *fortuna* does not discriminate between the deserving and the undeserving in her attacks is a familiar theme in Senecan tragedy (e.g. *Her. F.* 524 *o Fortuna uiris inuida fortibus* with Fitch (1987) 256), and here suggests a tragic dimension to the portrayal of Augustus. Because *fortuna* is indiscriminate in her workings, the *sapiens* is fortified by indifference to her (e.g. *Ep.* 15.9 *quam magnificum sit plenum esse nec ex fortuna pendere*, 98.2–6, 120.12); for all his stoical endurance, Augustus falls short of such standards in his yearning to escape from office.   **cui ... praestiterunt:** for the technique of emphasizing Augustus' *felicitas* before qualifying that picture, Plin. *N.H.* 7.147 *in diuo ... Augusto, quem uniuersa mortalitas in hac censura* [sc. *felicitatis*] *nuncupet, ... magna sortis humanae reperiantur uolumina* (a list of Augustus' tribulations follows in 147–50).   **non desît ... uicturum sibi:** the language of retirement (*quietem, uacationem, otium*) and of unceasing ambition towards that end (*non desît ... precari, omnis ... sermo, semper*) emphasizes Augustus' strength of desire; but the claim that he constantly wished to be free of office is an exaggeration, at least to judge by the evidence. Suet. *Aug.* 28.1 reports that Augustus twice seriously considered abdication, first in (perhaps) 29 BC (Dio 52.1.1 with Carter (1982) 127), and secondly when he fell gravely ill in 23 (Dio 53.30.1–3). When in 28–7 the Republic was 'restored' by constitutional settlement (Aug. *R.G.* 34.1, Vell. 2.89.4), Dio reports that Augustus dramatically announced to the Senate his intention to retire (53.4.3; cf. 53.8.7, 9.1); but the manoeuvre was apparently strategic (53.2.6) and achieved its goal when the Senate 'forced' Augustus to remain in power (53.11.4). The historians make no further mention of any plans to retire, sincere or otherwise; and S.'s report of Augustus' letter is itself by no means above suspicion (4.3n. on *in quadam ... epistula*).   **desît:** contracted perf. (= *desiit*).   **uacationem:** normally accompanied by the gen. in S. (20.3, *Apoc.* 11.5, *Ep.* 85.5, 92.11), but *Helu.* 2.4 *uacationem ... a grauissimis luctibus*. **sermo:** conversation of a private sort.   **reuolutus est** 'kept coming back to', pass. with middle sense (*OLD* 4c).   **ut:** epexegetic ('to the effect that ... '), defining *ad hoc*; *OLD* 39a.   **hoc ... solacio:** defined by *aliquando ... sibi* below (acc. and inf. in variation on epexegetic *ut* above). The sentence is artfully contrived if Augustus is taken as the subj. of *oblectabat*, *hoc* is abl. and distant agreement with *solacio* binds together the intervening construction; the unappealing alternative is to construe *hoc* as the nom. subj. of *oblectabat*, with *aliquando . . . sibi* set in apposition to it (i.e. 'this would relieve his toils with sweet even if illusory comfort, namely the thought that one day he would live for himself'). **se uicturum sibi:** so Hor. *Ep.* 1.18.107–8 *ut mihi uiuam | quod superest aeui*, Ov. *Tr.* 3.4.4 *uiue tibi*, both with Epicurean overtones. Augustus may have looked forward to 'living for himself' only in the (non-philosophical) sense of relinquishing office (Dio 53.9.1 ἐν ἡσυχίᾳ . . . καταβιῶναι), but for the Stoic application of the phrase, *Ep.* 55.4 (*sibi uiuere* the privilege of the self-sufficient *sapiens*).

4.3 in quadam . . . epistula: Augustus and later emperors frequently corresponded by letter with the Senate when they did not attend themselves (Talbert (1984) 230–1). In this case the letter is lost, S. our sole witness to its existence and (partial) content; its date is uncertain, and any coincidence with Suetonius' and Dio's reports of Augustus contemplating retirement in the first decade of his reign (4.2n. on *non desît . . . uicturum sibi*) can only be conjectured.   **non uacuam:** dignified understatement (litotes) in carefully chosen language; Augustus' retirement will be disengaged in one sense (4.2 *uacationem*) but not in another (i.e. 'not devoid of . . . ').   **dignitatis:** prestige and personal image; in conjunction with *requiem*, a possible adaptation of *cum dignitate otium*, the formula made famous by Cicero (e.g. *Sest.* 98, *De orat.* 1.1.1, *Fam.* 1.9.21), for whom it denoted 'above all tranquillity with dignity in the Roman State as well as in his own life' (Wirszubski (1954) 13).   **nec a . . . discrepantem** 'and not inconsistent with'; solemnly dignified in tone.   **sed . . . possunt** 'but these things can be made to happen more impressively than they can be promised'; fulfilment lies in the deed, not the word.   **rerum . . . adhuc** 'the joy of that reality is still slow in coming'; *rerum laetitia* in contrast to *ex uerborum dulcedine* below.   **praeciperem:** for the historic sequence following a pure perf. (*prouexit*), *Thy.* 891–2 *ne quid obstaret pudor, | dies recessit* (cited with other examples by Kenney (1962) 31 n. 4); K–S II 179. For the sense of the verb, Cic. *Phil.* 13.45 *praecipio gaudia*, Liv. 10.26.4 *tanta laetitia . . . fuit ut praeciperetur uictoria animis*.   **dulcedine:** 4.2 *dulci . . . solacio*.

4.4 tanta . . . res 'such a desirable thing', in apposition to *otium*. **usu** 'in practice' as opposed to *cogitatione* 'in thought'.   **non poterat:** sc. *sumere*, to be inferred from *praesumeret*; a bold ellipsis (Duff 106). **praesumeret:** variation on 4.3 *praeciperem*; so Plin. *Ep.* 3.1.11 (in reference to the aged Spurinna's enviable retirement) *hanc ego uitam uoto et cogitatione* *praesumo, ingressurus auidissime, ut primum ratio aetatis receptui canere permiserit. interim mille laboribus conteror* ....   **omnia ... pendentia:** Ov. *Tr.* 2.217 (also of Augustus) *de te pendentem ... dum circumspicis orbem.*   **qui ... dabat** 'who bestowed prosperity on individuals and nations'. Although *fortuna* can be used of both prosperity and its opposite (*OLD* 9, 10; Duff 107 renders *fortunam dabat* 'made happy or unhappy'), the phrase *fortunam dare* regularly denotes the granting of good fortune / success; e.g. Cato, *Orig.* 4 fr. 7 = p. 19.8–9 Jordan *dii immortales tribuno militum fortunam ex uirtute eius dedere*, Virg. *Aen.* 10.421–2, Man. 2.832, Curt. 6.5.8. The verb, often applied to the gods (*OLD do* 3a), suggests that Augustus exercised god-like authority over his subjects even before his apotheosis (4.2 *Diuus*).   **illum:** emphatic, 'that (longed for) day'.   **laetissimus:** in anticipation of the joyful reality projected in 4.3 *rerum laetitia*.   **cogitabat** 'he looked forward to'.   **quo ... exueret** 'on which to lay aside his greatness', final relative clause (G–L §630); the verb suggests 'throwing off' the unwelcome (so *Ep.* 24.2 *si uis omnem sollicitudinem exuere* ...).

4.5 S. surveys Augustus' rise to and consolidation of power. By moving from Augustus' exploits on the margins of Roman *imperium* to the near empire and then to domestic troubles at Rome itself and in the imperial household, S. portrays the emperor as threatened by dangers increasingly closer to home (4.2 intro.).   **quantum ... exprimerent, quantum ... tegerent:** the two clauses, balanced by anaphora (*quantum*), homoeoteleuton (*-erent*) and the same clausula in each (–∪–∪∪–), contrast brilliant appearance (*bona ... fulgentia*) and darker reality (*occultarum sollicitudinum*).   **exprimerent:** the bold image 'wrings out' the fig. sweat (*OLD* 1a), with the hint of reluctance on Augustus' part (cf. *Ep.* 82.7 *exprimitur sera confessio*, where a late confession is 'squeezed out' of the misguided).   **tegerent** 'veiled'.   **cum ciuibus ... fudit:** a summary of events from the aftermath of Julius Caesar's assassination in 44 BC to Antony's defeat at Actium in 31. The sequence here (*primum, deinde, nouissime*) is not strictly temporal but designed to portray a growing personal tragedy for Octavian as he battles first with his fellow citizens, then with his political colleagues, and finally with his own relatives. His 'enforced' (*coactus*) engagement in increasingly personal forms of conflict emphasizes the sweat involved in his early progress (*quantum ... exprimerent* above), while his bloodshed (*sanguinem fudit*) hints at the darker side of the picture (*quantum ... tegerent*; S. contrasts Augustus' hot-headed youth with his mildness as *princeps* at *Cl.* 1.9.1, 11.1). The darker implications of the passage are keenly pursued by Jal (1957) 250–1.   **ciuibus:** his fellow countrymen, slain during the civil wars at Mutina in 43 BC and at Philippi in 42 (Suet. *Aug.* 10.2–4, 13.1 with Carter (1982) 99–102, 103).   **collegis:** M. Aemilius Lepidus and Antony, partners with Octavian in the Second Triumvirate (43–33 BC). Relations with Antony were uneasy but finally broke down only in 32; after the final break, Antony was decisively vanquished at Actium in 31 (Carter (1982) 107–9 on Suet. *Aug.* 17.1–2). Lepidus was deposed by Octavian in 36 following their joint Sicilian campaign against Sextus Pompeius (Carter (1982) 106–7 on Suet. *Aug.* 16.4).   **affinibus** 'relations by marriage', incl. Antony who in 40 BC married Octavia (Octavian's sister) after the death of Fulvia, his third wife (Vell. 2.78.1, App. *B.C.* 5.64, Dio 48.31.3). S. may also be alluding to Octavian's Sicilian campaign against Sextus Pompeius, ending in 36 (Carter (1982) 104–5 on Suet. *Aug.* 16.1); for Octavian was related to Sextus by marriage to Scribonia, the aunt of Sextus' wife (App. *B.C.* 5.53).   **coactus:** in antiquity, an important emphasis in favourable interpretations of Augustus' role in the civil wars; so e.g. Dio 56.37.1–4 (part of Tiberius' funeral speech in praise of Augustus), 44.1 (the young Octavian's deeds attributed to force of circumstance). At *Ann.* 1.9.3 Tacitus reports the view that Augustus was driven to arms out of filial duty to Julius Caesar and because of national emergency (*necessitudine rei publicae*), only then to report the opposite view: lust for power was Augustus' real motive (1.10.1; for discussion of Tacitus' own inclinations, Goodyear (1972) 156 on 1.9.3).   **mari terraque:** modification of a phrase which, in reverse order, S. uses only twice elsewhere, on both occasions echoing a familiar peace formula (Momigliano (1942) 62–4) in Augustus' reported voice (*Cl.* 1.9.4 *terra marique pax parata est*, *Apoc.* 10.2; cf. [Sen.] *Oct.* 479–80). S. follows Augustus' own example (*R.G.* 3.1 *bella terra et mari . . . toto in orbe terrarum saepe gessi*, 4.2, 13, 26.4); but the Augustan echo here is modified in tone as well as word-order if the gruesome implications of *sanguinem fudit* are felt as keenly as Jal (1957) 251 proposes ('un pastiche particulièrement cruel du style triomphal d'Auguste').   **per Macedoniam . . . oras:** a survey of Octavian's itinerary during the civil wars. By *Macedoniam* S. refers to Philippi (42 BC), by *Siciliam* to Sextus Pompeius' defeat at Naulochus in 36. After Actium Octavian pursued Antony and Cleopatra to Egypt, settling affairs peacefully in Syria and Asia Minor en route (Suet. *Aug.* 17.3, Dio 51.5.2). He subsequently occupied Alexandria; after Antony and Cleopatra committed suicide (Vell. 2.87.1, Suet. *Aug.* 17.4, Dio 51.10.7–9, 13.5), he made Egypt into a province (*R.G.* 27.1, Suet. *Aug.* 18.2).   **oras** 'lands' (*OLD* 3a).   **circumactus** 'led on a circuitous course' by war, but the implication of circularity (*OLD circumago* 1b) is perhaps significant; Octavian's itinerary from Macedonia to Asia Minor is roughly circular in Senecan design.   **Romana . . . lassos:** perhaps a glance at the darker aspect of Augustus' *gloria* (*quantum . . . tegerent* above); to refrain from (Roman) slaughter through weariness hardly suggests virtuous restraint. Cf. *Cl.* 1.11.2 (on Augustus' moderation after the civil wars) *ego uero clementiam non uoco lassam crudelitatem*, [Sen.] *Oct.* 524–6.   **externa:** foreign as opposed to civil wars; Aug. *R.G.* 3.1 *bella . . . ciuilia externaque . . . saepe gessi.*   **Alpes pacat:** the Alpine tribes were pacified between 35 and 7–6 BC, an achievement recorded by Augustus at *R.G.* 26.3; in 7–6 a monument honouring him and listing forty-six subdued tribes was erected in the Maritime Alps (the text is recorded by Plin. *N.H.* 3.136–7 = E–J no. 40). The tone of *pacat* is neutral, allowing for both the official and rather more ironic versions of the Augustan 'achievement' in 'pacifying' allegedly troublesome peoples (Carter (1982) 115–16 on Suet. *Aug.* 21.2).   **immixtosque . . . hostes** 'enemies nesting in the heart of the peaceful empire'; if not an elaboration of *Alpes pacat*, then perhaps referring to troublespots 'pacified' by Augustus in his consolidation of the near empire; these included northern Spain, Aquitania, Dalmatia and Illyricum (Suet. *Aug.* 21.1).   **paci et imperio:** hendiadys; for the association, Virg. *Aen.* 6.851–2.   **ultra . . . mouet:** from the near empire S. moves to the margins to burden Augustus with distant responsibilities. Drusus (Tiberius' brother) and Tiberius made various expeditions across the Rhine, but the *clades Variana* of AD 9 effectively ended plans to extend the northern frontier beyond it. At *R.G.* 30.2 Augustus exaggerates in claiming that his armies had crossed the Danube and subjugated the Dacians; in S.'s time the Danube remained the acknowledged limit of empire (*Prou.* 4.14, *N.Q.* 1 *praef.* 9, 6.7.1). Beyond the Euphrates Augustus controlled affairs in Armenia and Parthia by installing compliant rulers (Aug. *R.G.* 27.2, 33, Suet. *Aug.* 21.3), but he annexed neither; S. elsewhere recognizes the Euphrates as the eastern limit of *imperium* (*N.Q.* 1 *praef.* 9).   **Murenae . . . acuebantur:** for lists of conspirators against Augustus, *Cl.* 1.9.6, Vell. 2.91.2–4, Suet. *Aug.* 19.1 with Carter (1982) 112–13. The plot of Varro Murena and Fannius Caepio was detected in 23 or 22 BC, that of M. Aemilius Lepidus (son of the triumvir) in 29 BC, that of M. Egnatius Rufus in 19.   **mucrones:** synecdoche, as *mucro* strictly denotes the point of a sword; cf. the words attributed to Augustus at *Cl.* 1.9.5 *ego sum nobilibus adulescentulis expositum caput, in quod mucrones acuant.*

4.6 nondum . . . mulier: in claiming that Augustus had not yet escaped the plots listed in 4.5 when the scandal concerning Julia, his daughter, broke in 2 BC (n. on *filia et . . . iuuenes* below), S. exaggerates the weight of domestic pressures 'simultaneously' burdening the emperor; the last of S.'s named conspirators, Egnatius, was exposed in 19, and the other plots mentioned by Suetonius (*Aug.* 19.1; cf. 4.5 *aliorum . . . mucrones*) appear to have occurred only late in the reign, well after 2 BC (Carter (1982) 112–13).

nondum . . . insidias: *nondum* and esp. *uixdum* often introduce a main clause followed by a subordinate *cum* + indicative clause (K–S II 339); but S. here avoids the more usual construction (i.e. *nondum . . . effugerat insidias cum . . .*) to heighten the dramatic effect through parataxis.   **filia et . . . iuuenes:** Julia was married first to Marcellus (Augustus' nephew), then to Agrippa and finally, in 11 BC, to Tiberius (Suet. *Aug.* 63.1–2); her scandalous behaviour led Augustus to banish her to the island of Pandateria in 2 BC (Suet. *Aug.* 65.1, 3; cf. *Ben.* 6.32.1–2). Velleius (2.100.2–5) names five of her lovers and alludes to others; acc. to Tac. *Ann.* 3.24.2 they were charged with sacrilege and treason and punished by death or banishment (cf. Vell. 2.100.5, Dio 55.10.15).   **adulterio . . . adacti** 'bound by adultery as if by an oath of allegiance'; such alliances were of potential danger to Augustus if, as Pliny reports, Julia actively plotted against her father (*N.H.* 7.149 *adulterium filiae et consilia parricidae palam facta*).   **iam . . . territabant:** *iam* qualifies *infractam* ('his now failing years'); the frequentative verb, not often in S. (*Ep.* 56.13, 74.5, 104.8), stresses constant alarm. The phrase is positioned between *filia et . . . iuuenes* and *Iullusque et . . . mulier* to convey the impression of Augustus' domestic enemies hemming him in on all sides. **Iullusque:** Waltz's proposal for *plusque* in the MSS, and preferable to Rubens' *Paullusque*. Iullus, the second son of Antony and Fulvia, was punished by death in 2 BC for adultery with the elder Julia (Tac. *Ann.* 4.44.3; acc. to Vell. 2.100.4 he committed suicide). Paullus would refer to L. Aemilius Paullus, husband of the younger Julia, Augustus' granddaughter (she was banished for adultery in AD 8; Suet. *Aug.* 65.1, Tac. *Ann.* 3.24.2, 4.71.4); Suetonius (*Aug.* 19.1) implicates Paullus, consul in AD 1, in a conspiracy against Augustus (its date and motive are unclear). However, the words *cum Antonio mulier* are much more apposite if *Iullusque* is read and *Antonio* is seen to refer not just to 'a man like Antony' but to one who really *was* an Antony. *-que* then proceeds from the general to the specific: after alluding to the elder Julia's various lovers (*tot iuuenes*) S. specifies Iullus in particular.   **iterum . . . mulier** 'a woman once again posing a threat

in the arms of her Antony'; the elder Julia is cast as a second Cleopatra.
haec ulcera ... absciderat 'he had cut away these sores limbs and all',
i.e. the conspiracies against Augustus were crushed, all the conspirators
from Murena to Iullus were executed, the elder Julia banished. S. draws
here on the familiar analogy of the state as the 'body politic' (e.g. *Cl.* 1.12.3,
Ep. 102.6; *OLD corpus* 6c). In imperial contexts the emperor is the master of
that body, his subjects its *membra*; *Cl.* 1.14.3 *tarde sibi pater membra sua abscidat,
etiam, cum absciderit, reponere cupiat, et in abscidendo gemat cunctatus multum diuque.*
subnascebantur 'kept growing up'; rare, late and paralleled in S. only at
Ir. 2.10.8, the ponderous verb here emphasizes slow but relentless growth.
For such resurgence see *iterum ... mulier* above (Iullus and Julia the 'new'
Antony and Cleopatra).   **uelut** qualifies *graue; pace* Duff 109 the clause
is not a simile but continues the preceding metaphor (i.e. 'as if overbur-
dened with blood, the body[-politic] was always ruptured by haemorrhage
somewhere').   **otium ... poterat:** 4.2; S. returns to his starting-point.
residebant 'found relief', from *resido* and not as listed at *OLD resideo* 2b;
for (i) the superior sense is that Augustus' labours were *eased* by hope and
thought of leisure, not that they 'were rooted in' or 'securely founded upon'
such hope and thought; (ii) S. tends to use *resido* in prose (*Ir.* 3.12.4, *Ep.* 66.11,
N.Q. 3.28.1), *resideo* in verse (*Ag.* 674, *Thy.* 583, *Oed.* 424); at *Tr.* 2.10 *nusquam
residentis* ('coming to rest') *animi uolutatio* and *Ben.* 5.24.1 *cum uelles residere* ('sit
down in rest') *feruentissimo sole*, the emphasis on action rather than state tells
in favour of *resido*; (iii) for *resido* applied to the alleviation of stress, e.g. *Ep.*
63.3 *acerrimi luctus residunt*, *N.Q.* 6.1.4; (iv) prose authors tend to avoid the
so-called 'heroic clausula', or prose rhythm emulating the end of a hexameter (9.3n. on *ipso fugiente*); *resideo* would here yield such a rhythm, *resido* the
familiar Senecan combination of cretic + spondee.   **uotum ... uoti:**
polyptoton (*Breu.* 1.1 n. on *uitae ... uita*), with irony in the contrast between
Augustus' ability to answer the prayers of others and his inability to fulfil his
own.   **uoti compotes** [sc. *homines*]: a common idiom (*OLD compos* 1a).

5 *Cicero*

The second *exemplum*, the late Republican orator and statesman M. Tullius
Cicero, offers a more ambivalent case than Augustus. While the latter seeks
(illusory) comfort in the anticipation rather than the fulfilment of *otium*,
Cicero languishes 'half-free' in his Tusculan retreat (5.2). *semiliber* is the key
word in the chapter: S. imposes his own interpretation on the Ciceronian

word to portray Cicero as falling far short of the Stoic ideal of complete and unconditional *libertas* (5.3n.). Far from being 'somewhat irrelevant here' (Duff 112), the introduction of the *sapiens* in 5.3 drives home the contrast between S.'s Cicero and the perfect Stoic.

5.1 A complex, not un-Ciceronian sentence, in which the final exclamation is preceded by five carefully balanced and contrasting units: a central clause, *dum fluctuatur . . . et . . . tenet* (with chiasmus), presents Cicero at the helm of the Roman ship of state; two surrounding pples. (*iactatus, abductus*) illustrate the violent pressures on him as they hem this clause in; each pple is followed by a qualifying phrase (*partim . . . partim, nec . . . nec*) with its own internal balance.   **Catilinas . . . Crassos:** in the first unit the central *iactatus* portrays Cicero as buffeted on both sides; first we have *Catilinas Clodios* ('the likes of Catiline' etc.; *Marc.* 20.5 *tantum Catilinarum* 'so many Catilines', *Ep.* 97.10), defined in the next unit as his 'declared enemies' (*manifestos inimicos*), and on the other side *Pompeios . . . et Crassos*, two allies subsequently branded as treacherous (*dubios amicos*).   **Catilinas Clodios:** as consul in 63 BC Cicero thwarted Catiline's infamous conspiracy. In 61 he took part in the prosecution of P. Clodius Pulcher, on trial for violating the mysteries of the cult of Bona Dea (among other charges; *Ep.* 97.2–6, App. *B.C.* 2.14, Dio 37.45.1–46.2); acquitted through bribery, Clodius later gained revenge when, as tribune in 58, he secured Cicero's exile (App. *B.C.* 2.15, Dio 38.14.1–17.7).   **iactatus** 'tossed', introducing the characteristic Ciceronian metaphor of the storm-tossed ship of state (Zetzel (1995) 97 on *Rep.* 1.1.3); the metaphor is continued in *fluctuatur, tenet* and *quietus* below.   **Pompeiosque et Crassos:** political allies (*OLD amicus²* 3a) with Julius Caesar (perhaps omitted here for symmetry and balance) in the First Triumvirate of 60 BC. Cicero found them *dubios* when he was faced with exile in 58 (Vell. 2.45.2, Dio 38.17.2–3), and was particularly critical of Pompey (*Q. fr.* 1.4.1).   **partim . . . partim** 'on the one hand . . . on the other'; a rare combination in S., paralleled only at 18.1, *N.Q.* 2.26.5.   **fluctuatur** 'tossed'. For the image, *Prou.* 5.9 *non erit illi planum iter: . . . oportet . . . fluctuetur ac nauigium in turbido regat, Ep.* 104.22, 111.4; at 2.3 fig. *fluctuantur* is less violent in connotation.   **illam . . . tenet:** Cicero 'kept the state from destruction', most obviously by thwarting Catiline in 63; cf. of Cato *C.S.* 2.2 *cadentem rem publicam . . . tenuit. tenet* in contrast to *fluctuatur:* Cicero is now a passenger on the storm-tossed ship of state, now its pilot (cf. *Diu.* 2.3 *cum gubernacula rei publicae tenebamus . . .*).

pessum euntem: lit. 'sinking to the bottom' (*N.Q.* 3.25.5, 7).
nouissime abductus 'finally swept away' as if by the turbulent waves;
if not an allusion to Cicero's exile in 58, then perhaps to his departure
from the political spotlight after the First Triumvirate was revived in the
spring of 56 (see Zetzel (1995) 2).   **nec ... quietus nec ... patiens:**
S. anticipates the contrast drawn in 5.3 between Cicero and the *sapiens*; for
the suggestion is that Cicero lacks Stoic calm (*Ir.* 3.6.1 *sublimis animus, qui-*
etus semper...) and endurance (*V.B.* 15.5 *quicquid euenerit feret* [sc. *uirtus*] *non*
patiens tantum sed uolens).   **nec aduersarum** [sc. *rerum*] **patiens:** cf.
Livy's epitaph on Cicero as reported by the elder Sen. at *Suas.* 6.22:
... omnium aduersorum [sc. exile, political failure, the death of his daughter]
nihil ut uiro dignum erat tulit praeter mortem.   **illum ... suum** 'that very
consulship of his'.   **non ... laudatum:** for Cicero's 'endless' praises
of his consulship, e.g. *Pis.* 3–7, *Flac.* 102, *Phil.* 2.11–12, *Att.* 1.16.6, 1.19.6;
in addition to his hexametrical *Consulatus suus* in three books (= frr. 5–13
Courtney), Cicero wrote a sketch (*commentarium consulatus*) in Greek (*Att.*
1.19.10, 20.6, 2.1.1 –2) and contemplated a Latin version (*Att.* 1.19.10; cf. *Fam.*
5.12.8). On his reputation for excessive boasting, e.g. Plut. *Cic.* 6.5, 24.1–3,
Dio 37.38.2, 38.12.7, Quint. *Inst.* 11.1.18 with Allen (1954).   **detestatur**
'curses'. S. exaggerates the μετάνοια here as he did in the case of Augustus.
Cicero's strongest comment is at *Q.fr.* 1.3.1 (at Thessalonica, June 58) *meus*
ille laudatus consulatus mihi te, liberos, patriam, fortunas [sc. *eripuit*].

5.2 flebiles uoces: a phrase quoted by Cicero from tragedy (Acc.
551 Ribbeck *ap. Tusc.* 2.33; cf. *De orat.* 3.217) and also used by S. at *Marc.*
13.2, *Ep.* 88.9.   **exprimit** 'wrung from himself' (4.5n. on *exprimerent*);
stronger than the usual (*e*)*mittere* (*Ben.* 2.5.2 *inde illae uoces, quas ingenuus dolor*
exprimit).   **in quadam ad Atticum epistula:** since the words reported below ('*quid ... semiliber*') are not found in Cicero's extant corre-
spondence with Atticus, S. either quotes from a letter which is now lost or
echoes Ciceronian language and (supposed) sentiment in words of his own
making (n. on *semiliber* below). Lipsius proposed *Axium* for *Atticum*, thereby
identifying the Senecan quotation as a fragment of Cicero's lost letters to
Q. Axius (= fr. 10.6 Watt); but his reasoning (if not to Atticus, Cicero *must*
have written the words to another addressee) unduly limits the possibilities.
iam uicto ... refouente: for two absolute pple phrases in combination
(and for examples of chiastic arrangement as here), Laughton (1964) 115–17.
After Pompey's defeat at Pharsalus in 48 BC and Caesar's further victory
over the surviving Pompeians at Thapsus (Tunisia) in 46, hostilities moved

to Spain. There, Pompey's elder son Gnaeus was commander-in-chief of
the forces decisively defeated by Caesar at Munda in 45; Gnaeus was killed
soon afterwards, but Sextus, his brother, continued Pompeian operations
in Spain until after Caesar's assassination in 44 (Hadas (1930) 48–55). By
adhuc ... refouente S. refers either (i) to Gnaeus' resistance down to Munda, or
(ii) to Sextus' prolongation of hostilities thereafter (*Pol*. 15.1 *post hunc ... casum*
[sc. Gnaeus' death] *Sextus Pompeius non tantum dolori sed etiam bello suffecit*). On
balance, a date before March 45 (Munda) appears more likely for the
Ciceronian letter allegedly quoted by S. (n. on *refouente* below).   **adhuc**
'still'; in reference to continuing action when cessation might have been expected, the adv. is avoided in the best Classical prose but found in Cicero's
letters (e.g. *Fam*. 9.2.3 *haec ego suspicans adhuc Romae maneo*) and in Silver
prose (*OLD* 3).   **refouente** 'reviving' the shattered arms; elsewhere in
Senecan prose only at *Helu*. 9.8, again in reference to the Pompeian resurgence (before Munda) in Spain: *illum* [sc. *Caesarem*] *... trahit Hispania, quae
fractas et afflictas partes refouet*.   **in Tusculano meo:** Cicero's beloved
(*Att*. 1.6.2, 2.1.11) estate at Tusculum in Latium, some fifteen miles SE of
Rome.   **semiliber:** i.e. neither fully at ease nor fully preoccupied at
his Tusculan estate, neither embroiled in nor completely detached from
the Caesarian/Pompeian strife. The adj. is paralleled in Cicero only at *Att*.
13.31.3 (at Tusculum, 28 May, 45), where its sense is different: *abiciamus
ista et semiliberi saltem simus; quod assequemur et tacendo et latendo* (i.e. 'let us give
up the pretence of having any influence over Caesar, and be at least half-
free by keeping silent and lying low'). If dated before Munda, the letter
quoted by S. is earlier than *Att*. 13.31 but falls into the same general period.
But since S. goes on in 5.3 to interpret *semiliber* in a partisan way, taking
Cicero to task for his lack of true Stoic *libertas*, the suspicion remains that
he saw the potential of the adj. in *Att*. 13.31, lifted it out of the original
and invented a new Ciceronian context for it in the words 'quoted' above.
alia ... desperat: a summary of further material contained in Cicero's
lost (or imaginary?) letter. Cicero's doleful reflection on the past, present
and future suggests the opposite of Stoic serenity; 10.5 *securae et quietae mentis
est in omnes uitae suae partes discurrere*, 15.5 *omnia illi* [sc. *sapienti*] *saecula ut deo
seruiunt* (the *sapiens* is god-like in his controlling perspective on the past,
present and future; contrast Cicero's resignation to lament, complaint and
despair).

5.3 semiliberum: emphatically placed as S. proceeds to impose
a Stoic interpretation on the adj.   **mehercules** 'needless to say',

colloquial (Summers 1, Hofmann 29–30); often in S. with *at* to mark
a strong qualification or objection (e.g. *Ep.* 50.5, 99.3, 110.7, 13).
numquam . . . procedet: the perfect Stoic 'will never resort to such a
lowly term [sc. *semiliber*]'. The verb is ironic, suggesting that the *sapiens*
will never 'advance' or 'develop' in such a negative direction; in this sense
(*OLD* 11a) more usually with *ad*, but for *in* + acc., Prop. 3.11.17 *Omphale
in tantum formae processit honorem.*   **numquam semiliber erit:** S. takes
philosophical issue with Cicero's use of the adj., but without pursuing the
Stoic notion of 'half-slavery', ἡμιδουλεία, attributed to Chrysippus at *SVF*
II 284.27; that refers to Chrysippus' 'soft determinism', or his attempt to
reconcile governance by fate with (limited) human autonomy (Sharples
(1983) 8–10).   **integrae . . . libertatis:** gen. of quality (G–L §365),
very common in S. (Summers lvi). Stoic freedom is complete and never
compromised; for its Senecan definition, *Ep.* 51.9 *quae sit libertas quaeris?
nulli rei seruire, nulli necessitati, nullis casibus . . .* , 75.18.   **solidae** 'unalloyed'; 17.3, *Prou.* 6.4 *non est ista solida et sincera felicitas, Ep.* 44.7, 74.16.
solutus 'not subject to any constraints', least of all the passions (*Ir.* 1.14.1
solutus . . . affectibus).   **sui iuris** 'his own master'; Ciceronian (e.g. *Verr.*
1.18) but mostly post-Augustan. For the Stoic application of the phrase,
Pol. 9.3 (of Polybius' brother, liberated by death) *nunc animus . . . uelut ex
diutino carcere emissus, tandem sui iuris et arbitrii, Ep.* 77.15, 94.74, [Sen.] *Oct.*
383–4. For a parallel idiom, 2.4n. on *suus nemo est.*   **altior ceteris**
'rising above all else' (i.e. things external to his own self-sufficiency); *V.B.*
11.1 *non uoco . . . sapientem supra quem quicquam est.*   **supra fortunam:** the
fortified position of the *sapiens* immune to the blows of fortune; *C.S.* 1.1, *Ep.*
41.2, 44.5, 63.1 (of grief held in control) *sed cui ista firmitas animi continget nisi
iam multum supra fortunam elato?.*

6 Drusus

The third *exemplum:* M. Livius Drusus. The radical social legislation which
Drusus introduced as tribune in 91 BC (6.1n. on *cum . . . mouisset*) met with
vigorous opposition and was eventually overturned by the Senate (6.1n.
on *exitum . . . peruidens*); Drusus was subsequently murdered, but S. uniquely
suggests that he committed suicide (6.2n. on *disputatur . . . collapsus est*). S.'s
rhetorical trio of *exempla* thus rises to a crescendo (Grimal (1960) 416, Mayer
(1991) 155); for by raising the possibility of suicide S. offers the most dramatic
illustration yet of escape at any cost from the pressures of high but perilous

responsibility, and also of the collapse of exceptional personal fortunes under their own weight (cf. 4.1). By stressing Drusus' hyperactive precocity, S. portrays that final collapse as the inevitable consequence of a life devoid of relieving *otium* and therefore of balanced perspective.

6.1 acer et uehemens 'vigorously energetic'; the pairing is standard with this sense (e.g. Cic. *Brut.* 113, 168, *Caec.* 28, V. Max. 3.7.6, Suet. *Gal.* 9.1). S. emphasizes from the outset the zeal which ultimately led to Drusus' (self-) destruction. Although exalted in some quarters for his eloquence, moral rectitude and championing of the Senate (Cic. *Mil.* 16, *Rab. Post.* 16, Diod. 37.10.1, Vell. 2.13.1, Plut. *Cato min.* 1.1), Drusus also won a reputation for being an obsessively ambitious and proud man of action (V. Max. 9.5.2, Flor. *Epit.* 2.6.4, [Vict.] *Vir. Ill.* 66.1).   **cum . . . mouisset** 'when he had brought forward seditious (*nouas*; *OLD* 10b) legislation and provoked the kind of social disturbance the Gracchi had'; syllepsis (Lausberg §1244 s.v. 1), as *moueo* is used in two different senses (*OLD* 18, 17b). Drusus strove to satisfy 'the poor with land and cheap corn, the Italians with the franchise, and the ruling oligarchy with control of the courts and a vast new citizen *clientela*, which would make its rule more stable than it had been for a generation' (Badian (1962) 225).   **mala Gracchana:** *Marc.* 16.4 *clarissimum iuuenem* [sc. *Drusum*] . . . *uadentem per Gracchana uestigia*, Flor. *Epit.* 2.5.6. S.'s emphasis on social unrest following the legislation of the Gracchi is designed to portray Drusus as a hyperactive agitator set on the wrong course. **stipatus** 'thronged about' by Italian supporters of Drusus' plan to extend the franchise; Vell. 2.14.1 (of Drusus when campaigning for his proposal) *immensa illa et incondita, quae eum semper comitabatur, cinctus multitudine*, Flor. *Epit.* 2.5.1 *totius . . . Italiae consensu.*   **exitum . . . peruidens** 'seeing no clear way out for his policies'. Acc. to App. *B.C.* 1.35, both the Senate and the Equites opposed Drusus' judicial legislation, the former indignant at the proposed elevation of 300 Equites to senatorial rank, the latter suspecting that they would lose control of the courts to the Senate. Fearful of having to give up land, the Italians were also made apprehensive by Drusus' agrarian and colonial policies (1.36); and Drusus' known association with Italian leaders such as Q. Pompaedius Silo (Plut. *Cato min.* 1.5) aroused suspicions of disloyalty and undermined support for Italian enfranchisement. At the instigation of L. Marcius Philippus (cos. 91), the Senate consequently invalidated all of Drusus' legislation (Cic. *Dom.* 41, Diod. 37.10.3); hence the impasse described by S. in *quas . . . relinquere* below.   **agere** 'carry through'.   **nec . . . relinquere** 'and which it was no longer an option to abandon'. *liberum est* lit. 'it is a matter of free choice' (*OLD* 10c); with an inf., Ciceronian (e.g. *Phil.* 1.12) and rare in S. (*Cl.* 1.7.4). Flor. *Epit.* 2.5.9 reports that the Italians, having supported Drusus' initial legislative successes, demanded Roman citizenship in return; Drusus had ignited a fire which could not be extinguished (Liv. *Per.* 71 *cum deinde promissa sociis ciuitas praestari non posset, irati Italici defectionem agitare coeperunt*); the Social War resulted (acc. to Vell. 2.15.1–2 it was directly precipitated by Drusus' murder).   **semel inchoatas** 'when once they had been entered into'; *semel* here of 'a single occurrence upon which some consequence ensues' (*OLD* 4).   **execratus:** cf. 5.1 *detestatur*. S. bears sole (and therefore suspicious) witness to Drusus' complaints against his life.   **inquietam a primordiis** 'constantly active from its very beginnings'. S. takes Drusus' reputation for precocity to the furthest extreme.   **dicitur dixisse:** a harsh repetition (Duff 113) designed to stress the 'objective' nature of S.'s reporting.   **ferias** 'a day of rest' (*OLD* 2). Drusus illustrates the opposite of the existence advocated at *Tr.* 17.4–8, where relaxation from mental exertion is made an integral part of the balanced life.   **et pupillus ... et praetextatus:** Drusus apparently pleaded his first cases at 16 (at most!). Assuming that he was born in 124 (*RE* XIII 1.861), he was 15 when made a ward (*pupillus*) after the death of his father in 109 while in office as *censor* (*RE* XIII 1.858); he would have assumed the *toga uirilis* (in place of the *toga praetexta*) by 17 (Courtney on Juv. 1.77). At *Inst.* 12.6.1 Quintilian sets no specific age at which orators should begin to plead cases; he goes on to list examples of youthful performance (at 18 or not much older; cf. Tac. *Dial.* 34.7), then adding that even greater precocity was heard of (*praetextatos egisse quosdam sit traditum*).   **iudicibus ... commendare:** far from embarking on his career in the manner prescribed by Quintilian (*Inst.* 12.6.6 *illum ... iuuenem ... incipere quam maxime facili ac fauorabili causa uelim*), Drusus acts precociously for the defence, a far more demanding task than prosecution (*Inst.* 5.13.2–3); often avoided by established orators, prosecuting was 'work for *adulescentuli* wishing to make a name for themselves' (Crook (1995) 138).   **gratiam ... interponere** 'to exert his special (*suam*; *OLD* 11) influence in the courts'; *foro* dat. dependent on *interponere*.   **efficaciter:** Livian (10.16.3) and mostly post-Augustan; rare in S. (*Ep.* 94.43; comparative at *Ep.* 80.7, 108.9, superlative at *Ir.* 3.27.4).   **quidem:** an instance of what Solodow (1978) 110–19 categorizes as 'extending *quidem*', reinforcing the general point (*ausus est ... interponere*) with specific evidence to prove the case.   **iudicia ... rapta:** verdicts 'captured' against the odds; Quint. *Decl.* 268 p. 86.16 Sh. B. *rapiunt* [sc. *oratores*] *malas aliquando causas.*

6.2 quo ... ambitio?: lit. 'in which direction was such premature ambition not likely to burst forth?' *erumperet* a potential subjunctive of the past (G–L §258); for pejorative *ambitio*, 2.1 n.   **scires** 'you might have known'; indefinite second pers. subjunctive.   **euasuram** [sc. *esse*] 'would result in'; so e.g. *V.B.* 14.2, but already Ter. *Ad.* 508–9 *nimia illaec licentia* | ... *euadet in aliquod magnum malum.*   **praecoquem audaciam:** *tam*, a late MS insertion before *praecoquem* to balance *tam immatura ambitio* above and printed by some editors, is superfluous; the stronger point is that *any* precocious presumptuousness courts disaster. *audaciam*, anticipated by 6.1 *ausus est*, is decidedly pejorative in tone (*OLD* 2).   **itaque:** 2.5 n. on *non ... quod.*   **querebatur:** either inceptive imperf. ('began to complain') or iterative ('kept complaining').   **seditiosus ... grauis** 'factious and bringing trouble to the forum'; *foro* (dat.; *Tr.* 1.6 *nec patrimonio nec corpori grauis* [sc. *cibus*], 3.6, *Helu.* 5.3) denotes the *rostra* (Duff 114), marking Drusus' progress from precocious performances in the law-courts (6.1 *foro*) to political activism.   **disputatur ... collapsus est:** no other source suggests that Drusus committed suicide, and at *Marc.* 16.4 S. himself reports that Drusus was murdered in his own home by an unknown assassin (so Cic. *Mil.* 16, *N.D.* 3.80, Liv. *Per.* 71, Vell. 2.14.1, [Sen.] *Oct.* 887–90, Flor. *Epit.* 2.6.3–4, App. *B.C.* 1.36). S.'s innovation is designed to illustrate the (lit.) self-destructive effects of a life burdened by preoccupation and by the weight of its own precocious success (4.1 *in se ipsa fortuna ruit*). Far from Stoic in his hyperactive ambition, Drusus gives only the illusion of 'true' Stoic action by suddenly (and by no means definitely) committing suicide; *subito* hardly suggests careful premeditation (contrast *Ep.* 70.5–6, where the *sapiens* will contemplate the possibility of suicide long before actually taking his life).   **uulnere per inguen accepto:** Vell. 2.14.1 (Drusus stabbed in the side by a small knife), App. *B.C.* 1.36 (a cobbler's knife allegedly found thrust into Drusus' thigh).   **aliquo ... an** 'some doubting whether ... '; *aliquo* (sing. for plur.) in contrast to *nullo* below (a familiar combination; *TLL* 1 1614.25–38). Wanting to stress the possibility of suicide, S. carefully plays down the general consensus that Drusus was murdered.   **nullo:** 3.1 n. **tempestiua:** ironic; the only timely event in Drusus' precocious life is his early death. Cf. Flor. *Epit.* 2.5.9 *imparem Drusum aegrumque rerum temere motarum matura, ut in tali discrimine, mors abstulit.*

6.3 superuacuum est ... plures: a strategic end to S.'s sequence of three *exempla*, 'proving' the rule by appeal to untold illustrations of the same (examples are elusive and conveniently left unnamed). **superuacuum:** first in verse in Horace, in prose in Livy (N–H on

C. 2.20.24), this poetical substitute for Classical *superuacaneus* came to be the preferred form in Silver prose (Krebs–Schmalz II 629); a favourite with S. (e.g. 6.4, 11.2, 13.3, *Tr.* 3.6, *Ben.* 2.34.4, *Ep.* 45.12, 48.12, *N.Q.* 3.16.1). **uerum testimonium:** testimony such as that which S. quotes from the letters of Augustus (4.3) and Cicero (5.2) and gleans from hearsay about Drusus (6.1 *dicitur... contigisse*).   **perosi** 'when they expressed intense (*per-*) hatred for ...'; the verb only once elsewhere in S., again of special loathing (*Phaed.* 124 *stirpem perosa Solis inuisi Venus*).   **omnem actum** 'every action' performed over the years; *Ep.* 76.19 *in omni actu uitae*, 120.10. **nec alios ... nec se ipsos:** i.e. because they fail to change themselves they have no salutary transforming effect on others.   **cum** 'as often as' (iterative; G–L §584), with the perf. indicative as at e.g. *Ep.* 21.9, 47.5, 52.8, 56.1; but possibly also with concessive force as at e.g. Ov. *Am.* 3.8.5–7 (... *cum bene laudauit, laudato ianua clausa est*).   **eruperunt:** the words 'burst forth', unable to be suppressed; cf. 6.2 for Drusus' 'bursting' ambition.   **affectus ... relabuntur** 'the passions revert to their habitual state'; *affectus* pejorative in connotation (1.1 n.).

6.4 S. takes his general audience to task for failing to seize each precious moment when life is so fleeting. The transition from the three preceding *exempla* is harsh (Duff 114) but strategic: S.'s fresh diatribe is arresting precisely because of the abruptness of its opening.   **Vestra:** 3.4 n. on *tamquam ... sit*.   **mehercules** 'in reality' (5.3 n.); for the position between adj. and noun and for the sense, Cic. *Att.* 1.8.1 *uir mehercule optimus* ('an excellent fellow really', Shackleton Bailey I 113). **uita ... contrahetur:** (i) *uita* = *spatium temporis*, the subj. of the clause *licet... exeat*; (ii) *uita* = 'that small part of life which is *really* lived' (2.2 n. on '*exigua ... uiuimus*'), the subj. of *contrahetur*; the paradoxical effect of the sentence derives from the shift in the sense of *uita* as we move from one clause to the next.   **exeat** 'go beyond'.   **in artissimum contrahetur** 'will be shrunk into the merest span of time'; most of life will be squandered.   **ista:** 2.5 n.; more accusing in tone than *uestra*.   **uitia:** for the wordplay as *uita* is assailed by *uitia*, 2.3 n. on *urgent... sinunt*.   **nullum non saeculum** 'every century' of the life which lasts a thousand years and more (*licet... exeat* above); for S.'s use of the strong affirmative, *Ot.* 5.4 n. and *Breu.* 2.1 n. on *numquam non*.   **deuorabunt** 'will swallow up'; the metaphorical use with an inanimate subj. is rare in S. (*Tro.* 400 *tempus nos... deuorat et chaos*).   **hoc ... dilatat** 'this span of time which, although it naturally hurries on, reason prolongs ...' For *natura* (abl.) used adverbially, *Ep.* 97.15; for *currit* applied to time's swift passage, 8.5n. The phrase *spatium currit* is unprecedented (cf. *Ep.* 99.7 *cogita breuitatem huius spatii per quod citatissimi currimus*) but no bolder than [*spatium*] *effugiat* below.   **uero** 'to be sure', underscoring the truth of the assertion (*OLD* 3). **ratio:** good management; since Stoic *ratio* determines appropriate action by recommending what to pursue and what to avoid (*Ep.* 82.6, 84.11), it 'prolongs' life by overseeing the wise investment of time (1.4 *aetas nostra bene disponenti multum patet*).   **dilatat:** before S., applied to time only by Vitruvius (9.8.10 *sol . . . dilatat contrahitque dies et horas*, 9.8.13); only two post-Senecan examples are listed at *TLL* v 1.1164.22–3.   **cito uos effugiat necesse est:** adversative in tone, i.e. '[this span of life which reason prolongs] must in your case however inevitably escape you quickly; for . . .' S. never uses *ut* to introduce a subjunctive clause dependent on *necesse est*. **apprenditis . . . retinetis** [sc. *uelocissimam omnium rem*] 'seize' in the moment and 'hold back' thereafter. Of time the first verb is unparalleled in Classical and Silver Latin but a natural companion to Horace's *carpe diem* (*C.* 1.11.8); for the second, *Ep.* 108.27.   **rei:** dat. dependent on *moram facitis*; *Helu.* 13.2 *moram tibi ambitio non faciet*.   **ut . . . reparabilem** 'as if it were something over-abundant which can be retrieved'. For *superuacuam*, 6.3n. Poetic *reparabilis* recurs in S. only at *Ep.* 1.3 (time contrasted with material things *quae minima et uilissima sunt, certe reparabilia*); contrast *Ep.* 123.10 *irreparabilis uita decurrit*, where the adj. is Virgilian (*G.* 3.284, quoted by S. at *Ep.* 108.24; *Aen.* 10.467–8).

7 *The art of living*

S. again (cf. 2.1–5) surveys 'misguided' attitudes and behaviour, on this occasion to demonstrate that the preoccupied know nothing of how really to live. The philosopher alone possesses such knowledge, setting a standard (7.5) which the rest of humanity manifestly falls short of in S.'s surrounding descriptions (7.1–4, 6–8) of life-sapping activity (and inactivity); the chapter ends with a contrasting picture of the philosopher's always complete existence. The uncompromising standards of the *sapiens* here establish a remote landmark of principle which disconcerts, even if it does not ultimately change, complacent or unquestioned attitudes to life.

7.1–2 Critics have argued either that 7.1–2 are misplaced in the transmitted text (e.g. Gertz (1874) 150, Albertini (1923) 179–81) or that another section of text is to be transposed to before 7.1 (Duff 115), thereby easing the apparent incoherence between 6.4 and the new chapter; for at the start of 7.1 S. abruptly locates the drunk and debauched among the worst of the wastefully preoccupied without having formally introduced that general class of *occupati* in an earlier chapter. Hence Duff 115 claims that 'neither *in primis* nor *et illos* can be explained here', adding that '*istorum* [7.2] has nothing to refer to'; but see in response 7.1 n. on *In primis . . . numero*, 7.2 n. on *omnia . . . excute*. In broader defence of the transmitted text, allowance has to be made for S.'s technique of abrupt and sometimes disconcerting transition from one stage of argument to the next. He also gives his strictures as wide an application as possible by varying the direction and scope of his forms of personal address (general intro. p. 27), so that in the last chapter the area of reference moves from the single individual (Drusus, 6.1–2) to *plures* (6.3) and then to S.'s general audience (*uos*) in 6.4. The theme of squandering one's energies and precious time (6.4) is taken up, with fresh emphasis, in the 'worst case' of the drunk and debauched in 7.1, where the area of personal reference changes again from *uos* (6.4) to *illos*; S. then turns to the more 'respectable' class of *occupati* (7.1 *ceteri*) before reverting to the more general *istorum* in 7.2. The disconcertingly unpredictable way in which S. varies the focal point of personal address in 6 is taken further in 7.1–2, where (short of transposing the passage) we may view the transition at best as unsubtle, at worst as a rare example in S. of a lack of organizing power.

7.1 In primis . . . numero 'In fact, among the worst cases I count also those who . . . ' *et* is not necessarily 'meaningless – no other class of *occupati* having been mentioned' (Duff 115); quite apart from the objection that at 2.1–5 S. surveys the lives of those who are *occupati* in all but name, *et* adds to, or stresses the membership of one group (*illos*) among, the specific class of *occupati* introduced at the start of the sentence. *autem* is explanatory (*OLD* 4a), supplying the link with 6.4: after S. has taken his general readership (*uos*) to task for wasting time, the particle amplifies the point by introducing a more specific and wretched case.   **uino ac libidini:** in familiar combination among the worst of base passions (*Ben.* 4.27.3 *hic uino, hic libidini deditus est*, *Ep.* 59.11, 17, 73.6, 99.13).   **uacant** 'give time to'.   **occupati:** apart from 2.4 *occupatio* (Gertz's plausible conjecture), the first appearance in the treatise of a key word on which S. now concentrates as a means of portraying both activity and inactivity of every (non-philosophical) kind as equally futile and ultimately frustrating.   **uana gloriae imagine** 'by the false semblance of glory'; *Ep.* 95.73 *o quam ignorant homines cupidi gloriae quid illa sit aut quemadmodum petenda!*   **speciose** 'in respectable fashion', relative to the behaviour of the grossly debauched.   **auaros ... iracundos:** S. aggravates the evil of 'wine and lust' by deliberately portraying as relatively seemly two vices which are themselves extreme. *auaritia* is *durissimum malum minimeque flexibile* (*Ir.* 2.36.6) and grouped with *luxuria, ambitio* etc. as diseases of the mind at *Ep.* 56.10, 75.11, 85.10, 106.6; but for anger as the most hideous and frenzied of all the passions, *Ir.* 1.1.1, 2.35.3–6, 3.1.3–5, 3.4.1–3. S. uses *iracundos* (as opposed to *iratos*) to stress the permanence of the condition; for *ira* and *iracundia* differentiated, *Ir.* 1.4.1.   **iniusta** qualifies both *odia* and *bella*. At *Ir.* 3.41.3 S. portrays anger which hardens into hate as incurable; for anger leading to war (public or private, national or individual), *Ir.* 3.5.6.   **uirilius** 'in more manly fashion'; for slavery to the appetites and lust (*uino ac libidini* above, *uentrem ac libidinem* below) is servitude to enervating pleasure (*V.B.* 13.4, *Ben.* 4.2.4, *Ep.* 104.34). **in ... proiectorum** 'abandoned to ... ' For the nuance (Ciceronian; *OLD proiectus*[1] 2), Tac. *Hist.* 5.5.2 *proiectissima ad libidinem gens*; for the combination of *uentrem ac libidinem, Ben.* 7.2.2, *Ep.* 55.5, 124.3.   **inhonesta labes est:** the predicative adj. in contrast to *speciose* above; *labes* ('stain') strongly pejorative as at *Marc.* 22.2, *Pol.* 3.5 *ab omni labe mens uacans, Ep.* 4.1.

7.2 omnia ... excute 'scrutinize every moment of such people's lives'. *istorum* (with derogatory force; *OLD* 5b) presumably refers to the *occupati* of all kinds, not just to the *isti* (7.1) who *uirilius peccant*; for having conceded that certain *occupati* are engaged in more seemly pursuits than others, S. now qualifies that picture by illustrating the overwhelming effects of *any* engrossment. **quam diu:** the start of an anaphoric sequence whose breathless progress reflects the suffocating engrossments of the *occupati*.   **computent** 'assess their gains', possibly alluding to the accountancy of the *auari* in 7.1; so *Ir.* 3.33.3 (of the gnarled usurer) *manibus ad computandum non relictis.* But the verb refers more generally to 'calculating the gains' of a given (often ruthless) action; e.g. *Ep.* 14.9 *plures computant quam oderunt* (i.e. more murderers assess the profits of their crime than kill out of hatred), Juv. 6.651.   **timeant:** *insidias* perhaps to be understood from *insidientur* (Duff 116), but the unaccompanied verb emphasizes ruling (*diu*) passion; for fear as one of the four cardinal Stoic πάθη along with desire, pain and pleasure, *SVF* III 92.16, 93.12, 94.7, 95.16.   **colant ... colantur:** 2.4 *ille illius cultor est, hic illius; suus nemo est.*   **quantum:** sc. *temporis.*   **uadimonia ... aliena** 'pledges given by the defendant and sought from others when he is the plaintiff'. A *uadimonium* was a promise made by a defendant already on trial, or by a debtor pursued by creditors, to (re-)appear before a magistrate on an appointed day; the promise could be strengthened by an oath or by bail (Berger 757).   **ipsa** qualifies *conuiuia*: 'dinner-parties which in themselves have become occasions for doing business', esp. for the kind of client-guest portrayed in e.g. Juv. 5 (12–13 *tu discumbere iussus* | *mercedem solidam ueterum capis officiorum*: the client pays, and is paid for, service).   **uidebis:** the apodosis after the protasis implicit in the imperatives *excute* and *aspice* above; 2.4n. on *interroga...uidebis*.   **respirare** 'to draw breath'. For the fig. usage, Ciceronian and Livian (*OLD* 2b), *V.B.* 2.2, *Ep.* 65.16; for combination with *sinant*, Cic. *Fin.* 1.53 *cuius in animo uersatur* [sc. *improbitas*]*, numquam sinit eum respirare*.   **uel mala...uel bona** 'their affairs, whether you call them bad or good'. *bona* ironic; S. refers back to 7.1 *speciose...errant* and *uirilius peccant*, now blurring the distinction between more and less respectable preoccupations to portray them all, relatively 'good' or not, as equally suffocating.

7.3–5 The *occupati* of all kinds are contrasted with the philosopher, who alone knows how 'really' to live.

7.3 Denique 'to sum up'. After portraying the *occupati* as suffocated by their many preoccupations, S. confidently establishes the general rule: those with divided interests adequately attend to none.   **nullam rem** 'no one area of study'.   **eloquentiam:** for the specialist status of rhetoric, Cic. *Off.* 1.115 *se alii ad philosophiam, alii ad ius ciuile, alii ad eloquentiam applicant*.   **liberales disciplinas:** for the phrase, *Pol.* 2.5. S. more often uses *liberalia studia* (e.g. 18.4, *Helu.* 6.2, 17.3, *Ep.* 36.3, 88.2, 20, 29), the Latin equivalent of ἐγκύκλιος παιδεία in Greek tradition (*Ep.* 88.23, Quint. *Inst.* 1.10.1) and embracing the seven liberal arts – a system which survived down to the Middle Ages in the form of the so called *triuium* (grammar, rhetoric, dialectic) and *quadriuium* (geometry, arithmetic, astronomy, music). **districtus** 'pulled in different directions'; so 10.6, 14.3, *Ben.* 5.23.1 *occupationibus districtus*, *Ep.* 56.9, 106.1.   **nihil...recipit** 'takes in nothing really deeply'; for the adv., *Ir.* 2.32.3, *Marc.* 23.1.   **sed...respuit** 'but rejects everything that is, so to speak, driven into it'. *respuit* in combination with *recipit* also at *V.B.* 21.4; for *inculco* of something forced on an unwilling recipient, *V.B.* 24.1, *Ben.* 6.24.1 *liberalia studia inculcant* [sc. *parentes*] *...nolentibus*.   **nihil...uiuere** 'there is nothing less characteristic of a person who is encumbered than a sense of how really to live'; for loaded *uiuere*, 2.2n. on *'exigua...uiuimus'*.   **difficilior** 'harder to acquire'.

scientia: knowledge of the sort acquired through philosophy at 19.2 (*uiuendi ac moriendi scientia*); *SVF* III 156.1–3 'The Stoics say outright that practical wisdom (τὴν φρόνησιν), which is knowledge of things that are good and bad and neither, is a skill relating to life (τέχνην ὑπάρχειν περὶ τὸν βίον).'   **uulgo** 'two a penny'; the adv. is virtually equivalent to an adj. (Bourgery (1922) 395).   **ex his:** sc. *artibus.*   **pueri admodum** 'mere boys'; so *Marc.* 24.3 *ut puer admodum dignus sacerdotio uideretur*, and for the adv. regularly applied to age, *OLD* 4.   **percepisse ... praecipere:** by the parisyllabic wordplay (Summers lxxxiii) young masters of the subject are portrayed as potential masters in the classroom. For the play, Nep. *Att.* 17.3 *principum philosophorum ita percepta habuit praecepta, ut...*; for the pupil graduating to teacher, *Marc.* 18.7 *disces docebisque artes*, *Ot.* 2.2 *discunt...et cum didicerunt docent.*   **possent:** imperf. subjunctive in primary sequence (*uisi sunt* = pure perf.) because the verb denotes present unreality (i.e. 'they could [now] be teachers but they are not').   **uiuere ... discendum est:** adversative asyndeton marks abrupt contrast with what precedes; *uiuere* ('the art of living') is set against *aliarum artium* above, the evolving process of life-long learning (*tota uita discendum est*) against the complete learning of 'mere boys' who quickly master the inferior arts. For the idea, *Ep.* 76.3 *tamdiu discendum est quemadmodum uiuas quamdiu uiuas.*   **tota uita:** the abl. of duration of time, occasionally in Classical prose (K–S I 360), occurs regularly in Silver Latin (e.g. *Cl.* 1.9.11, *Helu.* 20.2, *Ep.* 52.10, 77.20, *N.Q.* 6.17.3, cited by Summers lviii and Bourgery (1922) 326); for *totus* in the abl. denoting 'the whole of time within which', *OLD* 3b, adding e.g. Catul. 109.5–6 *liceat nobis tota perducere uita | ...foedus amicitiae* with Fordyce, Cic. *De orat.* 3.88.   **mori:** postponed to the end of the sentence to balance *uiuere* at the other extreme. S. repeatedly urges reflection on death (e.g. *Ep.* 26.8, 10 *meditare mortem*, from Epicurus (fr. 205 Us.), 70.18, 114.27, *N.Q.* 6.32.12); for to learn how to die is liberating (*Ep.* 26.10 *qui mori didicit seruire dedidicit*), anticipating the soul's release in death from bodily captivity (*Marc.* 23.2) and bringing freedom from the fear of death (*Ep.* 30.18 *mortem ut numquam timeas semper cogita*, 36.8, *N.Q.* 6.32.12). The Stoic notion of *meditatio mortis* is Platonic in origin (e.g. *Phd.* 67e 4–5 'true philosophers diligently practise dying'; cf. *SVF* III 190.36–7 'the Stoics understood philosophy to be a training for natural death'). But for Epicurean appropriation of the same idea (allowing S. to borrow the phrase *meditare mortem* at *Ep.* 26.8, 10), *Ep. Men.* 126 = L–S I 24A7 'to practise living well and to practise dying well are one and the same'.

7.4 tot maximi uiri: an unnamed generality of 'the greatest' in terms of philosophical endeavour and commitment; but whether they attain their ultimate goals is another matter (*plures . . . abierunt* below). **impedimentis:** obstacles to immersion in philosophy; *C.S.* 3.2 *omnibus relictis negotiis Stoicus fio, Ep.* 5.1 (cited with other parallels by Duff 117). **renuntiassent:** intrans. with dat. of the thing renounced, first found in S. (*Marc.* 8.3, *Tr.* 3.7, *Ep.* 108.15, *Ben.* 7.14.6).   **hoc unum . . . egerunt, ut** 'made it their sole aim to . . .'; 18.4n.   **in extremam usque aetatem:** for the position of *usque, Ben.* 5.2.4 *ad ultimum usque uitae diem stabit paratus, Ep.* 95.37, 98.1, 6, *N.Q.* 2.9.2, in contrast to its more familiar position at e.g. *Ot.* 1.4, 5.7, *Cl.* 1.6.3 *usque ad extremum aeui delinquemus*, 1.7.1, *Ep.* 104.28. When postponed, the word acquires additional stress ('right up to the end – the very end – of life').   **plures** 'the majority'.   **nedum ut isti sciant** 'still less do those others [sc. the *occupati*, non-philosophers by definition] know how to live'. *nedum ut* + subjunctive is Livian (3.14.6, 30.21.9) and post-Augustan (*C.S.* 8.3, Quint. *Inst.* 12.1.39, Tac. *Dial.* 10.2); the more usual construction in Classical and Silver Latin is *nedum* + subjunctive without *ut* (K–S II 67–8).

7.5 magni . . . uiri est . . . sinere: the familiar defining gen. with *est* is here extended to an unusual compass with the insertion of the colloquial *mihi crede* (18.3, *Marc.* 16.1, *Pol.* 9.5, 9, *Ep.* 8.6, 17.2; Hofmann 126) and the fig. variation *supra . . . eminentis* (*Pol.* 2.5, *Ep.* 36.6, 71.5); the elongated construction is appropriate to a context describing the Stoic philosopher's *uitam longissimam*, which is measured not in years but in his uninterrupted disposition to virtue.   **delibari:** lit. 'to be skimmed off', here denoting not even the merest diminution of perfect wholeness; so in relation to time Lucr. *D.R.N.* 3.1087–8 *nec . . . uitam ducendo* (i.e. 'by protracting life') *demimus hilum | tempore de mortis nec delibare ualemus.*   **quantumcumque . . . uacauit** 'however much or little time has been available, the whole of it has been free for his use'. S. measures the length of life by the amount of time devoted exclusively to oneself. For the idea and the temporal sense of *patuit, Ep.* 78.28 *ut Posidonius ait* [= fr. 179.4–5 E–K], '*unus dies hominum eruditorum plus patet quam imperitis longissima aetas.*'   **inde:** sc. *ex ea uita.*   **otiosumque iacuit:** Erasmus' conjecture, supplying a verb appropriate to the image of time lying 'barren' or 'fallow' like uncultivated land (*N.Q.* 3.6.2, 4A.2.9; already Virg. *G.* 2.37 *neu segnes iaceant terrae*); *otiosus* for unproductive land is unprecedented (*TLL* IX 2.1170.74–1171.1).   **sub** 'under the control of' (*OLD* 15). **neque . . . repperit** 'for he found nothing'; *neque enim* commonly used to

connect an explanatory sentence or clause with what precedes (K–S II 43).
dignum . . . permutaret 'worth exchanging for his time'. For the verb
with (*cum* +) abl. of the thing given in exchange, *OLD* 3a; the relative of
tendency is regularly used with *dignus* and other terms emphasizing character (G–L §631.1).   **eius:** sc. *temporis sui*; possibly governed by the adj. as
well as the noun (but S. never elsewhere uses *parcus* + gen.).   **itaque:**
2.5n. on *non . . . quod.*   **satis:** substantive, with *temporis* (partitive gen.)
understood.   **uero** 'however', pointing the contrast between *illi* and *iis*.
necesse est defuisse: sc. *tempus.*   **populus:** pejorative, suggesting
the 'crowd' of clients (2.4 *circumfusus clientium populus*) and other invaders of
time such as those described in 7.6–7.

7.6–8 In contrast to the philosopher's serene existence (7.5), S. revis-
its the pressures and frustrations of the *occupati*, enlivening his description
by affecting an urgent, abrasive tone. Brief sentences with little subordination, a volley of pointed questions in 7.7, the use of confrontational
second-person forms of address, the surveying of a diverse range of characters which, in 7.8, implicates even (or esp.) the most distinguished citizens
(consul, praetor, leading advocate) in the same general mass of *occupati* –
all these features contribute to the nervous stylistic energy of the section.
S. also draws on fresh evidence to support his argument: by 'quoting' their
expressions of anguish (e.g. 7.6 *'uiuere mihi non licet'*), he conveniently has the
occupati themselves bear dramatic witness to their frustrations.

7.6 nec est quod: 2.5n.   **illos non aliquando . . . suum** 'that
those people are not sometimes conscious of their loss'. *hinc illos aliquando*
MSS, but *hinc* ('from this circumstance'?) is sufficiently imprecise to be
suspect; hence Madvig's conjecture of *non* in its place (II 397). Unless the
negative is supplied either there or later in the phrase (*illos <non>* Reynolds),
an apparent contradiction arises between the statements (i) that there is no
reason to suppose that the *occupati* are sometimes conscious of their loss and
(ii) (*plerosque . . . licet* below) that 'you will certainly hear many of them occasionally exclaiming *uiuere mihi non licet*' (how then can they be unaware of
their loss in (i)?).   **plerosque:** 2.2n.   **quos . . . grauat:** 2.4 *aspice
illos ad quorum felicitatem concurritur: bonis suis offocantur*, where the same characters (the overworked advocate, the patron besieged by clients) appear as
here; but S. now gives them voice actively to complain (*'uiuere mihi non licet'*).
For *felicitas* weighing heavily upon itself/its possessor, *Ep.* 74.18 *ipsa . . . se
felicitas, nisi temperatur, premit*, 94.74 (4.1 above for the anxieties attendant
upon prosperous fortune).   **grauat:** of grievous affliction at e.g. *Her.*

F. 628 *quae domum clades grauat?, Phaed.* 859. **greges** 'hordes'; pejorative as at *Tr.* 1.16 *inter laudantium blandientiumque positus greges.* **causarum
actiones** 'pleadings of cases' (cf. *OLD causa* 3a); the formula is Ciceronian
(*Caec.* 4, *Deiot.* 7). **honestas miserias:** i.e. socially respectable forms
of occupational drudgery. **interdum** complements *aliquando* above:
the occasional outburst is prompted by occasional awareness of lost time.
'uiuere mihi non licet' 'I've no chance to live'; but if *mihi* is (also)
construed with *uiuere* ('live for myself'), the speaker inadvertently (?) uses
philosophically charged words (4.2n. on *se uicturum sibi*).

7.7 quidni non liceat? 'Of course you lack the chance!'; *Ot.* 7.3n.
te ... abducunt: sharp antithesis in two pairings (*sibi ... tibi, ad- ...
ab- ...*). For the meaning of *aduocant* in legal contexts, 2.4n. on *hic ... iudicat*;
sibi is dat. of advantage, *tibi* of disadvantage (*Ep.* 62.2 *cum me amicis dedi, non
tamen mihi abduco*, 88.34). But the legal nuance of *aduocant* is relevant only to
the first (*ille reus ... abstulit?*) of the five brisk questions which S. poses below;
for he moves from the legal arena to social summonses elsewhere, and the
initial addressee (*te ... tibi*) recedes into the diverse mass of *occupati* finally
addressed in *uos* below. All in their different ways are *aduocati* (i.e. 'called
upon' for legal or other social duty). **abstulit** 'took up' (*OLD* 14), but
with the added implication of 'took', 'snatched away' as at *Ep.* 1.1 *tempus
quod adhuc ... auferebatur ... collige.* **quot ... candidatus?:** canvassers
promoting candidates for election were known as *suffragatores*; 17.5 *candidati laborare desimus, suffragatores incipimus.* **efferendis ... lassa** 'worn
down by burying her heirs'. Legacy-hunters were notorious for preying
on the bereaved or childless (2.2n. on *affectatio*); but S. alludes here to the
manipulative power which the bereaved holds over her *captatores* (*C.S.* 6.1
diues aliquis regnum orbae senectutis exercens, Marc. 19.2, Plin. *N.H.* 14.5, Mart.
1.49.34). **ille ... aeger** 'that man who feigns illness in order to excite
the greed of legacy-hunters'; for the tactic, Petr. 117.9 *imperamus Eumolpo
ut plurimum tussiat* (i.e. to deceive the legacy-hunters of Croton), Mart.
5.39.5-6. **amicus:** ironic given what follows; one's more powerful
'friend' is an *amicus* in name only. **qui ... habet** 'who retains you not
for the purposes of true friendship but for show'; for the latter idiom (rare),
*OLD apparatus*² 2, incl. *Tr.* 9.5. **dispunge ... et recense ... dies**
'mark off and survey the days of your life' in an audit parallel to that conducted at 3.2-3. The first verb, post-Augustan and rare in S., lit. denotes
the weighing of income and expenditure (cf. *Ben.* 4.32.4); the second refers
to the review conducted after the initial accounting is done. **inquam:**

used to reinforce the imperative as at e.g. *Marc.* 12.4 *circumspice, inquam, omnes, N.Q.* 1.6.4; the emphasizing parenthesis is commonly found in both ordinary and more formal speech (Hofmann 125).   **uidebis:** 2.4n. on *interroga . . . uidebis.*   **paucos admodum** 'very few'; 1.1 *exceptis admodum paucis.*   **reiculos** 'worthless', an abusive application of the agricultural term for older animals due to be culled (Var. *R.* 2.1.24, 2.5.17), cleverly restored here by Erasmus; the shocking *reicula mancipia* ('worthless slaves') was similarly restored by Muretus at *Ep.* 47.9, where (as here) the MSS have a form of *ridiculus.* Summers xlvi (b) lists other agricultural terms used by S. and mostly or always avoided by 'the purely literary writers'.   **apud te resedisse** 'have been retained in your possession'; legal terminology fig. applied (*OLD resideo* 3b).

7.8 assecutus . . . ponere: *fasces* is postponed behind its dependent relative clause (*quos optauerat*) to give it central position within the phrase, consular office being the focal point of all administrative ambition; *assecutus* and *ponere* are polarized at either end of the construction to illustrate how what starts as the goal of one's ambition finally becomes an intolerable burden.   **subinde** 'repeatedly'; the nuance, frequent in S. (e.g. *Ep.* 13.13, 15.10, 32.3, 53.2), is not found in prose before Livy (e.g. 4.44.7, 9.16.4, 29.34.2).   **'quando . . . praeteribit?':** S. grants the consul a full – and long – year in office, but under the Empire several consuls normally held office consecutively in the same year. The first two (*consules ordinarii*) gave their names to the year but conventionally stepped down after two to four months, to be succeeded by *consules suffecti* (Talbert (1984) 21).   **ille:** the praetor; in 22 BC Augustus transferred responsibility for public shows from the aediles, and, although the consuls probably continued to contribute to the cost, the main burden of staging the games (*ludos circenses*) and/or theatrical shows (*ludos scaenicos*) fell upon the praetors (Talbert (1984) 59–64).   **quorum . . . aestimauit:** he greatly prized the fact that responsibility for the games fell to him; lit. denoting a duty assigned by lot, *sors* is esp. used of the dividing of duties among the praetors (Lewis–Short IIB).   **magno:** abl. of value (sc. *pretio*).   **istos:** derogatory (*OLD* 5b).   **diripitur:** lit. 'is torn to pieces', lionized by the entire forum (so *Ir.* 3.23.5 *Timagenes . . . tota ciuitate direptus est*); a Silver metaphor (*TLL* V 1.1261.45–54).   **omnia . . . complet** 'fills the whole place further than he can be heard'; *complet* balances *diripitur*, drawing together the crowd (with a play in <u>concursu . . . com</u>-) which 'tears to pieces' the star attraction; the marked repetition of long vowels, esp. *o* and *u*, may

echo the advocate's resonant delivery.   **'quando . . . proferentur?'**
'when will there be a vacation?'; for *res proferre* applied to the adjourn-
ment of public or legal business, *OLD profero* 10a. The orator's words echo
the cries of tedium of the consul (*'quando . . . praeteribit?'*) and the praetor
(*'quando . . . effugiam?'*), the cumulative effect being to highlight dramatically
the moment at which popular success turns to exasperation and disillusion.

praecipitat . . . taedio: after the three preceding *exempla*, S. defines the
common fault; but he makes no allowance for the possibility that the consul,
praetor, advocate or whoever else may experience only bouts of disillusion,
and that to hurry life on through a yearning for the future and weariness
of the present may be only a temporary and minor aberration (if such it is).

futuri desiderio . . . praesentium taedio: for anxiety about or yearning for the future as an impediment to fully living, 7.9n. on *nec optat . . . nec
timet*. The philosophical importance attached to seizing the moment extends back to Democritus (fr. 202 D–K); the convergence of Epicurean
and Stoic thinking on this point enables S. to declare 'excellent' (*insigne*) the
Epicurean saying which he renders at *Ep.* 15.9 *stulta uita ingrata est, trepida;
tota in futurum fertur* (= fr. 491 Us.).

7.9–10 An alternative perspective on life: after the preceding picture
of lives always hurried on through disillusion with the present, S. advances
the claims of the ever complete Stoic existence.

7.9 at ille qui: the *sapiens* in all but name.   **nullum non:** *Ot.* 5.4n.
in usus . . . confert 'devotes to his own needs' in the manner of the *magnus
uir* in 7.5.   **omnem . . . ordinat** 'organizes each day as if it were a
complete life'. *uitam* of the MSS contrasts with the dissatisfied, incomplete
life hurried on in 7.8 *praecipitat . . . suam*; for each day as a separate existence,
Ep. 61.1 *id ago ut mihi instar totius uitae dies sit*, 101.10. These parallels defend
uitam against *ultimum*, conjectured by Gertz (*ultimam* Bentley) on the analogy
of e.g. *Ep.* 12.8 *sic ordinandus est dies omnis tamquam cogat agmen et consummet atque
expleat uitam*, 93.6, M. Aur. 7.69.   **nec optat . . . nec timet:** the *sapiens*
is devoid of such πάθη as desire and fear; *V.B.* 5.1 *potest beatus dici qui nec cupit
nec timet beneficio rationis*, *Ep.* 121.4 (7.2n. on *timeant*). The *sapiens* never longs for
the future because, ever content with his present lot (*V.B.* 6.2, *Ep.* 74.12), he
always seizes the moment (*Ep.* 1.2 *sic fiet ut minus ex crastino pendeas, si hodierno
manum inieceris*), and so *lives* as opposed to always preparing to live (9.1, *Ep.*
45.12).   **crastinum:** either neut. or masc. (sc. *diem*), the adj. is more
commonly used as a substantive with *in* ('till tomorrow'; *OLD* 1c); but *crastinum* stands alone at *Ep.* 12.9, 32.4, 101.4 (Summers lxi on S.'s substantival

use of this and other adjs. denoting parts of the day or particular days). **nouae uoluptatis:** partitive gen. dependent on *quid*. The *sapiens* alone knows true pleasure, defined at *Ben.* 7.2.3 as *perturbatione carere*. Because such pleasure cannot be improved upon (*Ep.* 85.20), Stoic happiness is not enhanced by long duration (*Ben.* 5.17.6, Cic. *Fin.* 3.46, *SVF* III 14.1–4 = L–S 1 63I). For the parallel Epicurean notion that infinite time brings no increase in pleasure, Epic. *Ratae sententiae* 19 = L–S 1 24CI.   **ad satietatem ... sunt** 'have been enjoyed to the full', but not to excess (*Ir.* 2.17.2 *temperatus sit sapiens*); often used of 'being glutted with food' (*OLD* 2), *satietatem* anticipates the analogy drawn between appetite for life and for food.   **de cetero** 'for the future'; so used (*Ir.* 1.8.1, 3.36.4), not found before S. (*OLD* 3c).   **fortuna:** various editors read *fors fortuna*, *fors* being Muretus' conjecture for *foro* transmitted in some MSS. But S. never elsewhere uses the cultic title *fors fortuna* (for Roman worship of whom, *RE* VII 1.16–19) to denote Stoic τύχη. Hence the case for excising rather than emending *foro*, which may have entered the text through dittography (*for- fortuna*) and modification to agree with *cetero*.   **ordinet:** perhaps more forceful if construed as a jussive rather than a potential subjunctive.   **iam:** emphatic; whatever the future holds, the life of the *sapiens* is already complete. **huic** [sc. *uitae*] **... nihil** 'addition can be made to this life, nothing taken away from it'; understood with *detrahi*, *huic* is dat. of disadvantage. For *adici* applied to the prolongation of an already complete existence, *Ep.* 98.15 *ipse uitae plenus est, cui adici nihil desiderat sua causa sed eorum quibus utilis est*; for the impossibility of detraction from that completeness, *C.S.* 5.4 *sapiens ... nihil perdere potest ...*   **saturo ... aliquid cibi:** the *sapiens* has an appetite for life parallel to that of the sated eater who nevertheless has room for more without craving it; in neither case is consumption taken to excess. The combination *saturo ... ac pleno* is Lucretian (*D.R.N.* 3.960); for the 'banquet of life' motif in Lucretius and elsewhere, Brink III 444–6 appendix 20 on Hor. *Ep.* 2.2.214–16.   **nec ... et** 'while not craving it, yet at the same time ...'; for *et* (suppl. Madvig II 397–8) so used with *nec*, *Ir.* 3.8.5 *elige ... qui iram tuam nec euocent et ferant*, *OLD et* 14a. **capit** 'has room for'; 15.1, *Ep.* 47.2 *est* ('eats') *ille plus quam capit*, 88.41, 108.2.

7.10 non ... quod: 2.5n.   **canos:** as a substantive in prose (sc. *capillos*; *C.S.* 12.1, 17.2, *N.Q.* 3.29.3), once in Cicero (*Sen.* 62) and then post-Augustan (*TLL* III 298.2–40).   **non ... fuit:** *correctio* (not x but y) points the contrast between 'really' living (*uixit*) and merely existing (*fuit*). A familiar distinction, e.g. *Ep.* 49.10 *doce ... posse fieri ... ut qui diu uixit parum uixerit*, 93.3, 101.15.   **quid ... egit?:** illustration by analogy of the difference between *uixit* and *fuit*; really to live is likened to making real progress in a sea-voyage (*multum nauigasse*), mere existence to travelling in circles in the same storm-tossed waters. The analogy is not exact, however. The sailor who goes to sea presumably has a purpose and destination in mind, only to be frustrated by the storm. In terms of the *uita/nauigatio* analogy the equivalent of *multum iactari* is to be endlessly floating about in life with no meaningful objectives of any sort; which is different from the plight of the storm-tossed sailor who, through circumstances beyond his control, cannot reach his clearly defined goal.   **quid ... quem** 'for what if you should think that he had sailed far, he whom ... ?' (for *quid ... si, OLD quis*[1] 13a). The key word *multum* (adv.) is stressed by early position in the *si*-clause: far from making real progress, the sailor goes nowhere.   **saeua ... egit?:** the sentence gathers momentum as S. whips up a raging storm in vigorous, alliterative style with notable resonance of *s*, *t* and *u*; the descriptive force of the relative clause overwhelmingly answers the initial question (*quid enim si ... nauigasse ... ?*).   **a portu exceptum** 'caught [by the storm] as soon as he left harbour'.   **uicibus ... egit?** 'through alternations of the winds raging from different quarters, [the storm] drove him in circles over the same course'. The picture evokes poetic (esp. epic) storm images (e.g. Virg. *Aen.* 1.84–5, 116–17 *illam* [sc. *puppim*] *ter fluctus ibidem* | *torquet agens circum*, Ov. *M.* 11.490–1, *Tr.* 1.2.27–30). *ex diuerso* is contrasted by *per eadem spatia* as the winds conspire to dictate an (ironically) ordered course; *spatia* is ambiguous, denoting both the expanse of the sea (e.g. *Phaed.* 1057–8 *uia* | *uicina tangens spatia suppositi maris*) and the fig. circuits (*OLD* 1 b) of the voyage.   **non ille ... iactatus est:** in rounding off the analogy, parallel in structure to *non ille ... fuit* above.

8 *The value of time*

S. treats time in more abstract terms than before, emphasizing its intrinsic value in order to attack complacent perceptions of its cheapness and at best only casual appreciation of its real worth.

8.1 Elaboration of the argument partially developed in 3.1: because time is invisible and intangible (*incorporalis*), people fail to appreciate its precious value. S. here appears to be endorsing the early Stoic view of time as real

but not material and therefore to be granted 'the twilight reality of one of the incorporeals' (Rist 274; *SVF* II 117.19–23, 166.1, 8), the other three categories of ἀσώματα being the 'sayable', void and place (Rist 152–3 with L–S I 164–5). But 'for Zeno and Chrysippus time is viewed primarily as a problem in physics' and 'does not intrude upon the moral sphere' (Rist 287; Goldschmidt (1989) 49–54). For S., on the other hand, as later for Marcus Aurelius, time is itself a moral problem, the uses to which time is applied inevitably affecting (and being affected by) our moral condition and priorities in life. In contrast to earlier Stoic tradition, then, Senecan time *per se* is not an entity of value independent of what happens *in* time; so that S. takes liberties by styling as *pretiosissimum* an ἀσώματον which, like void and place, has no *intrinsic* worth acc. to early Stoic terms of definition.
Mirari soleo, cum uideo: S. again (3.1 n. on *Omnia . . . mirabuntur*) asserts the enlightened position from which, sage-like, he surveys the mass of misguided humanity.   **tempus petentes** 'requesting the time of others'; for *uideo* regularly with a predicative pple or adj., *OLD* 8.   **facillimos** 'most accommodating'; *Ot.* 5.7 n. on *facilitate . . . excidere.*   **spectat** 'only considers' (*OLD* 8a).   **ipsum quidem** [sc. *tempus*]: *quidem* adversative (Solodow (1978) 75–8) given the contrast between *illud* and *ipsum*, then *uterque* and *neuter*. For *ipsum* used to specify 'the (aforementioned) thing itself' (frequent in S.), *Ben.* 2.33.3 *debeo . . . quod extra beneficium est, ipsum quidem bene accipiendo persolui*, 4.9.3, *Ep.* 9.9, 22.9.   **quasi . . . petitur, quasi . . . datur** 'it is requested as if it were nothing, granted as if it were nothing'; the anaphoric repetition of *quasi nihil*, while accounting for each of the two parties merged in *uterque* and *neuter* above, redoubles the emphasis on time's devaluation before S. vindicates its worth in *pretiosissima* below.
re . . . luditur 'men trifle with the most valuable thing of all'. For the verb (here impersonal pass.) with the abl., 18.5 *C. Caesar . . . uiribus imperi ludit*, *V.B.* 26.3. *re* Muretus for *res* of the MSS; the nom. would distort the sense by portraying time as 'teased' or 'played false' in the manner of people, their feelings or actions (e.g. *Ag.* 17 (of Sisyphus) *redeunte totiens luditur saxo labor*; *OLD ludo* 9a).   **pretiosissima:** the first in a sequence of evaluative terms by which S. contrasts perceptions of material worth and the 'cheapness' of time; *pretiosus* of time only here, but the idea extends back to the sophist Antiphon (Plut. *Ant.* 28.1 = fr. 77 D–K '[Antony] spent and squandered that which Antiphon calls the costliest outlay, namely time'.
fallit [sc. *tempus*] 'escapes their notice' (*OLD* 6a).   **incorporalis:** not found before S., the adj. is equivalent to ἀσώματος in Stoic tradition; for its technical philosophical application, *Ep.* 58.11, 89.16, 90.29.

sub oculos non uenit 'it does not appear to the eyes'. The phrase
is Senecan (*Ben.* 1.5.6, *Ep.* 58.16), *cado* the more usual verb with
sub + acc. (of the senses); *OLD sub* 25a. Those blind to the immate-
rial see their material objectives clearly enough (contrast *spectat* above).
uilissime: in contrast to *pretiosissima*.   **immo:** *Ot.* 4.2n.   **paene
nullum...pretium est:** time has 'practically no value at all'. After
re...pretiosissima above, the opposite extreme; *pretium* of time also at *Ep.*
1.2 *quem mihi dabis qui aliquod pretium tempori ponat...?*

8.2 Because time is not valued, people waste it; but when they find
themselves in mortal danger, they spare no expense in order to stay alive;
hence S. rounds on their inconsistent attitude (*discordia affectuum*). An immediate objection, however, is that what most people would consider to
be a rational, logically defensible position is here unfairly presented as
reprehensible mindlessness. People take urgent measures to protect life
when it is in danger, and when it is not, they spend time to their own
satisfaction. For S.'s argument to convince, he would have to demonstrate
more successfully than here that this normal pattern of behaviour is *unde-
niably* absurd.   **annua, congiaria:** the substantive *annuum*, first used
by S. (*Ben.* 1.9.4, *Cl.* 1.15.2; *TLL* II 121.37–45), here appropriately measures time in terms of financial return rather than intrinsic value. *congia-
rium*, derived from *congius* (= a liquid measure), originally denoted a gift
of oil or wine distributed to the people as largess; but money, first offered in 46 BC by Julius Caesar, became standard. From Augustus onwards
congiaria were given not on fixed occasions but at the emperor's discre-
tion (in general, van Berchem (1939) 119–30).   **carissime accipiunt**
'set great store by'; the superlative adv. in contrast to *uilissime* above, material value to the 'cheapness' of time.   **illis aut:** Gertz's conjecture
((1874) 151n.) for *inis ut* (*uel sim.*) in the MSS; *illis* abl. of value (K–S 1
389–90), the continuing sense being 'they hire out (*locant*) their energies
etc. for them (sc. *annua, congiaria*)'.   **aut...aut...aut:** possibly dis-
tributive (= *alii...alii...alii*) as Duff 122 claims, but certainly suggestive
of great general exertion; Cic. *Att.* 4.1.1 *cognoram...te...plurimum...operae
studi diligentiae laboris ad conficiendum reditum meum contulisse* (further *TLL*
V 1.1174.42–51).   **nemo...tempus:** strongly adversative asyndeton.
aestimat 'values highly'; cf. 8.1 *uilissime aestimatur*.   **laxius** 'more than
lavishly', hence carelessly.   **quasi gratuito** 'as if it cost nothing'.
eosdem uidebis: *aegros* of the MSS is read before *uidebis* by most editors but rightly deleted by Reynolds. S. goes on to portray two kinds of

emergency which suddenly rouse the negligent to awareness of time's precious value, but only the first of them (*si...tangentes*) is precipitated by illness; the second (*si...impendere*) concerns those who, facing execution, go to any expense to defend themselves against the capital charge.   **uidebis:** most editors read either *uide* or *uides* (also in the MSS), but *uidebis* better anticipates the moment of rude awakening (i.e. 'when the time comes, you'll see those same people suddenly valuing life as the precious thing it is').   **admotum est:** with *propius* (adv.), lit. 'is brought closer', i.e. 'draws nearer'; first applied to (the danger of) death by S. (*Tro.* 575, *Ep.* 30.8, 98.18), the verb is mostly so used in Silver verse (*TLL* 1 774.72–82). **medicorum...tangentes:** S. dramatizes the scene by portraying the patients as anxious suppliants; a similar picture at Epict. fr. 24 Schenkl (of the old man who has no wish to live, still less to die): 'when death draws near he wants to live and sends for the doctor and implores him to spare no pains and effort'.   **capitale supplicium:** of the death penalty (so first at V. Max. 1.7 *ext.* 10), *Ir.* 3.32.2, *Ep.* 18.11, *N.Q.* 2.59.8.   **discordia affectuum** 'the inconsistency of their feelings' (Basore). As the opposite of Stoic harmony within the self, *Ep.* 34.4 *non est huius animus in recto cuius acta discordant*; for pejorative *affectus*, 1.1 n.

8.3 S. pursues the theme of time's invisibility (8.1 *fallit...non uenit*) in a different way: because the amount of time left to us cannot be foreseen, such a precious commodity is to be carefully conserved; hence the always 'complete' existence of the *sapiens* who makes the most of every living moment (cf. 7.9).   **quodsi...futurorum:** a carefully ordered correlative construction in which the words *annorum cuiusque numerus proponi* are common to both clauses, with preceding *quemadmodum* [sc. *potest*] *praeteritorum...* looking to the past and succeeding *sic* [*posset*] *futurorum* looking forward and completing the protasis.   **quomodo:** repeated anaphorically to redouble its exclamatory force; so used ('how...!'; 12.3, *Ep.* 77.18 with Axelson (1939) 188–9), found in comedy but avoided in more formal Classical prose (e.g. Pl. *Mil.* 462, Cic. *Att.* 7.2.5, 10.8.9, *Amic.* 9 *quomodo...mortem filii tulit* [sc. *Cato*]*!*).   **illis** [sc. *annis*] **parcerent** 'they would now be using them sparingly'; *parco/parce* (adv.) of (Stoic) thriftiness with time also at *Tr.* 3.8 *alii parce illo* [sc. *tempore*] *utimur, alii prodige*, *Ep.* 48.12, 88.39, 94.28.   **quamuis exiguum...certum est** 'to manage an amount, however small, which is clearly defined'. *dispensare* lit. 'pay out' (*OLD* 1), 'manage' by extension (2); of time, *Tr.* 3.7, *Ep.* 48.12.   **quod...deficiat** 'which may give out at any time'; *nescias* potential subjunctive.

8.4 S. rounds on the inconsistency of those who claim to value time and yet unconsciously give so much of it away to others; but for radical weaknesses in the argument here see nn. on *dant autem . . . detrahant* and *sed . . . nesciunt*.   **nec . . . quod:** 2.5n.   **ignorare** 'are wholly unaware of' (loaded in emphasis).   **quam cara res sit:** sc. *tempus.* In conceding that those who undervalue time are not wholly unaware of its worth, S. gives ground only to retrieve it in *dant . . . latentis* below. **dicere . . . dare:** so e.g. Argyrippus at Pl. *Asin.* 609–10 *quam* [sc. *Philaenium*] *si intellegam deficere uita, iam ipse* | *uitam meam tibi largiar et de mea ad tuam addam*; versions of the familiar saying (hence *solent*) at e.g. Hor. *C.* 2.5.14–15, Prop. 4.11.95, Ov. *M.* 7.168, Stat. *S.* 5.1.177–8.   **ualdissime:** the intensifying superlative only here in S. and otherwise rare.   **dant nec intellegunt** 'they *do* give [sc. a part of their lives] without knowing it'; without lit. shortening their years (as envisaged in *dicere . . . dare* above), they make an equivalent sacrifice in freely bestowing their time. For *nec* in this adversative sense, *OLD* 5.   **dant autem . . . detrahant** 'but they give in such a way that, without adding to [sc. the years of] their loved ones (*illorum*), they take away from themselves'. Blinkered logic: to devote time to loved ones is to deprive oneself, apparently without gain for the beneficiaries; but S. makes no allowance for the intangible benefits (e.g. deep personal satisfaction) which both parties surely stand to gain from the gift of time. **sed . . . nesciunt** 'but this very point, namely, whether they are depriving themselves, escapes them'. Another tendentious claim, at least in its sweeping generality: it need hardly be the case that those who devote time to their loved ones are either universally or permanently unaware of their own 'deprivation' (if they so regard it).   **ideo . . . latentis** 'and so they find bearable the loss of what goes unnoticed in the losing'. *illis* dat. with *tolerabilis*, which Alexander (1945) 84 faults on the grounds that it is logically inconsistent with what follows (to tolerate a loss is to notice it); but S. perhaps uses the word more ironically than loosely. The phrase *iactura detrimenti* has been faulted as tautological, but (i) unlike *detrimenti, iactura* has the added implication of loss through squandering (3.1 *simul ad iacturam temporis uentum est,* 9.1), and (ii) such pleonasm is not unparalleled in S. (e.g. *Ben.* 1.2.2 *multorum amissorum damna, Helu.* 17.5 *afflictationis irritae superuacua uexatio;* Axelson (1939) 229–30). *detrimenti,* though derived from *detero,* is also an assonant play on *detrahant* above (Traina 20).

8.5 Underneath a dozen and more variations in metaphor and angle of perception, the same basic idea persists ('time moves inexorably on'), so that the text mirrors both the tumult and unpredictability on the surface of life and the constant, relentless flow of time below. The images on the surface are bold and sometimes seem to be innovative (nn. below on *te tibi reddet, ibit . . . aetas, supprimet, tumultuabitur* and *sicut missa est*). In contrast, the smooth, regular movement of time is suggested by the series of five anaphoric pairings (*nemo . . . nemo, aut . . . aut, nihil . . . nihil, non . . . non, nusquam . . . nusquam*) and – in the wider context – by the recurrent evocations of Horatian imagery, theme and diction (nn. on *nihil . . . suae, tacita labetur, regis imperio . . . fauore populi* and *curret*).   **iterum:** with *reddet* below, emphatic.   **te tibi reddet:** the conventional phrase for 'bringing one back to one's real self/senses' (*Pol.* 8.3, *N.Q.* 6.29.2; already e.g. Cic. *Red. sen.* 1, Hor. *Ep.* 1.14.1) is here adapted to mean 'bring back one's former self' by the recovery of lost years.   **ibit . . . aetas** 'life will follow the path on which it started'; 1.3n. on *ire*.   **supprimet:** here fig., and uniquely, applied to the 'checking' of life's course. For the impossibility of time reversing itself, *Her. F.* 175–7, 181–2 *durae peragunt pensa sorores | nec sua retro fila reuoluunt.*   **nihil . . . nihil** 'not at all' (adverbial). **tumultuabitur:** rare with an abstract subj. (*Helu.* 3.2 *muliebris dolor tumultuatur*).   **nihil . . . suae:** hence the mindfulness urged by e.g. the town mouse at Hor. *S.* 2.6.97 *uiue memor, quam sis aeui breuis.*   **admonebit:** with gen., the usage preferred by S. (11.1), who only occasionally (*Ir.* 2.33.3, *Ben.* 2.6.2, *Ep.* 94.22) has Cicero's regular *de*, the older construction (Krebs–Schmalz I 99).   **tacita labetur:** poetic language, Horatian sentiment (*C.* 2.14.1–2 *eheu fugaces . . . | labuntur anni*). *tacitus* applied to time at e.g. Phaed. 775, Ov. *F.* 6.771, Col. 10.159; for *labetur,* Tib. 1.8.48, Ov. *Am.* 1.8.49–50, *Tr.* 4.10.27, with N–H on *C.* 2.14.2.   **regis imperio . . . fauore populi:** the chiastic arrangement polarizes the extremes, ruler and people. For the polarity in depictions of death's impartiality, Hor. *C.* 1.4.13–14 *pallida Mors aequo pulsat pede pauperum tabernas | regumque turres,* 2.3.21–4, 2.14.11–12. **sicut missa est** 'just as it was started', as if a runner in a race. The verb is technical (Var. *L.* 5.153 *unde mittuntur equi, nunc dicuntur carceres,* Hor. *S.* 1.1.114); fig. here, a bold and (acc. to *TLL* VIII 1174.40–54) unique usage.   **curret:** applied to life as in 6.4; with *aetas,* Horatian (*C.* 2.5.13–14 *currit . . . ferox | aetas,* where however *aetas* = 'time'; N–H *ad loc.*).   **nusquam . . . nusquam** 'nowhere', but additionally 'under no circumstances' (*OLD* 4).   **quid fiet?** 'What will the result be?'; after Horatian reflections on life's swift passage S. reverts in closing to a less poetic, more mundane style (n. on *uelis nolis* below).   **interim** 'all the while'.   **uelis nolis** 'like it or not',

a common colloquialism; *OLD uolo*[1] 7e with Eden (1984) 66 on *Apoc.* 1.2
uelit nolit.

9 Seizing the moment

Three stages of argument: (i) those who pride themselves on what, in Stoic
terms, is false *prudentia* (9.1 n.) waste their lives in always planning ahead,
never seizing the present; (ii) S. supplies the corrective, invoking Virgil
(9.2–3) to reinforce the imperative: seize the moment, 'for all life's best
days are always the first to flee for wretched mortals'; (iii) the preoccupied
bear out the need for Senecan (and Virgilian) admonition (9.4–5): as life
passes them by, old age arrives before they know it.

9.1 Potestne ... iudicio: the MSS have the impossible *potest ne quicquam
sensus hominum eorum dico* (or similar), but the required sense ('Can anything
be more misguided than the attitude of those people who boast of their
foresight?') is most succinctly conveyed in Housman's emendation (printed
by Duff 12 and reproduced here). But for Housman's *leuius* (insufficiently
strong) consider *dementius* (*amentius* Gertz (1874) 152), which accords more
closely with both the usual expressions of Senecan outrage like *quid est dementius quam...? (Ir.* 2.26.3, *Ep.* 41.6, 74.33, 99.7, *N.Q.* 6.2.6) and Ciceronian
precedents like *iis nihil potest esse dementius (Off.* 2.24; cf. *Rab. Post.* 24, *Dom.*
76, *Phil.* 2.19).   **prudentiam:** here simply 'foresight' as at *Ep.* 90.5
and esp. Cic. *Sen.* 78 *tanta memoria praeteritorum futurorumque prudentia*; not the
same as Stoic πρόνοια (*SVF* III 65.29–30), which uses foresight to exercise rational control over the present (*Marc.* 9.5 *aufert uim praesentibus malis
qui futura prospexit*); nor is it, as elsewhere in S., φρόνησις, one of the four
primary Stoic virtues (*Ep.* 90.46, 115.3, 120.11; *SVF* III 64.15–16, 65.6–7).
Those criticized here simply fret about the future as they lose sight of the
present (hence *Ep.* 5.8 *prouidentia, maximum bonum condicionis humanae, in malum
uersa est*).   **operosius** 'too busily'.   **impendio ... instruunt** 'they
plan out their lives at the cost of life itself'. For *impendio uitae, Marc.* 5.2
(*impendio* also with *pudoris* at *C.S.* 6.7, *temporis* at *Ep.* 45.12); polyptoton
(*uitae uitam*; 1.1 n.) underlines the paradox as at *Ep.* 45.12 ... *multos transisse
uitam dum uitae instrumenta conquirunt.*   **cogitationes ... ordinant** 'they
form their purposes with the distant future in view', misguided because
the future is so uncertain: *Ep.* 101.4 *o quanta dementia est spes longas in-
choantium*, where the sentiment is Horatian (*C.* 1.4.15).   **in longum:**

of the distant future, a Virgilian usage (*Ecl.* 9.56) entering Silver prose through Livy (5.16.4).   **porro** 'on the other hand' (*OLD* 6c). S. qualifies *cogitationes . . . ordinant* by presenting such foresight as mere postponement (*dilatio*); so *Ep.* 1.2 *dum differtur uita transcurrit*, 45.13, 101.7 *nihil differamus*. For the similar Epicurean position, *Sententiae Vaticanae* 14 'But you, who have no mastery over tomorrow, postpone your happiness [reading τὸ χαῖρον]; life is wasted in procrastination.'   **illa:** sc. *dilatio*. **primum quemque:** lit. 'each (day) as it comes to the fore', i.e. 'each in turn' (*OLD primus* 12); a parallel thought at *Ep.* 101.10 *in spem uiuentibus proximum quodque tempus elabitur* (i.e. 'the immediate future slips from grasp'). **extrahit** 'strips away'.   **illa . . . promittit:** chiastically arranged to juxtapose present and future; postponement 'snatches away' the present by anticipating the future (causal *dum*, *OLD* 4a).   **uiuendi** 'really living'; 2.2n. on '*exigua . . . uiuimus*'.   **expectatio . . . hodiernum:** whether in the form of anxious expectancy or apprehension about the future, an *affectus* to which the *sapiens* is immune; *Ben.* 7.2.4 *hic praesentibus gaudet, ex futuro non pendet*, *Ep.* 12.9.   **pendet . . . perdit:** for this class of parisyllabic word-play, Summers lxxxiii.   **in manu fortunae:** the image also at *C.S.* 8.3, Suet. *Nero* 23.3 *euentum in manu esse fortunae*, Plin. *N.H.* 37.4.   **disponis** 'map out', as at 1.4, 3.5.   **in tua** [sc. *manu*]: for the contrast with *in manu fortunae*, Liv. 30.30.19 *haec in tua, illa in deorum manu est*.   **dimittis** 'let slip'.   **quo spectas?** 'What are you aiming at?'; for the verb, *OLD* 9b. **quo te extendis?** 'What is your goal?'; *Ep.* 85.21 *se ad id quod est optimum extendet* [sc. *beatus*].   **protinus uiue:** equivalent to Horace's *carpe diem*, *quam minimum credula postero* at *C.* 1.11.8; for the Epicurean associations of the Horatian phrase, N–H *ad loc.*

   9.2 For S.'s strategic use of poetic quotation, *Ot.* 1.4n. on *quod . . . premimus*, and for his predilection for Virgil, *Ot.* 1.4n. on *disertissimus*. **clamat:** the Virgilian message is pressed on the reader as plain and incontrovertible. *clamo* in this sense is Ciceronian (e.g. *Fin.* 1.57 *clamat Epicurus*) and corresponds to the Greek (ἐμ)βοῶ; so *Marc.* 23.2 *Platon clamat*, with Pease on Cic. *N.D.* 1.86 and Traina (1987) 129.   **ecce** reinforces the solemn authority of the pronouncement; after the verb (more often in verse) at e.g. *Ir.* 3.43.1 *uenit ecce mors*, Sen. *Contr.* 1 *praef.* 8, 9.4.4, 10.6.1, Petr. 80.4.   **uelut . . . instinctus** 'as if inspired with divine utterance'. Dahlmann (1941) 103 compares *Tr.* 1.14 *sublimius feror et ore iam non meo*, 17.11 *cum . . . instinctu . . . sacro surrexit excelsior* [sc. *mens*], *tunc demum aliquid cecinit grandius ore mortali*, showing that the divine voice can inspire as successfully as the more usual divine *spiritus* (Liv. 5.15.10 *cecinerit diuino spiritu instinctus*, Quint. *Inst.* 12.10.24).   **optima ... fugit:** *G.* 3.66–7, also quoted at *Ep.* 108.24, 26.   **'quid ... fugit':** S. gives a relevant (hence *salutare* above) slant to lines which in their original context are quite different in tone and emphasis. Virgil (*G.* 3.49–71) is writing about cattle, not human beings, and pressing for the urgent selection of breeding stock to perpetuate the herd (60–5), for *optima quaeque dies ... | prima fugit* – the pathetic gnome embracing the animal and the human conditions (Thomas (1988) II 51). Again at *Ep.* 108.24–8 S. treats the lines in isolation from their context, distinguishing philological and philosophical approaches to their interpretation.   **occupas** 'seize'; of time, *Ep.* 108.28 (also applying the lesson of *G.* 3.66–7) *quod fugit occupandum est*; of opportunity, *Ben.* 1.7.1. For the pres. indicative as idiomatic in implicit threats and warnings, Kenney (1996) 182 on Ov. *Her.* 19.205.   **et** 'even'.   **occupaueris:** fut. perf.   **itaque ... certandum est** 'and so you must compete with time's swiftness in the speed with which you use it'; chiastic *celeritate ... uelocitate* sets the contending forces in balanced opposition.   **uelut ... hauriendum** 'you must draw quickly as if from a torrent that is fast moving and will not always flow'. *rapido* (after *torrenti*, tautological for emphasis) and *cito* carry forward the contrast between *celeritate* and *uelocitate* above.   **torrenti:** more commonly -*e* (e.g. *Ep.* 85.6, Liv. 33.18.15, Tac. *Dial.* 24.1); for such variations see G–L §82 n. 1, N–W I 363.   **ituro:** of flowing water or other liquids, mostly poetic and post-Augustan in prose (*OLD eo*[1] 3b).

9.3 hoc ... dicit: *hoc* is elucidated by *quod* ('the fact that') and is the object of *dicit*, which serves as verb in both clauses.   **pulcherrime** 'very aptly' (*OLD pulchre* 1b).   **exprobrandam ... cunctationem:** the succession of predominantly long polysyllables suitably protracts 'interminable delay'; *cunct-* is Gertz's convincing conjecture ((1874) 153; cf. 9.2 *quid cunctaris?*, *Tr.* 2.8) for *cognat-*, *cognit-* or *cogitat-* in the MSS.   **non ... dicit:** i.e. Virgil stresses the value of the living moment by narrowing his compass, specifying 'all life's best days' as opposed to 'stages' (*aetatem*).   **securus** 'nonchalant', unlike the *sapiens* who is *securus* in the positive sense of 'free from anxiety' (e.g. *C.S.* 13.5, *V.B.* 26.3, *Ep.* 12.9, 32.3).   **in tanta ... lentus** 'unconcerned (*OLD lentus* 9) when/even though (*OLD in* 4oc) time flies so quickly'; but the adj. also suggests slowness in contrast to *tanta ... fuga. temporum fuga* possibly from Horace, who first applies *fuga* to time (*C.* 3.30.5, where however *temporum* = 'the ages'); but for *fugio* already so used, Catul. 68.43 *fugiens saeclis obliuiscentibus aetas*.

menses . . . seriem: i.e. 'project (*exporrigis*) your life into the distant future' (cf. 3.4–5 on the folly of ambitiously planning for retirement). *tibi* dat. of advantage; *in* (Gertz (1874) 154) removes the objection that, if *et* of the MSS is read in its place, *longam seriem* is intolerably vague after *menses . . . et annos.*

utcumque . . . uisum est 'to whatever extent your greed sees fit'; the clause strategically separates *exporrigis* from *in longam seriem*, elongating the months and years indefinitely 'stretched out'.   **auiditati:** the opposite of Stoic continence; the *sapiens* has no such greed for life, living only as long as he ought (*Ep*. 65.22, 70.4 *sapiens uiuet quantum debet, non quantum potest*).

tecum loquitur: the verb regularly used of writings 'speaking' to their readers (*OLD* 1 c), and so of writers 'conversing' with us through their works.

hoc: S. changes the gender of *dies*, fem. (for metrical reasons) at *G*. 3.66. His use of the masc. here (but not always) coincides with the general rule in Classical prose, namely that the masc. denotes a specific day, the fem. the beginning or end of a given period of time (Fraenkel (1964) 54 on S. and other post-Augustan prose authors); so the fem. at e.g. *Ben*. 4.32.4 *aliis post longam diem repono* 'some I repay in the long term', *Marc*. 8.1, *Pol*. 18.2, *N.Q.* 3.19.2.   **ipso fugiente:** because of the break after *ipso*, not a pure example of the so-called 'heroic clausula', or prose rhythm emulating the end of a hexameter (Shipley (1911) 411, cautioning that 'not all combinations of –∪∪–∪ necessarily form the heroic clausula'); a pattern generally avoided by S. because of its closeness to verse (Bourgery (1922) 146), but here chosen to portray urgent flight in conspicuous, 'running' rhythm.

9.4–5 The Virgilian lesson re-applied (9.4; general intro. p. 28) and supported (9.5) by an elaborate crowning illustration (*quemadmodum . . . sic*) of life passing us by unnoticed – only for the shock of recognition upon arrival at the end.

9.4 mortalibus . . . occupatis: at *G*. 3.66 *miseris* describes the general human condition, but S. now uses the adj. predicatively, specifying 'mortals who are wretched, that is the engrossed'.   **quorum . . . opprimit:** old age 'takes their still childish minds by surprise'. For the verb, often of surprise military attack (*OLD* 7a), *Marc*. 11.5 *longa conantem eum mors opprimit*; the military nuance is reinforced by *imparati inermesque* below. **nihil . . . prouisum est:** ironic given S.'s portrayal of those who boast of their foresight in 9.1.   **illam:** sc. *senectutem*.   **inciderunt, accedere:** juxtaposed for contrast; the wordplay is typical (cf. *Ep*. 24.19) and unaffected by the variations in quantity (*incĭd-*, *accēd-*; Summers lxxxiii n. 1 on *V.B.* 3.4 *aut irritant nos aut territant*).   **cotidie:** contrasting with *subito*; stressed at e.g. *Ep.* 24.20 *cotidie morimur; cotidie enim demitur aliqua pars uitae*, 120.17. The general point is familiar from the moralists; Powell (1988) 106 on Cic. *Sen.* 4 *obrepere aiunt* [sc. *stulti*] *eam* [sc. *senectutem*] *citius quam putauissent.*

9.5 quemadmodum . . . sic: the elaborate comparison is built around the familiar image of the *iter uitae*, for which e.g. *Ben.* 3.31.5, *Ep.* 44.7 *per insidiosum iter uitae*, 99.7, 12, 107.2 (*TLL* VII 2.543.17–21). **decipit** 'beguiles'. **peruenisse ante sciunt quam appropinquare** 'they find that they have arrived at their destination before being aware of approaching it'. For *sciunt* understood after *ante . . . quam* cf. the parallel construction at *Pol.* 4.2 *lacrimae nobis deerunt antequam causae dolendi.* For *se* omitted, e.g. *Ep.* 1.4 *non possum dicere nihil perdere, Ben.* 7.26.3, Bourgery (1922) 357; found in Latin of all periods, the phenomenon is esp. common in colloquial usage (Löfstedt II 262; H–S 362). **assiduum et citatissimum:** for the thought, *Her. F.* 179 *properat cursu uita citato, Ep.* 99.7; for the combination of adjs., *Helu.* 6.8. **uigilantes dormientesque:** a possible play on lit. and fig. senses of both verbs; awake and asleep, whether alert to time's swift passage (*OLD uigilo* 4) or inert (*dormio* 2), all travel life's journey at the same pace. **non . . . in fine** 'becomes noticeable only at the end'. The final stroke of the chapter (and of the first thematic half of the treatise) is stylistically bold and as arresting as the end of their journey is to the distracted passengers; for *finis* used to end a section for effect, *V.B.* 7.4 *eo enim pertendit* [sc. transient pleasure] *ubi desinat, et dum incipit spectat ad finem.*

10 Stoic time in tripartite division

S. now shifts his line of attack on the *occupati* from the exhortatory approach to the dialectical, constructing his argument with the aid of various well-known philosophical definitions of 'parts' of time (10.2n. on *In tria .. futurum est*). There is no major change of direction here; the new line of attack deploys the same rhetorical skills for the same therapeutic purpose.

10.1 Quod proposui 'my subject', defined at the end of the sentence by *breuissimam . . . uitam*. The *propositio* (*Ot.* 2.1n. on *Nunc probabo*) follows on from the *exordium* (1) and *narratio* (2–9); for these divisions, Grimal (1960) 412. The language is deceptively intimidating, and meant to be, for there is in fact no fully developed *diuisio* here to succeed the *propositio*. S. is using the jargon of rhetoric as a weapon in his strategic armoury, and is about to reinforce this approach with an appeal to the tactical support of an accepted authority in the field.   **in partes . . . et argumenta diducere** 'to divide [sc. my subject] into categories with their separate proofs'; cf. Quint. *Inst.* 7.1.1 *sit . . . diuisio rerum plurium in singulas*, and for such *diuisio* in S., *Ot.* 2.1 n. on *hoc . . . partes*.   **occurrent:** after the subjunctive in the protasis (*si . . . uelim*), the indicative in the apodosis expresses S.'s confidence in his rhetorical skills were he to proceed with the conventional *diuisio*. For the difference of mood, found in early and Classical Latin but most often in circumstances which do not apply here (K–S II 394–5), *N.Q.* 1 *praef.* 10 *si quis formicis det intellectum hominis, nonne et illae unam aream in multas prouincias diuident?*   **per quae probem** 'through which to demonstrate'; final relative (G–L §630).   **Fabianus:** Papirius Fabianus, *c.* 35 BC – *ante* AD 35 (*RE* XVIII 3.1056–9), rhetorician and writer on political philosophy and natural science, whose wide-ranging interests provided a model for S., his student and admirer, with whom he may possibly have shared a Spanish origin (Griffin (1972) 16). He joined the eclectic philosopher Q. Sextius in what is said to have been Rome's only indigenous philosophical school (Griffin (1976) 37–40), where he deeply impressed both the youthful S. (*Ep.* 40.12, 58.6, 100.12) and his father (*Contr.* 2 *praef.* 1–2).   **his** 'of the present day' (*OLD hic*[1] 2a).   **cathedrariis philosophis** 'lecture-hall philosophers and rhetoricians' occupying professorial chairs (*cathedras*), and hence shallow, sophistic pedants (cf. Juv. 7.203 *paenituit multos uanae sterilisque cathedrae*). The contemptuous adj., only here before Sidonius, contrasts with *ueris* below.   **antiquis** 'old-fashioned', eschewing modern dialectic.   **contra affectus . . . non uellicari:** rightly taken by Griffin (1976) 15 n. 5 as virtually a verbatim quotation from Fabianus. For the pervasive military diction here see the extended fragment of Fabianus as reported by the elder Sen. at *Contr.* 2.1.10; both passages exemplify the forceful, more direct approach which S. commends in Fabianus with extended analysis in *Ep.* 100 (Leeman (1963) I 261–71).   **affectus:** 1.1 n.   **impetu:** rhetorical vigour of the sort affected by Fabianus himself (*Ep.* 100.3).   **subtilitate:** nicety of logic-chopping argument, too light a weapon for combat with the passions; so *Ep.* 117.25 *hoc est sapere, non disputatiunculis inanibus subtilitatem uanissimam agitare . . . remoue ista lusoria arma: decretoriis opus est*. S. generally disapproves of mere *subtilitas* as *inutilis* (*Ep.* 65.16, 82.24, 88.43).   **pugnandum:** sc. *esse*.   **minutis uulneribus** 'by pinpricks'. Beyond denoting light injury the adj. hints at the hair-splitting technique which inflicts mere pricks. So *Ep.* 82.24 *et aduersus mortem tu tam*

minuta iacularis?, where *minuta* refers to syllogistic subtlety as an ineffec-
tual weapon of argument against fear of death; disparaging also at Cic.
Parad. 2, *Tusc.* 2.42 *minutis conclusiunculis* ('quibbling syllogisms') ... *effici
uolunt* [sc. *Stoici*] *non esse malum dolorem.*   **incursu** 'by a frontal assault'.
Fabianus' military metaphor is not the one familiar from S., who uses the
noun to denote the onrush of passions etc. (e.g. 10.4 *morborum incursus, C.S.*
3.4, *Ep.* 59.8).   **auertendam aciem:** Livian (e.g. 7.11.7 *auertitur ... acies
Gallorum,* 9.19.17, 10.36.5, 30.35.1).   **non probat ... enim:** the MSS
offer *non probat* (or *probam*). *cauillationes enim,* whence Shackleton Bailey's
conjecture ((1970) 359) as given here. Most editors omit *non probat cauillationes* as a scribal interpolation which interrupts the *oratio obliqua* continuing
in *uitia ... uellicari*; but (i) *oratio recta* interrupting *oratio obliqua* is easily paralleled (e.g. Cic. *N.D.* 2.37 with Pease 631 on *ortus est*), and (ii) *cauillatio*
is unlikely to be a scribal gloss because it is a specialized term (*TLL* III
648.17–51) which does not so much supply an explanation as need one
itself. Shackleton Bailey supplies *uitia* to complete the sense; but S. in any
case generally avoids using *enim* in first position in a sentence (Bourgery
(1922) 400 for alleged exceptions).   **contundi ... non uellicari:** for
the ruthless suppression of *uitia, Marc.* 1.7. *contundi* combines the continuing
military metaphor (e.g. Virg. *Aen.* 1.263–4, Liv. 27.2.2, 40.52.6, Tac. *Ann.*
12.31.3) with fig. application to the passions (e.g. *Pol.* 14.2, *Ben.* 3.29.1; *OLD*
3a); *uellicari* 'to be merely nipped at' recurs in the gentle impression made
by a friend's death at *Ep.* 63.1 *illum quoque* [sc. *sapientem*] ... *ista res uellicabit,
sed tantum uellicabit.*   **tamen:** emphatic position, not uncommon in early
and Classical Latin (*OLD* 1a), and frequent in S. (e.g. *Ir.* 3.17.4, *Marc.* 14.3,
16.4, *Pol.* 15.3).   **ut ... deplorandi sunt** 'in order that they (*illis* [sc.
occupatis]) may be censured for their distinctive (*OLD suus* 11) failing, they are
to be instructed, not merely given up for lost (*deploro* 2a)'. *exprobretur* loaded
here ('constructively censured'), exposing the *occupati* not just to Fabianus'
brand of destructive criticism.   **illis:** the usual dat., with *exprobro,* of the
person reproached; *Tr.* 14.5, *Ben.* 1.11.6, *Ep.* 22.14 *exprobratur senibus infantia.*

     10.2–6 S. introduces the tripartite division of time, arguing that the
occupati lack the unified perspective which distinguishes the *sapiens*. The argument falls into two main parts: (i) unlike the present and future, the past
is certain and immutable but deliberately 'forgotten' by the *occupati* because
they can have no pleasant memories and are in any case too harried to
have time for leisurely recollection (10.2–5); and (ii) since the 'now' is all
but non-existent, the *occupati* who live only for the present are clutching at

moments in fleeting time (10.6). Significant weaknesses underlie S.'s arguments (10.3nn. on *inuiti . . . reuocant* and *nemo . . . retorquet*); but the confident
manner in which he draws on and manipulates technical Stoic – and, notably, Epicurean – material to support his case still makes for an impressive
tour de force.

   10.2 In tria . . . futurum est: philosophical reflection on time is of
great importance to the *sapiens* (*Ep.* 88.33), and S. doubtless recognized
that the superficially simple division here masks complex questions and
conflicting arguments, which had continued to interest philosophers since
Aristotle's paradoxes in *Physics* 4.10 had cast doubt on the reality of time;
for analysis of these paradoxes and for the ensuing debate down to the
Neoplatonists, Sorabji (1983) 7–63. Among the Stoics Chrysippus held
that no time is wholly present but composed of the past and future; the
present is 'real' only in the sense that it 'belongs' (ὑπάρχει) while the past
and the future merely 'subsist' (ὑφίστανται; general intro. p. 20). However, the likely intermediate source used by S. here is Posidonius (fr. 98.5–7
E–K = L–S 1 51 E3 'And he holds that that time which is thought of in terms
of "when" is partly past, partly future, and partly present'); but S. adapts
Posidonius' division to meet his requirements here, as he again does in the
different context of animal awareness of time at *Ep.* 124.17 *tempus . . . tribus
partibus constat, praeterito, praesente, uenturo.* The background to Posidonius'
division is explored by Kidd II 396–403, but see more generally Rist 273–88,
who prefers to discuss Marcus Aurelius rather than Seneca.   **futurum
est:** S. conveys the uncertainty of the future by using the periphrastic, not
the less remote fut. indicative; so also *quod acturi sumus* below (Westman
(1961) 56).   **quod** [sc. *tempus*] **agimus breue est:** the shortness of the
present time (10.6 *breuissimum*) was acknowledged by Posidonius (fr. 98.9–12
E–K = L–S 1 51 E4–5) as an aspect of his argument that the present (τὸ
νῦν) can be understood not only in the broader sense (ἐν πλάτει) necessary if time is thought of as a continuum, but also as 'the least perceptible
time' (τὸν ἐλάχιστον πρὸς αἴσθησιν χρόνον) between the dividing lines
of future and past. As Kidd II 402 points out, this least perceptible present
need strictly be no more than a (non-temporal) demarcation point (διορ
ισμὸς σημειώδης) between past and future, and to give it even the limited
temporal status envisaged here (i.e. to understand it ἐν πλάτει) 'is a loose
(i.e. imprecise) usage'. For Chrysippus' different emphasis, Kidd II 401 with
Rist 276–82.   **quod egimus certum:** so *Marc.* 22.1 *quod praeterit certum
est, Pol.* 10.2, *Ep.* 99.4; one can readily see how emphasis on the certainty

of past blessings is appropriate to these consolatory contexts. At *Ben.* 3.4.1 (= fr. 435 Us.) the idea is attributed to Epicurus, *qui assidue queritur quod aduersus praeterita simus ingrati, . . . cum certior nulla sit uoluptas quam quae iam eripi non potest . . .* Certainly, this fits well with the authentic Epicurean view that we experience time as incidental to our experience of events (Bailey (1928) 305–8 for a full discussion), but has nothing in common with the standard Stoic view that only the present is 'fully real' (Rist 278–9); n. below on *iniucunda . . . recordatio*.   **hoc** 'the last' (*OLD hic*[1] 10a).   **ius** 'control'; with *in* + acc., e.g. *Ep.* 57.3 *in quem* [sc. *sapientem*] *fortuna ius perdidit*.   **nullius:** 3.1 n. on *a nullo*.   **amittunt** 'lose sight of'; *Ep.* 98.6 *praesentia . . . amittet* [sc. *animus futuri anxius*].   **nec enim:** 7.5 n. on *neque . . . repperit*.   **si uacet . . . est:** *est*, not *sit*, because only their leisure is potential; their past folly is a continuing and inescapable fact. For the usage, usually with the imperf. indicative, K–S II 404.   **iniucunda . . . recordatio:** since the *occupati* have never been free from anxiety and/or vice-ridden distraction (cf. 10.4 *ille . . . effudit*), they can apparently never look back on the past with pleasure. Contrast *Pol.* 10.3 *in praeteritum tempus animus mittendus est, et quicquid nos umquam delectauit reducendum ac frequenti cogitatione pertractandum est*, where S. echoes the Epicurean view of *reuocatio* as consoling because it keeps alive the pleasure of past blessings; *Ben.* 3.4.1 (n. above on *quod egimus certum*), *Ep.* 63.4, Cic. *Fin.* 1.57, Epic. fr. 436 Us., *Sententiae Vaticanae* 55 'you must ease present misfortunes with the fond recollection of past blessings, and with the recognition that the past cannot be undone'. Any convergence of Epicurean and Stoic views here (also envisaged by Torquatus at Cic. *Fin.* 1.62) is more apparent than real. While Epicureans can compensate for present troubles by recollecting past pleasures and anticipating future ones (Cic. *Tusc.* 5.96), Stoics question the reality of past and future, and banish present misery by seeking self-fulfilment in every present moment (*Breu.* 7.9). Here, however, S. is deploying the Epicurean point to score the maximum advantage over the *occupati*.   **rei:** the past.

   10.3 inuiti . . . reuocant: for the idea, *Pol.* 18.7 *naturale est . . . ut semper animus ab eo refugiat ad quod cum tristitia reuertitur*, *Ep.* 63.4. But S. assumes (i) that the *occupati* will find their past uniformly regrettable; (ii) that memory cannot be distorted or regret diminished over time; and (iii) that it is inconceivable that anyone could live happily in/for the self-indulgent present; but cf. at least Ath. 12 544a–b on the Cyrenaic Aristippus, who held that happiness 'is for the single moment (μονόχρονον) . . . , regarding the memory of past joys as nothing to him any more than the anticipation of future joys, but judging the good by the sole criterion of the present' (= fr. 207 Mannebach).   **itaque:** 2.5n. on *non . . . quod.*   **male exacta** 'badly spent'.   **animum:** the seat of memory; *Ir.* 2.5.3, *V.B.* 15.5, *Pol.* 10.3, *Ben.* 1.12.2, 2.2.1, 3.5.2. The exact sense here is determined by *reuocant* (*OLD* 13a).   **nec audent:** made explicit in 10.4 *necesse est memoriam suam timeat.*   **retemptare** 'to re-explore' the past, perhaps with an echo of *tempora* above; applied fig. to memory, *Ep.* 72.1 *sed diu non retemptaui memoriam meam.*   **quorum:** sc. the *occupati.*   **etiam . . . surrepebant** 'even those which insinuated themselves by some allurement of pleasure in the moment'. *lenocinium* (lit. 'brothel-keeping') is used pejoratively in Classical and later Latin of what confers artificial attractiveness; *Helu.* 16.4 (of cosmetics) *non faciem coloribus ac lenociniis polluisti, Ep.* 80.9. For the verb, conjectured by Erasmus, *Tr.* 17.12 *surrepentibus uitiis, Ep.* 7.2, 90.6 (in the sense of 'insinuate itself', poetic and mostly post-Augustan in prose; *OLD* 2); these parallels defend the conjecture against *surripiebantur* of the MSS, read by most editors. The verb in no way detracts from S.'s view that responsibility for *uitia* belongs with human beings themselves, and should not be attributed to time or circumstances: *Ep.* 97.1 *hominum sunt ista* [sc. *uitia*], *non temporum,* a line consistently followed by Stoics of every period (Long (1986) 183–4). **retractando:** the extension of the verb to cover mental recollection is Ovidian (*M.* 7.714) and common thereafter.   **nemo . . . retorquet:** i.e. the *sapiens* whose every action has been subjected to his moral scrutiny can have no regrets. S. makes no allowance for matters decided under human self-scrutiny (*censura*) turning out on recollection to be occasions of regret, as either experience or new information modifies our outlook. To believe one was right *at the time* on the evidence then available may deliver one from guilt, but need hardly make much difference to the greater torment of remorse.   **quoi:** equivalent to *cui* (archaic; N–W II 453–4), dat. of agent with *acta sunt*; Gruter's conjecture for *quo* of the MSS (corrected to *a quo* in one late MS). S. still uses the form occasionally (e.g. *V.B.* 23.2 with Madvig's conjecture (I 68)), and Quintilian (*Inst.* 1.7.27) testifies that *grammatici* were teaching it when he was a boy, though he thought *cui* made clearer the sound distinction between the dat. and nom. masc. sing. Here the archaizing form, used in combination with the solemn double negative *nemo nisi,* lends special distinction to the *sapiens* (contrast the commonplace *ille qui* in 10.4, of the non-Stoic). For the dat. of agent, *Ot.* 3.4n. on *quietissimis.*   **sua:** in keeping with his general self-sufficiency (αὐτάρκεια), the *sapiens* answers only to his own conscience.   **numquam fallitur:** since Stoic virtue is founded on reason, it follows that the judgement and (here) the moral self-arbitration of the *sapiens* are infallible; *Ben.* 4.34.4 *non mutat sapiens consilium omnibus his manentibus, quae erant cum sumeret. ideo numquam illum paenitentia subit, quia nihil melius illo tempore fieri potuit quam quod factum est, nihil melius constitui quam constitutum est* (but n. above on *nemo … retorquet*).   **libenter:** in contrast to *inuiti* above.   **se … retorquet:** the fig. application of the verb to memory is first found in S.; *Cl.* 1.11.1, *Ben.* 3.3.4.

10.4 ille … effudit: a Stoic catalogue of *uitia*, in which the rapid sequence of six advs. and verbs overwhelms the subj. of *timeat* below with a mounting indictment of his past actions.   **ambitiose concupiit:** 2.1 n. on *ambitio*; for the verb denoting untrammelled greed, 3.4.   **superbe contempsit:** arrogant disdain of the sort that S. characterizes as an *affectus inflatus* at *C.S.* 11.1. For *superbia* classed as a branch of malice, itself a disease of the soul, *Ep.* 106.6; 2.5 above for a display of patronizing arrogance to a client.   **impotenter uicit** 'has recklessly prevailed' over all opposition. The adv. denotes the opposite of Stoic temperance, ἀκρασία in a parallel list of κακίαι at *SVF* III 65.19; hence S.'s characterization of *impotentia* as a *uitium mentis* along with greed and cruelty at *Ep.* 85.10 (associated with other *affectus* at e.g. *Ep.* 39.5, 92.8, 94.71, 100.10).   **insidiose decepit:** 7.2 *aspice … quam diu insidientur* [sc. *occupati*].   **auare rapuit:** 2.1 n. on *insatiabilis … auaritia.*   **prodige effudit** 'has extravagantly squandered' his resources; ἀκολασία listed in the 'front rank' of κακίαι at *SVF* III 65.18.   **timeat:** 10.3 n. on *nec audent.*   **atqui … possessio est:** essentially the same picture as that in 10.2, but here rhetorically elaborated in six units all of which support the same basic image, anaphoric *haec … haec* enclosing the tricolic anaphora *quam non … non … non … exagitet.* The effect is to elevate the memory of the *sapiens* as an inviolable treasure-house of his morally impeccable experience of life.   **dedicata** 'set apart', so that the past becomes consecrated ground, a place of sanctuary for the mind; for the bold image, Quint. *Inst.* 12.11.7 (of the retired orator, his fame secure) *iam secretus et consecratus.*   **supergressa** 'elevated above' human vicissitudes; a nuance not found before S. (*OLD* 3).   **extra … subducta:** lit. 'removed beyond the reach of fortune's sway' (10.2 *hoc est … perdidit*). Transcendent in one way (*supergressa*), the past is 'extricated' in another (*OLD subduco* 5), with the difference marked by the contrasting prefixes. *regnum* applied to the rule of fortune also at *Prou.* 6.7, *Marc.* 10.6, *V.B.* 25.5; of gods generally, poetic (*OLD* 2b).   **quam … exagitet:** relative clause of tendency (G–L §631).   **non inopia … incursus:** poverty and illness also feature among the most feared of life's possibilities in a tricolon at *Ep.* 14.3 *timetur inopia, timentur morbi, timentur quae per uim potentioris eueniunt.* Tricolic anaphora with *non* is poetic (e.g. Catul. 64.63–5, Virg. *G.* 3.520–1, *Aen.* 4.600–1, 10.358, *Ciris* 168–70, 433–6), the anaphora in any case more generally so because of its hymnic associations (N–H on *C.* 1.10.9 and 2.8.21).   **incursus:** 10.1 n.   **nec eripi potest:** more neatly at *Ep.* 98.11 *habere eripitur, habuisse numquam.*   **perpetua . . . possessio est:** *Ep.* 99.4 *nostrum est quod praeterît tempus nec quicquam est loco tutiore quam quod fuit.*   **singuli . . . sunt:** because 'days are present only one at a time, and these only minute by minute', those who live only for the present must lack any controlling perspective on life as a whole (*Ep.* 71.2 *non disponet singula* ('the details of life'), *nisi cui iam uitae suae summa proposita est*).   **per momenta:** 10.2 n. on *quod agimus breue est.* The present is here the 'least perceptible time' (Posid. fr. 98.11 E–K τὸν ἐλάχιστον πρὸς αἴσθησιν χρόνον); cf. 10.6.   **omnes** [sc. *dies*]: emphatic, contrasting with *singuli* above. **cum . . . patientur:** we can treat the past as our slave, but those who fluctuate with the present moment *are* slaves; *Ep.* 22.11 *paucos seruitus, plures seruitutem tenent.*   **iusseris:** fut. perf., with the second pers. distinguishing the initiated reader from the *occupati.*   **ad arbitrium tuum** 'to suit your wishes'.

   10.5 securae et quietae mentis: defining gen. (cf. 7.4), emphasizing two staple characteristics of the *sapiens*, freedom from care (*C.S.* 13.5 *securitas . . . proprium bonum sapientis est, Ep.* 44.7) and serenity (*C.S.* 9.3 *caret . . . perturbatione uir . . . altae quietis et placidae, Ir.* 3.6.1, *Ep.* 25.7). **discurrere** 'to roam freely' (*OLD* 2b); this positive nuance disappears when the verb and its cognates are applied to the *occupati* (3.2 *officiosa per urbem discursatio*, 14.3, *Tr.* 2.9).   **uelut . . . sint:** i.e. like an animal under the yoke, the preoccupied mind can only see ahead (cf. 7.8 *quisque . . . futuri desiderio laborat*, 9.1). *uelut* + subjunctive (without *si*) is rare in S. (*Ep.* 26.4, *N.Q.* 4B.13.8).   **respicere non possunt:** *Ep.* 83.2 *hoc nos pessimos facit, quod nemo uitam suam respicit.*   **abit . . . in profundum:** life for the *occupati* 'disappears into an abyss' of the forgotten past, but this abyss (M. Aur. 4.50 τὸ ἀχανὲς τοῦ αἰῶνος 'the yawning gulf of time') is elsewhere the inevitable receptacle of every present moment (*Ep.* 49.3 *quicquid temporis transît eodem loco est . . . omnia in idem profundum cadunt*).   **ut . . . transmittitur:** each clause in the second part of this carefully worked correlative construction parallels one in the first (*nihil prodest / per quassos . . . transmittitur; licet . . . ingeras / nihil . . . detur; si . . . seruet / si . . . subsidat*), with the six clauses so arranged

(1 2 3 2 3 1) that the two main ones are balanced for emphasis (on futility) at the opposite ends of the entire construction.   **ut . . . sic** 'just as it does no good, although you pour any amount [sc. of liquid into a vessel], if there is nothing at the bottom to receive and keep it, so . . . ' A probable allusion, extended in the second part of the correlative construction (n. on *per quassos . . . animos*), to the Danaids, punished in the Underworld for the murder of their new husbands by having constantly to draw water in leaking vessels or sieves. Proverbially a symbol of wasted effort (Aristot. *Oec.* 1.6.1, Xen. *Oec.* 7.40, Pl. *Ps.* 369), the vessel serves as an allegory for the insatiate, 'leaky' soul of the thoughtless in a famous Platonic passage (*Gorg.* 493a–d); hence the Lucretian echo at *D.R.N.* 3.935–7 *si grata fuit tibi uita anteacta priorque | et non omnia pertusum congesta quasi in uas | commoda perfluxere atque ingrata interiere . . .* The Lucretian allusion to the Danaids (taken up at 3.1003–10) illustrates a form of ingratitude and of an inability to be satisfied (ἀπληστία; Kenney (1971) 213 on 936–7 and 227 on 1003–10) which S. – whether or not directly influenced by Lucretius – may also impute to the *occupati* here; for by allowing each living moment to vanish into the abyss as if water were being poured into a bottomless vessel, they yearn insatiably for each new moment of fresh stimulus (cf. 7.8 *praecipitat . . . taedio*) with no grateful memory of the past.   **ingeras:** of pouring on liquid, *OLD* 1 b.   **quod . . . seruet:** final relative clause (G–L §630).   **nihil . . . quantum** 'it makes no difference how much'; parenthetical before the conditional construction (*si . . . transmittitur*).   **si . . . transmittitur** 'if there is nowhere for it to settle, it is allowed to pass through the cracks and holes of the mind'; the same combination of verbs at *Ep.* 22.17 *non . . . apud nos pars eius* [sc. *uitae*] *ulla subsedit: transmissa est et effluxit.*   **ubi:** with a final subjunctive, *OLD* 7 b.   **per quassos . . . animos:** two adjs. to parallel *securae et quietae mentis* above, both of them applicable to the leaky vessel presupposed in the first half of the correlative construction; for *quassus* of a broken vessel, Var. *L.* 5.137, Plin. *N.H.* 18.236, and for *foratos* (hence *Ep.* 99.5 *perforato animo*), *Med.* 748 *urnis quas* [sc. *Danaides*] *foratis irritus ludit labor.*

10.6 praesens . . . breuissimum est: S. develops his argument of 10.2 against the *occupati*, this time drawing on the other sense in which Posidonius defines the present moment (10.2n. on *quod agimus breue est*). Instead of interpreting the 'now' point broadly (ἐν πλάτει, fr. 98.9 E–K) to make possible a brief existing present extending into past and future, S. here describes it in Posidonius' other, rigorous and precise sense (κατ᾽ ἀπαρτισμόν, 10), which allows the present to be only a conceptual 'point-like division' (διορισμὸς σημειώδης, 8–9) between past and future. Posidonius inherited this idea of the 'now' (i.e. simply as a junction-point rather than as an existing time-span, however short) from a Stoic of the previous generation, Archedemus of Tarsus (*SVF* III 263.31–7, Kidd II 401), and its ultimate source is in the time-paradoxes of Aristotle's *Physics* (Sorabji (1983) 7–16). S. is not concerned here so much with the pedigree of these ideas as with deploying them persuasively. The general line of attack is the same, but with a sting in the tail: 'Time is pressing on while you fritter it away, *before* you can even fritter it away!'   **quidem** intensifies *adeo* with *ut* following. So in Velleius (e.g. 1.16.5, 2.9.3) and later (*TLL* I 611.16–35); for the combination, *Ir.* 3.30.2, *Ep.* 86.10, 117.16.   **ut ... uideatur:** by *quibusdam* S. refers to unspecified Stoics, perhaps incl. Zeno himself (*SVF* I 26.11–15; Rist 274 on time 'given the twilight reality of one of the incorporeals'), Archedemus of Tarsus (n. on *praesens ... breuissimum est* above) and, when seen from one angle, Chrysippus and Posidonius (Sorabji (1983) 22–7; Kidd II 397– 403). The 'apparent nothingness' of time was taken to be a consequence of the infinite divisibility of every moment, an idea which underlay the temporal paradoxes of Aristotle in *Physics* 4 (Sorabji (1983) 8–12). By here presenting the 'now' point as part of a continuum which is consistently in motion along with the Stoic universe (*in cursu ... manet* below), S. leaves no place even for that 'minimal' time (*SVF* II 165.40, Posid. fr. 98.11 E–K) or partless 'now' he made provision for in 10.2; he now allows only for movement *in* time.   **in cursu ... praecipitatur:** like the cosmos; *Helu.* 6.7 *caelestium ... natura semper in motu est, fugit et uelocissimo cursu agitur*.   **fluit** 'slips by'; of time, a Horatian usage (*Ep.* 1.1.23) introduced into prose by S. (*Ep.* 123.10, *N.Q.* 6.32.10; *TLL* VI 1.974.2–12).   **praecipitatur** 'hurries on' (pass. in middle sense as at Tac. *Hist.* 2.25.1 *Vitelliani ... ultro in insidias praecipitantur*); cf. 7.8. Because no word-break, not a pure example of the 'heroic' clausula (9.3n. on *ipso fugiente*), but the conspicuous verse-rhythm (–∪∪–∪) nevertheless suggests a running movement.   **ante ... uenit:** *uenit* perf., with tmesis of *antequam* anticipating the death of each living moment on its arrival; cf. *Pol.* 10.3 *uoluptas ... fluit et transit et paene antequam ueniat aufertur*.   **nec ... moram patitur:** contrast 10.4 *praeteriti temporis omnes* [sc. *partes*] ... *se ... detineri patientur*.   **mundus ... manet:** the Stoic cosmos is perpetually in motion and ever changing (*Helu.* 6.7–8, *Ep.* 36.11, 58.24, 71.12–14). Since time is 'the dimension of the world's motion' (L–S I 51A; Kidd II 396–7 on Posid. fr. 98.3–5), the present must itself be constantly in motion.   **sidera** 'heavenly bodies' (both stars and planets).

irrequieta . . . manet: the word order around *agitatio* (*irrequieta* in contrast to *in eodem uestigio*, *semper* to *numquam*) portrays the restless instability of the cosmos.   **irrequieta:** Ovidian (*M.* 1.579, 2.386, *Tr.* 2.236) and Silver in prose; *Pol.* 7.2 *quae* [sc. *sidera*] *irrequieta semper cursus suos explicant*, Plin. *N.H.* 2.6, 2.11.   **uestigio** 'position', as at e.g. Caes. *Gal.* 4.2.3, V. Max 8.13 *ext.* 1, Plin. *Ep.* 6.20.8.   **solum:** emphatic by position ('*alone* the present matters . . . ').   **arripi:** for the hint of urgency, *Ep.* 12.2 *occasionem . . . arripio*, 70.24.   **et id ipsum . . . subducitur:** the *occupati* have so many claims on their attention that, even if they *could* seize the moment, they are too distracted to make the most of it.   **illis:** dat. of disadvantage with *subducitur*.   **districtis in multa** 'pulled in many directions'; 7.3n.   **subducitur** 'is stolen away'; cf. 10.4 *subducta*.

11 Clinging to life

Since the *occupati* live for the (all too fleeting) present, they are taken unawares by death and plead in vain for each vanishing moment to continue. Contrast the serene end of the *sapiens*, whose wide perspective on life has always made allowance for its final scene.

11.1 Denique 'in short'.   **uis scire:** colloquial (Summers 305 on *Ep.* 88.4; *OLD uolo* 8) and common in S. (e.g. *Prou.* 3.9, *V.B.* 22.5, *Ep.* 32.4, 67.1, 94.58).   **quam non . . . diu uiuere:** the first *quam . . . diu* is in tmesis, 'how briefly they really live' (*Marc.* 21.1 *uidebis quam non diu steterint etiam quae* [sc. *urbes*] *uetustate gloriantur*, Cic. *Fam.* 11.3.4), so highlighting the parallel between *diu uiuant* and *diu uiuere*; the second *quam* qualifies not *diu* but *cupiant*, 'just see how they long to . . . ' For *uiuant/uiuere*, 2.2n. on '*exigua . . . uiuimus*'.   **decrepiti . . . mendicant:** the old are traditionally 'fond of life (φιλόζωοι), esp. in their last days' (Aristot. *Rhet.* 1389b 33; Powell (1988) 246–7 on Cic. *Sen.* 72 for parallels). Juvenal (10.188–288) expands S.'s outline sketch to devastating effect, and the possibility that he took it as his starting-point cannot be ruled out, esp. as Senecan influence on the tenth satire is recognized on other grounds as very likely (Dick (1969), esp. 238–9).   **decrepiti:** a colloquialism from early comedy (Summers xliv), before S. rare in reference to senility (*Ep.* 12.3, 26.1, fr. 69.20 Vottero). For the picture, Lucil. 331–2 Marx *quod deformis, senex arthriticus ac podagrosus* | *est, quod mancus miserque, exilis . . .* , but the elaboration in Juvenal (previous n.) is incomparable.   **paucorum . . . mendicant:** Juvenal (10.188) gives voice to these *uota* and makes them even more ambitious: *da spatium uitae, multos da, Iuppiter, annos.* Maecenas had asked for much the same (fr. 4 Courtney), with his poetic *uotum* for prolonged life at the cost of being crippled, deformed, even impaled: *uita, dum superest, benest* (3). S. found this contemptible (*Ep.* 101.13 *quid tam foeda uitae mendicatio?*), and, as here, attributes such cowardice to the fear of death (101.10–15).   **accessionem** 'addition'; Cic. *Amic.* 11 *quid . . . hunc* [sc. *Scipionem*] *paucorum annorum accessio iuuare potuisset?* **minores natu** 'younger (sc. than they really are)'.   **fingunt . . . sibi blandiuntur . . . se fallunt:** the three verbs cumulatively emphasize the extent to which the self-deception of the elderly prevents them from living in honesty conformity with nature. For resistance to ageing as an example of this, *Ep.* 47.7, 122.7 *non uiuunt contra naturam qui spectant ut pueritia splendeat tempore alieno?* **mendacio:** wordplay (*mendicant/mendacio*) gives the lie to the old men's appeal for more time.   **blandiuntur:** the reflexive use is Silver (*OLD* 2).   **quam . . . decipiant** 'as if at the same time (*una* adv.) they are cheating fate', rather than submitting to it stoically (*Ep.* 107.12 *hic est magnus animus qui se ei* [sc. *fato*] *tradidit*).   **uero:** adversative (*OLD* 7b).   **cum . . . admonuit** 'when some real illness has reminded them that they are mortal'. For this nuance of *aliqua, OLD aliqui*[1] 4a; *imbecillitas* is here a sudden reversal of health and not the slow degenerative disease of 20.4. For *admonuit* + gen., 8.5n.   **quemadmodum:** rare in the exclamatory sense required here (Axelson (1939) 189, comparing S.'s similar use of *quomodo* at 8.3 and elsewhere); *TLL* VIII 1283.48–55 (the present instance is tentatively, and surely wrongly, listed at 1284.81–3 = *tamquam, quasi*).   **non tamquam . . . sed tamquam:** with *correctio* (not x but y) to strong antithetical effect, favoured by S.; *Cl.* 1.22.3, *Ben.* 5.19.8, 6.16.2, *Ep.* 30.15, 99.32.   **exeant . . . extrahantur:** for the idea, *Ep.* 54.7, *Ep.* 107.11 *ducunt uolentem fata, nolentem trahunt* (apparently after Cleanthes).   **qui non uixerint** 'because they have not really lived' (causal relative; G–L §633); *qui* Madvig II 399 for *ut* of the MSS, which is awkward if taken as introducing a consecutive clause ('foolish to the degree that . . . ') without an antecedent.   **clamitant** 'cry out repeatedly'; rare in S. (*V.B.* 26.5, *Ep.* 104.1).   **si modo** 'only provided that' (*OLD modo*[1] 3a).   **euaserint . . . ualetudine:** *ualetudo* here = *imbecillitas* above, but at *Ir.* 3.13.5, *Tr.* 2.1, *Ep.* 65.1, 66.38 this negative sense is in each case defined by an appropriate adj.; *illa* serves that purpose here. For *euadere* of coming through an illness, *Marc.* 22.2 (*morbos*), Cic. *Diu.* 2.13 (*e morbo*).   **otio:** withdrawal from business and social duty

(3.5n.), not true philosophical retirement of the sort portrayed at 11.2, 14.1.
quam ... fruerentur 'how uselessly they made provision for things which
they would not [live to] enjoy'; for the fut. dimension of the imperf. subjunctive (= *fructuri essent*), K–S II 180–1.   **quam ... labor** 'how fruitless
all their toil turns out to be'. The poetic diction and motif emphasize the
tragic situation of those who 'wake up' too late. For the motif, Lucr. *D.R.N.*
2.1164–5 *suspirat arator* | ... *in cassum magnos cecidisse labores*, Virg. *G.* 4.491–2
ibi omnis | *effusus labor*, and for the tragic diction, *Aen.* 7.421 *Turne, tot in cas-
sum fusos patiere labores ... ?* Although *in cassum* was originally Plautine (*Poen.*
360) and entered Silver prose through Livy (2.49.8, 10.29.2), S. reserves it
elsewhere only for verse (*Med.* 26, *Ag.* 894), and here intensifies the effect
through alliteration (*cass-, ceci-, cog-*; the device determines the unusual
word-order) and proximity to *frustra* (cf. Lucr. *D.R.N.* 2.1060, 5.1002, 1430).

   11.2 After the panic of the *occupati* in the face of death, the serenity
of the *sapiens*.   **quibus:** dat. of agent with *agitur* (*Ot.* 3.4n. on *quietissimis*), perhaps here because of attraction (i.e. *iis a quibus*, where *iis* would be
dat. of advantage with *quidni ... sit?*).   **uita procul ... negotio:** not
just freedom from the grind of professional life (Hor. *Epod.* 2.1 *beatus ille
qui procul negotiis ...*, of the countryman far removed from the world of
the money-lender, of the soldier etc.), but specifically philosophical withdrawal.   **quidni:** *Ot.* 7.3n.   **spatiosa** 'ample'; of time, the adj.
enters Silver prose through Ovid (*OLD* 2).   **nihil ... superuacuum
est:** the anaphoric repetition of *nihil* (*Pol.* 3.5, *Ep.* 31.5) relentlessly drives
home the point.   **delegatur** 'is made over' to another. A bold image,
contrived from the technical meaning of the verb ('to transfer the ownership
of (property)', *OLD* 2d), by which S. (i) portrays time as a precious possession jealously owned by the *sapiens* and (ii) sets up a contrast with *spargitur*
below (time is neither 'given over' to anyone nor 'given away' rather more
indiscriminately); the image is sufficiently bold for the reading of the MSS
to have aroused suspicion (Reynolds *delibatur*, lit. 'is skimmed off', under
the influence of 7.5 *delibari*).   **alio ... spargitur** 'is scattered in one
direction and another'; of time also at *Ep.* 19.1 *satis multum temporis spar-
simus.*   **nihil ... traditur:** i.e. at every moment in life, whatever his
external circumstances, the *sapiens* is superior to fortune; *C.S.* 5.4 *omnia in se
reposuit, nihil fortunae credit, Ep.* 57.3 (in 10.2n. on *ius*).   **inde:** equivalent
to *ex illa* [sc. *uita*] above.   **interit** 'is wasted' through neglect, acc. to
Ep. 1.1 most shameful of all (*turpissima tamen est iactura quae per neglegentiam fit*).
largitione: free giving of the sort deplored in 3.1, 8.1.   **detrahitur** 'is

lost', 'subtracted'.   **nihil superuacuum est** 'it all serves some useful purpose'; the *sapiens* cannot be accused of letting any part of life slip by *ut rem superuacuam* (6.4). For the adj., 6.3n.   **in reditu est** 'yields a return', a financial idiom (e.g. Plin. *Ep.* 4.6.1); a bold (hence *ut ita dicam*) and apparently unprecedented metaphor.   **quantulacumque** 'however short', life is long enough if well invested; *Ep.* 93.5 *laudemus . . . eum cui quantulum-cumque temporis contigit bene collocatum est.*   **itaque:** 2.5n. on *non . . . quod.* **quandoque** 'whenever'; rare in Classical Latin, more common in Silver (Brink on Hor. *Ars* 359) but not often in S. (e.g. *Tr.* 11.2, *Helu.* 11.6, *N.Q.* 3.29.1).   **uenerit:** fut. perf.   **non cunctabitur . . . gradu:** since the *sapiens* lives each day as if a complete life (7.9n. on *omnem . . . ordinat*) and scorns death (*Prou.* 6.6 *contemnite mortem, Tr.* 11.6, *Ep.* 36.8, 78.5), he calmly meets his end (*Ep.* 61.2 *bene . . . mori est libenter mori*).   **certo gradu** 'sure-footed'; *Helu.* 8.5, *Ep.* 37.4 *uade certo gradu.*

12 Busy idleness, idle business

Definition, illustration and condemnation of the *occupati* busy in (misguided) *otium.* S. rounds on familiar targets in Roman diatribe-satire (see the introductory remarks below on 12.3, 4 and 5), affecting the tone of a stern moralist.

12.1 Quaeris . . . quos . . . uocem?: the mock-interrogative simply announces a new subject; a familiar Senecan technique (e.g. *Ep.* 7.1, 22.1, 29.1, 88.1, 109.1).   **uocem** 'designate as' (*OLD* 9a); so 12.2.   **non est quod:** 2.5n.   **a basilica:** here probably 'lawcourt', as at *Ir.* 3.33.2 *fremitu iudiciorum basilicae resonent.* If the sing. refers specifically to Rome, S. perhaps means the *basilica Iulia*, in his time the seat of the centumviral court (for proceedings there, Carcopino (1968) 187–9).   **immissi . . . eiciunt:** weighed down by court business, the lawyers leave the basilica only when the watchdogs are finally let in for the night. The Roman business day began at sunrise, lawsuits generally had to be started before noon, and proceedings ended with the declining afternoon sun; not even the Senate could convene after sunset (Dupont (1992) 188–9). For night watchdogs at Rome, Cic. *S. Rosc.* 56, Liv. 5.47.3.   **immissi:** of dogs let loose with hostile purpose, Virg. *G.* 3.371, Gell. *N.A.* 15.20.9.   **speciosius elidi:** patrons are 'crushed to death' by the crowd of their clients and hangers-on; the force of the comparative adv. is felt in the contrast with *contemptius* below ('crushed more with affected adulation in their own crowd, with greater scorn when they are part of another's'). For the hyperbole, Ov. *Pont.* 4.9.21 *nec querulus, turba quamuis eliderer, essem*, V. Max. 2.2.4, Suet. *Iul.* 39.4; for the patron so pressed, 2.4, 7.6, and for the *salutatrix turba*, Juv. 5.21.   **in aliena** [sc. *turba*]: when not besieged by clients, the patrons cultivate their superiors on the principle of 2.4 *ille illius cultor est, hic illius; suus nemo est.*   **officia:** the client's duties (e.g. *salutatio*), already characterized as *uoluntaria seruitus* in 2.1.   **ut ... illidant:** lit. 'in order to dash them [sc. the clients] upon other people's doors'; *alienis foribus dat.* (*Ep.* 77.14 *illisum parieti caput rupit*). The obvious hyperbole should be read in the light of the many other references to rough and violent behaviour on such occasions; Mayor 1 246–7 on Juv. 5.19, with *Tr.* 12.6 *multorum frustra liminibus illisus nomenculatores persalutauit.*   **quos ... exercet:** i.e. profiteers disreputably exploiting the praetorian auctions. At public auctions a spear was fixed in the ground, apparently after the ancient practice of selling the spoils of war under the victors' symbol of ownership (*sub hasta*; Courtney on Juv. 3.33); so *Marc.* 20.5 *hastam consularia spolia uendentem* (of the selling of Pompey's property after defeat by Caesar in 48 BC). The auctioneers presiding over the sale of state property and over the bidding for state contracts were known as *praecones publici* and were attached to the staff of important magistrates incl. praetors (Rauh (1989) 453); hence the phrase *hasta praetoris* (i.e. an auction conducted under the authority of the praetors).   **infami lucro:** strongly suggesting that this auction is offering goods at knock-down prices to a despicable *sector* (*OLD* 2) rather than allowing competitive tendering.   **quandoque** 'some day'; cf. the relative sense at 11.2.   **suppuraturo** 'bound to fester'; disreputable gain always ends in tears (*Ep.* 115.16 *nulla ... auaritia sine poena est ... o quantum lacrimarum, quantum laborum exigit!*). For the bold image, not found before S., *Ep.* 59.17 *cum uoluptates angusto corpori ... ingestae suppurare coeperunt*, 80.6; for the force of the fut. pple, Westman (1961) 141.

12.2 otium occupatum: the oxymoron, reversed in *desidiosa occupatio* below, emphasizes the basic contradiction in the lifestyles described here. **in uilla ... molesti sunt:** for the idea, *Tr.* 2.9, *Ep.* 55.8 *non multum ad tranquillitatem locus confert: animus est qui sibi commendet omnia. uidi ego in uilla hilari et amoena maestos, uidi in media solitudine occupatis similes.* S. recalls Lucr. *D.R.N.* 3.1063–7, where the opposite of Epicurean ἀταραξία is illustrated by restlessness invading the country-house retreat (Kenney (1971) 240–1 on 1068–9).   **lecto:** for recreational study; McKeown on Ov. *Am.* 1.9.42

lectus et umbra.   **quamuis . . . recesserint:** withdrawal is only the first stage (*Tr.* 14.2 *animus ab omnibus externis in se reuocandus est . . .*), and not sufficient in itself to produce the *sapiens.*   **quorum . . . occupatio:** the *correctio* (not x but y) lays emphasis on *desidiosa occupatio,* the key term defining S.'s subsequent illustrations (12.2–5); for the oxymoron, Mayer (1994) 194 on Hor. *Ep.* 1.11.28 *strenua . . . inertia.*   **Corinthia:** vessels and statues of Corinthian bronze, acc. to Plin. *N.H.* 34.6–8 an alloy with varying proportions of gold, silver and bronze allegedly first produced by accident when Corinth was burnt and sacked by L. Mummius in 146 BC (but Sherwin-White on Plin. *Ep.* 3.6.3). As antiques, they were highly prized by Roman collectors, Augustus apparently among them (Suet. *Aug.* 70.2); but for S.'s hostility to such collecting as decadent and trivial, *Tr.* 9.6, *Helu.* 11.3. **paucorum furore pretiosa** 'which the collecting mania of connoisseurs has made so expensive'. Cf. *Helu.* 11.3 *aes paucorum insania pretiosum*; already in Tiberius' reign the cost of Corinthian bronze caused concern (Suet. *Tib.* 34.1).   **anxia . . . concinnat** 'arranges with meticulous attention to detail', the verb pre-Classical and Silver (*OLD* 2).   **dierum:** i.e. 'of every day'.   **lamellis** 'strips of copper'; the diminutive (of *lamina*) reinforces S.'s superior condescension (cf. *V.B.* 21.3 *paucae argenti lamellae*). **ceromate** 'wrestling-ring' by metonymy, *ceroma* properly denoting the soft earth or mud forming the floor of the ring (Courtney on Juv. 6.246). S. makes first use of the derivative (= κήρωμα) to identify the specifically Greek character of the paedophilic voyeurism associated with the *palaestra,* where boys wrestled naked. For Roman contempt of the effeminate associations of Greek athletics, e.g. *Ep.* 88.18, Hor. *S.* 2.2.9–13, *C.* 3.24.54–7, Trajan *ap.* Plin. *Ep.* 10.40.2 *gymnasiis indulgent Graeculi* with Courtney on Juv. 3.68. The link with homosexual conduct is unscrupulously exploited as a target by Juvenal (e.g. 2.65–148) and stated unequivocally by Tac. *Ann.* 14.20.4 *ut . . . degeneret . . . studiis externis iuuentus, gymnasia et otia et turpes amores exercendo.* **(nam . . . laboramus):** the unusually strong tone of the parenthesis may be self-defensive, as it is philosophers, and esp. Stoics, whom Cicero and Martial among others accuse of hypocrisy because of their active homosexual behaviour. The *locus classicus* for these *tristes obsceni* in Latin is Juv. 2.1–35, but Courtney 120–1 on Juv. 2 refers to Lucian and Athenaeus as well as to the many Roman parallels. The satirists' caricature of homosexuality as an effeminate Greek *uitium* is uncritically adopted here to distance the Roman philosopher's *pudor uitiorum* (cf. fr. 77 Vottero) from the notoriety of his Greek counterparts.   **pro facinus!** 'for shame!'; *facinus* voc.

(K–S 1 274; Kurth (1994) 212 on *Pol.* 17.4 *pro pudor imperii!*).   **laboramus**
'we suffer from', with abl. (*OLD* 5).   **sectator** 'enthusiastic admirer';
only here in S., and ironic because of its popular use for a philosophy student
(*OLD* 1 b).   **rixantium:** more brawling than disciplined fighting. The
word reinforces S.'s contempt for both the young men and those who watch
them: there is no sporting skill to appreciate here.   **qui ... diducit?:**
just as the collector of Corinthian bronzes constantly fusses over their arrangement, so the devotee of wrestling spends his time busily dividing his
athletes into matching pairs.   **unctorum suorum greges** 'the troops
of his own oiled wrestlers'. For the substantival use of the pple (Dahlmann
(1949) 56 for *iunctorum* of the MSS), Vitr. 5.11.3 *ab unctis* [sc. wrestlers] *se
exercentibus* (Salmasius' necessary emendation of MSS *cunctis*); for *grex* applied to people, *Ep.* 95.24 *puerorum infelicium greges.* Some editors read *iumen-
torum* after Gertz ((1874) 155), but the context makes this much the less likely
option.   **aetatium ... paria** 'pairs of the same age and (skin-)colour';
so *Ep.* 95.24 (on male prostitutes laid on at a luxurious dinner-party) *agmina
exoletorum per nationes coloresque discripta.* In both contexts it was important to
match physique and experience.   **aetatium:** *aetas* takes both *-um* and
-ium in the gen. plur. (N–W 1 409; *Ot.* 3.4n. on *uirtutium*); for the former
(Ciceronian), *Ep.* 84.10, for the latter (Livian), *C.S.* 7.1, *Marc.* 26.5, *Ben.*
7.19.8.   **nouissimos:** the real enthusiast is always reinvigorating his
troop of athletes with the latest talent (Alexander (1945) 87). The athlete's
cultivation of physical rather than moral strength puts him well down in
S.'s scale of values; *Ir.* 2.14.2 *athletae ... in uilissima sui parte occupati, Ep.* 80.2,
88.18–19.   **pascit** 'maintains' (*OLD* 3a).

   12.3 On hairstyling. Here, and in the following sections, S. comes as
close as he does anywhere to the subject-matter and the tone of verse satire.
The fussy meticulousness is effeminate (*RAC effeminatus* 632–3), decadent
(Tib. 1.6.39, 8.9–10, Ov. *A.A.* 3.433–4) and contrary to Stoic principle
(*Ep.* 124.22). What is simply a topos in Tibullus and Ovid becomes a small
dramatic scene in S., where we meet the *tonsor* and his client, follow his
fingers over the hair and register (with mock horror) the client's shudder-
ing response to every small touch. Here again (cf. 11.1) Juvenal develops the
scene (6.487–507) with additional comic touches drawn from verse satire,
e.g. supplying a name for the hairdresser (491, 494) and a mock-epic dimension (502–3). For the Roman barber in action, Carcopino (1968) 157–64.
quibus: dat. of agent; *Ot.* 3.4n. on *quietissimis.*   **transmittuntur** 'are
allowed to pass'; in this sense not before S. (*OLD* 7).   **decerpitur:** of

superficial trimming also at *Ep.* 59.10 (on reluctance to confront our vices) *nemo nostrum in altum descendit; summa tantum decerpsimus.* 'The man who was rich enough to include *tonsores* in his household retinue put himself in their hands in the morning and again, if necessary, in the course of the day' (Carcopino (1968) 157). **proxima nocte:** 7.3n. on *tota uita.* **succreuit** 'has grown anew'. **in consilium itur:** witty use of a familiar phrase for judicial assessment (*OLD consilium* 1 a); so Juv. 6.497 *est in consilio materna* [sc. *ancilla*], where the maid 'sits as assessor' (Courtney) of her mistress's haircut and set. **disiecta** 'dishevelled', Ovidian (*Her.* 12.63, *M.* 11.385–6). **deficiens . . . compellitur:** thinning hair is combed forward from both sides of the head to disguise baldness; so Julius Caesar to conceal the *caluitii deformitatem* which made him the butt of popular jokes (Suet. *Iul.* 45.2). **quomodo:** 8.3n. **uirum** 'a real man'; *Ep.* 31.7 *non est uiri timere sudorem.* **excandescunt** 'blaze with rage', much stronger than *irascuntur* above; after Caelius (Cic. *Fam.* 8.12.2), the personal use develops in and after S. (*TLL* v 2.1200.82–1201.20). **iuba sua** 'their precious mane'; the rare application to human hair is contemptuous (Mart. 1.31.6). **extra ordinem:** of hair, Ov. *Am.* 1.11.1 with McKeown. **nisi . . . recciderunt!** 'if everything hasn't fallen back into its proper ringlets'. *anulus* for a ringlet of hair is not found before S. (the older word is *cincinnus*); the fashion was thought effeminate (Quint. *Inst.* 12.10.47). Martial (2.66.1–4) describes a show of more violent anger when Lalage finds a ringlet out of place. **istorum:** contemptuous (*OLD* 5b). **qui . . . comam:** for the idea, *Ep.* 77.17 *tanti . . . illam* [sc. *patriam*] *putas ut tardius cenes* (i.e. 'which is to be served first, your country or your dinner?'); so already e.g. Cic. *Att.* 1.18.6 (of self-interested aristocrats) *qui ita sunt stulti ut amissa republica piscinas suas fore saluas sperare uideantur*, Sall. *Cat.* 52.5. **non malit:** the usual subjunctive after *quis est qui . . . ?* and related negative expressions (e.g. *nemo est qui . . .*); K–S ii 306. **suam:** rightly placed (despite the doubts of some editors) to emphasize the point made at *Ep.* 66.26 *nemo . . . patriam quia magna est amat, sed quia sua*; for the phrase Reynolds in OCT 253 in app. compares Liv. 44.15.3, Plin. *Ep.* 7.15.2. **turbari:** of political disorder, Liv. 3.59.5 *turbato rei publicae statu*, 4.52.8, Virg. *Aen.* 6.857; of hair, *C.S.* 11.2, Phaed. 827 *decus omne turbat capitis* [sc. Phaedra]. **decore:** on the analogy of Phaed. 827 (previous n.), the abl. of *decus*, not of *decor*; acc. to *TLL* v 1.206.75 S. in his prose works (excl. *Apoc.*) shows a marked preference for *decus*, using it some 29 times (6 abl.), *decor* 12 (2 abl.). **salute:** sc. *capitis*, now in the extended sense of 'life'

(*OLD* 4a).   **comptior ... quam honestior** 'smarter in appearance
rather than of better character'; S. rarely uses the double comparative (*Ep.*
22.7 *cautiores quam fortiores sunt*; K–S II 474). For *comptus* 'well groomed', esp.
with reference to hair, *OLD* I c.   **pectinem speculumque:** for careful combing as effeminate, N–H on Hor. *C.* 1.15.14; for use of the mirror as
unmanly, *N.Q.* 1.17.10, Juv. 2.99–101 with Braund (1996) 149.

     12.4 Training of the singing voice is contrary to Stoic norms
(n. on *cuius ... fecit*) and condemned by the rhetoricians as another effeminate exercise (Sen. *Contr.* 1 *praef.* 8 *ad muliebres blanditias extenuare
uocem...*; Edwards (1993) 82), which helps to explain why Tacitus
reproaches Nero's public singing as a *foedum studium* (*Ann.* 14.14.1).
quid illi...? 'What of those...?', a common idiom (*OLD quis*[1] 12a).
componendis ... canticis: the anaphoric repetition of -*is* suggests the
rhythm of the songs; *cantica* originally denoted lyric sections of Roman
drama (esp. comedy) but has a wider application in Silver Latin (*OLD* 2).
operati 'absorbed in'. S. is among the last to use the word as an adj., which
from the elder Pliny on tends to become the past pple of the new verb *operari*
(*TLL* IX 2.689.75). At *Ben.* 7.14.6 he apparently opts for the more popular dependent dat.; hence the omission here (after Gruter) of *in* of the MSS before
the gerundives (cf. *Ep.* 117.26; McKeown on Ov. *Am.* 2.7.23–4 for '*operatus*
constructed with the dative of the gerundive').   **cuius ... fecit:** as in
the case of styled hair, the trained, artificial voice is *contra naturam*; at *Ep.* 15.7
S. advocates exercising the voice but not the performing of elaborate scales.
rectum: of even, 'natural' enunciation, e.g. *Ep.* 56.2 (*rectae uoces*, in contrast with *tenuem et stridulam uocem*), Cic. *De orat.* 3.45, Quint. *Inst.* 2.5.11.
simplicissimum: of 'natural' voice, e.g. Cic. *De orat.* 3.45, Quint. *Inst.*
1.11.6, 5.10.124.   **in flexus ... torquent** 'they twist the voice into sin-
uous turns of the most feeble crooning'. Inflection of the voice, like the
artful twisting of the *anuli* in 12.3, is a degenerate embellishment; *flexus* of
pitch-variation is Silver (first in S.; *OLD* 5).   **inertissimae:** three senses
coalesce to make this just the right word: (i) lit. *sine arte* (Maltby 302); (ii) 'unmanly', 'effeminate' (*OLD* 3, adding Stat. *Ach.* 1.848 *sexus iners*); (iii) 'weak',
'feeble' (e.g. Ov. *Am.* 1.15.2 *ingenii ... uocas carmen inertis opus* with McKeown);
of the voice, e.g. Virg. *Aen.* 10.322. Editors from Erasmus (*inept-*) emend
needlessly.   **quorum ... sonant** 'whose fingers are always snapping
in time to some song which they carry in their head'; cf. Quint. *Inst.*
9.4.51 *tempora ... metiuntur et pedum et digitorum ictu. intra se* of internalized
activity as at e.g. *Ben.* 2.1.4, 6.38.2 *omnes ... idem ... intra se optant*; Ovidian

(e.g. *Tr.* 3.4.69–70 *intra mea pectora quemque* | *alloquar*, 4.5.17).   **adhibiti sunt** 'they have been asked to attend to'.   **tacita modulatio:** for the humming or mental replaying of music as an untimely distraction at solemn moments, *Ep.* 123.9, Man. 5.334–5.   **iners negotium:** *uariatio* on 12.2 *desidiosa occupatio*.

12.5 Lavish banquets are a matter of intense concern, not pleasure, for the preoccupied host. S. conveys the harried *negotium* of such occasions by picturing in a busy sequence of uncoordinated clauses the anxious exertions involved. The concentration of the mind on ephemeral detail, frivolous embellishment and the anticipation of physical pleasure is the basis of the charge of *luxuria* which S. brings against banquets and rich eating as being contrary to nature; so *Helu.* 10.2–11, *Ep.* 78.23–4, 89.22, 95.15–19, 24–9, 110.12–13, 119.13–14. For food as a regular feature in attacks on luxury, Edwards (1993) 186. The gluttonous banquet is a recurring theme in verse and prose satire (Lucil. bks. 5 and 13, Var. Περὶ ἐδεσμάτων (see *Men.* 403 = Gell. *N.A.* 6.16.1–5), Hor. *S.* 2.8, Juv. 5 and esp. Petronius' *Cena Trimalchionis*), incorporating several of the extravagant details reproduced in S.'s satirical pictures here and at *Ep.* 47.5–8.   **conuiuia:** cf. 7.2 *aspice . . . quantum conuiuia* [sc. *occupent temporis*].   **mehercules:** 5.3n.   **non posuerim:** perf. potential subjunctive, equivalent in sense to the present; rare in early Latin but more frequent from Cicero's time (G–L §257 n. 1), it is common in S. (Summers lxiii).   **uacantia tempora:** *uariatio* for *otium*.   **cum:** causal   (*Ot.* 7.3n.).   **quam . . . ordinent:** cf. 12.2 (of bronzes), *V.B.* 17.2 *quare . . . nec temere et ut libet collocatur argentum sed perite struitur . . . ?*. For the luxury value of silver plate, *Helu.* 11.3, *Ep.* 5.3, 110.14, 119.13, Juv. 1.76 with Courtney.   **exoletorum:** male prostitutes (also *Prou.* 3.13), their tunics gathered up by a belt (cf. *V.B.* 17.2 *quare paedagogium pretiosa ueste succingitur?*) obviously for titillating effect; for slave boys providing sexual services as a sequel to feasting, e.g. *Ep.* 47.7, 95.24, Cic. *Phil.* 2.105, *Fin.* 2.23 (all cited by Edwards (1993) 188).   **suspensi** 'on tenterhooks'.   **quomodo . . . exeat:** commentators refer to Petr. 40.2–41.5 for the ultimate in culinary preparation and display as a huge wild boar is carved at Trimalchio's table and live thrushes emerge from inside. But the boar itself, *animal propter conuiuia natum* (Juv. 1.141), was often associated with luxury; so e.g. Hor. *S.* 2.8.6, Mart. 7.78.3, 9.14.3, 12.17.4, Juv. 5.116, and for a range of different ways in which boar could be prepared, Apic. 8.1. By S.'s time it was unremarkable for a whole boar to be served at table (Smith (1975) 93 on Petr. 40.3), a practice apparently begun in the late Republic by P. Servilius Rullus (Plin. *N.H.* 8.210).   **coco:** the familiar spelling *coquus* is relegated *apud antiquos* by Priscian at *GLK* II 36.13.   **exeat** 'turns out', a Silver use for *eveniat* (*OLD exeo* 11; Krebs–Schmalz I 548).   **signo dato:** military phraseology (*Ir.* 2.3.3, Liv. 2.25.1, 8.9.14), appropriate for an 'army' of slaves; so *Ep.* 95.24 *transeo ministratorum* [sc. *turbam*] *per quos signo dato ad inferendam cenam discurritur*, where (as here) the military associations are strengthened by *discurrere* (*TLL* V 1.1366.15 *praecipue de militibus*).   **glabri:** effeminate slaves, shaven or depilated (*Ep.* 47.7 *uini minister...glaber retritis pilis*), their smoothness a sign of *mollitia* (Edwards (1993) 68–9).   **scindantur:** for carving as a specialist skill, *V.B.* 17.2 *quare...est aliquis scindendi obsonii magister?*, *Ep.* 47.6, Petr. 36.6, and esp. Juv. 5.120–4, 11.136–41.   **in frusta non enormia** 'into carefully shaped portions', the virtual double negative carrying special force; the adj. not found before S. and Petronius (2.7 *enormis loquacitas*, of 'formless' Asiatic literary style).   **pueruli** 'slave boys', a rare Ciceronian usage (*S. Rosc.* 120). The degrading (*infelices*) duty of wiping up the disgorged spittle after the diners' wine-tasting is cited at *Ep.* 47.5 as contributing to the hostility of slaves towards their masters.   **ex his** 'by these means'.   **elegantiae...captatur:** since luxury is unnatural (*Ep.* 74.14), to seek a reputation for sumptuous living merely aggravates the initial vice; *Ep.* 114.9 *deinde ad cenas lautitia transfertur et illic commendatio ex nouitate et soliti ordinis commutatione captatur.*   **uitae secessus** 'life's quiet corners', invaded by *luxuria, ambitio* etc. so that even when dining alone one dines sumptuously; the Silver image also in Quintilian (*Inst.* 10.5.16 *studiorum secessus* 'bypaths of study'). The *sapiens* values a different *secessus* (*Ot.* 1.1).   **ambitione** 'ostentation', a post-Augustan nuance (*OLD* 6); cf. 20.5, *Helu.* 10.3, *Ir.* 3.34.1, *Tr.* 1.5. More basic appetites are easily satisfied: *Ep.* 119.13–14 *nihil praeter cibum natura desiderat...ambitiosa non est fames...*

12.6 Those who have slaves to attend to their every need are too reliant on others to be truly independent. From the Stoic perspective such an existence, including travel by litter or carriage, is *contra naturam*; *Ep.* 55.1 *labor est...et diu ferri, ac nescio an eo maior quia contra naturam est, quae pedes dedit ut per nos ambularemus, oculos ut per nos uideremus. debilitatem nobis indixere deliciae*, Plin. *N.H.* 29.19. Again, this self-indulgence is a regular target of satirists (e.g. Juv. 1.32, 64–5, 3.239–42, 7.139–43, 9.142–4, 10.36–7), who embellish the theme with accounts of vehicles stuffed with luxurious cushions (Courtney on Juv. 1.158), just as Cicero had already ridiculed Verres (*Ver.* 5.27 ... *ut mos fuit Bithyniae regibus, lectica octaphoro ferebatur, in qua puluinus*

erat . . . ; the hardy Roman governor should of course be seen on horseback).
For the theme elsewhere in S., *C.S.* 14.1, *Ep.* 22.9 and esp. 80.8, 110.17.
ne . . . quidem 'neither would I . . .' (*OLD ne*[1] 6b).   **numerauerim:**
12.5n. on *non posuerim*.   **sella . . . et lectica:** passengers sat in the former, reclined in the latter, though they are often grouped as here (e.g. Mart.
10.10.7, 11.98.11–12, Suet. *Claud.* 25.2; *RE* XII 1.1083).   **se . . . ferunt**
'move around'; a rare appearance of the reflexive form (*OLD* 3a) in Senecan
prose (cf. *N.Q.* 6.32.6).   **gestationum** 'rides', here in a sedan chair or
litter as at *Ep.* 15.6 and 55.1, but elsewhere also in a carriage or on horseback (*OLD* 1; *gesto* 3); the noun (post-Augustan) less often denotes place
('a drive'; *OLD* 2). Since outings in a litter were recommended for the sick
(Cels. 2.15.3 *genera . . . gestationis plura sunt . . . lenissima est naui uel in portu uel in
flumine, uehementior uel in alto mari naui uel lectica,* Plin. *N.H.* 26.13; Courtney on
Juv. 4.5–6), S. may refer here to exercise taken on medical advice (cf. *alius
admonet* below).   **quasi . . . non liceat:** the unexpected position of the
clause draws attention to the obsessive preoccupation with this one activity to the exclusion of all else.   **occurrunt** 'turn up' punctually; with
ad, *OLD* 2.   **quos . . . admonet:** for the same basic routine, but emphatically self-directed, Plin. *Ep.* 9.36.   **usque:** preceded in the MSS
by *et*, probably dittography after *admonet*; removed by Gertz (1874) 155.
usque eo . . . ut 'they are so enervated by the excessive sloth of a pampered
mind that . . .'; excessive dependence undermines firmness of character. For
delicatus associated with 'soft' living, e.g. *Ep.* 7.7, 87.9, 114.4; for the sense of
soluo (Livian and Silver), *Ep.* 82.2 *effeminatur animus atque in similitudinem otii
sui . . . soluitur, OLD* 8c.   **per se** 'by themselves' (*OLD per* 15b).

  12.7 As a climax, a dramatized example of extreme helplessness and af-
fectation, comparable with but outshining the satirical parodies of human
folly on the stage (12.8).   **audio quendam:** S. appropriately relies
on mere hearsay (*OLD* 9a) and cannot bring himself to name the character.   **deliciae** 'self-indulgence'; Isid. *Orig.* 10.70 follows S. in con-
necting the noun with *delicatus* (Maltby 179). Such patent irresponsibility
towards one's duty merits a much stronger noun; hence the force of *modo*.
uitam . . . dediscere 'to unlearn life and normal human practice', a paradox running counter to the principle established at 7.3–4 *uiuere tota uita discendum est . . .* For the phrase cf. Sen. *Contr.* 1 *praef.* 16 *Hispanae consuetudinis morem
non poterat dediscere* [sc. *M. Porcius Latro*].   **uocandae sunt:** the subj. is
dediscere below but the verb is attached to the nearer noun; G–L §211 with
K–S I 40–1 for a range of examples.   **inter manus:** of handling those

who (like S.'s bather) are otherwise helpless, e.g. Pl. *Mos.* 385, Cic. *Ver.* 5.28, Liv. 3.13.3, Phaed. 5.7.10.   **interrogando:** equivalent to *interrogantem*, a use of the abl. of the gerund which is found in all periods but is mainly post-Augustan; K–S 1 752–3.   **'iam sedeo?':** because, sitting still in his *sella*, he is still carried by his slaves.   **hunc tu:** emphatic juxtaposition ('Do *you* think that someone like *this* . . . ?').   **uiuat . . . uideat:** possible adaptation of the idiom *uiuus uidensque* 'alive and in possession of your faculties' (*OLD uiuus* 1 d); Otto 377 *uiuus* 3, and esp. Lucr. *D.R.N.* 3.1046 *mortua cui uita est prope iam uiuo atque uidenti* . . . with Kenney (1971) 237.   **dixerim:** 12.5n. on *non posuerim*.   **si hoc ignorauit** 'if he really did not know this [sc. *an sederet*]'; the indicative carries stress.

   12.8 quidem: equivalent to μέν, contrasting with *sed* (= δέ); Solodow (1978) 31–2, 47–53.   **sentiunt** [sc. *delicati*] 'genuinely experience'.   **imitantur** 'affect' [sc. *obliuionem*]; the verbs depicting human self-deception here (*finxit, imitantur*) anticipate the coming theatrical parallel (*mentiri* and *fingunt* below).   **quasi . . . argumenta** 'as evidence of their success'; from S.'s perspective *felicitatis* of course ironic.   **humilis et contempti:** more sarcasm, with a particularly insulting adj. combination which elsewhere (e.g. *Ir.* 3.43.1, *Ben.* 3.28.6) appears in earnest. For the defining gen., 7.5n. on *magni . . . uiri est . . . sinere.*   **facias:** 2.1n. on *si uti scias.*   **i nunc et . . . puta!** 'What folly to think . . . '. For the formula *i nunc*, an ironical exhortation first found in Augustan poetry (e.g. Virg. *Aen.* 7.425, Prop. 2.29.22, Hor. *Ep.* 1.6.17, Ov. *Am.* 1.7.35 with McKeown) and perhaps derived from everyday usage (Gagliardi (1978) 378), e.g. *Helu.* 6.8, *Ben.* 6.35.5, *Ep.* 88.37 *i nunc et longam esse uitam nega!* Here it presses home the new point with a triumphant rhetorical flourish.   **mimos:** actors in mimes, a theatrical medium for risqué, sententious and sometimes downright vulgar realism (Ov. *Tr.* 2.497, 515), which S. elsewhere (*Ep.* 8.8–9) presents as a vehicle for popular moral philosophizing, esp. in the hands of its famous Augustan exponent Publilius Syrus. For the historical background, Fantham (1989) with Beare (1964) 154–8.   **mentiri** 'feign', 'invent'.   **exprobrandam:** cf. 9.3. The moralizing emphasis given here to the treatment in mimes of such themes as extravagance, party-giving and adultery evidently survived when these themes were later incorporated into the genres of verse satire and the satiric novel.   **mehercules:** 5.3n.   **praetereunt** [sc. *mimi*] 'pass over'.   **tanta . . . processit:** S. often resorts to *conuicium saeculi* (e.g. *Ben.* 1.10.1–4, *Ep.* 75.15, 95.23–4,

N.Q. 1.17.10, 7.31.1–32.4). The rhetorical hyperbole is Ciceronian (e.g. *Ver.* 3.64 *hoc . . . nouum ac singulare atque incredibile genus iniuriarum contumeliarumque*), but S.'s *uitiorum copia* seems to be first here (cf. *Tr.* 11.8 *mala quorum ingens cotidie copia est*) and is perhaps echoed in Juv. 1.87.   **ingenioso . . . saeculo** 'in an age which has applied its fertile talents to this one area (i.e. creating new vices)'. *ingeniosus* with *in* + acc. is Ovidian (*Tr.* 2.288, 342, *Ibis* 188) and suggests 'bringing about consequences to the agent's (or another's) detriment' (e.g. *Helu.* 19.6; Williams (1994) 202–3).   **processit** 'has arisen', a nuance apparently not found in Classical Latin (*OLD* 6). **iam . . . neglegentiam** 'we can now fault the mime actors for disregarding them'; for the nuance of *arguere*, *OLD* 6b.   **esse aliquem qui** 'To imagine that there is anyone who . . . !'; acc. and inf. of exclamation expressing surprise, as at *C.S.* 18.2 *di boni, hoc uirum audire, principem scire, et usque eo licentiam peruenisse ut . . .*, and colloquial in tone (Bourgery (1922) 359). Often in comedy, the construction is Ciceronian but otherwise rare in Classical and post-Augustan prose (K–S 1 719–21).   **interierit** 'is finished off', anticipating 12.9 *mortuus*; the colloquialism mainly in comedy (*OLD* 1 c), which may explain S.'s use of it in a section devoted to the mime. **an . . . credat!** 'take another's word as to whether . . .'   **alteri:** equivalent to *alii*; Setaioli (1981 a) 28–30 with *Ot.* 4.1 n. on *alterius*.

12.9 Conclusion: self-delusion a form of living death.   **non est ergo . . . imponas:** the asyndeton is another colloquial feature (Summers xcii–xciii); the jussive use of the second pers. pres. subjunctive is mainly confined to comedy, Cicero's letters, verse and Silver prose (K–S 1 186).   **aeger:** not just physically weakened by a delicate lifestyle but sick in mind, a frequent emphasis in S. (e.g. *Ep.* 2.1, 15.1 *sine hoc* [sc. philosophy] *aeger est animus*, *Ep.* 74.34).   **mortuus** 'as good as dead'; rarely thus (*TLL* VIII 1496.52–65), but of gluttons at *Ep.* 60.4. In some cases the hyperbole is modified, as here by *semiuiuus* below; cf. *Ep.* 82.3 *otium sine litteris mors est et hominis uiui sepultura.*   **ille . . . sensus est:** a model *sententia* (Summers xxxv–xxxvii) supplies the corrective to the preceding *exempla* of *otium* misunderstood and misused.   **sensus** 'personal awareness' (*OLD* 5b).   **semiuiuus:** only here in S.; Ciceronian (e.g. *Ver.* 1.45, *Tul.* 21; cf. 5.2 *semiliber*).   **cui . . . opus est** balances *cui . . . sensus est*, contrasting that self-assurance with this excessive need for dependence. **habitus:** of posture, post-Augustan (*OLD* 2b).   **ullius . . . dominus esse:** use of time is one of the few areas where total control is within reach;

Ep. 1.3 *omnia... aliena sunt, tempus tantum nostrum est...* For the phrase, *Ep.* 101.4 *crastini... dominum, Anth. Lat.* 431.8 Sh. B. *dominus temporis ipse mei.*

13 Pointless learning

On the trivial pursuit of obscure, and often highly speculative, antiquarian knowledge; a pleasure (*uoluptas*) to some, but a form of *otium* flawed in Stoic terms because in reality it is just another engrossing preoccupation (*negotium*) with no enriching philosophical value whatsoever.

13.1 Persequi ... longum est 'it would be a long business to run through the individual cases', a familiar formula conveying the epic proportions of the rejected task; so e.g. Cic. *Phil.* 2.27, *N.D.* 2.159, Quint. *Inst.* 10.1.118 with Peterson (with the indicative 'the action is spoken of as still possible'). Parallel expressions at *Ir.* 1.3.3, *Ben.* 3.12.4, *N.Q.* 5.17.5 (*TLL* VII 2.1640.9–14). **quorum ... uitam:** the hyperbaton, whose effect is heightened by the postponed *cura*, works with the heavy guttural alliteration to emphasize the seemingly limitless capacity for devising ways of wasting time. **latrunculi:** lit. 'robbers', pieces in a board-game (*ludus latrunculorum*) resembling draughts; for a description, Austin (1934) 25–30. Cf. *Tr.* 14.7 and, given the emphasis here, esp. *Ep.* 106.11 *latrunculis ludimus. in superuacuis subtilitas teritur: non faciunt bonos ista sed doctos.* **pila:** popular with both young and old at Rome; on the variety of games played, Owen (1924) 260 on Ov. *Tr.* 2.485. **excoquendi ... cura:** enjoying bright sunshine (*apricitas*) was highly recommended for sustaining and restoring health in men of all ages. Hence *Tr.* 3.1 *quidam sole atque exercitatione et cura corporis diem educunt* (with Courtney on Juv. 11.203); for taking the sun before ball exercises, Plin. *Ep.* 3.1.8. **excoquendi:** of 'baking' the body thoroughly, colloquial in tone; Ter. *Ad.* 849 *tam excoctam* [sc. *psaltriam*] *reddam atque atram quam carbost.* **consumpsere** 'have used up the whole of...' Duff 141 gives copious parallels from S., but the sense is found more widely (*OLD* 5c, 6a and esp. Sall. *Jug.* 98.2) and here has the added implication of 'squandered' (*OLD* 7). **quorum ... habent:** S. introduces his new subject. **habent** 'entail'. **operose nihil agant:** for the oxymoron, 12.2 *otium occupatum est* and *desidiosa occupatio.* **litterarum inutilium studiis:** the pedantic interests of the *grammatici* ignore the real relevance (*utilitas*) of literature and philology in forming mature judgement. S.'s point is well illustrated by Gellius' story (*N.A.* 4.1.1–19) of how the philosopher Favorinus responded to an

unsolicited lecture from an unnamed *grammaticus* on the various genders
and endings of the noun *penus* ('provisions') with observations on the social and moral dimensions of semantic accuracy: *sic Fauorinus sermones ... a
rebus paruis et frigidis abducebat ad ea, quae magis utile esset audire ac discere* (19).
S. was always ready with such a response himself, as he shows with his
assertions at *Ep.* 108.24–35 of the superiority of the philosophical reading
of Virgil and Cicero over the purely grammatical. For this contemptuous
attitude towards the *grammatici* in the early Empire, Kaster (1988) 54–63.
detinentur 'are kept busy'.   **quae** anticipates *manus* ('group') by being
attracted into its gender and number; *constructio ad sententiam* (K–S I 30–2).
magna: on the growing number of *grammatici* in Rome in the first century
AD, Kaster (1988) 51–7. Later emperors copied Vespasian, who in 74 offered immunity from taxation and other burdens to attract to Rome the
best *grammatici* from all over the empire (Kaster 223–6).

13.2–8 Pointless learning exemplified in a tone of superior condescension.

13.2 Graecorum ... fuit 'It was once the well known (*iste*) failing of
the Greeks ... ', *fuit* putting current (*iam*) Roman experience into a context;
for *morbus* 'foible' (already e.g. Cic. *Ver.* 1.91, Catul. 39.7, Hor. *S.* 2.3.121),
Ben. 1.14.1 *morbo suo morem gessit* 'he indulged a personal weakness', *Ep.* 79.4
with Summers 272. Of the Greeks S. presumably has in mind esp. the line
of Alexandrian grammarians which included Aristarchus (*c.* 216–144 BC),
Didymus (*c.* 65 BC – AD 10) and Apion (Didymus' pupil). All three wrote
extensively on Homer, and S. rounds on them as pedants at *Ep.* 88.37,
39–40, echoing the cynic Diogenes who 'would wonder that the grammarians were inquiring into Odysseus' hardships while they were ignorant of
their own' (D.L. 6.27).   **quem ... habuisset:** presumably as he lost
them little by little over successive stages of the journey. This is the 'How
many children had Lady Macbeth?' approach to literature, which one of
Gellius' friends (*N.A.* 14.6.3) carried to the point of naming the six oars-
men plucked by Scylla at *Od.* 12.245–50. For further *quaestiones* of this type,
Suet. *Tib.* 70.3, Juv. 7.233–6 with Courtney, and esp. *Ep.* 88.6–8 (with the
emphatic contrast drawn in e.g. 8 *quid inquiris an Penelopa impudica fuerit?
... doce me quid sit pudicitia*), 37–41.   **prior ... Odyssia:** for this debate
in antiquity, e.g. [Longin.] 9.11–15 with Russell (1964) 95–6. The modern
consensus agrees with [Longin.] (*Iliad* earlier); Heubeck in Heubeck *et al.*
(1988) 12–14.   **praeterea ... auctoris:** the general consensus in antiquity was that both were composed by the same poet (so [Longin.]

9.12–13); the so-called 'chorizontists', Alexandrian scholars such as Xenon and Hellanicus, who denied that the *Odyssey* was Homeric, were exceptional. For the controversy, and a summary of the issues from the perspective of a modern chorizontist, Heubeck in Heubeck *et al.* (1988) 7, 12–18. **alia:** e.g. (*Ep.* 88.6) who wrote first, Homer or Hesiod? Why does Hecuba, though younger than Helen, seem older? What are the relative ages of Achilles and Patroclus?   **huius notae** 'of this stamp', defining gen.; S. favours the phrase (e.g. *Cl.* 2.2.2, *C.S.* 10.2, *Ben.* 1.11.3, *N.Q.* 1.16.2). **contineas** 'keep to yourself' (*OLD* 5d), as opposed to *proferas* ('come out with'); Cic. *De orat.* 1.206 *ea quae continet neque adhuc protulit* [sc. *M. Antonius*]. **nihil . . . iuuant** 'in no way enhance your purely private, unspoken knowledge'; for the nuance of *conscientiam*, *OLD* 2b.   **non doctior . . . sed molestior** 'more of a pedant than a true scholar'; S. modifies the more usual double-comparative construction (*molestior quam doctior*; cf. 12.3 *comptior . . . quam honestior*). For the nuance of *molestior*, *Ep.* 88.37 *ista liberalium artium consectatio molestos . . . facit*, Quint. *Inst.* 9.4.53 *molestos . . . grammaticos*, Suet. *Gram.* 22.

13.3 inuasit 'has attacked' like a disease (13.2 *morbus*); *Ep.* 54.1, 91.5. **superuacua** 'useless', 'redundant', reinforcing *inane* (cf. *Ep.* 88.36 *in superuacua litterarum supellectile*); *Breu.* 6.3n.   **his diebus** 'only a few days ago', as at *Ep.* 117.23 (*OLD hic*[1] 3a).   **audiui quendam referentem:** very likely a simple rhetorical device for introducing the point in colloquial tone (cf. 12.7, *N.Q.* 6.31.3), but as S. sometimes identifies his interlocutor in a way which effectively rules out a mere fictional strategy (e.g. *Prou.* 4.4, a named gladiator; *N.Q.* 6.8.3, two centurions sent by Nero to discover the source of the Nile), it has been misguidedly concluded that where the source is not named S. must be concealing its identity. Some of the facts 'heard' by S. here also appear in Pliny's *Natural history*, which leads Herrmann (1936) to suspect that S. refers to Pliny himself. Since the portrayal of S. in the *Natural history* (14.51) is arguably hostile, *Breu.* 13 has also been viewed as a thinly veiled critique of Pliny's own *inane studium* (Citroni Marchetti (1991) 37–43; cf. the balanced view of Griffin (1976) 433–40). Any point of this kind would depend on the allusion being unmistakably identified, which can hardly have been the case in antiquity if even today we can name several plausible candidates. And if the identity had for some reason to be concealed in this case, why arouse needless curiosity by referring to an informant at all, esp. as S. regularly makes historical points without naming his sources? For S.'s method in assembling historical *exempla*,

Griffin (1976) 182–3 with references.   **primus ... fecisset** 'had been
the first to do'. In naming these Roman pioneers S. draws on the genre
of 'l'heurématologie', or research into inventions and their discoverers;
along with aetiology, a thriving branch of antiquarian enquiry, esp. in the
Julio-Claudian age (Poucet (1992) 281–2).   **primus ... uicit:** Gaius
Duilius, consul in the First Punic War, led Rome's fleet to victory over the
Carthaginians off Mylae (Sicily) in 260 and celebrated the first naval triumph in 259; the inscription to commemorate this on the *columna rostrata* in
the Forum was renewed in the early Empire (Broughton I 205 for sources).
primus ... elephantos: M'. Curius Dentatus triumphed for the third
time in his consulship of 275 after defeating Pyrrhus, the Molossian king of
Epirus (*CAH²* VII 2.482–3 with Broughton I 195 for sources). For the four elephants first paraded at Rome in Curius' triumph, Flor. *Epit*. 1.13.28, Eutrop.
2.14.5.   **etiamnunc** 'thus far' in S.'s treatment of pointless learning; so
Pol. 7.1, but for a complex range of senses, Duff 143.   **ueram gloriam:**
i.e. Stoic virtue; cf. *Ep*. 79.13 *gloria umbra uirtutis est: etiam inuitam comitabitur*.
circa ... uersantur '[these cases] nevertheless involve models of service
to the state'; *uersor* with *circa* + acc. (post-Augustan; Summers lxviii) at
e.g. *Marc*. 19.5, *Ep*. 88.3, 44, Quint. *Inst*. 2.15.15, 6.2.20.   **non est**
profutura: the periphrastic fut. lends emphasis as at *Ir*. 2.13.3 *tota dimittatur*
[sc. *ira*], *nihil profutura est* (Westman (1961) 65–6).   **quae ... detineat**
'of the sort to hold our interest because the subject-matter, although empty,
is appealing'. Relative clause of tendency (G–L §631); for *speciosa* (abl.), *Pol*.
9.5 *speciosa sed fallaci uoluptate*, and for *detineat*, 13.1.

    13.4 remittamus 'excuse' (potential) with the usual dat. (*OLD*
14b); post-Augustan (*Ir*. 3.24.4, *N.Q*. 2.2.4; pass., 13.6).   **nauem**
conscendere: i.e. use a naval force. The inf. after *persuadere* for *ut* +
subjunctive is generally in verse until Silver prose (Krebs–Schmalz II
289).   **(Claudius ... uocantur):** S. caricatures the futile accumula-
tion of factual knowledge by exhausting the subject (and reader) with this
convoluted explanation. V. Max. 2.4.7 presents Caudex in just the way S.
has in mind, while Gell. *N.A*. 17.21.40 includes him in an excursus on relative chronologies.   **Claudius:** Appius Claudius Caudex, cos. 264 BC,
crossed to Sicily in the First Punic War to counter the alliance of Hieron
II of Syracuse and the Carthaginians (*CAH²* VII 2.542–5 with Broughton I
203 for sources). Polyb. 1.12.5 describes this action as 'the first crossing from
Italy with an armed force'; an exaggeration given the evidence of fourth-
century interest in naval defence (*CAH²* VII 2.410).   **ob hoc ipsum**

anticipates *quia*.   **plurium . . . contextus:** the structure formed by joining together several wooden boards, here of course boat-planks; hence the *cognomen*.   **caudex** = *codex* (Maltby 138), created (by the first century AD) when the waxed wooden panels of hinged writing tablets gave way to parchment (*OCD*³ 252). <u>*contextus caudex*</u> juxtaposed to hint at an etymology which is otherwise unattested.   **publicae tabulae:** public records and official statutes (cf. *Ir.* 2.28.2; *OLD tabula* 9), here written down as opposed to engraved on metal or carved in stone (*RE*² IV 2.1959), and stored in the official registry (*tabularium*).   **nunc quoque** 'even today' (*OLD quoque* 4c).   **ex** 'in accordance with'.   **subuehunt** 'convey upstream', i.e. from Ostia to Rome, as at e.g. Tac. *Ann.* 15.39.2 *subuecta . . . utensilia ab Ostia*, Suet. *Cal.* 15.1.   **codicariae:** with *naues*, hauled barges of joined timbers (Fest. 40.13 Lindsay *caudicariae naues ex tabulis grossioribus factae*), the adj. perhaps distinguishing such craft from more primitive types hollowed from tree-trunks (Meiggs (1973) 293 n. 2).

13.5 sane 'doubtless', continuing the caricature with a hint of irony (*OLD* 7).   **ad rem pertineat** 'might be of relevance', a common idiom (e.g. 13.6, *Ep.* 19.12, 87.8, 88.6).   **Valerius Coruinus:** M'. Valerius Maximus Messalla, cos. 263, in that year forced Hieron II of Syracuse to reach terms with Rome and celebrated a triumph in part for his capture of Messana (*CAH*² VII 2.545–6 with Broughton I 203–4 for sources); hence his *cognomen ex uirtute*.   **Coruinus** has not been satisfactorily explained; possibly a slip on the part of S. or his source (*RE*² VIII 1.123), or an attempt to show how easily such a confident parade of historical learning can be open to muddle and error (the 'real' Messalla Coruinus was a contemporary of Augustus).   **primus . . . uicit:** i.e. no Roman had captured the city before (there was no subsequent Roman capture). S. (or his source) sides with the version which credited Valerius, not Appius Claudius before him (13.4n.), with success at Messana (*CAH*² VII 2.545 with Walbank (1957) 66–7 on Polyb. 1.15.1–11). Narrative historians conflated often irreconcilable family traditions in just this way, and S. parodies the procedure here.   **urbis . . . nomine:** despite the appearance at Liv. 2.33.5 of Cn. Marcius Coriolanus, Valerius' is possibly the earliest *cognomen ex uirtute* taken from a captured city (Ogilvie on 2.33.5).   **permutante:** for such mutation, e.g. Plin. *N.H.* 4.114 *prodidere* [sc. geographers] *. . . ibi gentem Artabrum . . . manifesto errore. Arrotrebas enim . . . hoc in loco posuere litteris permutatis*. Acc. to Meister (1916) 130–1 *Messanan(a)s* mutated by dissimilation (i.e. the differentiation of two like sounds within a word), *n* changing to *l* on the analogy of e.g.

nympha becoming *lympha* (Var. *L.* 7.87; G–L §9.5 with Palmer (1954) 231).
Messalla: the spelling reported in most MSS and strongly attested in inscriptions, but *Messala* is also found; Eden (1984) 117 on *Apoc.* 10.2.

13.6 num: the tone becomes more impatient.   **curare** 'regard with interest' (*OLD* 8a).   **quod . . . iaculatoribus?:** as *praetor urbanus* in 93 BC L. Cornelius Sulla gave the *ludi Apollinares* on an extravagant scale, with 100 lions supplied for the occasion (Plin. *N.H.* 8.53). Acc. to Plin. *ibid.*, lions were first exhibited in games at Rome in 104 BC, when Q. Mucius Scaevola was aedile; they were apparently leashed (*alligati*), allowing Sulla later to lay on a novel display of *leones soluti*. For the vast array of exotic animals exhibited at Rome and for the kinds of combat presented (armed men against animals, animals fighting against each other, unarmed men exposed to animals), Wiedemann (1992) 56–62.   **dedit:** often used of 'putting on' games and (as here) animal-shows etc. (*OLD* 5a); *edo* provides a variant below.
cum: concessive.   **alioquin** 'as a general rule' (*OLD* 1 b); rare in poetry, the word enters prose through Livy and is then frequent in S., Quintilian and the younger Pliny (*TLL* 1 1591.11–14).   **ad conficiendos eos:** for the specialist meaning of the verb, Don. *ad* Ter. *Eun.* 926 (= 1 465 Wessner) *proprie hoc uerbum* [sc. *conficere*] *conuenit gladiatoribus*; related *confector* at e.g. *Ir.* 3.43.2, Suet. *Aug.* 43.2, *Nero* 12.1.   **missis . . . iaculatoribus:** more tangential detail for the collector of facts. The *iaculum* was 'a typically Moroccan weapon' (N–H on Hor. *C.* 1.22.2). Bocchus, Jugurtha's father-in-law (Plut. *Sull.* 3.2, Flor. *Epit.* 1.36.17; read *Bocchi* at Sall. *Jug.* 80.6), had been persuaded by Sulla to betray his son-in-law to the Romans; becoming a 'friend of the Roman people', he remained on good terms with Sulla after the end of the Jugurthine War (*CAH*² ix 28–31).   **hoc** refers back ('all right, let's allow that as well').   **sane:** 13.5n.   **remittatur:** 13.4n.
num 'but can it be said that . . . ?' (*OLD* 3a). After the ironic concession, *num* requires an adversative emphasis to stress the change of tone to outright scepticism.   **et Pompeium primum . . . edidisse:** the acc. and inf. construction is the subj. of *pertinet*. Asconius agrees (*Pis.* 14 = p. 16.5–6 Clark) that elephants first fought in the circus at the games which Pompey put on in 55 BC, during his second consulship, to celebrate the opening of his new stone theatre in the Campus Martius; but for at least one variant, Marshall (1985) 114. Cicero's report (*Fam.* 7.1.3) that the crowd was moved to feel kinship with the persecuted elephants (*quandam illi beluae cum genere humano societatem*) is reflected here in S.'s own protest (13.6–7; cf. Plin. *N.H.* 8.21, Dio 39.38.2–3). Most scholars infer from S.'s depictions of the cruelty and

morally degrading consequences of gladiatorial combat (e.g. *Ep.* 7.3–5, 95.33) that he was firmly opposed to the institution; Wistrand (1990) 43–4 surveys opinion but argues to the contrary, straining in the process to explain away S.'s outraged tone here.　　　**edidisse:** of 'putting on' a public display, *Ben.* 1.12.3 *munere edito*; *OLD* 12a.　　　**commissis . . . hominibus** 'non-criminals set to fight them in mock battle'. *innoxiis* Gertz (1874) 155–6; MSS *noxiis* turns the contest into a form of execution of those condemned of capital crimes, but (i) Pliny (*N.H.* 8.20) claims that Pompey used against the elephants not criminals but Gaetulians armed with javelins, and (ii) (more important) by specifying non-criminals S. sharpens his emphasis on the inhumane excesses of the occasion (no need to stress the guilt of the combatants if they had been criminals).　　　**ad . . . rem . . . pertinet:** 13.5n. **princeps . . . homines** introduces a moralizing aside; S. returns to his argument (13.8 *Sed . . . decessi*) after a seemingly irrelevant digression. But the aside offers its own oblique commentary on 'the vain passion for useless learning' criticized above: whereas a trivial fact about Pompey strictly belongs to the category of *inane studium*, the ability to use that fact – as S. himself does here – to draw conclusions about human behaviour and tendency (13.7 *o quantum . . . felicitas!*) distinguishes the very different category of *utile studium.*　　　**princeps ciuitatis:** a Republican term and Ciceronian label used (with variations) esp. of Pompey; e.g. *Dom.* 66, *Sest.* 84, *Prou.* 41 *principem ciuium.* S. varies the phrase for Pompey at *Marc.* 20.4 *populi Romani princeps.*　　　**antiquos:** simply 'former' (*OLD* 3).　　　**fama:** the Augustan tradition from Livy on was sympathetic to Pompey; Syme (1958) 140, 433. **bonitatis eximiae:** gen. of quality (G–L §365) forming with *ciuitatis* a neat syllepsis after *princeps.* Elsewhere (e.g. *Cl.* 1.1.5, 6, 2.2.1, 2.6.3) S. presents *bonitas* as a key quality in the good ruler, but here it is set in pointed contrast to Pompey's cruel streak (*memorabile . . . exterantur*); Alexander (1948) 21–2. Griffin (1976) 189–90 explains that S. has a consistent conception of Pompey – a great man whose faults nevertheless 'more than outweigh his merits' – which qualifies the favourable Augustan image.　　　**nouo** 'unheard of' (*OLD* 3).　　　**perdere** 'kill', with the underlying implication of squandering (*OLD* 6a) valuable human lives (*homines* stressed by position); the inf. here the substantival obj. of *putauit* in apposition to *memorabile genus* (K–S I 665–6).　　　**'depugnant? . . . exterantur':** prosopopoeia if (with Gertz) Pompey is heard deliberating with himself. For the rejection of one cruel extreme for another, *Thy.* 257 (Atreus ponders what instrument of revenge to use against Thyestes) SAT. *ferrum?* AT. *parum est.* SAT. *quid*

ignis? AT. *etiamnunc parum est*; so already the elder Sen. at *Contr.* 10.5.1.
depugnant?: often used of fights to the death in the arena; *Ep.* 76.2 *nullum par* (i.e. a pair of gladiators) *sine me depugnabit, OLD* 2.   **lancinantur?**
'Are they torn to pieces?', mostly post-Augustan (*OLD*); used both of animalistic savagery (Plin. *N.H.* 8.33, 9.13, 10.181) and of depraved human
violence (*Ir.* 3.19.5, 40.4, *Thy.* 778 with Tarrant (1985) 202).   **mole** of
elephants, e.g. Liv. 27.49.2 *in tantae molis belua*, Man. 4.237, Curt. 8.13.10,
9.2.21.   **exterantur:** usually a gradual process, but for sudden obliteration ('utterly crushed'), *Ep.* 57.7.

   13.7 satius . . . ire 'it would certainly be preferable . . .', an early
colloquialism (Summers l) common in S. (e.g. 13.9, *Ep.* 9.2, 19.6, 25.7,
63.12).   **ista** 'such stuff'; contemptuous (*OLD* 5b).   **postea:** attributive and quasi-adj., a common usage since Livy (K–S I 218), here
with the sense 'after Pompey's time'. Like other moralists of the period
S. supposed that such spectacles had become more inhumane; *Ep.* 7.3
*quicquid ante pugnatum est misericordia fuit; nunc omissis nugis mera homicidia
sunt* (13.6n. on *et Pompeium primum . . . edidisse*).   **inuideretque** 'envy',
with a view to emulation.   **o quantum . . . felicitas!:** for the dangers
and self-delusions of great prosperity, much advertised in Graeco-Roman
tragedy (Tarrant (1976) 182–3 on *Ag.* 57–107), e.g. *Prou.* 4.10, *Ep.* 39.4, 91.5
with 7.6n. on *quos . . . grauat*. With a possible play on his *cognomen* in *magna
felicitas* S. perhaps alludes to Pompey's stunningly successful early life, as
exploited by Cicero in a famous passage (*Man.* 47–8); in his fall Pompey
supplied an esp. striking example of life's vicissitudes (*Marc.* 20.4, *Ep.*
94.64–5; N–H on Hor. *C.* 2.1.3).   **caliginis:** 3.1n.   **obicit** 'causes',
esp. of misfortunes (*OLD* 4).   **tunc . . . cum . . . obiceret:** the indicative would be more usual (G–L §580), but for the subjunctive in examples
from all periods stressing the special features of a particular time, K–S
II 332.   **cum . . . cum . . . cum:** the anaphoric sequence of clauses
builds up an impressive dossier of evidence against Pompey.   **tot:** with
cateruas.   **cateruas:** of gladiators, Caecil. 38 Ribbeck, Plin. *N.H.* 8.20.
sub . . . natis: cf. Liv. 5.54.3 *hoc caelum sub quo natus educatusque essem.*
beluis: of elephants, *OLD* 2b.   **obiceret:** here the regular word for
throwing human victims to beasts in the arena (*OLD* 1b).   **animalia:**
incl. man, as at e.g. *Cl.* 1.3.2, *Tr.* 8.8, 11.5, *Ben.* 7.1.7; *TLL* II 78.73–79.19.
in conspectu 'before the very eyes of . . .', a familiar idiom (*TLL* IV 491.80–
492.34) preferable to *in conspectum* 'for the gaze of . . .' (*TLL* IV 490.73–
491.19 and in the *Ambrosianus*, doubtless anticipating *multum*).   **multum**

sanguinis: Summers lv; the substantival *multum* with partitive gen. is not common until Livy and subsequent prose. Tacitus (*Ann.* 12.56.3) even has *multum uulnerum.*   **mox ... coacturus:** i.e. during the civil war and esp. at Pharsalus in 48 BC (for the Roman losses on both sides there, App. *B.C.* 2.79–80, 82). The fut. pple forms an adj. clause (seemingly parenthetical; Westman (1961) 119) effectively comparing the carnage of civil war with that of the arena, which is itself given an international dimension (*sub alio caelo natis*) in readiness for the comparison.   **ipsum:** sc. *populum Romanum.*   **at idem ... praebuit:** almost seven weeks after his defeat Pompey arrived off Egypt, where he expected protection from Ptolemy XIII, his *cliens* and possibly his ward (Woodman (1983) 100), but while going ashore at Alexandria he was murdered in the boat by a group of soldiers who included the commander of Ptolemy's army. Accusations of Egyptian *perfidia* entered the tradition at an early stage (Caes. *B.C.* 3.104.1–3).   **ultimo mancipio** 'the meanest of his chattels' (*OLD ultimus* 9b), dat. with both *transfodiendum* and *praebuit;* of slaves, *Ir.* 3.37.2 *extremo mancipio, Ep.* 70.25, but here the phrase is an abusive slur against Ptolemy for betraying his duty as Pompey's *cliens.* This identification is secured and filled out by Vell. 2.53.2 *princeps Romani nominis imperio arbitrioque Aegyptii mancipii ... iugulatus est,* where Woodman (1983) 100–1 shows that *mancipium* is an 'uncomplimentary equivalent' to *cliens* (S. had himself recognized Ptolemy as Pompey's *cliens* at *Tr.* 16.1). Duff 146 and others here take *mancipium* to refer to Ptolemy's commander Achillas, who was among those who actually carried out the murder; but to make its point the insult needs to be directed at a more prominent target, and Woodman *ibid.* collects several parallels (incl. *Tr.* 16.1) for the notion that Ptolemy was, in effect, the murderer by proxy. **transfodiendum:** predicative gerundive expressing purpose; for the use with *se praebere,* K–S I 731.   **se praebuit** 'laid himself open' (*OLD* 3); the phrase need not suggest voluntary submission.   **inani iactatione:** so *Ben.* 2.11.6, but here the adj. is predicative. Pompey supplied rhetoricians as well as moralists with an obvious example of *commutatio fortunae;* Woodman (1983) 101.   **cognominis sui:** for the allusion to *Magnus/magnus,* n. above on *o quantum ... felicitas!;* also *Marc.* 14.3, *Ben.* 4.30.2 *unius uiri magnitudo tanta quondam, Ep.* 94.64–5, Luc. 1.135 *stat magni nominis umbra* with Feeney (1986), esp. p. 243 n. 15.

13.8 Sed ... decessi: variation on a familiar Senecan mannerism; e.g. *Ben.* 4.27.4 *ut ad propositum reuertar, Ep.* 59.4, 65.23, *N.Q.* 3.19.1, 4B.12.1, 5.16.1. **illo:** equivalent to *illuc,* often in S. but rare in Classical Latin (*TLL*

VII 1.385.14–16).   **decessi:** of digressing in writing or speech, first in S. (*OLD* 5b).   **materia** 'subject-area' (*OLD* 7a).   **superuacuam:** 6.3n.   **quorundam:** sc. *Romanorum* (cf. 13.3).   **diligentiam:** obsessive nit-picking over trivia (Quint. *Inst.* 1.6.17 *molestissima diligentiae peruersitate*, 5.13.37). We may therefore expect that the following examples will illustrate details (e.g. the number of Metellus' elephants, the precise conditions for extending the *pomerium*) which were already contentious in S.'s own day and which he thought should be irrelevant (*superuacua*) to any serious-minded person.   **idem:** the unnamed source (*quendam*) introduced in 13.3.   **Metellum:** L. Caecilius Metellus, cos. 251 BC, won an important victory over Hasdrubal at Panormus (modern Palermo) in 250 (*CAH*² VII 2.559–60 with Broughton I 213 for sources); the number of captured Carthaginian elephants allegedly paraded in his triumph ranges from a high of 142 or 140 (Plin. *N.H.* 8.16) to 120 (Liv. *Per.* 19, Zon. 8.14) to a low of 60 (Diod. 23.21; Walbank (1957) 102–3 on Polyb. 1.40.15). Given that elephants had already been paraded in M'. Curius Dentatus' triumph of 275 (13.3n. on *primus . . . elephantos*), the novelty of Metellus' display presumably lay in the large number of animals on show.   **unum . . . Romanorum** 'alone of all Romans'; for the idiom, e.g. Catul. 1.5, Cic. *Sest.* 133, Liv. 23.30.19 *unus Romanorum imperatorum*. The focus of antiquarian enquiry now shifts from 'Who was the first Roman general to . . . ?' (13.3–6) to 'Who was the only Roman to . . . ?' to (*Sullam . . . fuit* below) 'Who was the last Roman to . . . ?'   **duxisse** 'conducted'; though *egisse* would be more logical, *ducere* is here appropriated from its conventional use for conducting a triumph or any kind of procession (*OLD* 7a, b).   **Sullam . . . fuit:** the *pomerium* in Rome was the sacral boundary, ploughed and then marked by stone pillars (*cippi*), 'demarcating an augurally constituted city. The area so defined marked the limit of the *auspicia urbana*. Within all was hallowed and under divine surveillance, outside was profane. The army as such could never cross the *pomerium*' (Ogilvie on Liv. 1.44.3). That Sulla extended the area (at an unknown date) is also reported by Tac. *Ann.* 12.23.2 and Gell. *N.A.* 13.14.4; but later extensions are attributed to Julius Caesar (Gell. *N.A.* 13.14.4, Dio 43.50.1, 44.49.2), Augustus (Tac. *Ann.* 12.23.2, Dio 55.6.6) and Claudius (between 25 January 49 and 24 January 50; n. below on *numquam . . . acquisito*). S.'s reference to Sulla as 'the last of the Romans' to extend it would therefore seem to be contradicted by the evidence; and so various explanations have been advanced to exonerate S. and/or his antiquarian informant (Griffin (1976) 401–6), of which the most plausible is

to find in the phrase *numquam prouinciali sed Italico agro acquisito* 'a traditional
ground for extension used by Sulla [contrasted] with an illegitimate one
not sanctioned by tradition: he [sc. S.'s informant] claimed that, by ancestral custom, the *pomerium* was moved when Italian territory was added,
not provincial' (Griffin (1976) 402, echoing (1962) 109–11 after Herrmann
(1937) 109–10). The debate should not lose sight of S.'s rhetorical strategy:
through his informant he provocatively advances views on controversial
facts to expose the insignificance of the issues.   **pomerium:** possibly
an Etruscan word wrongly derived by traditional etymology (Maltby 483)
from *post* or *pone* + *murum* (*RE* xxi 2.1870–1).   **quod:** obj. of *proferre*
below.   **numquam . . . acquisito:** S.'s aggressive tone vividly reproduces a point from a lively contemporary debate. Acc. to Tac. *Ann.* 12.23.2
extension of the *pomerium* was indeed justified by provincial acquisition:
pomerium urbis auxit Caesar [sc. *Claudius*], *more prisco, quo iis, qui protulere imperium,*
etiam terminos urbis propagare datur, where reference to provincial expansion
(to Britain) is paralleled by the words *auctis populi Romani finibus* on the *cippi*
set up by Claudius (*CIL* vi 1.1231, vi 4.31537; also Gell. *N.A.* 13.14.3). Julius
Caesar's extension 'was based, like Claudius', on a claim of provincial
acquisition' (Griffin (1976) 404). But since (*pace* Tac. *Ann.* 12.23.2) Sulla
made no provincial gains, and since the words *Italico agro acquisito* coincide
with his probable change (for administrative reasons) of the Italian boundary with Cisalpine Gaul (Badian (1968) 34), S.'s informant pedantically
cites Sulla's extension as the last of an antiquated, traditionally sanctioned
kind, bringing out the questionable and almost obscurantist nature of the
debate S. is criticizing. For a vigorous defence of the view generally followed here against the objections of Hambüchen (1966) 51–61 see Griffin
(1976) 402–3.   **moris . . . fuit** 'it was customary', a common predicative gen. (*OLD mos* 3b) elsewhere in S. only at *Ben.* 5.6.3 but generally
more frequent in Silver Latin (Löfstedt ii 408–9).   **hoc:** *Sullam . . . fuit.*
Auentinum . . . non addixissent: the antiquarian enquiry also at Gell.
N.A. 13.14.4 *propterea quaesitum est ac nunc etiam in quaestione est, quam ob causam*
ex septem urbis montibus, cum ceteri sex intra pomerium sint, Auentinus solum . . . extra
pomerium sit.   **Auentinum . . . esse:** the Aventine, Rome's southern-
most hill, was in fact included in the *pomerium* by Claudius' extension of AD
49–50 (Gell. *N.A.* 13.14.7, confirmed by the location of one of the terminal
cippi; see H. F. Pelham's note in Furneaux (1907) ii 87). Since S.'s informant,
only recently heard (13.3 *his diebus*), apparently still located the Aventine *ex-*
tra pomerium, the treatise (it has been argued) must have been composed

before January 50 (see e.g. Grimal (1947) 166 with Giancotti (1957) 392);
but a date *after* 50 becomes possible if the passage is interpreted ironically.
So Griffin (1962) 110–11 (following Herrmann (1937) 109–10 and (1948)
226): 'The pedant was protesting against the illegality of Claudius' extension by insisting that what *ought not* to be the case *was not* the case. Claudius
had already extended the Pomerium to include it, as Seneca knew, but our
pedant insisted that the Aventine *was not* within the boundary, whatever
the Emperor said, because it *could* not be.'   **affirmabat** suggests that
S. doubts his informant (*TLL* I 1222.67–8, of asserting *rem incertam falsam
addubitatam*; Griffin (1962) 109).   **plebs eo secessisset:** acc. to one tradition the *plebs* twice withdrew to the Aventine, 'the plebeian hill' (Ogilvie
on Liv. 2.32.1 and 446–7 on 3.31.1), first in 494 BC (Liv. 2.32.3) and again in
449 (Liv. 3.50.13); cf. Sall. *Jug.* 31.17.   **quod . . . non addixissent:** the
explanation for the Aventine's position *extra pomerium* apparently favoured
by Valerius Messalla Rufus (cos. 53 BC and augur for 55 years; Griffin (1962)
109), cited as Gellius' authority at *N.A.* 13.14.5–6. For the story (Remus defeated in the contest to become Rome's founder when, taking auspices on
the Aventine, he counted six birds, Romulus on the Palatine twelve), Liv.
1.6.3–7.3 with Ogilvie on 1.6.4; but for Romulus placed on the Aventine
in earlier tradition, Skutsch on Enn. *Ann.* 76.   **illo loco:** sc. on the
Aventine; *loco* often without *in*, esp. when accompanied by an adj. (K–S
I 348–9).   **non addixissent** 'had not been propitious'. Of augury, a
technical application of the verb (*OLD* 4) drawn from Livy, who prefers an
accompanying pple in the dat. with an indirect obj. (22.42.8, 27.16.15 *Fabio
auspicanti . . . aues . . . non addixerunt*); hence Wesenberg's emendation of *auspi-
cante* in the MSS, which was doubtless attracted into the abl. by the phrase
following it.   **alia . . . similia** 'beyond that countless other items [sc. of
pointless information] which are either crammed with lies or improbable'.
Various editors emend *farta* of the MSS because of the rare metaphorical
use (so Reynolds after Abel *falsa sunt aut mendaciis similia*). But (i) *farta* is more
likely to have been corrupted into a simplifying gloss such as *falsa*, Erasmus'
ficta or Gertz' *fulta* than vice versa, and (ii) for the metaphor see the parallels
(mostly later) at *TLL* VI 1.280.60–6 and *Ep.* 76.4 *illud* [sc. *theatrum*] *quidem
fartum est* ('is full to overflowing'). For [*mendaciis*] *similia*, *Ep.* 83.8 *quae* [sc.
probationes 'proofs'] *ut sint uerae, tamen mendacio similes sunt*; *mendaciis* abl. with
farta, dat. with *similia*.

13.9 Conclusion: such learning contributes nothing to moral improvement.   **ut . . . ut** 'even supposing' in both cases.   **eos:** sc. collectors

of obscure antiquarian facts.   **ad praestationem scribant** 'they guarantee the truthfulness of their writing'. *praestatio* (post-Augustan and only here in S.) lit. denotes a payment in settlement of an obligation (*OLD* 1); rarely it covers 'the action of guaranteeing (against)' (2). **cuius ... minuent?** 'whose mistakes will such items of information make fewer?'; the first of three rhetorical questions by which S. drives home the point that trivial antiquarian learning does nothing to promote the four primary Stoic virtues, *iustitia, prudentia, temperantia* and *fortitudo* (*Ep.* 90.46, 115.3; L–S 1 61 c1–2, d2–5, h1–6). The *sapiens* is saved from lapses of judgement (*errores*) by prudence (*ratio*, φρόνησις), defined (L–S 1 61 h1) as 'the science of what should and should not be done and of neutral actions, or the science of things that are good and bad and neutral...' (cf. *SVF* 11 297.13, 111 65.8–9, 22, 42).   **ista:** contemptuous (*OLD* 5b). **cuius ... prement?** 'Whose passions will they hold in check?' *cupiditas* (ἐπιθυμία), an 'irrational stretching' for something (2.1 n.), is restrained by prudence and moderation (σωφροσύνη), which is defined (L–S 1 61 h2) as 'the science of what should be chosen and avoided and of neutral situations' (cf. *SVF* 1 85.37–8, 111 65.23, 67.35–6).   **quem ... quem ... quem:** the tricolon reinforces the rhetorical crescendo.   **fortiorem:** a Stoic virtue (ἀνδρεία); Sphaerus' definition (L–S 1 61 h4 'courage is the science of things that are fearful and not fearful and neither of these') is elaborated by Cicero (*Tusc.* 4.53 = L–S 1 32h) and by S. (*Ep.* 85.28 [*fortitudo*] *scientia est distinguendi quid sit malum et quid non sit*, 113.27, *Ben.* 2.34.3).   **iustiorem:** a virtue (δικαιοσύνη) defined as 'the science concerned with distributing individual deserts' (L–S 1 61 h3), *iustitia* is given a central moral role in Cicero (*Off.* 3.28 *omnium est domina et regina uirtutum*; cf. *Leg.* 1.48, *N.D.* 1.4 with Pease), who links it to Roman *pietas* (*N.D.* 2.153 with Pease) as S. also does (*Ep.* 90.3, 92.19).   **liberaliorem** 'more obliging', 'open-handed'; *liberalitas*, counted with *frugalitas, continentia, tolerantia* etc. as lesser Stoic virtues after the primary four at *Ep.* 115.3 (cf. 66.13), denotes 'the disposition from which the act of conferring a *beneficium* is derived' and is 'important in that its right distribution helps to bind the human community together' (Manning (1985) 73); also Dyck 155 on Cic. *Off.* 1.42–60 on *liberalitas* as a sub-category of Stoic *iustitia* (hence perhaps the Senecan sequence *iustiorem ... liberaliorem*).   **interim** 'at times' (4.1 n.), by position qualifying *dubitare* more naturally than *aiebat*.   **Fabianus:** 10.1 n.; his reported words are charactistically trenchant (cf. 10.1 *solebat ... non uellicari*).   **satius esset:** 13.7 n.   **admoueri** 'to apply oneself to'

(pass. with middle sense), with dat. (*OLD* 7c).   **implicari** 'to be embroiled in' (*OLD* 7b).

14 Society and countersociety

Anaphoric *soli* in the opening sentence offers a solemn introduction to a
contrasting picture. People are side-tracked by the superficial preoccupations of social involvement at every level, enhancing their prospects with
skills and knowledge which are in reality harmful to them. The *sapiens* stands
in contrast to all this, isolated from surrounding society and substituting for
it a 'society of the imagination' in which we mingle at leisure among minds
from many ages and places (general intro. pp. 23–4).

14.1 Soli . . . soli: the primary sense here ('only') already anticipates the
way in which the true *sapiens* must be said to live 'alone' in an intangible society of his own construction. As the philosophical life is his only
concern (cf. *Ep.* 53.9 *omnia impedimenta dimitte et uaca bonae menti*), the second *soli* carries an additional ambiguity: it not only emphasizes the nom.
plur. by repeating it but also refers back to the dat. sing. *sapientiae* to
suggest '. . . who give their time to the philosophical life, who live for
that only' (for *uiuere* + dat. in this sense, *OLD* 9b).   **otiosi:** i.e. '*truly*
at leisure'.   **sapientiae uacant:** contrast 7.1 *illos . . . qui nulli rei nisi
uino ac libidini uacant*; S. tends to think in terms of these polar opposites.
uiuunt 'really live'; 2.2n. on '*exigua . . . uiuimus*'.   **nec enim:** 7.5n. on
neque . . . repperit.   **aetatem** 'life-time', opposed to *aeuum* ('epoch') below
as at *Ep.* 91.14, 99.31, 102.2, *N.Q.* 7.25.4 (cf. 1.1n. on *aeui*).   **tuentur**
'attend to', 'look after'.   **omne . . . adiciunt:** exactly what the *occupati* cannot do; cf. 10.2–5, esp. 2 *nec enim illis uacat praeterita respicere* (the
theme is developed at 15.5).   **annorum:** the indefinite plur. = *temporis*
(*OLD* 2c).   **illis acquisitum est** 'has been added to *their* lives as well';
illis dat. of advantage.   **ingratissimi:** in Senecan terms no small dis-
grace; *Ben.* 3.1.1 *non referre beneficiis gratiam et est turpe et apud omnes habetur* [sc.
turpe].   **sacrarum . . . conditores** 'founders of the revered schools of
thought'. S. represents philosophy as inspiring religious awe (19.1, *V.B.* 26.7,
N.Q. 7.30.6), distinguishing it from basic moral instruction: *Ep.* 95.64 *aperta
sunt* [sc. *praecepta*], *decreta uero sapientiae in abdito. sicut sanctiora sacrorum tantum
initiati sciunt, ita in philosophia arcana illa admissis receptisque in sacra ostenduntur.*
The model figure offered there is Posidonius (95.65), but the *conditores* of

the schools like Epicurus and Zeno merited special respect (cf. *Ep.* 64.7) and are here contrasted with the achievers of 'firsts' in merely trivial areas (13.3 *quae primus quisque ex Romanis ducibus fecisset*).   **uitam** 'a model for living', a possible echo of Lucr. *D.R.N.* 5.9–10 *qui* [sc. *Epicurus*] *princeps uitae rationem inuenit eam quae | nunc appellatur sapientia*; but for the general debt owed to past philosophers, *Ep.* 39.2   **ad res … erutas:** another Lucretian echo; *D.R.N.* 3.1–2 (on Epicurus) *O tenebris tantis tam clarum extollere lumen | qui primus potuisti …* The influence of the Senecan reminiscence here may have promoted the Renaissance reading *E tenebris tantis …* which was only recently supplanted by the *O* of the MSS. For this and the opposition of light and darkness, common in philosophical literature, Kenney (1971) 74 on *D.R.N.* 3.1 with (on light/dark) *Cl.* 1.1.4, *Ep.* 79.12, 102.28, 120.13, *N.Q.* 1 *praef.* 2.   **pulcherrimas** 'morally elevating', as sometimes in Cicero (e.g. *Amic.* 26) and often in Quintilian, e.g. *Inst.* 1.2.22 (opp. *turpe*), 12.1.37, 2.9, 11.4 (*pulcherrimis uitae praeceptis*), 11.26 (as a substitute for *honestum* at Cic. *Orat.* 4).   **ex tenebris … erutas:** cf. *Ben.* 3.32.5 … *nisi illos filiorum gloria e tenebris eruisset et adhuc in luce retineret?*; but the full image is already in Hor. *Ep.* 2.2.115–16 *obscurata … bonus eruet atque | proferet in lucem … uocabula* (with Brink for discussion).   **deducimur:** of an intellectual journey, *OLD* 11 b.   **nullo … interdictum est** 'from no age are we debarred'; *nobis* the usual dat. of pers. with *interdico* (*OLD* 3a; *Ir.* 3.23.5, 8 *illi domo mea interdicam*). For the idea, *Helu.* 11.7 *cogitatio eius* [sc. *animi*] *circa omne caelum it, in omne praeteritum futurumque tempus immittitur, Ep.* 102.22.   **omnia:** sc. *saecula.*   **admittimur:** *OLD* 5; S. anticipates the contrast drawn below (14.3–5) between clients who struggle to gain access to their patrons, and philosophers, never refused admission to *their* masters (Zeno, Pythagoras etc.).   **magnitudine animi:** i.e. breadth of perspective, freeing the mind from the narrowness of ordinary human vision; cf. *Ep.* 102.21 *dic potius quam naturale sit in immensum mentem suam extendere. magna et generosa res est humanus animus; nullos sibi poni nisi communes et cum deo terminos patitur*, 110.9, *N.Q.* 1 *praef.* 7–13, but S. is here perhaps influenced by Lucr. *D.R.N.* 1.72–4. In S. *magnitudo animi* regularly of the virtuous, high-minded *sapiens* (*C.S.* 9.4, 15.3, *Ir.* 1.20.1–2, *Ep.* 87.16, 92.3).   **egredi** 'transcend'.   **humanae … angustias:** *N.Q.* 1 *praef.* 5 *o quam contempta res est homo, nisi supra humana surrexerit!*; for *angustiae* applied to limited mental horizons (here in chiastic contrast to *magnitudine*), *Ep.* 88.35.   **per … spatiemur** 'for us to range over', final relative clause (G–L §630); of the mind, Ovidian (*Tr.* 4.2.59 *illa* [sc. *mens*] *per immensas spatiatur libera terras*).

14.2 The *sapiens* at leisure to converse with philosophers of every past era; *Ot.* 1.1 *quid quod secedere ad optimos uiros . . . licet?*, *Ep.* 62.2 *cum optimo quoque sum; ad illos, in quocumque loco, in quocumque saeculo fuerunt, animum meum mitto*, 104.21–2. By envisaging dialogue with the different philosophical schools, each characterized by his choice of distinctive verb, S. acknowledges their influence without compromising his mainly Stoic allegiance (cf. *Ep.* 64.9–10). Diversity is stressed here to emphasize the philosopher's freedom of movement in contrast (14.3–4) to the suffocating routine endured by Roman clients.   **disputare:** of Socrates' dialectical method in debate, *Ep.* 24.4, Cic. *Parad.* 23, *Ac.* 1.16 *ita disputat ut nihil affirmet ipse, refellat alios, Tusc.* 5.11. Socrates heads the list out of respect (*Ben.* 7.8.2, *Ep.* 104.27–8), not just because of chronology.   **dubitare cum Carneade:** acc. to Cic. *Tusc.* 5.11 Socrates was effectively the originator of the sceptical Academy, Carneades of Cyrene (214–129 BC) his outstanding successor and founder of the New Academy (D.L. 4.62); S. perhaps reflects that relationship in naming Carneades after Socrates. By *dubitare* he refers to the anti-dogmatic approach (ἐποχή) of the Academy, not least towards Chrysippus' redefinition of Stoic positions (see Sharples (1996) 9–10).   **quiescere:** on the Epicurean's freedom from inner disturbance (ἀταραξία) cf. Cicero's sarcastic picture at *De orat.* 3.63 *in hortulis quiescet suis . . .*; for cognates (*quies, quietus*) in this Epicurean sense, *V.B.* 19.1, *Ep.* 66.47, 88.5. **hominis . . . excedere:** the Stoic *sapiens* holds the natural passions in check by reason (e.g. *Ir.* 2.12.3–6) but 'the Stoic doctrine of ἀπάθεια never was a doctrine of impassivity' because 'the scars of πάθη remain in [the wise man's] soul' (Rist 72; *Ir.* 1.16.7 *sentiet* [sc. *sapiens*] *. . . suspiciones quasdam et umbras affectuum, ipsis quidem carebit*). For the Cynics, on the other hand, the *sapiens* is ἀπαθής (*Ep.* 9.1 *animus impatiens*) in the more extreme sense of 'totally detached', even 'unemotional' (Rist *ibid.*); hence they surpass the Stoics in 'going beyond' (*excedere*) human nature (cf. *Ep.* 9.3).   **cum:** causal (*Ot.* 7.3n.).   **consortium** 'common possession'; with gen., Livian and post-Classical (*OLD* 2a).   **patiatur:** sc. *nos.*   **incedere:** for the fig. use with *in*, 3.1.   **quidni:** *Ot.* 7.3n.   **exiguo et caduco:** contrasted with *immensa* and *aeterna* below (cf. V. Max. 1.6 *ext.* 3); in combination, cf. *Marc.* 21.1 *omnia humana breuia et caduca sunt, N.Q.* 6.1.14. **transitu:** of time, *Ep.* 49.2.   **in illa** [sc. *tempora*]: the past.   **toto:** emphatic by position.   **quae . . . quae . . . quae:** the formally structured climax (anaphoric tricolon with homoeoteleuton in -*a . . . -a . . . -(i)a*) supports the solemn tone.   **cum melioribus communia** 'shared with our betters', i.e. with Socrates, Carneades, Epicurus etc.

14.3–4 In contrast to the 'timeless' philosophical relationship envisaged in 14.2, the ordinary client is starved for time with *his* patron; the manoeuvres on both sides – the client to gain access to his patron, the latter to escape – are described with familiar satirical colour.

14.3 isti: contemptuous (*OLD* 5b).   **qui ... qui ... cum ... cum ... cum:** the elongated sequence of subordinate clauses conveys the exhausting, repetitive and seemingly interminable routine of the clients' daily exertions.   **discursant:** for the sense, 3.2 *officiosa ... discursatio* and Juv. 1.86 *discursus* with Courtney. The verb, only here in S. and not found before him, is rare afterwards (*OLD*), but parallel frequentative formations (e.g. *incurso*) are commonly Livian and post-Classical revivals of pre-Classical usage (cf. Löfstedt II 297–8).   **se ... inquietant:** contrast 14.2 *cum Epicuro quiescere*; the Stoic *sapiens* too neither feels nor causes disquiet (*Cl.* 2.5.4 *serena eius mens est...* , *Ep.* 59.14). The verb is post-Augustan; with *discursare*, cf. *Cl.* 1.3.5 *inquieti discurrimus*, *Ep.* 2.1.   **aliosque:** the clients' besieged patrons. **cum bene insanierint** 'when they'll have thoroughly indulged their madness' (fut. perf., as in the two following *cum* clauses). For the nuance of *bene*, *TLL* II 2117.34–44; for the verb (hyperb.), *Ben.* 7.26.4, *Ep.* 81.27, 115.8. **perambulauerint:** of 'doing the rounds' on distasteful business, Catul. 29.7 *perambulabit* [sc. *cinaedus*] *omnium cubilia*; multiple calls made by the busy client (*Tr.* 12.6, Mart. 10.10.2, 12.29.1) in contrast to the more leisurely associations of 14.1 *spatiemur*.   **nec ... praeterierint:** contrast the advice given at *Ep.* 84.12 *praeteri ... magno aggestu suspensa uestibula ... huc potius te ad sapientiam derige*.   **diuersissimas** 'very distant from one another' (*OLD* 3a).   **meritoriam** 'money-making'; only twice in S., who adapts the derogatory Classical sense ('hired out for gain', usually of persons; *TLL* VIII 843.50–5) to other areas which deserve contempt (*Ep.* 88.1 *meritoria artificia*, on liberal studies as but 'money-making skills'). On the *sportula* given in return to the client (lit. 'little basket', in effect 'dole'), Courtney on Juv. 1.95.   **quotum quemque** 'how few will there be whom ... ?'; *quemque* here a pronoun (*OLD quotus* 2a), as opposed to the adj. at 3.3. **ex tam immensa ... urbe:** contrast the vast temporal landscape (14.2 *immensa*) over which the *sapiens* ranges unrestricted.   **immensa:** of Rome, *Helu.* 6.2.   **districta:** for the nuance, 7.3n.   **uidere** 'even to catch sight of' (*OLD* 5), stressed by position.

14.4 quam multi [sc. *patroni*]: 2.4n.   **illos:** the clients. **quorum ... qui:** relative clauses of tendency (G–L §631).   **somnus:** Mart. 9.6.3 *'non uacat' aut 'dormit' dictum est bis terque reuerso*.   **luxuria:** as a

vice which can absorb all one's time, *Helu.* 10.2–12.7, *Ep.* 51.3–13 (at Baiae),
110.12–20.   **inhumanitas** 'discourtesy', Ciceronian (*OLD* 1; add *C.S.*
13.4).   **torserint:** by keeping them waiting; for similar use of the fut.
perf., *Ep.* 84.1 *sunt autem . . . necessariae* [sc. *lectiones*] *. . . ut, cum ab aliis quaesita
cognouero, tum . . . de inuentis iudicem, Prou.* 5.2, *Marc.* 16.6, *N.Q.* 3.27.1 (all cited
by Waldaestel (1888) 39).   **simulata festinatione:** cf. 7.7 *simulatus
aeger.*   **transcurrant** 'pass without taking real notice', a Silver usage
(*OLD* 4a).   **atrium:** the first main room, used for receiving visitors; for
clients crowding the *atrium* and/or *uestibulum* ('forecourt'; Courtney on Juv.
1.132), *Marc.* 10.1, *Pol.* 4.2, *Ep.* 84.12, Juv. 7.91 with Mayor 1 291 for extensive parallels, esp. in Martial.   **uitabunt:** with a complementary inf.
(*Ep.* 81.22, 114.4), apparently not in prose before S. (K–S 1 675; Summers
lxv).   **per obscuros . . . profugient:** i.e. escape by a rear exit (cf. Hor.
Ep. 1.5.31 *atria seruantem postico falle clientem*); verbal symmetry (*per . . . prodire,
per . . . profugient*) balances the patrons' options.   **obscuros** 'hidden from
view' (*OLD* 3a).   **quasi:** often used to introduce an ironic comment
(*OLD* 2); for a contrasting view, *Ir.* 2.24.1 *in quibusdam rebus satius est de-
cipi quam diffidere.*   **inhumanius:** cf. *inhumanitas* above.   **excludere:**
of clients, *Marc.* 10.1.   **hesterna . . . graues** 'half-asleep and weighed
down by the effects of yesterday's drinking'. The patrons' sluggishness is
reflected in the ponderous rhythm, esp. in *-a . . . -a . . . -es . . . -es*; given *Ep.*
122.1 *turpis qui alto sole semisomnus iacet*, S. uses the adj.'s alternative form in
-somnis, nowhere else attested, to enhance the aural effect. For the lingering
effects of high living, Hor. *S.* 2.2.77–8 *corpus onustum* | *hesternis uitiis animum
quoque praegrauat una.*   **crapula:** *Ep.* 122.2 *oculos hesterna graues crapula;*
2.1 n. on *alius . . . madet.*   **illis:** sc. the clients; dat. with *nomen . . . reddent.*
suum . . . expectent 'cutting short their own sleep in order to wait on
another's'. For clients rising early to attend the *salutatio,* 19.3 *ad alienum
dormiunt somnum,* Mart. 10.82.2 *mane uel a media nocte togatus ero,* Juv. 3.127–
8; for the phrase *somnum (ab)rumpere* in this context, Mart. 12.29.7, Juv.
5.19–20 with Mayor 1 247.   **expectent:** i.e. 'await the end of', a rare
nuance; Petr. 17.2 *expectauimus lacrimas ad ostentationem doloris paratas.*   **uix
alleuatis . . . reddent!** 'with a really disdainful yawn will address clients
[sc. *illis*] by the right name – a name whispered to them a thousand times
over by lips which hardly move'. The phrase *uix alleuatis labris* surely refers
to the *nomenclator,* for whose duties as guest-announcer and prompter of
his master at *salutationes* etc. e.g. *Ben.* 1.3.10, *Ep.* 27.5, Plin. *N.H.* 29.19
aliena memoria salutamus; for whispering, Paul. *Fest.* 78.27–8 Lindsay *fartores*

nomenclatores, qui clam uelut infercirent nomina salutatorum in aurem candidati (cited by Traina 35, who argues successfully against earlier interpretations and unnecessary emendations). Duff 151, misled by Juv. 3.185 where a parallel phrase depicts quite a different situation, takes the lips to be those of the patron but cannot explain how a virtually sealed mouth is compatible with a really mighty (*superbissima*) yawn.   **miliens:** hyperb. (*OLD* 1 a). **nomen...reddent:** lit. 'will utter a (client's) name in reply to a greeting'; so *C.S.* 13.4, *Ep.* 27.5, *Ben.* 1.3.10, Petr. 44.10.   **oscitatione:** post-Augustan; as a sign of boredom, Mart. 2.6.4 *longas trahis oscitationes*, Gell. *N.A.* 4.20.9. For the patrons' arrogant disregard cf. 2.5 *insolenti... respexit.*

14.5 The contrasting experience of the philosophical *cliens*.   **hos:** the clients of 14.3–4.   **ueris** 'proper', 'morally commendable' (*OLD uerus¹* 9a).   **morari** 'spend time on', with *in* + abl. (*OLD* 11 b). **putamus?...dicamus:** only interpretation solves all the problems raised here by the reading... *morari putamus licet dicamus qui...* of the MSS. Emendation has favoured excising *putamus* as a gloss on *licet dicamus* (less often *uice uersa*, sometimes with a change to the verb, e.g. Reynolds' *puta*). But (*a*) such a gloss is improbable as there is no real difficulty to explain here; (*b*) *hos* most naturally refers back to the clients of the preceding sentence, to be contrasted with a different group now to be introduced; (*c*) a strong adversative (*autem, potius*) should mark the contrast. Courtney's interpolation ((1974) 104), adopted here, answers these requirements while enabling us to see that the error first arose through haplography (*putamus*/*potius*). **Zenonem...Theophrastum:** varying the list at 14.2.   **Zenonem:** in deference to S.'s own school Zeno of Citium (335–263 BC) naturally heads the list as its founder (not Zeno of Elea, the dialectic philosopher born *c.* 490 BC; *Ep.* 88.44).   **Pythagoran:** his blend of mysticism and mathematics, dating from the later sixth century, was revived at Rome in Cicero's time allegedly by Nigidius Figulus (but cf. Rawson (1985) 291–4), but the only written material surviving from the master even then was the dubiously authentic list of sayings called *acusmata* (Guthrie I 155, 183–4). Roman familiarity with Pythagoras may have been derived from a treatise on his teachings by Philolaus, himself a Pythagorean and a contemporary of Socrates (Guthrie I 330).   **cotidie:** the philosopher-'client' *never* lacks access to *his* 'patrons'.   **Democritum:** fifth-century atomist from Abdera who wrote extensively on physics, cosmology and ethics. S. quotes from him at *Tr.* 13.1, *Ep.* 7.10, *N.Q.* 4B.9, 5.2, 6.20.1; cf. *Prou.* 6.2, *Ir.* 3.6.3, *Tr.* 2.3 (a *uolumen egregium* on εὐθυμία).   **antistites:** an echo of 14.1 *illi...sacrarum* *opinionum conditores*; for the priest-like philosopher-teacher, *V.B.* 26.7 *professores eius* [sc. *uirtutis*] *ut antistites colite*, *Ep.* 52.15, *OLD* 2.   **bonarum artium:** esp. philosophy; 19.2, *Ot.* 3.4n.   **Aristotelen et Theophrastum:** 1.2n. on '*aetatis . . . stare*'; master and student are again paired at *N.Q.* 6.13.1. **quam familiarissimos:** for the phrase, Cic. *Fam.* 11.27.5; for the bond of shared philosophical interests, *Tusc.* 3.22 *Peripatetici, familiares nostri.* **nemo . . . non:** S. favours the strong positive formation (e.g. 20.5, *Ep.* 4.8, 7.2, 30.11, 33.10; 2.1n on *numquam non*), here varied (*nemo . . . non, nemo non, nemo*) for effect within the climactic anaphoric tricolon.   **uenientem ad se** 'a visitor'; for the wider Silver use of the pres. pple in the sing. as a noun, Summers lix-lx, G–L §437 n. 1.   **beatiorem:** here used with its common philosophical emphasis; Mankin (1995) 64–5 on Hor. *Epod.* 2.1 *beatus ille*.   **sui:** possibly the philosopher-'patron' but more likely his 'client', who departs more at ease with himself. For 'being one's own friend' / 'devoted to oneself' as a Stoic goal, *V.B.* 2.3 *mihi ipse nondum amicus sum, Ep.* 6.7 (S. renders a saying of Hecaton of Rhodes) '*quaeris*' *inquit* '*quid profecerim? amicus esse mihi coepi*'; also mined by Hor. *S.* 1.2. 19–20, *Ep.* 1.18.101 (with Mayer (1994) 255).   **uacuis . . . manibus** 'empty-handed' (*OLD uacuus* 4a).   **conueniri** 'to be approached' (*OLD* 2a) by night or by day (*interdiu*), in contrast to the negligent patrons in 14.4. For the pass. (only here in S.), e.g. Cic. *Fam.* 6.19.2, *Att.* 9.6.1, Liv. 1.58.6, 7.5.3, 33.35.7.

15   The advantages of philosophical clientela

The alternative *clientela* of the philosopher's 'society of the imagination' more closely resembles true friendship than conventional clientship (15.1–2). Adoption into one's philosophical *familia* of choice (15.3) thus opens the way to freedom and immortality won through philosophy (hence S.'s *laudes philosophiae* in 15.4), and to a 'whole' perspective on the unity of past, present and future time (15.5) that the *occupati* inevitably lack (16.1).

15.1 Horum: sc. *philosophorum.*   **te . . . contribuet:** asyndeton and wordplay (*nemo/omnes, coget/docebunt, conteret/contribuet*) emphasize the contrasts; mortal danger was not among the usual hardships attending the *sportula*, but for the extreme case, Juv. 3.249–67 with Mayor I 209–10. **docebunt** [sc. *mori*]: 7.3 *tota uita discendum est mori* and n. on *mori.* **contribuet:** sc. *quisque*, understood from *nemo* as at *Ep.* 53.8 *quare uitia sua nemo confitetur? quia etiamnunc in illis est* [sc. *quisque*]; H–S 825. In the sense of 'give to' / 'share with' (*OLD* 3) the verb is found before S. only in verse (Tib. 1.6.63–4, Ov. *M.* 7.231); the rare usage suggests that wordplay influences his choice.   **nullius:** 3.1n. on *a nullo*.   **sermo** 'conversation with' (+ gen., *Tr.* 7.3, *Ep.* 123.8).   **periculosus:** because of informers and accusers (*delatores*), notorious under the early emperors after Augustus; so e.g. *Ben.* 3.26.1 (under Tiberius) *excipiebatur ebriorum sermo, simplicitas iocantium; nihil erat tutum*.   **capitalis** 'life-threatening' (*OLD* 2); conspicuous cases at e.g. Tac. *Ann.* 5.8.1, 15.71.3 (Decimus Nouius Priscus exiled *per amicitiam Senecae*), 16.14.1, 16.18.3 (Petronius).   **nullius . . . obseruatio** 'close attendance upon none of them will cost you dear'; *obseruatio* unprecedented in this sense (*TLL* IX 2.200.76–84). The *cliens* expecting the *sportula* had to go to the considerable expense of keeping clean the *toga* customarily worn at *salutationes* etc. (Juv. 1.119, 3.180); paying off slaves to gain admission to his patron was only one of other frequent costs (Juv. 3.184–9 with Braund (1996) 205).   **quicquid uoles:** in contrast to the *sportula* of usually 25 asses, a very small sum (Courtney on Juv. 1.95).   **per illos . . . haurias** 'they will not be at fault if you do not drink in the very fullest amount you have room for'. The construction with *stare* (*OLD sto* 22), only here in S., is a legal formula used widely in prose (H–S 680).   **quantum plurimum:** Muretus' transposition of *plurimum quantum* in the MSS, which is first paralleled only at Flor. 2.13.74 *plurimum quantum fauoris partibus dabat fraternitas ducum*, where the elliptical construction ('very great is the amount of popularity which . . . '; K–S 1 14) is in any case quite different from the Senecan case if *plurimum quantum* is read with Grimal 60. But for *quantum plurimum* as a Senecan mannerism, albeit usually with acc. of extension with *licet/potest*, *Marc.* 21.1, *Ben.* 7.23.1, *Ep.* 8.3, 91.8, 124.23; *plurimum* then rightly emphasizes not the fullest capacity of drinking (*haurias*) but the fullest capacity of the space to be filled (*quantum ceperis*).   **ceperis:** fut. perf.; for the sense, *Ep.* 108.2 *non quantum uis sed quantum capis hauriendum est* (Axelson (1939) 43 n. 17); 7.9n.   **haurias:** S. favours the image, e.g. *Helu.* 17.4, *Ep.* 59.9, 84.6, 99.5, 108.2.

    15.2 felicitas: in contrast to the misery of ordinary clients (14.4 *miseris*) because founded upon virtue (*V.B.* 16.1 *in uirtute posita est uera felicitas*), which is itself inseparable from the study of philosophy (*Ep.* 89.8, 90.3).   **pulchra:** meditation on death (*Ep.* 26.8–10, 70.17–18) makes for an old age blissfully free from the anxieties described in 11.1.   **manet** 'lies in store (for)' (*OLD* 4).   **se . . . contulit** 'has put himself under the patronage of . . . ' Ciceronian (*S. Rosc.* 106 *se in Chrysogoni fidem et clientelam* *contulerunt*); the fig. use of the noun, finally spelling out the analogy between the ordinary and the philosopher-client, is not found before S. (also *Ir.* 1.10.2).   **habebit . . . effingat:** in this informal *De amicitia* (cf. *Tr.* 7.3, *Ep.* 3.2–3, *Ep.* 9; Vottero 37–41 on frr. 58–60) the relationship envisaged between the philosopher-'client' and his patrons bears the stamp more of 'true' Roman friendship than of clientship; cf. Cic. *Amic.* 22 *quid dulcius quam habere quicum omnia audeas sic loqui ut tecum?*; 88 *et monendi amici saepe sunt et obiurgandi, et haec accipienda amice cum beneuole fiunt,* 89 all possible care must be taken *primum ut monitio acerbitate, deinde ut obiurgatio contumelia careat.* As frankness comes without insult, so praise without flattery: 91 *habendum est nullam in amicitiis pestem esse maiorem quam adulationem blanditiam assentationem*; and the true friend is a model for oneself: 23 *uerum . . . amicum qui intuetur, tamquam exemplar aliquod intuetur sui* (with Powell (1990) 91 on the Stoic and Aristotelian associations of the idea). This integration of the Roman *amicitia*-model with the philosopher–'client' relationship (perceived by Motto–Clark (1993) 97) is made easier because the Stoic *sapiens* is in theory the equal of his 'patrons': D.L. 7.124 = L–S 1 67P Stoics 'say that friendship exists only among the virtuous, on account of their similarity', *Ben.* 7.12.2 *hoc inter sapientes solum consortium est, inter quos amicitia est.*   **cum quibus:** S. never uses *quibuscum*, frequent down to Cicero, less so later (K–S 1 585 with Duff 153).   **deliberet** 'consult' (*OLD* 1b).   **a quibus** 'from whom' with *audiat*, 'by whom' with *laudetur.*   **contumelia:** relatively mild compared with *iniuria*; *C.S.* 5.1.   **adulatione** 'fawning', to be distinguished (Powell (1990) 115 on Cic. *Amic.* 91) from *blanditia* (ingratiating speech) and *assentatio* (toadyism).   **ad quorum . . . effingat:** *Ot.* 1.1 *quid quod . . . licet?* with nn.   **ad . . . similitudinem:** Ciceronian (*OLD similitudo* 1d).   **effingat:** of imitating a model, *V.B.* 16.1, *Ep.* 65.7 *humanitas, ad quam* ('after which') *homo effingitur.*

15.3 The greater advantages in selecting (cf. *ad nostrum arbitrium*) a substitute parent were already illustrated in Aesop's fable of the dog and the lamb which Phaedrus had adapted for a Roman audience (3.15, esp. 18 *facit parentes bonitas, non necessitas* (= 'kinship')). For the pedagogic emphasis in S., Quint. *Inst.* 2.9.1 *discipulos . . . moneo, ut praeceptores suos . . . ament et parentes esse non quidem corporum, sed mentium credant,* Fronto p. 65.23 van den Hout² *a meo magistro et parente Athenodoto.* In comedy a parental title was widely conferred on benefactors (Lindsay on Pl. *Capt.* 444 *tu patronus, tu pater*), a dilution of the 'natural' sense which Horace (*S.* 1.6.93–7) firmly resists. **solemus dicere:** *Ot.* 5.1 n.   **potestate** 'power to choose' (*OLD* 6a).

sortiremur: the *sors nascendi* of *Ir.* 2.22.1, *Ep.* 79.12. **forte:** emphatic, with strong instrumental force as at *Cl.* 1.6.3 *alii ex destinato, alii forte impulsi.*
nobis uero: the adversative particle (*OLD* 7) contrasts proverbial wisdom (*solemus . . . nobis datos*) with an alternative possibility for us all (*nobis uero . . . licet*): 'our parents come to us by chance, but *in actuality* we can be born according to our own choosing' (Alexander (1945) 89). It is much less likely that two almost juxtaposed instances of *nobis* should refer to distinctly different groups, the common mass of humanity and the philosophically enlightened, however strong the adversative. **nasci:** a bold image extended below in fig. adoption into a philosophical school (*familia*) of choice.
nobilissimorum ingeniorum: the resonant wording with homoeoteleuton combines the adj.'s senses of '(intellectually) distinguished' (e.g. *Ep.* 44.2, 5 *animus facit nobilem*) and 'well-born', though the superlative can strictly apply only to the former; the contrast is exploited more extensively at *Ep.* 44.5–6, *Ben.* 3.28.1 *nemo altero nobilior, nisi cui rectius ingenium et artibus bonis aptius.* **familiae:** philosophical 'schools' (*N.Q.* 7.32.2) as well as adoptive 'families'. **ascisci:** of adoption, semi-technical (*OLD* 1 c) and a Silver replacement for the older *adoptare*; childless nobles found heirs, emperors successors, through the important expedient of adoption, often of adults (Wiedemann (1989) 34–5 with Crook (1967) 111–12). **in nomen . . . adoptaberis:** for the formula, e.g. Liv. *Per.* 116 *in nomen adoptatus est* [sc. *C. Octauius*], Suet. *Iul.* 83.2, *Gal.* 17 *in bona et nomen ascitum* [sc. *Pisonem*]; but here by *nomen* S. means 'Stoic', 'Epicurean' etc. In the Republic and early Empire the adoptee regularly assumed the *tria nomina* (*praenomen, nomen gentilicium* and *cognomen*) of the adopter; so e.g. L. Iunius Gallio Annaeanus, who as Annaeus Nouatus (S.'s brother) was adopted by L. Iunius Gallio (cited *inter alios* by Salomies (1992) 20–2). **bona:** lit. 'property', but here also with an obvious ethical dimension which is developed more explicitly at *Ep.* 31.3. **sordide . . . custodienda** 'to be hoarded in a miserly or mean spirit'. For the nuance of *sordide, V.B.* 20.4; for *maligne,* 1.1 n. on *malignitate.* **maiora . . . quo . . . diuiseris:** S. favours ellipsis in the correlative (*eo*) . . . *quo* construction (K–S II 484); e.g. 17.4, *Ben.* 2.27.3, 5.12.6, *Ep.* 19.11, cited with other examples by Bourgery (1922) 405. **quo . . . diuiseris:** lit. 'the more people you'll have shared them with'; for the benefits of philosophy as available to all, *Ep.* 44.2 *bona mens omnibus patet, omnes ad hoc sumus nobiles. nec reicit quemquam philosophia nec eligit: omnibus lucet,* 90.1. For *diuido* with dat. (*OLD* 6b), *Marc.* 20.5, *Ep.* 77.8, *N.Q.* 2.5.1.

15.4 In praise of philosophy as a release from ordinary mortal restrictions. S. draws on familiar (esp. poetic) topoi (nn. on *honores . . . non potest*, *nulla abolebit . . . deminuet* and *quoniam . . . miramur*), but for his *laudes philosophiae*, well worn in Aristotelian and later protreptic tradition (e.g. Cic. *Hort.* frr. 106–15 Grilli; cf. *Leg.* 1.58–63 with Vottero 57–64 on S.'s own *Exhortationes* (= frr. 76–89)), cf. *Helu.* 20.1–2, *Ep.* 65.16–24, 88.28, *N.Q.* 1 *praef.* 3–17.   **hi . . . subleuabunt:** reapplication of a motif which S. favours esp. in *consolatio*, where genre may help to explain his uncharacteristic portrayal of the soul as apparently immortal (19.1 n. on *quis . . . componat*); so *Marc.* 24.5 *ipse quidem* [sc. Marcia's son] *aeternus meliorisque nunc status est . . . nititur illo unde demissus est. ibi illum aeterna requies manet ex confusis crassisque pura et liquida uisentem*, *Pol.* 9.7 *ne . . . inuideris fratri tuo: quiescit . . . tandem aeternus est.*   **iter:** *aeternitas* is attained at the end of the *iter uitae*; cf. *Pol.* 11.2 *tota uita nihil aliud quam ad mortem iter est* with Kurth (1994) 138. **illum locum . . . deicitur:** like the position of safety which the *sapiens* attains above the blows of fortune; C.S. 1.1 *qui* [sc. *editus uertex*] *adeo extra omnem teli iactum surrexit ut supra fortunam emineat.* The image extends back to Lucretius (*D.R.N.* 2.7–10 with Lyne (1978) 104 on *Ciris* 14–17). **haec . . . uertendae:** i.e. by living virtuously in accordance with reason the *sapiens* gains access to immortality (i.e. undying glory) and a god-like state in life (ὁμοίωσις θεῷ; cf. Pl. *Tht.* 176b 1); Vottero 298–9 on fr. 62 (= Lact. *Inst.* 3.12.11) *una . . . res est uirtus quae nos immortalitate donare possit et pares diis facere.*   **una ratio** 'the only means', with the usual gen. (*OLD ratio* 14b). **extendendae . . . uertendae:** solemn in tone, suitably mannered in its chiastic arrangement and polysyllabic wordplay (*Ot.* 5.7 n. on *immortalium*). **honores . . . non potest:** endorsing the familiar *lex mortalitatis* that *debemur morti nos nostraque* (Hor. *Ars* 63; cf. 68, Lucr. *D.R.N.* 5.311), S. invokes the celebratory topos of literary monuments as more lasting than the pyramids etc. (e.g. Hor. *C.* 3.30.1 *exegi monumentum aere perennius . . .* , Prop. 3.2.18–22, Ov. *M.* 15.871–2 etc.); so S. himself in *Ep.* 21.3–5 and, in epigrams attributed to him, *A.L.* 415–16 Sh. B.   **quicquid . . . extruxit:** elaboration of *honores, monumenta*, the former bestowed in *quicquid . . . iussit*, the latter erected in *quicquid . . . ambitio . . . operibus extruxit.*   **decretis:** sc. *senatus* (*OLD* 3b).   **ambitio . . . extruxit:** *Pol.* 1.1 *septem illa miracula et si qua his multo mirabiliora sequentium annorum* <u>extruxit ambitio</u> *aliquando solo aequata uisentur*, where, as here, *ambitio* (hinting also at 'ostentation'; *OLD* 6) is pejorative in connotation (cf. 2.1 n.).   **subruitur:** of time's attritional effect, Senecan (*Phaed.* 775 *tempus te tacitum subruit*).   **nihil non . . . uetustas:**

so in consolation *Marc.* 26.6 *omnia sternet abducetque secum uetustas*; a much used topos in all periods (*OLD uetustas* 3).   **nihil non:** rare in S., *non* qualifying *demolitur*; for the strong positive emphasis, e.g. *Ben.* 2.29.5, 6.30.6, *N.Q.* 5.18.15.   **demolitur:** only here in S.; of time (rare), Ov. *M.* 15.228–9. **mouet** 'transforms'; for the nuance, Ov. *M.* 8.729 *forma semel mota est*, Liv. 34.54.8, and for the idea, Virg. *Aen.* 3.415 *tantum aeui longinqua ualet mutare uetustas* (quoted at *N.Q.* 6.30.1). The change of idea after *demolitur* defends *mouet* against calls for emendation on the grounds that it is anti-climactic after the stronger verb (cf. Gertz (1874) 157).   **consecrauit** 'has hallowed', bestowing immortality on 'sacred' ideas (14.1 *sacrarum opinionum*); Ciceronian (*Tusc.* 5.11 *cuius* [sc. *Socratis*] . . . *ingenii magnitudo Platonis memoria et litteris consecrata* . . . , with other examples at *TLL* IV 384.43–70).   **non potest:** sc. *uetustas*; Vitr. 1.5.3 *ei materiae nec caries . . . nec uetustas potest nocere.* **nulla abolebit . . . deminuet:** poetic in feel, Ovidian in confident prediction (*M.* 15.871–2 *iamque opus exegi, quod . . .* | *nec poterit ferrum nec edax abolere uetustas*).   **deminuet:** i.e. 'reduce *at all*', let alone destroy (*abolebit*). **sequens . . . ulterior** 'the next [sc. *aetas*] and each one after that' in an unbroken line.   **aliquid . . . conferet** 'will enhance the respect in which they are held'; with *ad* + acc., in Celsus and then favoured by S., *C.S.* 1.1, *Ir.* 1.20.1, *Ep.* 55.8 (with other examples at *TLL* IV 186.12–59). After *consecrauit* above, *uenerationem* develops the religious connotation (cf. *Ep.* 41.4). **quoniam . . . miramur:** Vell. 2.92.5 *praesentia inuidia, praeterita ueneratione prosequimur*; for the familiar topos that the great suffer less from envy after death, McKeown on Ov. *Am.* 1.15.39–40.   **in uicino** 'close at hand'; first in Velleius (2.70.2; *OLD* 3c).   **simplicius** 'with less reserve'; *Helu.* 19.5 *simplex admirandis uirtutibus . . . antiquitas* ('frank in admiration of . . .'), cited by Duff 154.

15.5 Conclusion: the *sapiens* lives long by embracing past and future within a single 'eternal present'.   **multum . . . uita:** 1.4n. on *aetas . . . patet.*   **terminus:** of life, *Ot.* 5.7n.   **cludit:** *Ot.* 5.6n. **solus . . . soluitur:** by winning glory and traversing all ages, past, present and future, the *sapiens* attains through philosophy the immortality envisaged at 15.4 *hi . . . uertendae*; for his special status, emphasized by *solus* echoed in *soluitur* and by the ambiguity of *generis humani* ('alone of the human race [*OLD solus* 5a] he is exempted from the laws of the human race'), *Ben.* 7.3.2, *Ep.* 124.23 *animus . . . super humana se extollens.*   **soluitur:** of legal exemption, semi-technical (*OLD* 14d).   **omnia . . . seruiunt:** cf. 14.1 *nec enim . . . adiciunt* and esp. *nullo . . . interdictum est* with n. For the *sapiens* as god-like, *Prou.* 1.5 *bonus tempore tantum a deo differt*, *C.S.* 8.2, *Ep.* 59.14 *cum dis ex pari uiuit*, 73.12–14 (the *sapiens* compared and contrasted with Jupiter), 87.19, 92.29; 15.4n. on *haec . . . uertendae.*　　**seruiunt:** the *sapiens* is *temporis dominus* (12.9, adduced by Duff 155).　　**transit:** *transît* Reynolds with other editors; but in using the present tense (so also *comprendit*) S. embarks on a sequence of present verbs which build up over the divisions of time to represent the 'eternal present' (cf. *omnium temporum in unum collatio* below) in the *diuina mens* of the *sapiens.*　　**comprendit:** of memory, *OLD* 11 b (Ciceronian); 10.2–5 for the contrasting *iniucunda recordatio* of the *occupati.*　　**instat:** of pressing time, *OLD* 6c.　　**utitur:** whereas the *occupati* are too distracted to use the present before it is snatched away (10.6 *subducitur*).　　**praecipit** 'he anticipates' (cf. 4.3). Freed by foresight from fears and hopes for the future (7.9n. on *nec optat . . . nec timet*), the *sapiens* is ready for all eventualities; cf. Cic. *Off.* 1.81 *illud . . . ingenii magni est, praecipere cogitatione futura* with Dyck 213 on the Stoic terminology (= προλαμβάνειν). **collatio:** i.e. 'the combining' into one of past, present and future, a rare usage (*OLD* 1b) here set in emphatic contrast to the *disunity* of the three times as pictured below (16.1 *Illorum . . . timent*).

16　*The disunity of times in uneven lives*

The unity of times experienced by the *sapiens* (15.5) contrasted with the fragmented existence of the *occupati* (16.1), whose 'irrational' condition is demonstrated by examples of their paradoxical (16.2n. on *mortem . . . timent*), even unnatural (16.4n. on *at . . . exigunt!*) behaviour, and by the impossibility of satisfaction in lives where time moves now too slowly, now too quickly, never evenly (16.3–4).

16.1 Illorum . . . timent: for the division of times, 10.2. For the *occupati* thus deprived, Plut. *Tranq. an.* 14 = *Mor.* 473c, possibly after Panaetius, but the extent of Stoic influence on the treatise remains controversial (Babut (1969) 97–101): ' . . . the foolish overlook and neglect good things even when they are present, because their thoughts are ever intent upon the future, but the wise by remembrance make even those benefits that are no longer at hand to be vividly existent for themselves [10.2n. on *quod egimus certum*]. For the present good, which allows us to touch it but for the smallest portion of time and then eludes our perception, seems to fools to have no further reference to us or to belong to us at all . . . '

(trans. W. C. Helmbold).   **breuissima:** because the *occupati* have no grasp of the complex of times which 'prolongs' life (15.5 *longam... collatio*); Plut. *Tranq. an.* 14 = *Mor.* 473d 'forgetfulness... does not allow life to become unified (τὸν βίον ἕνα γενέσθαι), when past is interwoven (συμπλεκομένων) with present' (trans. W. C. Helmbold).   **qui... timent:** the variety of construction (verbs with gen., acc. and *de* + abl.) itself underscores the disunity of times.   **de futuro timent:** unlike the fearless *sapiens* (7.9n. on *nec optat... nec timet*, 15.5n. on *praecipit*).   **extrema** 'death', a usage favoured by S. (*Cl.* 1.6.3, *Ep.* 26.1, 54.7, 101.7).   **sero:** as in the case of Livius Drusus (6.2 *sero... contigisse*), prominently positioned to dramatize the quasi-tragedy (cf. *miseri*).   **nihil agunt, occupatos:** paradoxical, portraying the irrational condition of the *occupati* themselves; for the trope in S., Summers lxxx.   **agunt:** for the retained indicative with *dum* in *oratio obliqua*, K–S II 544 ('more often post-Classical').

    16.2 nec est quod: 2.5n.   **hoc** 'the following', anticipating *quia*. **inuocant:** of death, first in Publilius Syrus (M5 Meyer *mori est felicis antequam mortem inuoces*) and then in the elder Pliny (*N.H.* 7.167) and S., who may possibly echo Publilius given his familiarity with the *Sententiae* (*Marc.* 9.5, *Tr.* 11.8, *Ep.* 8.9, 94.28, 43, 108.9).   **uexat... timent:** almost a catalogue of Stoic *fugienda* (opp. *petenda*, *Ot.* 1.3n. on *laudandum petendumque*).   **uexat:** emphatic by position; of Stoic disturbance, *Ot.* 1.2, *Tr.* 2.6, *Ep.* 39.5, *Ag.* 63. **imprudentia:** the reverse of one of the four primary virtues (φρόνησις); 9.1n. on *prudentiam*.   **incertis:** in contrast to *constantia*, for which e.g. *Ep.* 111.4, 120.19, *N.Q.* 2.36.1 *sapientis quoque uiri sententiam negatis posse mutari*; wordplay with *incurrentibus* (Summers lxxxiv 2b).   **affectibus:** instrumental abl.; 1.1n.   **incurrentibus** 'rushing into'; for the hint of recklessness, *Cl.* 1.12.5 *incurrere in pericula iuuat*.   **mortem... timent:** paradoxical. The idea, which extends back to Democritus (68b 203 D–K 'in avoiding death men pursue it'), may here be derived from Epicurus; *Ep.* 24.22 (= fr. 496 Us.) and esp. 23 (= fr. 498 Us.) *'quid tam ridiculum quam appetere mortem, cum uitam inquietam tibi feceris metu mortis?'* (cf. *Ep.* 70.8 *stultitia est timore mortis mori*, and also Lucr. *D.R.N.* 3.79–84 with Kenney (1971) 86).   **mortem... optant:** perverse, as the *sapiens* who lives *quantum debet, non quantum potest* (*Ep.* 70.4) will never merely pray for death but will commit suicide at the appropriate time; *Ep.* 117.22–4 *nihil mihi uidetur turpius quam optare mortem... imbecillae mentis ista sunt uerba* [sc. *'Ita quam primum moriar'*] *et hac detestatione misericordiam captantis: non uult mori qui optat.*

16.3 illud ... quod 'There is no reason to suppose that this too is evidence that they live long, the fact that...' Variation on the construction at 16.2 *nec est quod ... uitam*; for *argumentum* with a gen. pple phrase for compression (S. favours the device), Duff 155–6, adding *Ep.* 6.1. **saepe ... dies:** contrary to the (Stoic) active life (*Ep.* 122.3 *nullus agenti dies longus est*) with its dedication to philosophy; *Tr.* 3.6 *si te ad studia reuocaueris, omne uitae fastidium effugeris nec noctem fieri optabis taedio lucis.* **quod, dum** 'or the fact that until'; complementary to, not an explanation of, *quod ... dies.* **condictum** 'appointed' (*OLD* 3a). **cenae:** gen., not dat. (*OLD tempus*[1] 8b), given e.g. *Ep.* 36.4 *discendi tempus*, 122.9 *somni*. The *cena* did not normally begin until the ninth or tenth hour (Courtney on Juv. 6.419). **ire:** 1.3n. **deseruerunt** 'have failed', 'left in the lurch'; the *sapiens* of course 'abandons' such *occupationes*, not they him. **relicti:** in two senses, as 'abandoned' by their preoccupations they are 'left with nothing to do' (Basore; *OLD relinquo* 9b). **aestuant:** of emotional turbulence, Ciceronian (*TLL* I 1114.28–36) and rare in S. (*Ep.* 13.13, 74.8); for combination with *queror*, *Med.* 390. **extrahant** 'drag out'. **aliquam:** effectively 'some other' (K–S I 636). **quod interiacet:** before its antecedent (*tempus*) in keeping with the sense; of time, the verb first in S. (*TLL* VII 1.2198.49–51). **tam ... quam cum** 'precisely as they do when ...' For colloquial *mehercules*, 5.3n.; with *tam ... quam*, favoured by S. (*Cl.* 2.6.4, *Ep.* 66.10, 87.17, 95.60, *Ben.* 6.6.1). **cum ... uolunt:** S.'s disapproval elsewhere of the cruelties of the arena (13.6–7, *Cl.* 1.25.1, *Ep.* 7.2–5, 95.33) and of the pleasure-seeking crowd (*Ep.* 80.2) casts its shadow over this passage; the restless *occupati* are just the sort to relish the cruelty of the games. **dies ... edictus est:** Ciceronian and esp. Livian (*TLL* V 1.1050.34–6); but S. departs from Livy by making *dies* masc. (Liv. 23.31.5 *edicta dies erat*, 41.10.12; 9.3n. on *hoc* for the general rule). **alterius:** equivalent to the gen. of *alius*, and rare in combination with *aliqui* (adj.); *Ot.* 4.1n. **expectatur:** not Stoic; 9.1n. on *expectatio ... hodiernum.* **constitutum** 'the appointed time'. Colloquial in tone (in Varro and Cicero's letters, then post-Augustan; *OLD* 1a); separated from its dependent gens. by the intrusion of *expectatur* to re-create the deferral of anticipated fulfilment. **transilire:** of 'leaping over' time in between, *Ep.* 74.34.

16.4 omnis ... dilatio: application of the theme of *dilatio* as *iactura uitae* in 9.1; the emphasis there is on postponement as an obstacle to *carpe diem* (9.1n. on *porro*), here on *dilatio* itself as feeding the frustration it engenders. **illud tempus:** sc. *spectaculi uel uoluptatis.*

amant (Muretus, *amanti* MSS) 'they enjoy' (*OLD* 9); less forced than Alexander's tentative 'but that occasion which they desire' ((1945) 90). **breue...praeceps:** 10.2n. on *quod agimus breue est*, 10.6n. on *praesens...breuissimum est*); S. starves the *occupati* of pleasure even in the long-awaited moment.   **breuiusque...uitio** 'and made far shorter by their own fault'; 10.6n. on *et id ipsum...subducitur.*   **aliunde...non possunt:** for the lack of Stoic constancy, 2.2n. on *plerosque...deprendunt.* **aliunde...transfugiunt:** they fig. 'desert' (cf. *Ot.* 1.4) one pleasure for another – after their own *occupationes* have deserted *them* (16.3). **aliunde...alio:** not found in combination before S.; *Helu.* 6.7, 8, *Ep.* 64.2, 69.1, 88.34.   **consistere** 'dwell on', with *in* + abl. (*OLD* 4). **cupiditate:** pejorative; 2.1n.   **inuisi:** stressed by *correctio* (not x but y) to suggest esp. intense loathing (so *Her. F.* 824 *diem inuisum*, [Sen.] *Oct.* 20); in retrospect, perhaps with a play on *inuisus* 'unseen' if the nocturnal revellers below (next n.) rarely wake to see the light of day (cf. Fitch (1987) 294 on *Her. F.* 664 *Ditis inuisi* with Hardie (1994) 166 on *Aen.* 9.496). **at...exigunt!:** for the hint of the unnatural turning of night into day, *Ep.* 122.2, 5, 9 *cum instituerunt omnia contra naturae consuetudinem uelle, nouissime in totum ab illa desciscunt. 'Lucet: somni tempus est. quies est: nunc exerceamur, nunc gestemur, nunc prandeamus...'*, 15–16.   **exiguae noctes:** in the contrast with *longi dies*, rare enough to be counted as another Senecan reminiscence of Virgil (*G.* 2.201–2; cf. 9.2 and *Ot.* 1.4n. on *disertissimus*).   **scortorum aut uino:** a cliché in combination, e.g. Liv. 23.45.2 *uino et scortis.*

16.5 For the Stoic rejection of certain poetry as immoral and harmful (in contrast to S.'s appeal to Virgil in 9.2) see De Lacy (1948) 266, and also *Ben.* 1.4.5–6, *Ep.* 115.12 with Mazzoli (1970) 74–9. For S.'s impatience with poetic depictions of Jupiter which merely give people an excuse to behave in the same way, *V.B.* 26.6, and against false characterizations of Jupiter, Vottero 342–3 on fr. 93 (= Lact. *Inst.* 1.16.10). S. here follows Cic. *N.D.* 1.42.   **inde:** elliptical (no verb) for sharp effect, as often (*V.B.* 1.4, *Tr.* 2.10, *Ep.* 95.16, 71).   **furor:** of poetic inspiration, e.g. Cic. *De orat.* 2.194, *Diu.* 1.80, Stat. *Silu.* 2.7.76; but here plain 'madness' predominates.   **fabulis:** pejorative (*Ot.* 5.1n.).   **alentium:** fig. of nurturing error, vice etc. (common), e.g. *Ir.* 1.1.5, 2.20.2, 25.4, *Tr.* 2.10.   **quibus:** sc. *poetis*; dat. with *uisus est* ('[poets] who have actually imagined that...'). **Iuppiter...noctem:** on his visit to Alcmena, wife of Amphitryon. **concubitus:** the sexual act, which Plautus makes Jupiter openly admit to Alcmena's husband at *Am.* 1136 *concubitu grauidam feci filio.* S. in principle objects to *uilis uoluptas* being ascribed to Jupiter (cf. *Ep.* 74.14); for the many similar *fabulae*, Pease on Cic. *N.D.* 1.42 *cum humano genere concubitus* [sc. *deorum*]. **duplicasse noctem:** the version followed elsewhere by S. (*Her. F.* 24–6), but for the night tripled in other versions, Tarrant (1976) 326 on *Ag.* 815. **quid aliud est ... quam** 'All this inflaming of our worst passions amounts to nothing else but ... ' **uitia ... incendere:** *Ep.* 115.12 ... *carmina poetarum, quae affectibus nostris facem subdant*; for the verb of inflaming passion, vice etc. (*OLD* 5), e.g. *Ir.* 2.19.5, *Ep.* 83.19, 104.20. **auctores ... deos:** lit. 'to record the gods as setting a precedent' (*OLD inscribo* 5a), perhaps with the added nuance of 'record as responsible for' (5b, incl. Ov. *M.* 15.127–8 *ipsos | inscripsere deos sceleri*). **morbo:** of the passions, vice etc. (common; *OLD* 2a), e.g. *Cl.* 1.17.1, 25.2, *Ep.* 7.1 with Summers 157, 106.6 (but for 'foible', 13.2n. on *Graecorum ... fuit*). **exemplo ... licentiam:** *V.B.* 26.6 *quibus* [sc. *ineptiis poetarum*] *nihil aliud actum est quam ut pudor hominibus peccandi demeretur, si tales deos credidissent*; for *excusatam licentiam, Ir.* 2.13.1. **diuinitatis:** the metonymy (= *deorum*) is rare; apparently first in Vitruvius (*TLL* v 1.1616.24–75). **istis:** contemptuous (*OLD* 5b). **noctes:** of love-making, *OLD* 3c. **quas ... mercantur?:** the full extent of the cost is described in *diem ... metu* below. **care:** a pun on the financial/ amatory aspects of the affair, as at Prop. 2.23.11 *quam care semel in toto nox uertitur* ('comes round') *anno!* **diem ... metu:** the chiastic arrangement around *perdunt* brings the chapter to an elegant close but is at odds with the disordered routine; for the disabling combination of expectancy and fear, 7.9n. on *nec optat ... nec timet*. **expectatione:** 9.1n. **perdunt ... metu:** *Ep.* 24.1 *quid ... necesse est ... praesens tempus futuri metu perdere?*

17 Anxious prosperity, restless ambition

Another change of direction, as S. meets the possible objection that the pleasures of prosperity and prestige won through *occupatio* may outweigh its disadvantages. The fear of losing those shallow (17.3) advantages, and therefore the anxiety of safeguarding them (17.4), undermine their enjoyment; and the ambition which won them is in any case too restless ever to allow any calm withdrawal into *otium* (17.5–6).

17.1 trepidae: marked by apprehension through fear of loss. **terroribus:** the combination with *uoluptates* fails to agitate the philosopher;

Ep. 75.17 *inagitati terroribus, incorrupti uoluptatibus, nec mortem horrebimus nec deos.*
subitque 'steals in on' (*OLD* 11); with *cogitatio*, 20.1, *Ben.* 1.11.3. **cum maxime exultantes** 'at the very moment when they are rejoicing'. As an *affectus*, *exultatio* itself has its dangers; *Ir.* 2.21.5 *exultationem tumor et nimia aestimatio sui sequitur*, *V.B.* 10.2. **cum maxime:** common in S. (Summers 161 on *Ep.* 7.6); with a pple, *OLD maxime* 6d, adding e.g. *Pol.* 9.4, *Ben.* 3.33.1. **haec** 'the present circumstances' (*OLD hic*[1] 9). **quam diu?:** ellipsis of the verb is colloquial (e.g. Cic. *Att.* 12.40.5 *quod quaeris quam diu hic: paucos dies*); for self-questioning of this type, e.g. *Tr.* 2.15. **ab** 'as a direct result of' (*OLD* 15a). **affectu:** pejorative (1.1 n.). **reges ... potentiam:** variation on the familiar topos (not least in Senecan tragedy) of the dangers/anxieties of high position (e.g. *Pol.* 9.5, *Ep.* 94.72–4); 4.1 n. on *si tuto liceat*. **magnitudo fortunae:** of 'exalted station', *Ben.* 5.5.1, *Ep.* 47.20; Livian (39.50.2) and in Velleius (2.100.3). **uenturus ... finis** [sc. *fortunae*] 'the end to which it must at some point come'; for the fut. pple predicting a sure or destined eventuality, Westman (1961) 149–50. **exterruit:** while intensifying the alarm (e.g. *Ep.* 71.30, 85.11, 104.10), the prefix also balances *exultantes*, weighing fear against joy.

17.2 A stock *exemplum* (Mayor II 127–8 on Juv. 10.173–84), slanted here to make Xerxes' lack of self-knowledge an important contributory cause of his catastrophic failure (cf. *Ben.* 6.31.1 *animum tumentem oblitumque quam caducis confideret*). S.'s emphasis is different from Herodotus' (7.45–6), probably his main source (Setaioli (1981b) 383–4, (1988) 489); but an intermediary Roman tradition cannot be ruled out given Plin. *Ep.* 3.7.13 and esp. the thematic and verbal coincidences with V. Max. 9.13 *ext.* 1. **comprenderet:** of gauging number, Virg. *G.* 2.104, Ov. *A.A.* 2.447, 3.151, *Tr.* 5.11.19; of size, capacity etc., Gell. *N.A.* 1.1.3, Fron. *Aq.* 67.9, 73.6, but a possible play on the verb ('enclose', 'surround'; *OLD* 7a) also suggests the way Xerxes estimated the total number (Herod. 7.60.2–3). **Persarum rex:** as often, e.g. *Ir.* 3.20.1, *N.Q.* 5.18.10. S. rarely names Xerxes directly (*Ir.* 3.16.4, *Ben.* 6.31.1, 11). **insolentissimus:** position and degree (superlative only here in S.) recall the 'immoderate' (*OLD* 3) scale of the expedition (*Ben.* 6.31.3, *N.Q.* 5.18.10) and the familiar moral that *nihil tam magnum est quod perire non possit, cui nascitur in perniciem ... ex ipsa magnitudine sua causa* (*Ben.* 6.31.10). The adj. further suggests arrogance (*OLD* 4; twice of Xerxes in V. Max. 9.5 *ext.* 2) and overbearing hybris; *C.S.* 11.1, *Ir.* 2.21.3, *V.B.* 10.2, *Ep.* 83.20 *crescit insolenti superbia*, 87.35 with N–H on Hor. *C.* 2.3.3. **lacrimas profudit:** so exposing the hollowness of his quasi-divine

pretensions, since 'gods cannot weep' (Feeney (1991) 203, quoting Ov. *M.*
2.621–2). The phrase also suggests pity for doomed youth at *Med.* 542–3.
quod . . . esset: Herod. 7.46.2; S. departs from his probable source text
before Artabanus answers unhelpfully (at least from the Senecan/Stoic
perspective) that, despite its brevity, life's ordinary afflictions make it seem
too long, death desirable (7.46.3–4).   **iuuentute:** i.e. men of military
age (*OLD* 1b.)   **superfuturus esset:** subjunctive in partial *oratio obliqua* (G–L §508.3).   **at:** emphatic, marking the turning-point (even the
tragic περιπέτεια in Xerxes' drama.   **admoturus:** 8.2n. on *admotum
est*; the first of three fut. pples. which suggest that Xerxes' actions are inevitable, even destined (Westman (1961) 73–4).   **perditurusque:** of
losing troops under one's command, *OLD* 3b; but for the hint of waste-
ful destruction, 1a.   **alios . . . alios . . . alios . . . alios:** the anaphoric
sequence breaks down the grand total Xerxes was a moment ago count-
ing up.   **alios in mari . . . proelio:** most obviously at Thermopylae
and Salamis in 480, in 479 at Plataea. The combination *in mari . . . in terra*,
only here in S. and rare elsewhere (K–S 1 348), specifies 'on' (as opposed
to *terra marique* 'by') land and sea.   **alios proelio, alios fuga:** ironic
given the Persians' earlier presumption (*Ben.* 6.31.1 *alius aiebat non laturos*
[sc. *Graecos*] *nuntium belli et ad primam aduentus famam terga uersuros*).   **fuga**
perhaps extends to desertion (*OLD* 3a); of Persian ships, Herod. 8.8.1, 11.3,
82.1, 87.4.   **consumpturus** 'set to destroy' all his men (*OLD* 1b), fulfilling the worse connotation of *perditurus*.   **quibus . . . timebat** 'for
whom he was afraid a century hence'; i.e. he was afraid they would be
dead a hundred years later, but in fact they would die *intra exiguum tempus*.
For the construction, *OLD timeo* 2b with Skutsch on Enn. *Ann.* 262 *metuo
legionibus labem*.

17.3 Not only are their pleasures subject to sudden loss (17.1) but so
are their joys.   **quid quod:** *Ot.* 1.1n.   **quoque** 'even' (*OLD* 4a).
trepida: 17.1n.   **solidis:** i.e. not generated from within the self as
in the case of the *sapiens*; 5.3n., *Ep.* 23.5, 27.3 *nullum . . .* [sc. *bonum*] *est
nisi quod animus ex se sibi inuenit*, 98.1.   **innituntur** 'rest on', with
dat. (*C.S.* 8.3 *rationi innixus*); fig. usage from Livy (*TLL* VII 1.1699.29–58).
eadem . . . turbantur 'they are disrupted as frivolously as they are produced'; for *uanitate* (lit. 'emptiness', here set against *solidis causis*), 13.3,
OLD 1a.   **qualia . . . sincera sint?:** just how wretched are their
times of admitted misery, if even in happier times their joys are impure?
ipsorum confessione: Ciceronian; *TLL* IV 189.14–18 (+ subj. gen.).

misera: with *tempora.*   **cum:** causal (*Ot.* 7.3n.).   **haec:** sc. *gaudia* (Duff, Basore), not *tempora* (Dahlmann (1949), Traina); more aptly described as *sincera, gaudia* better anticipates *se . . . efferunt* (nn. below).   **quoque:** as above.   **quibus . . . efferunt:** ironic; the heights of 'sublime' joy to which the *occupati* rise are illusory. Only the *sapiens* can be transported so far *super hominem* (*C.S.* 6.3, *Ep.* 66.31, 111.3–4) and attain true joy (*Ep.* 59.2, 17–18).   **se attollunt:** of persons, first and often in S. (*TLL* II 1153.26–33).   **se . . . efferunt:** with joy, *C.S.* 9.3 *gaudio elatus* [sc. *sapiens*]; but here the verb shares the negative connotation (from a Stoic perspective) of *elatio* at e.g. Cic. *Fin.* 3.35 ἡδονήν . . . *quasi gestientis animi elationem uolup-tariam, Tusc.* 4.13 (Inwood (1985) 174–5 for fuller discussion).   **sincera** 'pure', as if 'unalloyed'; n. above on *solidis, Prou.* 6.4 *solida et sincera felicitas.*

17.4 The never-ending price to be paid by the *occupati* who rely on fortune for the 'joys' and *bona* of their superficial lives; cf. *C.S.* 5.7 *omnium . . . extrinsecus affluentium lubrica et incerta possessio est.*   **bona:** not of the philosophical kind (15.3n.).   **nec . . . creditur:** the play on related words (*minus bene / optimae*; cf. *pessimus* and *optimus* juxtaposed at *Tr.* 16.1, *Ben.* 2.24.1, 31.4) contributes to the aphoristic tone; hence the suggestive coinci-dence between *fortunae creditur* and Pub. *Sent.* v12 Meyer (16.2n. on *inuocant*). For S.'s own apparent cautiousness, *Helu.* 5.4 *numquam ego fortunae credidi, etiam cum uideretur pacem agere.*   **felicitate . . . felicitatem:** to be distin-guished from the true *felicitas* of the *sapiens* (15.2n.). The polyptoton (*Prou.* 6.5 *non egere felicitate felicitas uestra est*) conveys the ingrained dependence; for the idea, *Pol.* 9.5 *ipsa . . . magnae felicitatis tutela sollicita est, Ep.* 98.1.   **pro** 'instead of'.   **successere** 'have turned out well' (*OLD* 7a, adding *Ben.* 6.27.5).   **uota:** prayers seek by divine gift what the *sapiens* derives from within; *Ep.* 31.5 *quid uotis opus est? fac te ipse felicem,* 72.7.   **fortuito** 'under fortune's influence'.   **obuenit:** esp. of chance events, as at *Ben.* 4.1.3, *Ep.* 72.8, 90.2 (*OLD* 3).   **instabile:** of fortune, prosperity etc., surprisingly rare (*OLD* 4); conspicuous in dramatic and declamatory contexts (Pac. *Trag.* 369 Ribbeck *insanam* [sc. *fortunam*] . . . *esse aiunt, quia atrox incerta instabilisque sit,* Sen. *Contr.* 1.1.3 *omnis instabilis et incerta felicitas est*), and so perhaps also here with special colour.   **et quo . . . in occasum:** as often, conventional wisdom reinforces S.'s case; for the idea, intimately connected with revolv-ing *fortuna* (N–H on Hor. *C.* 1.34.12) and long associated with diatribe and Roman declamation (Fantham (1982) 249 on *Tro.* 253), e.g. *Tr.* 10.5, *Pol.* 15.1, *Ben.* 6.30.6, *Ep.* 8.4 and esp. *Ag.* 100–1 *quicquid in altum | Fortuna tulit, ruitura leuat* with Tarrant (1976) 183 (e).   **quo:** correlative with ellipsis; 15.3n.

on *maiora . . . quo . . . diuiseris.*   **surrexerit:** fut. perf., the subj. to be inferred from *omne . . . obuenit* above.   **opportunius** 'more susceptible to';
with *in* + acc. only here in S. (with *ad, Cl.* 1.8.6, *Ir.* 2.19.1) and suggesting
the rapidity of the fall (cf. Liv. 10.42.1 *praeceps in occasum sol erat*).   **porro**
introduces the minor premiss in a syllogism, as at *Ep.* 66.12 . . . *bonum omne
diuinum est. nullum porro inter diuina discrimen est; ergo nec inter bona.*   **casura**
'what is subject to imminent collapse'; the fut. pple turns the likely into the
inevitable. For the nuance and the substantival use cf. *Ep.* 74.11 *abitura*, cited
with *casura* by Westman (1961) 185.   **miserrimam . . . uitam esse:**
having set out in 10.1 to prove *breuissimam esse occupatorum uitam*, S. now draws
the tragic inference.   **qui . . . possideant:** for the idea, *Pol.* 9.5 *omnia
ista bona quae nos speciosa sed fallaci uoluptate delectant . . . cum labore possidentur*,
taken up by Juv. 14.303–4 (with Mayor II 344).   **magno . . . maiore:** in
combination, *Tr.* 4.4.   **parant . . . possideant:** for this class of wordplay, Summers lxxxiv 3.   **quod . . . possideant:** relative clause of tendency; G–L §631.

   17.5 Anxiety never ends because ambition always seeks new advancement (cf. *Ep.* 115.17).   **assequuntur** 'acquire'; in combination with
uolunt, Ciceronian (*TLL* II 860.81–3).   **anxii:** so also 17.1 *trepidae* (cf.
17.3), *inquietae* and *sollicita* (cf. 17.4).   **nulla . . . ratio est:** like the *occupati*
at e.g. 3.4–5, 6.4 and 8.4–5, they lack awareness of time's value; for the
homespun ideal, *Her. F.* 175–7 *nouit paucos secura quies,* | *qui uelocis memores
aeui* | *tempora numquam reditura tenent* with Fitch (1987) 176 on the Epicurean
overtones of 175.   **numquam amplius:** in combination, *OLD amplius* 5b, adding *Helu.* 17.5; with the fut. pple, emphatically portraying
time's irretrievability (Westman (1961) 148).   **ratio** 'consideration of'
(*OLD* 8a).   **nouae . . . substituuntur:** *Ep.* 72.2 *numquam . . . non succe-
dent occupationes nouae: serimus illas, itaque ex una exeunt plures.*   **ueteribus:**
dat. (*OLD substituo* 4).   **spes . . . ambitio:** the chiasmus matches up the
two deleterious *affectus.* The *sapiens*, unconcerned with the future (*V.B.* 26.3,
Ben. 7.2.4), never hopes (*C.S.* 9.2, *V.B.* 15.5; 9.1 n. on *cogitationes . . . ordinant*);
for *ambitio*, 2.1 n., and for its self-reproduction, *Ep.* 115.17.   **excitat:** of
arousing the passions / being aroused, e.g. *Cl.* 1.19.7, *C.S.* 9.3, *Ep.* 95.15.
miseriarum . . . mutatur: possibly influenced by Epicurean wording
given *Ep.* 17.11 *multis parasse diuitias non finis miseriarum fuit sed mutatio* (fr.
479 Us.).   **materia** 'source', 'cause' (*OLD* 8a); so *Ir.* 3.30.2, *Tr.* 8.1
aerumnarum materiam, 17.1 *sollicitudinum.*   **nostri . . . distinetur:** asyndeton hastens the breathless movement from one (pre)occupation to the

next. For the draining effects of busy professional life, 2.4, 7.6–8; but here
the Roman career-structure (for the *cursus honorum*, *OCD*[3] 415) conveniently
lends itself to S.'s argument.   **nostri nos:** the shift to the first person is
dramatically timed, confronting each reader (esp. Paulinus) with complicity
in the general fault.   **honores** 'public office' (*OLD* 5a).   **torserunt:**
cf. 2.1 *torquet*; pure perf. denoting action that is 'over and gone' (G–L §236.1),
i.e. '*non iam torquent*' (Duff 159). S.'s own alliterative *contortio litterarum* (*nostri nos
honores* . . .) supports the point.   **alieni:** sc. *honores*.   **auferunt:** 7.7n.
laborare: with the added suggestion of attendant anxiety/distress
(*OLD* 4, 7) and even of 'being in (electoral) difficulties' (*Ep.* 118.2
quis candidatus laboret).   **desîmus:** 4.2n.   **suffragatores:** 7.7n. on
quot . . . candidatus?   **accusandi . . . molestiam:** Ciceronian (*Mur.* 46
ego expertus . . . accusandi molestiam); that prosecution was less glamorous than
defence (6.1n. on *iudicibus . . . commendare*) may have contributed to the nui-
sance.   **iudicandi:** cases were typically heard by a single judge (*iudex
unus*), not necessarily a professional lawyer but perhaps a distinguished juror,
or orator such as Pliny (*Ep.* 6.2.7); Crook (1967) 78–83.   **desît:** 4.2n.
quaesitor: a magistrate presiding over a *quaestio*, or a commission set up to
investigate a particular case; the first of several 'standing courts' (*quaestiones
perpetuae*) was introduced by the *lex Calpurnia* of 149 BC, the chairman usually
taken from among the praetors (Crook (1967) 69 with Tarrant (1976) 171
on *Ag.* 24).   **alienorum . . . consenuit:** a *procurator omnium bonorum* was
employed by the wealthy as a general manager of their property (Berger
654). If working for pay (*mercennarius*) he was presumably inferior in status, if
unpaid either a freedman owing services or an equal; but already in Cicero's
time the social distinctions were fluid (Crook (1967) 238–9).   **consenuit**
'has spent all his working life' (*OLD* 2).   **distinetur** (Gruter, *dest-* MSS)
'is diverted' from looking after other people's property to looking after
his own (*TLL* v 1.1523.74–5), the diversion well staged in the opposition of
alienorum and *suis*. *det-* Reynolds after Erasmus, but the relatively rare *dist-* is
more likely to have received a simplifying gloss; the verb's frequent use with
occupationibus/negotiis further supports the reading (e.g. Cic. *Att.* 2.23.1 *quanta
occupatione distinear*, *Fam.* 12.30.2, Vitr. 5 *praef.* 3, Plin. *Ep.* 6.18.1).

17.6 Three Republican *exempla* (cf. 4.2–6.2), the number again following
rhetorical convention (Mayer (1991) 155–6). While the earlier trio reaches a
climax in Drusus' suicide (6.2), this one is not chronological and culminates
in an extended treatment of P. Cornelius Scipio Africanus after brief men-
tion of Gaius Marius and L. Quintius Cincinnatus. Incapable of simply

retiring, they are continually distracted by new *occupationes* or fresh *ambitio*. As before (and often) S. emphasizes and oversimplifies his point more than the fuller historical picture bears out. Little or no allowance is therefore made for the possibility that Marius became consul (107 and six times thereafter) and Cincinnatus dictator for the second time (439) not to fulfil an otherwise empty life but from a combination of patriotic service and the desire to excel, or that Scipio may have gone into self-imposed exile out of more than restless *ambitio* of an exhibitionist kind. Moreover, to evaluate on exactly the same moral terms a patrician of the mid-fifth century, a *nobilis* of the late third and an *eques* of the late second is to de-contextualize ethical judgements to an extent which renders them almost meaningless. But S.'s aim is not a 'truer' perspective on the past but effective moral exhortation in the present. As at 4.2–6.2, the *exempla* here have significant implications for Paulinus (4.1 intro.): by retiring from his own high position (cf. 18.1) he can impress by demonstrating that, unlike such illustrious figures as Marius, Quintius and Scipio, he is no slave to self-perpetuating *occupatio/ambitio*.

Marium . . . exercet: after serving under Q. Metellus (cos. 109) against Jugurtha, Marius won election (despite Metellus) as consul for 107 with popular and equestrian support; assigned Africa as his province by a plebiscite, he took over Metellus' command (*CAH²* IX 89–91); after Jugurtha's defeat he was elected again in 104 and then four more times down to 100 (again in 86). The full impact of S.'s allusion lies in Marius' multiple consulships, and not just in his transition from soldier to consul, as an illustration of how (17.5) *nouae occupationes ueteribus substituuntur*. S.'s own 'senatorial prejudice' (Alexander (1947) 41) may explain his consistent hostility to a *nouus homo* rising to consul from modest origins (*Ir.* 2.2.3, *Ben.* 5.16.2, *Ep.* 94.66; Tac. *Hist.* 2.38.1 *e plebe infima*).   **caliga:** lit. 'soldier's boot', 'military service' by metonymy (first in S.); Erasmus' conjecture for *caligo* in the MSS, supported by *Ben.* 5.16.2 *C. Marius ad consulatus a caliga perductus*, where (as here) *caliga* as 'common boot' may contain a slur at Marius' origins (Kühnen (1962) 57–8).   **dimisit** 'has discharged'; of military service, *OLD* 2a. **exercet** 'keeps him busy'.   **Quintius . . . reuocabitur:** acc. to tradition L. Quintius Cincinnatus was appointed dictator in 458 BC (defeating the Aequi in fifteen days and then laying down his office) and again in 439 (against the seditious Sp. Maelius); Powell (1988) 219 on Cic. *Sen.* 56. The legend that he was called from the plough is usually linked with his first dictatorship; but by following the tradition which ties the legend to the second dictatorship, and by strategically overlooking the distance between

458 and 439, S. suggests that Cincinnatus was restless after stepping down
from his first dictatorship and quickly sought new office to replace the
old.   **properat:** by writing in the present and then 'predicting' the future in *reuocabitur*, S. creates the illusion that Cincinnatus' hasty withdrawal
from office anticipates a foreseeable result. The effect is taken further in
the case of Scipio below (n. on *ibit*).   **peruadere** 'get through', with
difficulties implied; Sall. *Rep.* 1.6.3 *capesse... rem publicam et omnia aspera, uti
soles, peruade.*   **ibit ... ambitio:** P. Cornelius Scipio Africanus, b. 236
BC, was appointed at 26 to the command against the Carthaginians in
Spain, receiving the *cognomen* Africanus after defeating Hannibal at Zama
(202). As legate serving under his brother, L. Cornelius Scipio Asiagenes,
he negotiated peace-terms after Antiochus III's defeat at Magnesia in 189.
But resentment at his successes and prestige may have fuelled the charges
of financial dishonesty which resulted in the so called 'trials of the Scipios'
in the 180s (*CAH²* VIII 179–80). Embittered, Scipio withdrew to Liternum
(on the coast of Campania) in 184, where he died in the next year. S.
generally admires him (*Ir.* 1.11.6, *Tr.* 17.4, *Ben.* 3.33.1–3, 5.17.2 and esp.
Ep. 86.1–5), but here the picture is more mixed: for all his achievements
(*uictor... sponsor*), not least his modesty in resisting the ultimate comparison
(but see n. on *ni... reponetur*), he is driven by a self-perpetuating ambition
(cf. 17.5 *ambitionem ambitio* [sc. *excitat*]) which works against him.   **ibit:**
the effect of casting Scipio's *exemplum* in the future is to suggest that his pre-
cocious *ambitio* follows an all too predictable course (n. above on *properat*).
nondum ... rei: ominously like Livius Drusus (6.2 *quo non erumperet tam
immatura ambitio?*).   **uictor ... uictor:** the first victory (Zama) military,
the second (Magnesia) diplomatic, as illness kept him out of the battle
(Liv. 37.37.6–8).   **sui:** i.e. *in his own case* he conferred distinction on the
office of consul (*OLD decus¹* 3) in 205 and 194, then acting as 'surety' for his
brother's consulship (*OLD sponsor* 1b) when he accompanied L. Cornelius
Scipio Asiagenes to the East against Antiochus III.   **ni ... reponetur**
'but for his own objections, he [i.e. his statue] will be placed in the company
of Jupiter' in the Capitoline temple; Liv. 38.56.12 *prohibuisse* [sc. *Scipionem*]
statuas sibi in comitio, in rostris, in curia, in Capitolio, in cella Iouis poni [sc. *ait
Ti. Gracchus* in 187, contrasting Scipio's arrogance with his earlier mod-
esty], V. Max. 4.1.6. On Scipio's 'considerable skill in neither affirming
nor denying' stories that he was of divine origin, Walbank (1967), esp.
54–6 with *CAH²* VIII 441.   **ni:** very rare in Senecan prose (*C.S.* 18.3,
N.Q. 3.27.13).   **per ipsum mora sit:** *Ot.* 6.3n.; mere delay, given the

placing of Scipio's image *in cella Iouis* after his death (V. Max. 8.15.1, App. *Hisp.* 23).   **ciuiles ... seditiones:** in the 'trials of the Scipios' (Liv. 38.50–3; n. above on *ibit ... ambitio*); the adj., emphatic by position, in contrast with the foreign campaigns.   **seruatorem:** given *cum Ioue* above and *dis aequos honores* below, both this and *uictor* possibly play on Jupiter's titles. For *Seruator, CIL* IX 4852, Germ. *Arat.* 410; *Victor,* Ov. *Fast.* 4.621–2, *OLD* 4.   **post ... ambitio:** turning down the honour of a statue with exemplary *modestia* and *temperantia* (cf. Liv. 38.56.11), Scipio marginalizes himself through the recurring cycle of *ambitio* in old(er) age (he died in his early fifties).   **dis:** i.e. *deorum honoribus*; for the elliptical comparison (*comparatio compendiaria*), *C.S.* 6.8, Juv. 4.71 with Courtney.   **contumacis** 'proud', 'stubborn', pejorative (*OLD* 1); his exile is hardly a retreat into Stoic *otium* (Grimal 68). But since Scipio left for Liternum rather than answer the charges brought against him in 184, the further implication is that he was 'wilfully disobedient to judicial orders' (*OLD* 2; Berger 415 *contumacia*).   **ambitio:** more 'show' (*OLD* 6) than the zeal for advancement and glory which drove him in youth.   **numquam ... optabitur:** in advance of S.'s appeal to Paulinus to retire (18.1), the conclusion not just to 17 but to the general examination of *occupatio* from 10.2 onwards.   **felices** 'resulting from prosperity'.   **trudetur** 'will be driven on' in a succession of (*OLD per* 8b) *occupationes* (cf. 17.5 *nouae ... substituuntur*); for the suggestion of 'a mechanical sequence', N–H on Hor. *C.* 2.18.15 *truditur dies die.*   **otium ... agetur:** before S., mostly poetic (*TLL* 1 1384.32–6). **optabitur:** 4.6.

18 The call to withdraw

Paulinus finally urged to withdraw to still greater things (18.2 *maiora*) in philosophical retirement. Even if unrealistic in one way (how many people, ancient or modern, are in a position simply to abandon their practical responsibilities?), S.'s exhortation hits home by disconcerting settled attitudes to life: there *is* another way. Whether or not Paulinus heeded S.'s recommendation, its wider relevance lies in the radical self-examination it provokes in *any* reader by challenging our accepted *status quo* with the claims of 'the view from above' (general intro. pp. 24–5).

18.1 Excerpe ... te uulgo: the goal is retreat into a self-sufficient inner life (*Ot.* 1.1), reinforced here as the last word in the sentence mirrors

and strengthens the first.   **Excerpe ... te:** of detachment, with dat., *Ep*. 5.2 *nos hominum consuetudini ... excerpere*, *Tr*. 13.3.   **itaque:** 2.5n. on *non ... quod*.   **in ... portum ... recede:** after a lively passage through descriptions of the storm-tossed lives of the *occupati*, Paulinus is urged into port with reassuringly familiar (and notably Ciceronian) imagery, here perhaps topically loaded given his origins at Arles, a city of navigational importance on the Rhone (Grimal 2, D'Escurac (1976) 320), and given his responsibility as *praefectus annonae* for the importation of grain by sea. The Graeco-Roman tradition of the λιμήν/ὅρμος and *portus* as a haven of *otium* (e.g. Cic. *Brut*. 8), solitude (*De orat*. 1.255), death (*Sen*. 71), exile (*Caec*. 100) etc. is well surveyed by Bonner (1941); for application by S. to the inner life, *Tr*. 5.5, *Ep*. 14.15, 72.10, 104.22, all cited with wider coverage of the motif by Armisen-Marchetti (1989) 153–4, 271.
non ... spatio 'excessively for the time you have lived', lit. 'not in proportion to ...' (*OLD pro* 12a).   **iactatus:** like Cicero (5.1; cf. 7.10).
recede: of (philosophical) retirement, *Tr*. 3.2, 17.3, *Ep*. 7.8, 25.7, 103.4; *OLD* 7a.   **tempestates ... priuatas:** unknown, but Grimal 68–9 suspects an allusion to possible tribulations as a ship-owner (*nauicularius*) at Arles.   **partim ... partim:** 5.1n.   **in te conuerteris** 'have brought upon yourself' (with damaging effect; *TLL* IV 860.45–9).   **satis iam:** with emphasis on *satis* (cf. *Marc*. 22.6 *iam satis*, *Thy*. 899); found esp. in comedy, rare in prose (mostly in Livy; *TLL* VII 1.117.24–34).
per ... documenta exhibita uirtus est: in accordance with *Prou*. 4.12 *numquam uirtutis molle documentum est*. Paulinus' is not Stoic *uirtus* (= *recta ratio*, *Ep*. 66.32; cf. 71.32, 76.10, 15–16), but has more in common with the secular use at e.g. Cic. *Rep*. 1.33.2, where 'public service demonstrates the possession of *uirtus* and is a duty of the person who possesses it' (Zetzel (1995) 124).
inquieta 'unceasing'.   **exhibita ... est:** of virtue 'displayed', *Prou*. 4.2, *Helu*. 19.7.   **experire ... tibi:** i.e. become a κοσμοπολίτης (*SVF* III 82.30), having earned the privilege portrayed at *Ot*. 2.2 *ut possit hoc* [sc. retirement to a life of philosophical contemplation] *aliquis emeritis iam stipendiis, profligatae aetatis, iure optimo facere ...*   **faciat** 'achieve' (*OLD* 11a).
melior: of a time of life, *OLD* 10b; a philosophical perspective would judge differently.   **est:** Madvig's substitute (II 400) for *sit* in the MSS better suggests the finality of the break with years of service: **aliquid ... tibi:** possible even in public life, unless (*Ot*. 6.1) *semper inquietus sis nec tibi umquam sumas ullum tempus quo ab humanis ad diuina respicias*; but for the freedom into which S. means to release Paulinus here, *Ep*. 73.10 *pingue otium et* <u>*arbitrium*</u>

sui temporis et imperturbata publicis occupationibus quies.   **aliquid . . . tui:** i.e.
after Paulinus' 'prime of life' in office; this despite S.'s biting portrayal (3.5)
of the *occupatus* who foolishly defers until retirement his plans for philosophical study (already a nudge to Paulinus).   **sume** 'take possession
of' (with dat., *OLD* 5a) in order to 'spend' (9b) on yourself.   **etiam** 'as
well'.

18.2 Paulinus is steered towards the 'active' philosophical life *in otio*,
for which *Ep.* 55.4 *multum . . . interest utrum uita tua otiosa sit an ignaua*, 82.2–3.
For the traditional Roman distinction between 'respectable' and 'waste-
ful' *otium*, Sall. *Cat.* 4.1, Cic. *Brut.* 8 *in portum confugere . . . non inertiae neque
desidiae, sed oti moderati atque honesti* with Zetzel (1995) 96–7 on Cic. *Rep.*
1.1.2. There is no implied suggestion of an attack on Epicureanism here,
which can also interpret *otium* positively; *Ot.* 7.2–3 with André (1966) 539–
40 and Grilli (1953) 65.   **segnem aut inertem:** a complementary
and strongly pejorative pairing; Tib. 1.1.58 and esp. Cic. *Fin.* 1.5 *inertissimae
segnitiae*, 5.56.   **turbae:** dat. with *caris*.   **indolis uiuidae** 'lively energy'; the full force of the adj. lies in the contrast between Paulinus and
the slothful *occupati*, already dead in life (*Tr.* 5.5 *ultimum malorum est e uiuorum
numero exire antequam moriaris, Ep.* 60.4, 77.18).   **mergas** 'drown', supple-
menting the sea-imagery in 18.1; in (abl.) sleep, pleasures etc., Livian (*TLL*
VIII 834.64–79).   **istud:** emphatic, contemptuous in tone (*OLD* 5b).
acquiescere 'to find peace of mind'; in this absolute form, Ciceronian
(*TLL* I 423.38–45).   **maiora** [sc. *opera*] 'more important' (*OLD* 5) because, from a cosmopolitan perspective, ultimately of greater benefit to
mankind (cf. *Ot.* 3.5 *hoc nempe ab homine exigitur, ut prosit hominibus . . .*); Vottero
324 on fr. 79 *faciet . . . sapiens . . . etiam quae non probabit, ut . . . ad maiora transitum
inueniat*.   **strenue:** the adv. only here in S., the adj. at *Ep.* 9.19, 22.7,
77.6, *Ben.* 5.24.2, in each case commending a Stoic virtue (= σπουδαῖος,
SVF III 50.1–2) in familiar (*OLD* 1b) combination with *fortis*; hence com-
plimentary here.   **quae . . . agites:** final relative clause (G–L §630);
quae with *maiora*.   **repositus** 'in seclusion'.   **agites** 'busy yourself
about' (*OLD* 11a) presses the point that *ne contemplatio quidem sine actione est*
(*Ot.* 5.8).

18.3–4 In terms of the 'two commonwealth' theory of *Ot.* 4.1–2,
Paulinus admirably serves the localized *res publica* in managing the imperial
accounts (*orbis terrarum rationes*). But S. steers him towards *ratio* of a more
introspective kind (*uitae suae*), and hence to contemplation of the greater
Stoic 'commonwealth' (cf. 19.1).

18.3 quidem 'it is true' (*OLD* 4), making a concession in advance of *sed tamen* below; 12.8n.   **orbis ... rationes:** Rickman (1980) 218–20 and esp. 81–2: 'they [sc. *praefecti annonae*] were experts in the keeping of accounts and that must have been their primary personal duty ... When it is realized that even in the case of corn the sources of supply could range from taxes in imperial or senatorial provinces, produce and rents of imperial possessions, to private purchases by the state or by individuals, it is obvious that the system of accounts for which the prefect was responsible must have been both complicated and sophisticated. At his desk in Rome the prefect was the one man who was supposed to have a complete picture in his files of what was going on around the Mediterranean [cf. *orbis terrarum*].'
tam abstinenter ... publicas: an unremitting dependability is conveyed in the triple anaphoric structure; for the effect cf. *Helu.* 14.3 *tu patrimonia nostra sic administrasti ut tamquam in tuis laborares, tamquam alienis abstineres.*   **abstinenter** 'scrupulously', 'with self-restraint' (ἐγκρατῶς), in Chrysippean terms an important indicator of virtuous action (κατόρθωμα); Plut. *Mor.* 1041a = *SVF* III 73.15–17.   **quam alienas** 'as you would a stranger's'.   **diligenter:** of careful management, *OLD diligens* 3, *diligentia* 2.   **religiose** 'conscientiously' (*OLD* 3a).   **publicas:** accounts of a more general kind (here perhaps of the *aerarium Saturni* or public treasury) than those relating specifically to the *annona*; with *rationes*, Caes. *B.C.* 2.20.8, *Gal.* 6.14.3.   **consequeris:** pres.; Paulinus has already won affection.   **odium ... difficile est:** so 18.5 *cogita ... esuriens*; for popular protests against shortages of grain and rising prices under the early emperors, Garnsey (1988) 218–24 (the first known *praefectus annonae*, C. Turannius, was appointed between AD 8 and 14; 20.3n.).   **odium:** in the pass. sense (*OLD* 3a).   **mihi crede, satius est:** colloquial; 7.5n., 13.7n.   **uitae suae rationem** 'the balance sheet of one's life' (Hadas 71), an image (cf. *Ep.* 1.4 *ratio ... impensae*, of time) here developed out of *rationes* above; but for *ratio uiuendi* as a (Stoic) science in its own right, *Ot.* 2.1n. and Vottero 331 on fr. 82 *philosophia ... nihil aliud est quam recta ratio uiuendi uel honeste uiuendi scientia uel ars rectae uitae agendae* (also 6.4n. on *ratio*).

18.4 istum 'that of yours', emphatic.   **uigorem:** cf. 18.2 *indolis uiuidae.*   **capacissimum** 'most qualified' for high office, esp. by intellect (Tac. *Ann.* 1.11.1 *solam ... Augusti mentem tantae molis capacem*, with other examples at *OLD* 3b) but here also 'most capable' of the important business (cf. 18.2 *maiora* [sc. *opera*]) of philosophy.   **ministerio:** even in high equestrian office (D'Escurac (1976) 47) Paulinus remains a subordinate

functionary (*OLD* 2). But for distinctions of social rank as unrelated to 'true'
freedom, *Ep.* 44.6, 80.4–6, *SVF* III 86.27–88.30 with Inwood (1985) 109–10.
honorifico: unphilosophical, as the *sapiens* sets no store by titles, honours
etc. (*C.S.* 13.2 *honores . . . nihilo aestimat*, *Ep.* 76.32, 81.28, 94.8).   **quidem
sed:** 12.8n.   **beatam uitam:** attainable only through philosophy; *V.B.*
3.3–4, *Ep.* 16.1, 92.3–4, 27.   **id egisse te . . . ut** 'that you did not make
it your aim . . . that'; for the construction, 7.4 (with *hoc*), *Pol.* 2.6, *Helu.* 5.1, *Ep.*
113.29 (*OLD ago* 27a).   **cultu** 'training in' (+ gen., *Ot.* 6.2); instrumental abl.   **studiorum liberalium:** 7.3n. Paulinus' commitment to, and
consequent dependence on, his *ministerium* are unworthy of his early education; *Ep.* 88.2 *quare liberalia studia dicta sint uides: quia homine libero digna sunt.
ceterum unum studium uere liberale est quod liberum facit, hoc est sapientiae . . .* (also
Summers 220 on *Ep.* 51.9).   **multa milia:** sc. *modiorum* ('measures');
a different harvest from that promised by Paulinus' early training (*cultu*).
promiseras 'had shown promise of', 'caused expectation of'; in prose,
a post-Augustan usage (*OLD* 7a).   **et frugalitatis . . . et . . . operae**
'men of both scrupulous good character and diligent service' (gen. of quality; G–L §365), their reliability discreetly underlined by the homoeoteleuton
in *-ae*. The hint of condescension is more marked if, as Duff 162 suggests,
S. commends these honest administrators as *frugi*, 'an epithet often applied to freedmen and slaves . . . , though not confined to them' (Shackleton
Bailey III 299 on Cic. *Att.* 7.4.1).   **tanto:** equivalent to *multo* (cf. 1.2).
aptiora: here with dat. (*Ir.* 2.15.2, *Ep.* 51.11, *Ben.* 3.28.1) for variation on
ad + acc. above and to avoid a confusing run of the same neut. plur. endings.   **portandis:** Madvig II 401. *exp-* MSS, but despite *exporto* used
of trade (incl. *frumentum*; *TLL* v 2.1769.55–73), *oneribus* denotes by analogy
the administrative burdens (cf. *sarcina* below) to be shouldered (*portari*) by
solidly competent officials (*tarda iumenta*); it does not refer to the actual loads
of grain presupposed by *exp-*.   **iumenta:** of horses/mules as opposed
to better horses, *TLL* VII 2.646.35–40.   **nobiles** 'well bred'; of animals,
OLD 5e, adding (also for the human analogy) *Cl.* 1.24.2. For the implied
compliment to Paulinus' own superior character, *Ep.* 95.67 *putas utile dari
tibi argumenta per quae intellegas nobilem equum, ne fallaris empturus . . . ? quanto hoc
utilius est excellentis animi notas nosse . . .*   **generosam:** i.e. resulting from
good breeding; of horses, *Cl.* 1.24.2. Here, by implication, also of Paulinus
(*OLD* 2b, adding e.g. *Ep.* 39.2, 44.5, 76.30).   **sarcina:** for Paulinus' fig.
burden cf. *Pol.* 3.2, *Ep.* 65.16 *graui sarcina pressus* [sc. *animus*, weighed down by
bodily imprisonment], *Ben.* 2.35.3, 6.35.2 (Armisen-Marchetti (1989) 83).

18.5–6 The public servant suffers the greatest stress when vulnerable to simultaneous attack from above (here Caligula) *and* below (*populus esuriens*). As at 4.2–6.2, 17.2 and 6, S. manipulates historical fact and chronology to cast Caligula in a particular light (18.5n. on *dum . . . ludit*); for S.'s consistently hostile treatment of Caligula, Griffin (1976) 213–15.

18.5 ad tantam . . . obicere 'to subject yourself to such a heavy responsibility' (*OLD moles* 6), *te* positioned between *tantam* and *molem* (cf. *tibi* below) to illustrate the pressure on Paulinus from all sides; *molem* also spells danger (*OLD* 7a), and for the verb used of exposure to risk, *OLD* 6a. **cum uentre . . . negotium est:** a thankless task, as hunger inflames the passions (*Ir.* 3.9.4) of the 'irrational'; as insistent as the appetite driving them (*Ep.* 21.11 *uenter praecepta non audit: poscit, appellat*), they are animal-like in their *uentri oboedientia* (Sall. *Cat.* 1.1, adapted by S. at *Ep.* 60.4). **cum . . . tibi . . . negotium est** 'you have to deal with', a vulgar idiom to match the subject, first in Cicero's letters (*OLD negotium* 10a); the further implication is 'have trouble with' (Krebs–Schmalz II 140; *Ep.* 21.1 with Summers 186).   **nec rationem . . . flectitur:** each unit of the tricolon stiffens the single-minded resolve of the hungry, impervious to reason as their passions rise (cf. *Ep.* 85.8 *quantuscumque est* [sc. *affectus*], *parere nescit, consilium non accipit*); 'any entreaty' (*prece*) marks a last desperate measure, as they are no more responsive to appeals for composure (*OLD aequitas* 2) than for philosophical reflection on their condition. So, famously, Cato the Censor: 'it is difficult, citizens, to argue with the belly as it has no ears' (Plut. *Cato mai.* 8.1).   **patitur** 'submit to', 'listen to'.   **modo modo** 'only recently'. Post-Augustan (*OLD* 5a, adding *Helu.* 2.5) and colloquial (Hofmann 60, 190); too vague to be of much help in dating the treatise.   **intra . . . perît** 'within those few days after Gaius Caesar died' (assassinated 22 or 24 January 41); for the abl. idiom, *quibus* here arguably evolving by attraction from *a* (*OLD* 5a) *die quo* (Duff 162), K–S I 356 with parallels from Cicero and Caesar.   **perît:** syncopated perf. (cf. 4.2 *desît*).   **si quis . . . est:** possibly barbed, qualifying Caligula's pretensions to divinity in life (for which Barrett (1989) 140–53).   **hoc grauissime ferens, quod uidebat:** if *gratissime* is read with the MSS, Caligula was delighted to see that Rome faced starvation; but Erasmus' *grauissime*, with *ferens* a much more familiar idiom (*OLD grauiter* 6), adds the still more malicious twist of resentment that the survivors of his reign have resources to last them for *as many as* eight days. Castiglioni's *uidebat* is one of several conjectures for *dicebat* in the MSS (Reynolds 263 in app.);

but *discebat* ('he came to hear', 'ascertained'; *OLD* 3) might also be considered.   **populo . . . superstite:** abl. abs., but *superstiti* (conjectured by
Gertz) is attractive, supplying a dat. with *superesse* below (cf. *Ep.* 93.1 *quae* [sc.
aequitas] *tibi . . . in omni negotio superest*). And yet S. may have avoided the obvious dat. construction to give Caligula double distress: the Roman people
not only survived him but even had a few days' supply of food in hand –
the last straw. And this despite Caligula's notorious wish *ut populus Romanus
unam ceruicem haberet, ut scelera sua tot locis ac temporibus diducta in unum ictum et
unum diem cogeret* (*Ir.* 3.19.2; cf. Suet. *Cal.* 30.2). In Stoic terms Caligula, a
tyrant rather than a (*rex/*)*princeps* (for the distinction, *Cl.* 1.11.4, 12.1–13.5, *Ep.*
114.24), perverts the natural law of good government (Griffin (1976) 204–10).
septem . . . superesse: while the more extreme accounts of Caligula's
disruption of the Roman food-supply may well be doubted (n. below on
dum . . . ludit), 'a food crisis in the winter of 40–41 can be accepted as genuine'
(Garnsey (1988) 223). Claudius responded in 42 by planning a new harbour
at Ostia (Dio 60.11.1–3), and the *Ceres Augusta* coinage marking the first year
of his reign offered symbolic reassurance about the corn-supply (Garnsey
(1988) 223 n. 12 with Rickman (1980) 74–5).   **aut . . . certe** 'or at all
events'; for the nuance after *aut* or *uel*, *OLD certe* 2c.   **cibaria** 'rations';
for their size and content, Rickman (1980) 10.   **dum:** causal, the action
of the main verb (*aderat*) resulting from that in the *dum* clause (*OLD* 4a).
dum . . . ludit: according to Dio (59.17.1–11) Caligula built his notorious
bridge of boats across the Bay of Naples in AD 39; its length and exact
location are disputed (Barrett (1989) 212). But if Dio's date is correct, and
even if he rightly reports that a severe food-crisis resulted from the comman-
deering of so many ships (59.17.2, perhaps corroborated by Suet. *Cal.* 19.1–2
and 26.5; Lindsay (1993) 95), it is hard to believe that Caligula's bridge was
directly responsible for the crisis which S. locates substantially later in 41, immediately after Caligula's assassination in late January. A convenient con-
flation by S. of events in 39 and 41 is more likely.   **pontes . . . iungit:**
i.e. 'joins' to land at both ends; for the phrase, *Med.* 585, Tac. *Hist.* 3.6.2
ponte iuncto, *Ann.* 1.49.4. If not plur. for sing., *pontes* exaggerates Caligula's
extravagance; or, given Suetonius' report that the ships were anchored
in a double line (*Cal.* 19.1 *ordine duplici*), the plur. may denote a 'double'
bridge.   **uiribus** 'assets', 'resources', financial and otherwise; *OLD* 26
(in prose, Livian and post-Augustan).   **ludit:** 8.1n.; for other tyran-
nical acts affecting the food-supply, Suet. *Cal.* 26.5, 39.1.   **ultimum
malorum:** rare in S., special in emphasis (*Tr.* 5.5, *Ep.* 39.6).   **obsessis**

quoque 'even for people under siege', dat. with *aderat*; Caligula is a perverse aggressor against his *own* city, his *own* people. For the nuance of *quoque*, *OLD* 4a.   **egestas:** of basic provisions (defining gen.), Sallustian (*TLL* v 2.246.56–71).   **exitio paene ... constitit ... imitatio** 'his imitation was at the cost almost of mass destruction'; *OLD consto* 11a (with abl. of price).   **exitio ... ac fame:** i.e. death by starvation (hendiadys) in keeping with Caligula's character-portrayal: *Pol.* 17.3 *quem* [sc. *Gaium*] *rerum natura in exitium opprobriumque humani generis edidit*. **rerum ... ruina** 'general catastrophe'.   **furiosi ... imitatio:** Suet. *Cal.* 19.3 *scio plerosque existimasse talem a Gaio pontem excogitatum aemulatione Xerxis, qui non sine admiratione aliquanto angustiorem Hellespontum contabulauerit* (in 480 BC). For Xerxes' bridge as a familiar 'paradigm of arrogance', Fantham (1992) 212 on Luc. 2.672–7, and cf. 17.2 intro.   **furiosi ... superbi:** each adj. has a special resonance for Caligula, who allegedly compounded his emulation of Xerxes here with aspirations to a Persian style of government (*Ben.* 2.12.2 *homo natus in hoc, ut mores liberae ciuitatis Persica seruitute mutaret*). **furiosi:** with reference to Caligula, *Pol.* 17.5, *Ben.* 2.12.2 (equivalent terms at *C.S.* 18.1, *Ir.* 1.20.9, *Tr.* 14.5, *Ben.* 7.11.2); on his mental state, Barrett (1989) 214–16.   **externi:** not just 'from abroad' but also 'alien' or 'irrelevant' to us. A Roman sense of superiority and general disdain for foreigners fits comfortably with this range of connotations, so that the combination of alcohol and Cleopatra can bring Mark Antony *in externos mores ac uitia non Romana* (*Ep.* 83.25); and in extreme cases '*externus* carries connotations of treachery' (Coleman (1988) 169 on Stat. *Silu.* 4.5.46). S.'s use here savours of all these ingredients.   **infeliciter superbi:** again with implications for Caligula. For his arrogance, *C.S.* 18.5, *Ir.* 3.19.1, *Ben.* 2.12.1–13.1, *Pol.* 17.5 *secundarum* [sc. *rerum*] *elatus euentu super humanum intumescebat modum* (swelling to divine pretension at *Ir.* 1.20.8–9); but *infeliciter* because of his bloody end (*C.S.* 18.3, Suet. *Cal.* 58.2–3, Dio 59.29.6–7).   **imitatio** puts the final touch to the picture of Caligula's moral decrepitude; cf. *Helu.* 16.3 *non te* [sc. *Heluiam*] ... *periculosa etiam probis peiorum detorsit imitatio*.

18.6 animum 'feelings', 'frame of mind' (*OLD* 10a).   **illi:** the *praefectus annonae* (presumably C. Turannius; 20.3) and lesser officials. **saxa ... excepturi:** trouble on two fronts; on one, a public riot (*saxa ... ignes*; for such disturbances, *Ir.* 3.41.3 *ferrum et ignes*, [Sen.] *Oct.* 688–9), on the other, Caligula, the ultimate threat (cf. *Ir.* 3.19.1, of instruments of torture which he had allegedly used against senators: *fidiculis, talaribus, eculeo, igne, uultu suo*).   **excepturi** 'destined to face' (*OLD* 11a; for the hint of inevitability, Westman (1961) 115). **dissimulatione** 'concealment'. **tantum . . . mali** 'such a great sickness [sc. the shortage of grain] lurking amid the state's innermost organs'; concealment at this deep level of the body politic (*OLD uiscus*¹ 2b) quells the rumblings of the public *uenter* (18.5). **cum ratione scilicet** 'with good reason, to be sure', a pragmatism which underscores in what follows the difference between the *praefectus annonae* and the *sapiens*. On a practical level (the argument goes) it would be folly not to hide the full seriousness of the food-crisis (*quaedam . . . sunt*); the truth revealed, panic and riot follow (*causa . . . nosse*). For the *sapiens*, however, self-knowledge is all: 'knowing what ails him' (*morbum suum nosse*) may become a *causa moriendi* (i.e. through suicide; *Ep.* 58.35–6, 98.16); but (self-) deception compromises the rational control exercised over every area of existence. **curanda** 'are to be treated' (for 'cure', *Cl.* 1.17.2). **morbum . . . nosse:** *Ir.* 3.10.4 *prodest morbum suum nosse et uires eius antequam spatientur opprimere* – a form of self-knowledge lost on the public with whom the *praefectus annonae* has to contend.

19 The view from above

Paulinus' official tasks, however important from one perspective, appear mundane, even trivial, when observed from the transforming perspective of 'the view from above' (general intro. pp. 24–5; 19.1 n. on *quae . . . miraculis?*).

19.1 haec: i.e. the benefits of philosophical retirement. **tranquilliora . . . maiora:** the haven's calm is underscored by homoeoteleuton and graded syllabic shortening, its *securitas et perpetua tranquillitas* (*Ep.* 92.3) resulting from a safe (cf. *tutiora*) indifference to fortune (*V.B.* 4.5, *Ep.* 74.6). **maiora:** 18.2n. **simile . . . accedas:** for the contrast between 'mundane' duties and the intellectual life, Epict. *Diss.* 1.10.10 (cited by Viansino II 760): 'Is it, then, the same thing to receive a petition from someone and to read in it "I entreat you to allow me to export a small amount of grain"; and one to this effect: "I entreat you to learn from Chrysippus what is the administration of the world and what place within it the rational animal holds; and consider who you are and what the nature is of your good and evil"?' Given that Epictetus shows little or no sign of familiarity with S.'s writings, it must remain a coincidence that Epictetus also features (1.10.2–6) a *praefectus annonae* (unnamed) whose ambition to devote himself to philosophy was soon forgotten when he was offered his high position

(hence the allusion at 1.10.10).   **simile ... esse** 'that it amounts to the
same thing' (*OLD similis* 7b).   **incorruptum ... a** 'not damaged as
a result of'.   **fraude ... neglegentia:** countering both was a prime
responsibility of the *praefectus annonae* (Rickman (1980) 86). Papyri from
Egypt illustrate the stringent documentation required of shippers as a safe-
guard against fraud, esp. the adulteration of grain with e.g. earth or barley;
sealed samples of cargo (δείγματα) were in common use as proofs of quality (Rickman 121–2). Negligence in transit: allowing grain to grow damp
(the cargo would then swell, possibly endangering the ship); bad storage,
causing the cargo to shift and the ship to list or worse; failing carefully to separate in the hold grains of varying quality (Rickman 132–3).
transfundatur: lit. 'transferred by pouring'; in this sense in Cato, then
post-Augustan (*OLD* 1 a).   **horrea:** granaries and storehouses, esp. the
vast structures at Rome and at the major points of entry (Ostia, Portus,
Puteoli); see on their size, construction, types and management Rickman
(1980) 21–4, 135–41.   **ne ... concalescat:** excessive moisture would
produce mildew, attracting weevils etc.; the grain also had to be kept
cool (below 60 °F), as overheating would lead to infestation by insects
and allow vermin to breed (Rickman (1980) 21, 134; Plin. *N.H.* 18.301–8).
concepto umore 'by absorbing moisture'; Lucretian (*D.R.N.* 6.628),
then in Columella and S. (*TLL* IV 58.11–13).   **concalescat:** of
grain, also in Pliny (*N.H.* 18.304 *spissitate sua concalescit* [sc. *triticum*]).
ut ... respondeat: special officials (*mensores frumentarii*) assessed the quantity and quality of imported grain by weighing and measuring the cargo
both at points en route and esp. on arrival in Italy; charges of fraud
ensued if the grain did not 'correspond' (*OLD respondeo* 14b) to the dimensions (*ad mensuram pondusque*) declared in the cargo's documentation
(n. above on *fraude ... neglegentia*). Fraud on the part of the *mensores* themselves was a major concern of the *praefectus* (Rickman (1980) 20, 86, 204).
sacra et sublimia: devotion to philosophy (*Ep.* 55.4 *sacrum quiddam ... et
uenerabile*) resembles initiation into a mystery cult (*Ep.* 95.64, quoted in
14.1 n. on *sacrarum ... conditores*); *sacra* also anticipates inquiry into god below
(*quae ... forma*), *sublimia* inquiry into (Stoic) cosmology (*quid sit quod ... excitet*).
accedas 'occupy yourself with' (*OLD* 9a), denoting positive intellectual
development towards knowledge (*sciturus*), as opposed to the narrower
concerns in *cures* above.   **sciturus:** purpose, with certainty expressed
(Westman (1961) 120).   **quae ... miraculis?:** S. here concentrates on
physics (natural philosophy), one of the three familiar divisions of Hellenistic

philosophy (*Ot*. 4.2n. on *ut*); of the two subdivisions of natural philosophy distinguished at *Ep*. 89.16 *corporalia et incorporalia*, he restricts himself here to *corporalia* (L–S 1 272–4 with Long (1986) 152–8). Investigation of such wide-ranging questions liberates the mind of the *sapiens* from the embodied self (*Ot*. 4.2, 5.5–6, *Helu*. 20.1–2, *Ep*. 65.16–22, 110.9, 117.19), but Paulinus' *curae* are at the other end of the scale of values: he concentrates on the grain-supply while the philosopher investigates god (*quae . . . forma*), he oversees transport-vessels (*ut . . . in horrea*) while the *sapiens* charts the soul's journey through life and beyond (*quis . . . componat*), he concerns himself with the weight and measurement of grain (*ut . . . respondeat*) instead of the physical properties and dimensions of the universe (*quid . . . excitet*), and he supervises 'the accounts of the whole (Roman) world' (18.3 *orbis terrarum rationes*) while the philosopher contemplates the *ratio* (= λόγος, *deus, natura*; *Ben*. 4.7.1–2, 8.2–3, *Ep*. 65.12, *N.Q*. 2.45.1–3) of the entire cosmos.   **quae . . . forma:** *Ot*. 4.2, *Ep*. 65.19, 23–4, *N.Q*. 1 *praef*. 3, 13–14, 16.   **materia . . . dei:** i.e. that *in* which the activity of an intelligent god is evident, and *except through* which we can have no perception of that intelligence; for Zeno 'designing fire', for Chrysippus pneuma (*Ot*. 5.5n. on *altior aliqua uis*).   **uoluntas:** divine governance (*Ben*. 6.23.1 *sua illis* [sc. *dis*] *in lege aeterna uoluntas est. statuerunt quae non mutarent*) and providence (L–S 1 42D2, 54A–B); *uoluptas* in the *Codex Ambrosianus* is a common corruption (Owen (1924) 199 on Ov. *Tr*. 2.357).   **condicio** 'general character' (*OLD* 8), e.g. how powerful is god? Is he a part or the whole of the universe? Does he do whatever he wishes?; cf. *Ot*. 4.2, *N.Q*. 1 *praef*. 3, 16, and esp. Cic. *N.D*. 2 for full discussion.   **forma:** often perceived as spherical (*rotundus*) like the Stoic cosmos, with whom god was identified (*Ep*. 113.22, *Apoc*. 8.1 with Eden (1984) 100, Cic. *N.D*. 1.24 with Pease); but not all Stoics agreed (Cic. *N.D*. 1.37 *qui* [sc. Ariston of Chios] *neque formam dei intellegi posse censeat . . .* with Pease).

quis . . . componat: cf. *Ep*. 65.20, the theoretical link with physics being that the human soul, as a portion of the divine breath (pneuma) pervading the universe (*Ot*. 5.5n. on *homines . . . haesisse*), does not perish with the body. Elsewhere the picture is complicated by S.'s blending of Stoic and other (esp. Epicurean) elements to meet the needs of the context, e.g. *consolatio* (Fantham (1982) 263–4 with Hoven (1971) 109–26). We may return to the non-existent state of our pre-birth (*Pol*. 9.2, *Marc*. 19.5, *Ep*. 54.4–5, 99.30, an Epicurean idea; cf. Lucr. *D.R.N*. 3.862–9), or rise to a better existence in the celestial home of the blessed (*Marc*. 23.1–2, 24.5–25.2, *Pol*. 9.3, *Ep*. 71.16), or return to 'mingle in nature' (*Ep*. 71.16; i.e. the soul is reabsorbed in the universal pneuma). For subsequent reincarnation by metempsychosis, *Ep.* 36.10.   **casus** 'outcome' (*OLD* 6).   **dimissos** 'released'; of the soul from bodily imprisonment, *Ep.* 65.16.   **componat** 'settles' us (*OLD* 4a), with a play on 'laying to rest' in burial (4c).   **quid ... excitet:** i.e. what principle ordains and gives coherence to the four elements, earth and water on the heavy side, air and fire on the light (cf. *Ir.* 2.19.1)? For post-Chrysippean Stoics it is pneuma (n. above on *materia ... dei*), itself comprising the 'active' pair of fire and air and holding together the 'passive' pair (earth and water) within the universal sphere (Long (1986) 156 with sources). **mundi** 'the enclosed universe' (*Ot.* 4.2n. on *toti inditus*), within which for Stoics 'uppermost is the fire [*in summum ... ferat* below] called "aether" in which the sphere of the fixed stars is first created, and next the sphere of the planets. After this the air [*leuia*], and then the water, and as foundation of everything the earth [*grauissima quaeque*, incl. earth and water], which is at the centre of all things [*in medio*]' (L–S 1 47B2 = *SVF* II 180.10–13). **grauissima ... leuia:** cf. *Ot.* 5.5 *grauia ... leuia.* Weightless, air and fire move away from the centre, counterbalancing the centripetal tendency (cf. *in medio*) of earth and water and uniting the centre with the circumference of the universe. Cosmic stability and coherence arise out of this natural disposition of the four elements (L–S 1 297).   **sustineat** 'holds in place'. **supra:** adv. (*pace* Duff 166).   **leuia:** although weightless, the air is cold (*N.Q.* 2.10.1 with Hine (1981) 213) and so below fire.   **sidera:** stars as well as planets, located in the uppermost zone with fire (n. above on *mundi*) and in constant motion (10.6n. on *mundus ... manet, Pol.* 7.2); on the complex nature and direction of star/planetary motion, Hine (1981) 221–3 on *N.Q.* 2.11.2.   **uicibus:** lit. 'changes' (of heavenly bodies, *Ben.* 4.23.1, *Ep.* 88.15, *N.Q.* 3.29.3), here in a regular sequence (cf. Fantham (1982) 379); dat. with *excitet* ('rouses to'; cf. Col. 10.109).   **cetera:** obj. of *sc-iturus* above.   **ingentibus ... miraculis:** an impressive close, with a favoured clausula (double cretic) and *plena* positioned centrally to maximize the equal emphasis on adj. and noun; for *miracula* of natural marvels, *Ep.* 90.43, *N.Q.* 6.4.1, 7.20.2.   **plena:** also with the gen. in S. (e.g. *Marc.* 24.4, *Ep.* 10.3, 12.4, *N.Q.* 6.16.3); but the abl. here illustrates the shift in post-Classical usage on which Quintilian remarks at *Inst.* 9.3.1.

19.2 uis tu 'You really ought (to)'. Colloquial in tone, peremptory in force; *OLD uolo* 8, adding e.g. *Marc.* 9.3, *Tr.* 1.13 with Summers 213 on *Ep.* 47.10.   **relicto solo:** so as to contemplate 'higher things' (*sublimia*, both lit. and fig.); in anticipation of its eventual release from the body, the philosopher's *animus liber* (*Ep.* 65.21) transcends the human condition by studying the universe (*Ep.* 110.9, *N.Q.* 1 *praef.* 11–13, 17 *haec inspicere . . . nonne transilire est mortalitatem suam et in meliorem transcribi sortem?*). **mente . . . respicere** 'cast your mind's eye'.   **dum calet sanguis** 'while enthusiasm is still fresh', far preferable to Duff's 'before you are too old' (166) and confirmed by Nemes. *Cyn.* 288–9 (of horses) *mox sanguis uenis melior calet, ire uiarum | longa uolunt . . .*   **uigentibus** 'those with an active interest'; liable to deletion (suggested by Reynolds 263 in app.) as simply explanatory of the preceding clause, though it helpfully supplies out of that clause a dat. of the agent defining the intellectual elite to which Paulinus will surely wish to belong.   **genere** 'mode' (sc. *meliore*); of life, *Tr.* 10.1, *Ep.* 5.1, 24.22.   **multum** 'a great array', enumerated in the following phrases; with gen. plur., Plin. *Ep.* 3.7.8, Gell. *N.A.* 12.9.2.   **bonarum artium:** esp. philosophy; 14.5, *Ot.* 3.4n. **amor:** of the virtues, *Ot.* 6.2, philosophy itself being *sapientiae amor* (*Ep.* 89.4). **uirtutium:** for the form (-*ium* as opposed to -*um*), *Ot.* 3.4n.; homoeoteleuton after *artium* here perhaps influences S.'s choice. The plur. here spans the four 'primary' Stoic virtues, moderation, justice, prudence and bravery (13.9n. on *cuius . . . minuent?*).   **usus** 'practice'; on the analogy of *sapientia/ sapere* at *Ep.* 117.15–17, virtue itself and acting virtuously are separate goods, the former undesirable without the latter.   **cupiditatium:** i.e. base passions (13.9n. on *cuius . . . prement?*); for -*ium*, *Ot.* 3.4n. on *uirtutium*. **uiuendi . . . scientia:** 7.3nn. on *scientia, uiuere . . . discendum est* and *mori*. **ac:** variation after cognate *atque*; S. follows the principle of *atque* before a vowel, *ac* and *atque* both being regular before a consonant.   **alta rerum quies:** *alta* Erasmus for *alia* of the MSS; of the *sapiens*, *C.S.* 9.3 *uir ereptus erroribus, moderator sui, altae quietis et placidae. rerum* is not superfluous to the sense; beyond providing symmetry with the preceding gens. and contributing to one of S.'s two favourite *clausulae* (double cretic), it here denotes not only Paulinus' prospective 'circumstances' in retirement but also his relief from 'public business' (*OLD res* 14a; *quies* 2c, + gen.).

19.3 The treatise draws towards its close with a panoramic vision: the plight of ordinary clients reinforces the point that *occupatio* is a major source of anxiety pervading every social level regardless of rank (incl., of course, that of *praefectus annonae*; cf. 18.1). The widening area of reference near the climax tells decisively against Duff's objection (167) that this section, because it is 'not specially true of the *occupatio* of Paulinus', is 'unsuited to the place it occupies'.   **condicio** 'plight' (*OLD* 6b).

misera: trumped by *miserrima*; for the technique, *Marc.* 12.4, *V.B.* 14.1.
tamen: δέ after *quidem* (μέν); 12.8n.   **qui ... occupationibus:** Paulinus' category, albeit at the higher end (18.1; Augustus sets the ultimate
example at 4.2–6).   **laborant** 'exert themselves' and in the process
'suffer strain from' (+ abl.; *OLD* 3a, 4).   **ad alienum ... somnum:**
of *salutatores*, 14.4n. on *suum ... expectent*; *ad* lit. 'so as to suit' (*OLD* 34b).
ad alienum ... gradum: clients/supporters escorting their patron after the morning *salutatio*, their pace regulated by his (or by that of his
litter); as a mark of honour (the larger the retinue the better), e.g. *Ep.*
22.9, 68.11, Cic. *Mur.* 70, Q. Cic. *Pet.* 34, 36, Juv. 1.46 with Braund
(1996) 87.   **amare ... iubentur:** the client–patron relationship dictated political (esp. in voting) and social allegiance (*OLD amo* 7 with e.g.
Dupont (1992) 18–20); in contrast to the *libertas* of the *sapiens* (*C.S.* 19.2,
Ep. 8.7, 51.9), abject slavery (cf. Mat. *Fam.* 11.28.3 *at haec etiam seruis semper
libera fuerunt, <ut> timerent gauderent dolerent suo potius quam alterius arbitrio*);
even an emperor could be enslaved in this respect (Tac. *Ann.* 12.3.2 *cui*
[sc. *Claudio*] *non iudicium, non odium erat nisi indita et iussa*, cited by Duff 167).
ipsorum: in place of the reflexive (2.5n. on *ipsis ... uolentibus*), which is
reserved for emphasis in the following clause.   **ex quota ... sit:** lit. 'in
what proportion to the total (*OLD quotus* 1b) it is their very own' (cf. 3.3
quotus ... dies).

20 The view from below

Crowning illustration of the quasi-tragedy of those who, consumed by ambition for wealth, position etc., are incapable of retiring if and when they attain their goals, have nothing to retire to even if they *could* make that change,
and invariably lack all balance and perspective in life because they are im-
prisoned by their obsessions; however long their lives, they barely live at all.

20.1 Lives driven by *ambitio* are never *really* lived.   **uideris:** fut. perf.
itaque: variable in position (2.5n. on *non ... quod*); cf. with no apparent shift
of emphasis *Prou.* 1.6 *itaque cum uideris bonos uiros ... laborare ...*   **praetextam:** bordered with purple, the toga worn by consuls, praetors and other
high magistrates (D–S v 349).   **saepe iam** 'often before now' (*TLL*
VII 1.115.29–40), i.e. the successful candidate has already completed the
lower stages of his political career.   **sumptam:** of donning robes
of office, *OLD* 2b.   **celebre ... nomen:** i.e. a 'name' (*OLD* 17a)
distinguished for political oratory and/or 'in the courts' (cf. Cic. *Brut.* 314

cum essem biennium uersatus in causis et iam in foro celebratum meum nomen esset . . .). For *celebre nomen* in combination, *TLL* III 740.15–19; for the pressures weighing upon such 'names', 2.4 *quam multorum . . . educit!*, 7.8 *diripitur . . . 'res proferentur?'*   **ne inuideris:** with a play on *uideris*. S. frequently appends a curt imperative *uel sim.* to a temporal (fut. perf.) *cum* clause (e.g. *Ep.* 2.4 *cum multa percurreris, unum excerpe . . .*, 3.2, 68.6, cited with other examples by Waldaestel (1888) 34–5), but *ne* + perf. subjunctive only here.

uitae . . . parantur 'are bought (*OLD paro* 4) at the cost of "really" living' (2.2n. on *'exigua . . . uiuimus'*); *damno* a usual abl. of price (G–L §404).

uitae damno: the cost might also, of course, be measured more literally; Caligula apparently thought of executing the entire senate (*Ir.* 3.19.2, Suet. *Cal.* 48.2), but the most celebrated individual martyrdom is that of Thrasea Paetus in AD 66 (general intro. p. 9).   **illis:** the *consules ordinarii* (7.8n. on *'quando . . . praeteribit?'*), after (*ab*) whom the year of their office was dated (*Ir.* 3.31.2 *a me numerari uoluit annum, Marc.* 14.1).   **quosdam . . . quosdam . . . quorundam:** a grouping which will constitute the first element in a tripartite structure, narrowing the focus on the addressee at each stage: (i) three general *exempla*; (ii) three singular *exempla* in 20.2 *foedus ille quem . . .*, *turpis ille qui . . .* and *turpis quem . . .*; (iii) Turannius in 20.3, the single named addressee and (presumably) Paulinus' predecessor as *praefectus annonae*.   **ambitionis:** 2.1n.   **eniterentur** 'struggle up', a rare fig. usage (*OLD* 1a), the effort lingering in *inter*.   **prima:** opp. *summum*; for the pairing (after Hor. *Ep.* 1.1.1), Quint. *Inst.* 10.1.21.   **luctantes:** Lucretian, *D.R.N.* 5.1132 *angustum per iter luctantes ambitionis* (Duff 168); for initial faltering, *Ep.* 101.1 *facilius . . . crescit dignitas quam incipit*, Quint. *Inst.* 12.10.78 (Duff 168).   **reliquit:** of life 'deserting' one, *Pol.* 11.4; Lucretian (*D.R.N.* 5.63).   **consummationem:** 1.3n.   **dignitatis . . . indignitates:** S. exploits the proverbial *digna indigna* (Serv. on *Aen.* 12.811; Otto 117). For shameless behaviour as a prerequisite for reaching high office, *Ep.* 95.3, 115.9, *N.Q.* 1 *praef.* 6 *ambitio quae te ad dignitatem nisi per indigna non ducet* (all cited by Viansino II 761), and for added venom, Juv. 1.73–8 with Braund (1996) 93 on 74.   **erepsissent** 'had clambered up' (fig.; *Ep.* 76.19, 101.2); Pincianus' emendation for *erupissent* in the MSS (cf. 6.2; as a simplifying gloss on *erepo* elsewhere, *TLL* V 2.748.73–4).   **misera . . . cogitatio:** 17.1 and n. on *subitque*.   **laborasse . . . sepulcri:** the final placing of *sepulcri* enacts for the reader the sense of shock which eventual realization of their actual destiny arouses in the very people (*ipsos*, for *se*; 2.5n. on *ipsis . . . uolentibus*) who expect their careers to be crowned by some uncommon distinction. The effect is supported by the ambiguity of *titulum:* (i) 'honour', 'distinction' (*N.Q.* 1.17.9), frequent with a defining gen. (e.g. Liv. 7.1.10 *gloriae*; *OLD* 7b); (ii) 'commemorative inscription' (*OLD* 2b), but esp. 'epitaph', e.g. Plin. *Ep.* 6.10.3 *neglectum... cinerem sine titulo sine nomine iacere.*   **ultima** 'the final stage of'; Livian (4.33.12; *OLD* 4d) for Classical *extremus.*   **dum... disponitur:** *Ep.* 13.17 *quid est... turpius quam senex uiuere incipiens?*; for Stoics a fundamental departure from the *constitutio naturae: Ep.* 121.15 *unicuique aetati sua constitutio est, alia infanti, alia puero, alia seni: omnes ei constitutioni conciliantur in qua sunt.* We should welcome the inevitable (*Ep.* 71.13 *nulli non senectus sua est*) for the benefits it can bring (*Ep.* 68.13 *haec aetas optime facit ad haec studia* [sc. *sapientiae*]); but the *occupati* inevitably *cum aetate luctantur* (cf. *Ep.* 47.7, expanded with poetic lyricism at 122.8–9).   **disponitur:** of time, 1.4.   **improbos** 'immoderate', 'asking too much' (*OLD* 5a, adding *Ir.* 3.7.2).   **inualida defecit** 'has succumbed to weakness', with heavy endings (*-us... -os... -os*) weighing down the close.

20.2 Those who die while still engrossed in their life-long pre-occupations.   **foedus ille quem... turpis... turpis:** 20.1 n. on *quosdam... etc.*; inversion of the μακαρισμός *felix/fortunatus ille qui...* (e.g. Virg. *G.* 2.490, 493 with Mynors). For *foedus* and *turpis* in combination, *TLL* VI 1.1001.4–8, incl. *Ir.* 2.11.2.   **ignotissimis** 'perfectly unknown' to him; the occasional appearance for friends would be more excusable (Duff 168).   **litigatoribus:** in Cicero's letters (*Fam.* 12.30.1) after Cato (cf. Plin. *N.H. praef.* 32), but mostly post-Augustan.   **grandem natu et... captantem:** it is easy to see how a pres. pple (*perorantem* Reynolds, *declamantem* Gertz) balancing *captantem* may have dropped out after *grandem natu*, but the supplement detracts from the dramatic centrality of these words in the sentence's structure and thought, and is in any case unnec-essary if *et* is taken as heightening the dramatic tension, i.e. '*even* at the very moment when he was winning the applause...' (cf. Virg. *Aen.* 2.49 *timeo Danaos et dona ferentes*).   **coronae:** the circle of onlookers at a trial (*OLD* 4a; Summers 346 on *Ep.* 114.12), here with emphasis on his playing to an impressionable (*imperitae*) audience (*Ir.* 1.12.3 *relicto iudice ad coronam uenis*, 2.7.3 *corona... bona patroni uoce corrupta*).   **assensiones captantem:** for the phrase, *Ep.* 20.2, and for the plur., Cic. *Brut.* 290.   **spiritus** 'life' (*OLD* 3b).   **uiuendo:** sc. to an advanced age.   **officia:** 3.5 n.   **collapsus est** 'dropped dead'; cf. 6.2.   **accipiendis... rationibus** 'in the act of going over his accounts' (dat.); post-Augustan (*Helu.* 17.2,

Ep. 14.18, 122.15).   **immorientem:** Horatian (*Ep.* 1.7.85) and mostly
post-Augustan (*OLD* 2), its position illustrating its sense.   **tractus** 'kept
waiting' (*OLD* 18b), but also 'drawn', 'lured' by the prospect of eventual gain
(9), the *heres* is tantalizingly held back until the final word; for *captatio*, 7.7 n.
on *efferendis . . . lassa* with 2.2 n. on *affectatio*.   **risit:** a malicious touch; the
tables are turned at Hor. *S.* 2.5.57 *captator . . . dabit risus Nasica Corano*.

    20.3–4 Inability to retire; the case of C. Turannius, Paulinus' predeces-
sor as *praefectus annonae* (20.3), brings the point close to home.

    20.3 praeterire . . . exemplum non possum: a variant *praeteritio*
formula is S.'s common lead-in to a specific case, as at e.g. *Pol.* 16.3, *Ben.*
3.26.1, *Ep.* 8.10 (Ciceronian, e.g. *Clu.* 134, 139, *Phil.* 13.27, 14.31, *Brut.* 273
etc.).   **quod mihi occurrit:** cf. 10.1; ironic if C. Turannius will already
have occurred to S.'s contemporary audience as an obvious case of long
life consumed by *occupatio*.   **C. Turannius:** *praefectus annonae* in AD 14
(Tac. *Ann.* 1.7.2; as the first known holder of the office, D'Escurac (1976) 317)
and, still in office in 48, a confidant of Claudius (*Ann.* 11.31.1). Since he
can also be plausibly identified as prefect of Egypt between 7 and 4 BC
(D'Escurac (1976) 317 and n. 4), an office entered when he was presumably at least 30 (Grimal 77), his age in AD 48 may be set at least at 85,
possibly even 90. If, however, S. is correct to put him *post annum nonagesimum* when Caligula pensioned him off before he would quickly return to
office, and even if these events happened soon before Caligula's death in
early 41, Turannius would seem to have reached his hundredth year in or
around 48. For this reason Gertz and others follow the MSS in reading
S(extus) Turannius here, assuming a reference to an otherwise unknown but
equally long-serving office holder only marginally different in name and
age from the well-attested Caius. But as soon as allowance is made for S.'s
tactical exaggeration of Turannius' age (Duff xiv, D'Escurac (1976) 318;
for the Senecan tendency, 3.2 *centesimus . . . annus*) in order to emphasize his
extreme reluctance to retire, this highly improbable duplication becomes
unnecessary. Even less likely, with the inverted *praeteritio* highlighting the
example, is Reynolds's suggestion (326 in *Ind. nom.* Turannius) that the error in the MSS may be the author's own rather than a scribe's.   **exactae**
'complete', 'proven' (18.4, *Ep.* 71.28 *uirtutis exactae*, 74.29).   **diligentiae:**
cf. 18.3.   **uacationem:** 4.2 n.   **procurationis:** seized upon by e.g.
Lenzen (1937) as evidence that S.'s Turannius held an office (*procurator
a rationibus*) different from that of his Tacitean namesake (n. above on
C. *Turannius*); but *procuratio* is used in connection with the corn-supply

by Cicero (*Har.* 43 *frumentaria procuratione, Att.* 4.1.6) and can be plausibly explained here by supposing (i) that the recent office of *praefectus annonae* (with C. Turannius its first holder) had yet to establish itself fully in terms at least of nomenclature, and/or (ii) that in this non-technical essay S. may in any case have avoided the strictly official term (*praefectus*) in favour of a more familiar alternative (D'Escurac (1976) 55).   **ultro:** i.e. on Caligula's initiative; *OLD* 5b for the usage with pass. verbs (*ab . . . accepisset* here 'pass. in implication'; *OLD ab* 20b). Caligula's intervention proves the high distinction of Turannius' office (Dahlmann (1941) 105).   **componi . . . iussit:** mock funeral rites, often compared with *Ep.* 12.8 *Pacuuius* (formerly legate in Asia) *. . . cum uino et illis funebribus epulis sibi parentauerat, sic in cubiculum ferebatur a cena ut inter plausus exoletorum hoc ad symphoniam caneretur:* βεβίωται, βεβίωται. *nullo non se die extulit*, and esp. with Trimalchio's performance in Petronius (78.5–8; cf. 71.1–4, 72.1 with Smith (1975) 211 on 78). But whereas the latter are related examples of 'the intimate link between the banquet of the living and the funerary ceremonies of the dead', or of 'the popular comparison between life and a banquet, which leads to recommendations to leave life like a guest withdrawing sated from a symposium' (Dunbabin (1986) 194; 7.9n. on *saturo . . . aliquid cibi*), Turannius' mock-theatrical performance stands apart, his ignorance of how (in Senecan terms) 'really' to live and to prepare for death (19.2 *uiuendi ac moriendi scientia*) giving a different significance to his perverse ceremony.   **componi:** as if in preparation for burial (*OLD* 4c).   **lecto:** as if a bier (*OLD* 3).   **uelut exanimem:** but indeed as good as dead from a Stoic/Senecan perspective (12.9 *semiuiuus* and n. on *mortuus*).   **familia:** i.e. relatives, friends and slaves.   **plangi:** elsewhere in S. only in verse; post-Augustan in prose (*OLD* 3a).   **lugebat:** first for emphasis, with *otium* as paradoxical obj.   **domus** = *familia* (*OLD domus* 6a); the wordplay with *domini* (Summers lxxxiv) imitates ritual repetition in the funeral lament.   **labor:** his usual 'task' (*OLD* 3a), but also in familiar contrast with *otium* (*TLL* IX 2.1186.79–81).   **adeone . . . mori?:** with the adv. in leading position, an epigrammatic rounding-off favoured by S. after esp. the earlier books of Livy (*TLL* I 606.58–607.44; Krebs–Schmalz I 87).   **occupatum** 'in harness'.

20.4 plerisque: 2.2n.   **animus** 'feeling' (18.6n.).   **cupiditas . . . laboris:** pejorative (2.1n. on *praeceps cupiditas*); *labor* itself is an indifferent (cf. 3.3n. on *uanus . . . conuersatio*): *Ep.* 31.3 *in eorum numero habitus quae neque bona sunt neque mala.*   **facultas** 'capacity for' (+ gen., *Marc.* 21.4, *Ep.* 90.1).   **imbecillitate:** 11.1n. on *cum . . . admonuit.*   **nullo . . .**

nomine 'for no other reason'; with *quam quod*, post-Augustan (*OLD nomen* 26a).   **seponit** 'it removes' them finally from office.   **lex . . . non legit:** the ordinary age of military discharge had been 46, traditionally (but no longer in Cicero's time) marking the beginning of *senectus* (Powell (1988) 231 on *Sen.* 60); but already in the Republic soldiers could in emergencies serve until 50 (Livy 40.26.7, 42.31.4, 33.4, cited by Balsdon (1969) 392 n. 1), apparently the standard age of discharge in Quintilian's time (*Inst.* 9.2.85, cited by Duff 169). **legit** Bongars (MSS *tegit, cogit*); of military recruitment, *OLD lego²* 6d. The play on *lex* reflects etymological speculation on the derivation of noun from verb (Maltby 336) – an enduring controversy (Palmer (1954) 25–6).   **a sexagesimo . . . non citat:** 3.5n. on *sexagesimus . . . dimittet*.   **citat:** technical (*TLL* III 1200.38–1201.16).   **a se . . . impetrant:** Ciceronian, then post-Augustan (*TLL* VII 1.601.38–41).

20.5 The general fault: a lack of perspective on life.   **interim dum** 'all the time while' (*OLD interim* 1b), introducing an elaborate explanation of the preceding paradox.   **rapiuntur . . . exequias:** constant fluctuation in both subj. and verb, from pass. to act., sing. to plur., negative to affirmative, vividly expresses the lack of focus and consistency which diverts the *occupati* from a clear perspective on life. In the first anaphoric sequence (*dum . . . dum . . . dum*) their instability is also reflected in dazzling wordplay (*rapiuntur/rapiunt, alter alterius*, both with polyptoton) and alliteration (*rapi-, alt-, mutuo miseri*); the second (*sine . . . sine . . . sine*) emphasizes cumulatively the scale of their deprivation, with the preposition followed by respectively two, four and eight syllables.   **rapiuntur et rapiunt:** i.e. 'swept along' by the uncontrollable tide of their preoccupations (cf. *Ep.* 108.24 *inscii rapimur* [sc. by time]), they rob others of *their* time. For the agitation conveyed by combined act. and pass. forms of the same verb, 7.2 *colant . . . colantur, Ep.* 108.24 *agit nos agiturque uelox dies*.   **rumpit** 'breaks in upon' (poetic; *OLD* 7b), thus 'cutting short' (cf. 14.4 *suum somnum rumpentibus*).   **mutuo** 'jointly'; in Cicero's letters and *B. Alex.* 48.1, then post-Augustan.   **fructu** 'profit'.   **uoluptate:** least of all the serene pleasure of the *sapiens*, defined at *Ben.* 7.2.3 as *perturbatione carere*. **profectu** 'improvement'; *Ot.* 6.3n.   **nemo . . . habet:** for *meditatio mortis*, 7.3n. on *mori*.   **in conspicuo:** C. Turannius can be said to have contemplated his (mock-)death *in conspectu* (sc. *familiae*, 20.3), and so S. here uses a phrase (rare, first in V. Max.; *TLL* IV 499.44–8) which emphasizes clarity of (inner) vision over private spectacle.   **nemo non:** 14.5n.   **procul**

spes intendit: for the general fault, 9.1 n. on *cogitationes . . . ordinant*; for the verb ('directs'), *Ep.* 65.18, 123.9. **disponunt . . . sunt:** after 1.4 *aetas nostra bene disponenti multum patet*, a distraction from the organization of time *in* and *for* the 'full' life. **magnas . . . exequias:** the elongated sequence (. . . *et . . . et . . . et . . .*) and the resonant polysyllabic wording with extensive homoeoteleuton (*-um, -as, -es*) themselves suggest 'endless' and grand ambition. Trimalchio's proposed monument (Petr. 71.5–7) is characteristically extreme in size and decoration (Toynbee (1971) gives extensive illustrations of tombs of various kinds and dimensions); but against extravagance in such matters, Cic. *Leg.* 2.62–8, and for Senecan antipathy, *Pol.* 18.2 (marble monuments etc. lack the longevity of *ingenium*), *Ep.* 90.15 ('we can live without the marble-mason . . . '). S. was as good as his word: Tac. *Ann.* 15.64.4 *sine ullo funeris sollemni crematur. ita codicillis praescripserat, cum etiam tum praediues et praepotens supremis suis consuleret.* **dedicationes:** in honour of the dead, Plin. *Ep.* 5.11.1 with Sherwin-White. **ad rogum** 'for (the purpose of) the funeral' (*OLD ad* 44a). **munera:** gladiatorial shows, long associated with the more expensive Roman funerals as a way of honouring the dead (Balsdon (1969) 248–9) as well as publicly expressing the importance and wealth of the deceased's family (Wiedemann (1992) 5–7); for an esp. clear statement of the association, Plin. *Ep.* 6.34.1 (cited by Duff 170) with Sherwin-White. **ambitiosas** 'ostentatious'; in this sense (12.5n. on *ambitione*), post-Augustan in prose (*OLD* 5; Brink on Hor. *Ars* 447). **at mehercules** 'in truth'; 5.3n. **minimum** 'for the briefest span', the adj. surely serving as a noun (*TLL* x 1.559.80–560.2; *Ep.* 83.3 *minimum* ('the briefest time') *exercitationi corporis datum*) rather than as an adv. (*OLD minimum* 1b). For life so shortened by preoccupation, *Ep.* 22.14 (after Epicurus; fr. 495 Us.) *nemo non ita exit e uita tamquam modo intrauerit*, 15. **ad faces et cereos:** children's funerals took place at night by torchlight and taper to avoid attention, a suitable ending for those like Turannius who stubbornly refuse to adapt themselves to progression through the natural stages of life; for the phrase, *Tr.* 11.7, *Ep.* 122.10 (both cited by Duff 170). **ducenda:** of a funeral 'led', 'conducted', *OLD* 7a.

BIBLIOGRAPHY

Works listed here are cited by author and date in the introduction and commentary, e.g. Griffin (1976).

Albertini, E. (1923). *La composition dans les ouvrages philosophiques de Sénèque.* Paris.

Alexander, W. H. (1945). 'Seneca's *Dialogues* I, II, VII, VIII, IX, X (miscellaneous moral essays): the text emended and explained', *University of California Publications in Classical Philology* 13: 49–91.

   (1947). 'Seneca the philosopher in account with Roman history', *TRSC* 41.3: 20–46.

   (1948). 'References to Pompey in Seneca's prose', *TRSC* 42.3: 13–29.

Allen, W. (1954). 'Cicero's conceit', *TAPhA* 85: 121–44.

André, J.-M. (1962). *Recherches sur l'otium romain.* Annales littéraires de l'Université de Besançon 52. Paris.

   (1966). *L'otium dans la vie morale et intellectuelle romaine des origines à l'époque augustéenne.* Paris.

Armisen-Marchetti, M. (1989). *Sapientiae facies: étude sur les images de Sénèque.* Paris.

   (1995). 'Sénèque et l'appropriation du temps', *Latomus* 54: 545–67.

Arnold, E. V. (1911). *Roman Stoicism.* Cambridge.

Austin, R. G. (1934). 'Roman board games I', *G&R* 4: 24–34.

Axelson, B. (1939). *Neue Senecastudien: Textkritische Beiträge zu Senecas Epistulae Morales.* Lund.

Babut, D. (1969). *Plutarque et le stoïcisme.* Paris.

Badian, E. (1962). 'From the Gracchi to Sulla (1940–1959)', *Historia* 11: 197–245.

   (1968). *Roman imperialism in the late Republic.* 2nd edn. Oxford.

Bailey, C. (1928). *The Greek atomists and Epicurus.* Oxford.

Balsdon, J. P. V. D. (1969). *Life and leisure in ancient Rome.* London.

Barnes, J. (1989). 'Antiochus of Ascalon', in M. T. Griffin and J. Barnes, eds., *Philosophia togata.* Vol. I. *Essays on philosophy and Roman society*, 51–96. Oxford.

Barrett, A. A. (1989). *Caligula: the corruption of power.* London.

Barton, C. A. (1992). *The sorrows of the ancient Romans: the gladiator and the monster.* Princeton.

Baumgarten, H. (1970). 'Vitam breuem esse, longam artem. Das Proömium der Schrift Senecas De breuitate uitae', Gymnasium 77: 299–323.

Beare, W. (1964). The Roman stage. 3rd edn. London.

Bellincioni, M. (1979), ed. Lucio Anneo Seneca, Lettere a Lucilio. Libro XV: le lettere 94 e 95. Brescia.

Bérenger, A. (1993). 'La commission financière extraordinaire de 62 ap. J.-C.', MEFRA 105: 75–101.

Bignone, E. (1973). L'Aristotele perduto e la formazione filosofica di Epicuro. 2 vols. 2nd edn. Florence.

Bogun, V. (1968). Die ausserrömische Geschichte in den Werken Senecas. Köln.

Bonner, C. (1941). 'Desired haven', Harvard Theological Review 34: 49–67.

Bonner, S. F. (1949). Roman declamation in the late Republic and early Empire. Liverpool.

Borgo, A. (1989). 'Allusione e tecnica citazionale in Seneca (Breu. 1, 1; Sall. Iug. 1, 1)', Vichiana 18: 45–51.

Bornecque, H. (1907). Les clausules métriques latines. Lille.

Bourgery, A. (1910). 'Sur la prose métrique de Sénèque le philosophe', RPh 34: 167–72.

(1922). Sénèque prosateur. Paris.

Braund, S. Morton (1996), ed. Juvenal: Satires Book I. Cambridge Greek and Latin Classics. Cambridge.

Brunt, P. A. (1975). 'Stoicism and the Principate', PBSR 43: 7–39.

Carcopino, J. (1968). Daily life in ancient Rome: the people and the city at the height of the Empire. Ed. H. T. Rowell and trans. E. O. Lorimer. New Haven and London.

Carter, J. M. (1982), ed. Suetonius: Divus Augustus. Bristol.

Citroni Marchetti, S. (1991). Plinio il Vecchio e la tradizione del moralismo romano. Pisa.

Coleman, K. M. (1988), ed. Statius: Siluae IV. Oxford.

Coleman, R. (1974). 'The artful moralist: a study of Seneca's epistolary style', CQ 68: 276–89.

Commager, S. (1962). The Odes of Horace: a critical study. New Haven and London.

Costa, C. D. N. (1994), ed. Seneca: four Dialogues. Warminster.

Courtney, E. (1974). 'Conjectures in Seneca's prose works', BICS 21: 100–6.

Crook, J. A. (1967). Law and life of Rome. Ithaca, NY and London.

(1995). Legal advocacy in the Roman world. Ithaca, NY.

Currie, H. M. (1966). 'The younger Seneca's style: some observations', *BICS* 13: 76–87.

(1973). *The individual and the state*. London and Toronto.

Dahlmann, H. (1941). 'Drei Bemerkungen zu Seneca, *De Breuitate Vitae*', *Hermes* 76: 100–6.

(1949), ed. *L. Annaeus Seneca, De Breuitate Vitae: Über die Kürze des Lebens*. Munich.

De Lacy, P. (1948). 'Stoic views of poetry', *AJPh* 69: 241–71.

D'Escurac, H. Pavis (1976). *La préfecture de l'annone: service administratif impérial d'Auguste à Constantin*. Paris.

Devine, F. E. (1970). 'Stoicism on the best regime', *JHI* 31: 323–36.

Dick, B. F. (1969). 'Seneca and Juvenal 10', *HSCPh* 73: 237–46.

Dionigi, I. (1980). '*L'epistola* 1, 1 di Orazio e il proemio del *De otio* di Seneca (tradizione filosofica e riflessi autobiografici)', *BStudLat* 10: 38–49.

(1995). 'Il *carpe diem* di uno stoico', in I. Dionigi, ed., *Protinus uiue: colloquio sul De breuitate uitae di Seneca*, 15–26. Bologna.

Dunbabin, K. M. D. (1986). '*Sic erimus cuncti* . . . : the skeleton in Greco-Roman art', *JDAI* 101: 185–255.

Dupont, F. (1992). *Daily life in ancient Rome*. Trans. C. Woodall. Oxford and Cambridge, Mass.

Düring, I. (1961). *Aristotle's Protrepticus: an attempt at reconstruction*. Studia Graeca et Latina Gothoburgensia 12. Göteborg.

Eden, P. T. (1984), ed. *Seneca: Apocolocyntosis*. Cambridge Greek and Latin Classics. Cambridge.

Edwards, C. (1993). *The politics of immorality in ancient Rome*. Cambridge.

Erskine, A. (1990). *The Hellenistic Stoa: political thought and action*. London.

Fantham, R. E. (1982), ed. *Seneca's Troades*. Princeton.

(1989). 'Mime: the missing link in Roman literary history', *CW* 82: 153–63.

(1992), ed. *Lucan: De bello ciuili II*. Cambridge Greek and Latin Classics. Cambridge.

Feeney, D. C. (1986). '*Stat magni nominis umbra*: Lucan on the greatness of Pompeius Magnus', *CQ* 36: 239–43.

(1991). *The gods in epic: poets and critics of the classical tradition*. Oxford.

Fitch, J. G. (1987), ed. *Seneca's Hercules Furens*. Ithaca, NY and London.

Fraenkel, E. (1964). 'Das Geschlecht von Dies', in his *Kleine Beiträge zur klassischen Philologie*. 2 vols. 1 27–72. Rome. First published in *Glotta* 8 (1917) 24–68.

Furneaux, H. (1907), ed. *The Annals of Tacitus*. 2nd edn, rev. H. F. Pelham and C. D. Fisher. 2 vols. Oxford.

Gagliardi, D. (1978). '*I nunc* ... Per la storia di uno stilema poetico', in E. Livrea and G. A. Privitera, eds., *Studi in onore di Anthos Ardizzoni*. 2 vols. I 373–9. Rome.

   (1998). *Il tempo in Seneca filosofo*. Naples.

Galasso, L. (1995), ed. *P. Ouidii Nasonis Epistularum ex Ponto liber II*. Florence.

Garnsey, P. (1988). *Famine and food supply in the Graeco-Roman world: responses to risk and crisis*. Cambridge.

Gertz, M. C. (1874). *Studia critica in L. Annaei Senecae dialogos*. Hauniae.

Giancotti, F. (1957). *Cronologia dei 'Dialoghi' di Seneca*. Turin.

Goldschmidt, V. (1989). *Le système stoïcien et l'idée de temps*. 4th edn. Paris.

Goodyear, F. R. D. (1972), ed. *The Annals of Tacitus*. Vol. I. *Annals 1.1–54*. Cambridge Classical Texts and Commentaries 15. Cambridge.

Gosling, J. C. B. and Taylor, C. C. W. (1982). *The Greeks on pleasure*. Oxford.

Griffin, M. T. (1962). '*De Breuitate Vitae*', *JRS* 52: 104–13.

   (1972). 'The elder Seneca and Spain', *JRS* 62: 1–19.

   (1976). *Seneca: a philosopher in politics*. Oxford.

   (1984). *Nero: the end of a dynasty*. London.

   (1988). 'Philosophy for statesmen: Cicero and Seneca', in H. W. Schmidt and P. Wülfing, eds., *Antikes Denken – Moderne Schule*. Gymnasium Beiheft 9. 133–50. Heidelberg.

   (1989). 'Philosophy, politics and politicians at Rome', in M. T. Griffin and J. Barnes, eds., *Philosophia togata*. Vol. I. *Essays on philosophy and Roman society*. 1–37. Oxford.

Grilli, A. (1953). *Il problema della vita contemplativa nel mondo greco-romano*. Milan.

Grimal, P. (1947). 'La date du *De Breuitate Vitae*', *REL* 25: 164–77.

   (1960). 'Le plan du *De Breuitate Vitae*', in *Studi in onore di Luigi Castiglioni*. 2 vols. I 407–19. Florence.

   (1978). *Sénèque ou la conscience de l'Empire*. Paris.

Hadas, M. (1930). *Sextus Pompey*. New York.

Hadot, P. (1995). *Philosophy as a way of life: spiritual exercises from Socrates to Foucault*. Trans. M. Chase. Oxford.

   (1998). *The inner citadel: the Meditations of Marcus Aurelius*. Trans. M. Chase. Cambridge, Mass. and London.

Hahm, D. E. (1977). *The origins of Stoic cosmology*. Columbus, Ohio.

Hambüchen, B. (1966). *Die Datierung von Senecas Schrift Ad Paulinum De Breuitate Vitae*. Diss. Köln.

Handford, S. A. (1947). *The Latin subjunctive: its usage and development from Plautus to Tacitus.* London.

Hardie, P. R. (1994), ed. *Virgil: Aeneid IX.* Cambridge Greek and Latin Classics. Cambridge.

Herrmann, L. (1936). 'Sénèque et Pline l'ancien', *REA* 38: 177–81.

(1937). 'Chronologie des œuvres en prose de Sénèque', *Latomus* 1: 94–112.

(1948). 'L. Antistius Vetus et le Pomoerium', *REL* 26: 222–8.

Heubeck, A., West, S. and Hainsworth, J. B. (1988). *A commentary on Homer's Odyssey.* Vol. 1. *Introduction and books I–VIII.* Oxford.

Hijmans, B. L. (1966). 'Drama in Seneca's Stoicism', *TAPhA* 97: 237–51.

(1991). 'Stylistic splendor, failure to persuade', in *Sénèque et la prose latine.* Fondation Hardt entretiens sur l'antiquité classique 36. 1–37. Geneva.

Hine, H. (1981), ed. *An edition with commentary of Seneca: Natural Questions, Book 2.* New York.

Housman, A. E. (1927), ed. *M. Annaei Lucani Belli Civilis libri decem.* 2nd edn. Oxford.

Hoven, R. (1971). *Stoïcisme et stoïciens face au problème de l'au-delà.* Paris.

Ingrosso, M. T. (1988). 'Connotazioni politiche del linguaggio Senecano (*Dial.* VIII)', *Rudiae* 1: 105–14.

Inwood, B. (1985). *Ethics and human action in early Stoicism.* Oxford.

(1995). 'Seneca in his philosophical milieu', *HSCPh* 97: 63–76.

Jal, P. (1957). 'Images d'Auguste chez Sénèque', *REL* 35: 242–64.

Joly, R. (1956). *Le thème philosophique des genres de vie dans l'antiquité classique.* Brussels.

(1961). '*Curiositas*', *Ant. Class.* 30: 33–44.

Kaster, R. (1988). *The guardians of language: the grammarian and society in late antiquity.* Berkeley and Los Angeles.

Kenney, E. J. (1962). 'The first satire of Juvenal', *PCPhS* 8: 29–40.

(1971), ed. *Lucretius: De rerum natura Book III.* Cambridge Greek and Latin Classics. Cambridge.

(1996), ed. *Ovid: Heroides XVI–XXI.* Cambridge Greek and Latin Classics. Cambridge.

Kindstrand, J. F. (1976). *Bion of Borysthenes: a collection of the fragments with introduction and commentary.* Uppsala.

Kühnen, F. J. (1962). *Seneca und die römische Geschichte.* Köln.

Kurth, T. (1994). *Senecas Trostschrift an Polybius, Dialog 11: ein Kommentar.* Stuttgart and Leipzig.

La Penna, A. (1956). 'Due note sulla cultura filosofica delle *Epistole* oraziane', *SIFC* 27: 192–201.

Laughton, E. (1964). *The participle in Cicero*. Oxford.

Leeman, A. D. (1963). *Orationis ratio: the stylistic theories and practice of the Roman orators, historians and philosophers*. 2 vols. Amsterdam.

Lenzen, H. (1937). *Senecas Dialog De breuitate uitae*. Leipzig.

Liebeschuetz, J. H. W. G. (1979). *Continuity and change in Roman religion*. Oxford.

Lindsay, H. (1993), ed. *Suetonius: Caligula*. Bristol.

Lindsay, W. M. (1894). *The Latin language*. Oxford.

Löfstedt, E. (1911). *Philologischer Kommentar zur Peregrinatio Aetheriae*. Uppsala and Leipzig.

Long, A. A. (1986). *Hellenistic philosophy: Stoics, Epicureans, Sceptics*. 2nd edn. Berkeley and Los Angeles.

Lyne, R. O. A. M. (1978), ed. *Ciris: a poem attributed to Vergil*. Cambridge Classical Texts and Commentaries 20. Cambridge.

Mankin, D. (1995). *Horace: Epodes*. Cambridge Greek and Latin Classics. Cambridge.

Manning, C. E. (1985). '*Liberalitas*: the decline and rehabilitation of a virtue', *G&R* 32: 73–83.

Marastoni, A. (1979), trans. *Lucio Anneo Seneca, i Dialoghi*. Milan.

Marshall, B. A. (1985). *A historical commentary on Asconius*. Columbia, Missouri.

Mayer, R. G. (1991). 'Roman historical *exempla* in Seneca', in *Sénèque et la prose latine*. Fondation Hardt entretiens sur l'antiquité classique 36. 141–76. Geneva.

  (1994), ed. *Horace: Epistles I*. Cambridge Greek and Latin Classics. Cambridge.

  (2001), ed. *Tacitus: Dialogus de oratoribus*. Cambridge Greek and Latin Classics. Cambridge.

Mazzoli, G. (1970). *Seneca e la poesia*. Milan.

Meiggs, R. (1973). *Roman Ostia*. 2nd edn. Oxford.

Meister, K. (1916). *Lateinisch-griechische Eigennamen, I: altitalische und römische Eigennamen*. Berlin.

Millar, F. (1992). *The emperor in the Roman world*. Ithaca, NY 1977; repr. 1992.

Momigliano, A. (1942). '*Terra marique*', *JRS* 32: 53–64.

  (1969). 'Seneca between political and contemplative life' (unpublished lecture, 1950), in *Quarto contributo alla storia degli studi classici e del mondo antico*, 239–56. Rome.

Moore, C. H. (1917). 'The decay of nationalism under the Roman Empire', *TAPhA* 48: 27–36.

Motto, A. L. and Clark, J. R. (1993). 'Seneca on friendship', *A&R* 38: 91–8.

Nussbaum, M. C. (1994). *The therapy of desire: theory and practice in Hellenistic ethics*. Princeton.

Oltramare, A. (1926). *Les origines de la diatribe romaine*. Lausanne.

Owen, S. G. (1924), ed. *P. Ovidi Nasonis Tristium liber secundus*. Oxford.

Palmer, L. R. (1954). *The Latin language*. London.

Pembroke, S. G. (1971). 'Oikeiosis', in A. A. Long, ed., *Problems in Stoicism*, 114–49. London.

Picard, G. C. and C. (1968). *The life and death of Carthage: a survey of Punic history and culture from its birth to the final tragedy*. Trans. D. Collon. London.

Pichon, R. (1912). 'Les travaux récents sur la chronologie des œuvres de Sénèque', *Journal des Savants* 10: 212–25.

Pittet, A. (1955). 'Le mot *consensus* chez Sénèque: ses acceptions philosophiques et politiques', *MH* 12: 35–46.

Poucet, J. (1992). 'Les préoccupations étiologiques dans la tradition "historique" sur les origines et les rois de Rome', *Latomus* 51: 281–314.

Powell, J. G. F. (1988), ed. *Cicero: Cato maior de senectute*. Cambridge Classical Texts and Commentaries 28. Cambridge.

   (1990), ed. *Cicero: Laelius, On friendship and The dream of Scipio*. Warminster.

Rauh, N. K. (1989). 'Auctioneers and the Roman economy', *Historia* 38: 451–71.

Rawson, E. (1985). *Intellectual life in the late Roman Republic*. London.

Reynolds, L. D. (1968). 'The medieval tradition of Seneca's *Dialogues*', *CQ* 18: 355–72.

   (1974). 'Some notes on the text of Seneca's *Dialogues*', *CQ* 24: 269–75.

   (1983). 'The younger Seneca: *Dialogues*', in L. D. Reynolds, ed., *Texts and transmissions: a survey of the Latin classics*, 366–9. Oxford.

Reynolds, L. D. and Wilson, N. G. (1974). *Scribes and scholars: a guide to the transmission of Greek and Latin literature*. 2nd edn. Oxford.

Rhodes, P. J. (1981). *A commentary on the Aristotelian Athenaion Politeia*. Oxford.

Rickman, G. (1980). *The corn supply of ancient Rome*. Oxford.

Rist, J. M. (1972). *Epicurus: an introduction*. Cambridge.

Rorty, A. O. (1980). 'The place of contemplation in Aristotle's *Nicomachean Ethics*', in A. O. Rorty, ed., *Essays on Aristotle's Ethics*, 377–94. Berkeley.

Russell, D. (1964), ed. *'Longinus': On the sublime*. Oxford.

Rutherford, R. (1989). *The Meditations of Marcus Aurelius: a study*. Oxford.

Salomies, O. (1992). *Adoptive and polyonymous nomenclature in the Roman Empire.* Commentationes Humanarum Litterarum 97. Helsinki.

Sambursky, S. (1959). *Physics of the Stoics.* London.

Sandbach, F. H. (1985). *Aristotle and the Stoics. PCPhS* suppl. vol. 10. Cambridge.

(1989). *The Stoics.* 2nd edn. London.

Schmidt, E. G. (1961). 'Die Anordnung der *Dialoge* Senecas', *Helikon* 1: 245–63.

Schofield, M. (1999). *The stoic idea of the city.* Chicago and London.

Setaioli, A. (1965). 'Esegesi virgiliana in Seneca', *SIFC* 37: 133–56.

(1980). 'Elementi di *sermo cotidianus* nella lingua di Seneca prosatore, I', *SIFC* 52: 5–47.

(1981a). 'Elementi di *sermo cotidianus* nella lingua di Seneca prosatore, II', *SIFC* 53: 5–49.

(1981b). 'Dalla narrazione all' *exemplum.* Episodi erodotei nell' opera senecana', in *Atti del convegno internazionale 'Letterature classiche e narratologia'*, 379–96. Perugia.

(1988). *Seneca e i Greci: citazioni e traduzioni nelle opere filosofiche.* Bologna.

Shackleton Bailey, D. R. (1970). 'Emendations of Seneca', *CQ* 64: 350–63.

Sharples, R. W. (1983), ed. *Alexander of Aphrodisias: On fate.* London.

(1996). *Stoics, Epicureans and Sceptics: an introduction to Hellenistic philosophy.* London and New York.

Shaw, B. D. (1985). 'The divine economy: Stoicism as ideology', *Latomus* 44: 16–54.

Shipley, F. W. (1911). 'The heroic clausula in Cicero and Quintilian', *CP* 6: 410–18.

Smith, K. F. (1913), ed. *The elegies of Albius Tibullus.* New York; repr. Darmstadt 1964.

Smith, M. S. (1975), ed. *Petronii Arbitri Cena Trimalchionis.* Oxford.

Solodow, J. B. (1978). *The Latin particle quidem.* American Classical Studies 4. Boulder.

Sorabji, R. K. (1983). *Time, creation, and the continuum: theories in antiquity and the early Middle Ages.* Ithaca, NY.

(1988). *Matter, space and motion: theories in antiquity and their sequel.* London.

Syme, R. (1958). *Tacitus.* 2 vols. Oxford.

Talbert, R. J. A. (1984). *The senate of imperial Rome.* Princeton.

Tarrant, R. J. (1976), ed. *Seneca: Agamemnon.* Cambridge Classical Texts and Commentaries 18. Cambridge.

(1985), ed. *Seneca's Thyestes*. Atlanta.

Thomas, R. F. (1988), ed. *Virgil: Georgics*. Cambridge Greek and Latin Classics. 2 vols. Cambridge.

Toynbee, J. M. C. (1971). *Death and burial in the Roman world*. Ithaca, NY.

Traina, A. (1987). *Lo stile 'drammatico' del filosofo Seneca*. 4th edn. Bologna.

van Berchem, D. (1939). *Les distributions de blé et d'argent à la plèbe romaine sous l'Empire*. Geneva.

Vander Waerdt, P. A. (1991). 'Politics and philosophy in Stoicism', *Oxford Studies in Ancient Philosophy* 9: 185–211.

Walbank, F. (1957). *A historical commentary on Polybius*. Vol. 1. Oxford.

(1967). 'The Scipionic legend', *PCPhS* 13: 54–69.

Waldaestel, O. (1888). *De enuntiatorum temporalium structura apud L. Annaeum Senecam*. Diss. Halle.

Weber, H. (1895). *De Senecae philosophi dicendi genere Bioneo*. Diss. Marburg.

Westman, R. (1961). *Das Futurpartizip als Ausdrucksmittel bei Seneca*. Helsinki.

Wiedemann, T. (1989). *Adults and children in the Roman Empire*. New Haven and London.

(1992). *Emperors and gladiators*. London.

Williams, G. (1978). *Change and decline: Roman literature in the early Empire*. Berkeley and Los Angeles.

Williams, G. D. (1994). *Banished voices: readings in Ovid's exile poetry*. Cambridge.

Wirszubski, C. (1950). *Libertas as a political idea at Rome during the late Republic and early Principate*. Cambridge.

(1954). 'Cicero's *cum dignitate otium*: a reconsideration', *JRS* 44: 1–13.

Wistrand, M. (1990). 'Violence and entertainment in Seneca the younger', *Eranos* 88: 31–46.

Woodman, A. J. (1983), ed. *Velleius Paterculus: the Caesarian and Augustan narrative (2.41–93)*. Cambridge Classical Texts and Commentaries 25. Cambridge.

Woodman, A. J. and Martin, R. H. (1996), eds. *The Annals of Tacitus: Book 3*. Cambridge Classical Texts and Commentaries 32. Cambridge.

Wright, J. R. G. (1974). 'Form and content in the Moral Essays', in C. D. N. Costa, ed., *Seneca*, 39–69. London.

Zetzel, J. E. G. (1995), ed. *Cicero, De re publica: selections*. Cambridge Greek and Latin Classics. Cambridge.

INDEXES

1 General

ablative: gerund, 196; instrumental, 98, 239; of place, 94, 209; of price, 87, 242, 249; of time, 101, 157, 191; of value, 161, 166

adoption, 217, 220

Aesop, 67, 219

alliteration, 31, 79, 117, 133, 164, 186, 198, 232

ambiguity, 70, 76, 211, 250

analogy, 130, 131, 132, 163, 164, 174

anaphora, 29, 30, 31, 65, 79, 81, 98, 108, 119, 123, 127, 129, 133, 140, 155, 165, 167, 169, 180, 181, 186, 192, 205, 211, 213, 217, 229, 238, 253

Annaeus Serenus, 12–13, 15, 109

antimetabole, 29, 66

Antiochus of Ascalon, 87

antitheton, 101

Appius Claudius Caudex, 201

'appropriation' (Stoic οἰκείωσις), 69

archaism, 31, 179

Archedemus of Tarsus, 183

Aristotle, 14, 82, 83, 84, 85, 86, 87, 97, 100, 106, 107, 114, 118, 120, 177, 183, 217

assonance, 31, 117, 168

asyndeton, 29, 123, 197, 217, 231; adversative, 31, 121, 132, 157, 166

Athenodorus of Tarsus, 15–16, 76, 78, 81

Athens, 5, 6, 14–15, 80, 114, 115, 116

attraction, 186, 199, 240

auctions, 188

Augustus, 7–8, 11, 15, 28, 29, 81, 137–44, 166, 189, 207, 248

Aventine, 208–9

banquets, 193

Caecilius Metellus, L., 207

Carneades, 213

Carthage, 5, 14–15, 80, 114, 115, 116

centenarian, 132

chiasmus, 30, 77, 93, 101, 102, 111, 113, 119, 130, 145, 146, 169, 171, 172, 212, 221, 227, 231

Chrysippus, 4–5, 17, 20, 69, 71, 79, 80, 82, 94, 101, 104, 105, 106, 112, 122, 148, 165, 177, 183, 213, 238, 243

Cicero, M. Tullius, 6–7, 25, 28, 29, 81, 104, 105, 111, 144–8, 213, 232

Claudius, 1, 12, 15, 135, 207, 208, 209, 241, 251

clausulae, 31–2, 69, 106, 125, 127, 140, 144, 173, 183, 246, 247

Cleanthes, 23, 86, 105, 106, 132, 185

clients/clientela, 23, 123, 127, 128–9, 156, 187–8, 212–17, 218, 248; philosophical clientela, 217–19

Codex Ambrosianus, 3, 13, 32–3, 117–18

colloquialism, 30, 70, 71, 79, 86, 104, 105, 106, 112, 117, 121, 130, 132, 133, 148, 158, 161, 170, 174, 184, 197, 198, 200, 205, 225, 228, 238, 240, 246

comparative, 187–8, 192, 200

compound verb, 118, 152

constructio ad sententiam, 199

consul, 161 (ordinarius/suffectus), 249

contemplation: of truth, as a prelude to the active life, 72; itself 'active' and inseparable from actio, 17–18, 85, 99–100

conuicium saeculi, 196–7

Cornelius Scipio Africanus, P., 28, 232, 233, 234–5

Cornelius Sulla, L., 203, 207, 208

correctio, 71, 104, 105, 121, 163, 185, 189, 226

2 Latin words

3 Greek words